"I AM A PHENOMENON
QUITE OUT OF THE ORDINARY"

The Notebooks, Diaries, and Letters of
DANIIL KHARMS

Cultural Revolutions: Russia in the Twentieth Century

"I AM A PHENOMENON QUITE OUT OF THE ORDINARY"

The Notebooks, Diaries, and Letters of
DANIIL KHARMS

Selected, Translated and Edited
by Anthony Anemone and Peter Scotto

BOSTON
2013

The publication of this book is supported by the Mikhail Prokhorov Foundation (translation program TRANSCRIPT).

 transcript

Library of Congress Cataloging-in-Publication Data:
A catalog record for this title is available from the Library of Congress.

ISBN 978-1-936235-96-4 (cloth)
ISBN 978-1-618113-72-6 (paperback)
ISBN 978-1-61811-146-3 (electronic)

Cover design by Sasha Pyle
Published by Academic Studies Press in 2013
28 Montfern Avenue
Brighton, MA 02135, USA
press@academicstudiespress.com
www.academicstudiespress.com

For our fathers.

"Translations that are more than transmissions of subject matter come into being when in the course of its survival a work has reached the age of its fame."

−Walter Benjamin

Contents

Acknowledgements

E very work of scholarship rests on the work of others in the field. What we have done here would not have been possible without the dedication and hard work of those scholars who rescued Kharms and his artistic legacy from decades of oblivion. When Mikhail Meilakh, Vladimir Earl, Aleksandr Aleksandrov, and Vladimir Glotser started studying Kharms's life and work in the late 1960s, he was almost completely unknown. Thanks to their multiple editions, scholarly articles, and books, today Kharms's works are acknowledged classics of twentieth-century Russian literature. Another generation of Russian scholars and researchers, including Aleksandr Kobrinsky, Andrei Ustinov, Aleksei Dmitrenko, Anna Gerasimova, Andrei Krusanov, Evgenia Stroganova, and Valery Shubinsky, has continued the recovery of Kharms, contributing immeasurably to our understanding of his life and work, and maintaining the high standards set by their predecessors.

We owe a special debt of gratitude to Valery Sazhin of the Russian National Library in Saint Petersburg and Jean-Phillipe Jaccard of the University of Geneva for their invaluable publication of the full corpus of Kharms's notebooks and diaries in Russian.

We would also like to thank: Andrei Ustinov for his meticulous reading and constructive criticism of a long and complicated manuscript and his generous sharing of photographs from his private collection; Dr. Gabriel Griffin for help identifying some of Kharms's maladies, imagined or otherwise; Eugene Hill of Mount Holyoke College for his encouragement and careful reading of early drafts of this work; Bella Ginzbursky Blum of the College of William and Mary, Boris Wolfson of Amherst College for their helping untangle some especially tricky passages in the Russian; F. F. Morton of South Hadley for his gentle instruction in the art of translation; Marietta Turian of Saint Petersburg for her support and inspiration over the years; Mikhail Vorobyov of Saint Petersburg for sharing family memories and photographs of some of the people in this book; Anaida Bestavashvili and Vladimir Livshits of Moscow for their enthusiasm and support of the project; Dmitry Sokolenko of Saint Petersburg for his enthusiasm for all things OBERIU; Susan Downing for her help compiling the Glossary; Stanley Rabinowitz, director of the Amherst College Center for Russian Culture, for allowing us access to rare items in the ACRC collection; Mike Blum of the College of William and Mary, for (always) much-needed technical assistance; Sasha Pyle for her cover design; Val Vinokur of the New School for good advice and even better friendship; Robert Pyle, Elisabeth Pyle, and Robinson Pyle for their help explaining the finer points of mathematics and music; Shoshana Lucich and Michaela Beals of Stanford University for last-minute research assistance; and our editor at Academic Studies Press, Sharona Vedol.

We are also grateful to Mount Holyoke College for a 2011-2012 sabbatical award; to the Mount Holyoke Faculty Grants Committee for providing material support for this research; to the New School for Public Engagement for supporting this research with a sabbatical award in 2011-2012; to the Interlibrary Loan Departments at Mount Holyoke College, the New School, and Bobst Library of New York University.

Finally, we would like to thank our patient and long-suffering mothers, without whom none of this would have been possible.

Last, and most of all, we thank Vivian Pyle and Amy Gershenfeld Donnella for their unflagging love and unfailing support.

A.A. and P.S.

Introduction

On February 2, 1942, Daniil Kharms died in the psychiatric section of an NKVD prison hospital in Leningrad. He was barely 36 at the time, a year or so younger than Aleksandr Pushkin was when he had died 105 years earlier, almost to the day, of a gunshot wound to the stomach in a better part of town.[1] Given the desperate conditions in Leningrad during the first winter of what would drag on to be a 900-day siege by the Wehrmacht, it is assumed that as the city slowly starved to death around him, Kharms did too. Like Pushkin, Kharms got it in the stomach.

During his lifetime, Kharms was known as a failed avant-garde poet and dramatist who had some notable, if brief, success writing poems and stories for children. However, for more than two decades following his death, his name and his works were consigned to an enforced oblivion. Today, after a heroic recovery operation mounted by dedicated friends, family members, scholars, and critics over the course of decades, he is read and remembered as a major voice of twentieth-century Russian literature.

Russians now know Kharms not only as the author of classic children's verse, but also as a central figure in a vibrant post-revolutionary avant-garde that was the contemporary of Dada and Surrealism and anticipated the "Theater of the Absurd"; as the author of poems that built upon the linguistic innovations of Russian Futurism; as the creator of a genre of mini-stories beneath whose disjointed and darkly comic surfaces the violence of the Stalinist world shimmers; as one more victim of a state whose tolerance for deviation of any kind was strictly limited, and whose carnivorous appetite is only too well-known. His posthumous glory is such that editions of his works, both scholarly and popular, have been published in print runs numbering into the thousands and tens of thousands[2] and, with the advent of the internet, there are now dozens of websites dedicated to preserving and promulgating his legacy.

Kharms's recovery is all the more remarkable when one considers that during his lifetime, he managed to publish only two of his works "for adults."[3] The rest had to wait for better days.

* * *

In a penetrating essay on Kharms, Yakov Druskin (1902-1980) noted that if there are some authors whose work can be understood apart from their personal lives, there are others whose "inner" life and "outer" work are so intimately connected that, without knowing their lives, it is not possible to comprehend their work in full.[4] Druskin placed Kharms squarely among the latter. If he is right—and we think he is—then the notebooks and diaries that make up the largest part of this translation represent our best chance to recover the inner life of Daniil Kharms.

Druskin was in a position to know. A philosopher, musicologist, and theologian, he first met Kharms sometime in the first half of the 1920s when both men were in their early twenties. The two became especially close during the 1930s, and Druskin remained Kharms's friend to the end—and beyond. According to one version, sometime after Kharms's arrest on August 23, probably in October 1941, Druskin heard from Marina Malich (Kharms's second wife) that the building where she had lived with her husband had been damaged by a bomb. What remained of Kharms's archive was still there, but in disarray following his arrest and a search of the apartment by the NKVD. An ailing Druskin made his way to the apartment, and working together with Malich stuffed a small suitcase with manuscripts and took it back home, thereby saving Kharms's archive for posterity.[5] Among the papers he kept safe for decades were notebooks, diaries, unpublished works, and letters that he then had the opportunity to contemplate at length before reaching the conclusion he did.[6]

1905–1924: From Daniil Yuvachev to Daniil Kharms

Daniil Ivanovich Kharms was born Daniil Ivanovich Yuvachev in Saint Petersburg at the very end of 1905. The widespread upheavals of that year (registered famously in the first chapters of *Doctor Zhivago*) are known to history as the "Revolution of 1905." They marked the beginning of a turbulent two decades that would see the world Kharms was born into remade by war and revolution, and his city's name changed from Saint Petersburg to Petrograd (1914), and finally to Leningrad (1924).

Daniil was the first child born to Ivan Pavlovich Yuvachev (1860-1940) and Nadezhda Ivanovna Koliubakina (1869-1929), both of whom seemed

Daniil Yuvachev, 1912.

eminently respectable members of the Petersburg *intelligentsia*. His father, then employed by the State Directorate of Savings Banks, in 1899 had been elected a Corresponding Member of the Main Geophysical Observatory of the Academy of Sciences for contributions to science. However, in his youth Ivan Pavlovich had been a naval officer in the Black Sea Fleet and had joined *The People's Will*, the revolutionary-terrorist group responsible for the assassination of the Emperor Aleksandr II in 1881. In August 1883, Ivan Pavlovich was arrested and incarcerated in the Peter-Paul Fortress and subsequently brought to trial for his alleged participation in a plot against Aleksandr III. Convicted of revolutionary agitation, he was sentenced to death by hanging on September 28, 1884. Fortunately, his sentence was commuted to 15 years exile and hard labor. He served out the first two years of his sentence in solitary confinement in Schlüsselburg Fortress (one of the most notorious and storied prisons in Russia), and the rest in exile on Sakhalin Island, Russia's newest, most distant, and most brutal penal colony in the Pacific Far East.[7] By that time he had undergone a profound religious conversion. By his own account, it had taken place during his time in solitary confinement, and may have been accompanied by a mental breakdown. At least that's what his revolutionary comrades suspected. In any case, the Ivan Yuvachev who returned to Saint Petersburg in or shortly after 1899 was a devout Christian, a pacifist, and an ascetic. Solitude had also uncovered the writer in him: he had begun writing in prison and continued to do so during his years in exile. After his return to Petersburg, his vocation for literature came into its own and, along with memoirs of prison and exile and an account of a pilgrimage to Jerusalem, he published more than 25 books and brochures on devotional topics.[8]

Kharms's mother, Nadezhda Ivanovna Koliubakina, was the daughter of a distinguished noble family from Saratov province. She was a graduate of Petersburg's Smolny Institute for Well-born Girls, the oldest educational institution for young women in Russia. Founded by Catherine the Great, the school continued to enjoy imperial patronage up until the Revolution. She later worked in a shelter (also supported by imperial patronage) for women released from prison, first as the director of the laundry and then, between 1900 and 1918, as the director of the entire shelter. In 1903, at the age of 33, she married ex-prisoner Ivan Yuvachev, and two years later gave him a son.[9]

* * *

In September 1917, a few months shy of his twelfth birthday and a few weeks before the Bolsheviks seized power in October, Daniil Yuvachev entered the *Realschule* of the prestigious Saint Petersburg Peterschule: prior to that he would have received his elementary education at home.[10] The Peterschule had been in existence since at least 1709 under the auspices of the city's Lutheran community, and was among the oldest schools in the city. It conducted classes in German and could boast one of the city's largest school libraries. The *Realschule* differed from the classical Gymnasium (another part of the school) in its emphasis on science and mathematics rather than the humanities, and on modern rather than classical languages. According to school records, in his first year (1917-18) Daniil was not an outstanding student. Nevertheless it was at this institution that German became his second language, though the same records indicate he had serious deficiencies in spelling.[11] Along with English (which he began studying at home), German (often misspelled) would make its appearance in Kharms's notebooks.

Young Daniil's education was interrupted in the spring of 1918 when his parents sent him to live with his mother's relatives in Saratov to escape the growing hunger and disorder that engulfed Petrograd in the wake of the October Revolution. He would remain in Saratov for more than a year, and was brought back to Petrograd in the summer of 1919, this time to escape the horrors of the Civil War then raging along the Volga.[12]

After returning to the city, Daniil continued his education for the next three years at the Peterschule, by then renamed "Unified Labor School No. 4."[13] By the end of his third year, his performance in all subjects, including German and English, had deteriorated to the point that he was required to leave the school.[14]

By September 1922, he was in Detskoe Selo ("Children's Village"), continuing his education at the "Second Children's Village Unified Labor School," where his maternal aunt and godmother, Natalia Ivanovna Koliubakina (1868-1945), was the director as well as the teacher of Russian literature. Neither the school nor the town in which it was located had escaped the orgy of renaming that followed the Revolution: until 1918 "Detskoe Selo" (located some fifteen miles to the south of Saint Petersburg) had been an imperial residence known as "Tsarskoe Selo" ("Royal Village"), while the school directed by his aunt had been the "Empress Maria Gymnasium for girls."

Not even the sixteen-year-old Daniil Yuvachev retained the name he had begun with. Sometime in 1922, under a hand-copied text of a humorous poem then a favorite among male adolescents, he placed the initials "DCh." (in Latin, not Cyrillic, letters).[15] The name lurking behind them, "Daniel Charms" (again in Latin letters) appears in full in 1924 on the first page of the earliest notebook to have come down to us.

Much scholarly ink and ingenuity has been spilled over the origin and meaning of this pseudonym. Transcribed from its Cyrillic rendering "Хармс" into English as "Kharms," it can be and has been plausibly derived from English "charms" (in its magical meaning), or from French "*charme.*" It may have been a tribute to a German teacher at the Peterschule named "Harmsen," or perhaps it paid homage to a literary idol, Sherlock Holmes. With an eye towards English "harm," he might have meant it to stand over and against his father's pseudonym "Miroliubov" ("Peace and Love").[16] His choice, in fact, seems drastically overdetermined, and he continued

Self portrait with pipe, 1923.

to brood on it for the rest of his life, inscribing it in manifold variations on the pages of his notebooks and his works. Kharms, who dabbled in the Kabbalah, was alive to the magic of names, and quite clearly he interpreted and reinterpreted his own over the course of years. The name became so much a part of him that it seems wrong even to speak of it as a pseudonym. It was more in the nature of a discovery.[17]

Daniil and his aunt were close: he had spent the summer of 1919 with her in Detskoe Selo, and during the two years he lived there finishing up his schooling they must have grown even closer. Clearly, they shared an enthusiasm for language, literature, and words. Trained as a philologist, Natalia Ivanovna would later work as a lexicographer for the Leningrad Division of the Academy of Sciences,[18] and she is remembered as the hostess of lively "literary evenings" at her house at 27 Malaya (renamed Revolution) Street, and as "loving to read Pushkin aloud."[19] Kharms remained close to his aunt throughout his life, continuing to visit her in Detskoe Selo. She makes numerous appearances (under the diminutive "Natasha") on the pages of Kharms's notebooks, where he evinces a special care and concern for her that is not accorded to the other members of his family. (His father is present, not without gentle irony, as an admired mentor and authority figure, while his mother is, strangely, hardly mentioned at all.)

After his graduation from school, the eighteen-year-old Kharms left Detskoe Selo and returned to Leningrad in the summer of 1924. (For those inclined to see fatality in such things, the distance covered is a species of topographic rhyme: in 1817, at age 18, after his graduation from the Lyceum in Tsarskoe Selo, Aleksandr Pushkin had removed to Saint Petersburg to take up a post as a collegiate secretary in the Ministry of Foreign Affairs.) In September 1924, with the help of his father, Kharms enters the Leningrad Electro-Technical College on Vasilievsky Island.[20]

DaNiil KHaRMS aNd His NoTebooks

It is with the autumn of 1924 that the record of the surviving notebooks begins. In all, 38 notebooks and a diary have come down to us. They cover the years 1924-1940 with notable gaps: little or nothing has survived for the years 1936, 1938, and 1941. We do know from official documents that at least six notebooks were confiscated by the state security apparatus, one after a first arrest in 1931 and five during a search of his apartment at the time of his final arrest in 1941. They have never been found.

* * *

Strictly speaking, in Russian a "notebook" (*zapisnaia knizhka*) is not something purchased, but something made. You can buy a *tetrad'* (a composition book, either stapled or sewn through the fold) or a *bloknot* (a pad, glued, stapled, or spiral bound)[21] and turn it into a *zapisnaia knizhka* by making notes (*zapisi*) in it on whatever you need to remember or whatever interests you, occurs to you, or you happen to be working on at the moment. Although notes can be dated, they need not be, and the *zapisnaia knizhka* does not have to adhere to the daily chronological sequence of a diary (*dnevnik*). It may be thought of as a genre as much as a thing, moreover a genre that is part of an established tradition in Russian literature. As Valery Sazhin, Kharms scholar and editor of the Russian edition of the notebooks, has justly observed, "A notebook is a natural attribute of the life of a writer."[22] They were for Kharms.

The 38 notebooks (*zapisnye knizhki*) that have survived are as motley a collection of documents as has ever been archived. They include *tetradi*, *bloknoty*, and even a pocket day planner (*karmannyi kalendar'*), in various states of preservation. Sheets are falling out, torn out, or otherwise missing, and there are scraps of writing inserted among the pages of the notebooks. Like chapters and verses in the Bible, numbers and dates have been assigned by scholars. "Notebook 38" is no more than a conventional designation for a bundle of loose pages with notes from various years. In addition to the notebooks there is also a true *dnevnik* from 1932-33, which Kharms kept on the pages of a standard large-format office ledger, possibly left over from his father's days as a bank examiner.[23]

One way to think of the notebooks is as a mapping of the topography of Kharms's mind: a mapping of the world through which he moved and of the pathways along which his thinking travelled. The landscape includes names, addresses, phone numbers, chess problems, shopping lists, "to do" lists, accounts of money spent and money owed, reading lists, drawings, poetry, stories, literary plans and projects, philosophical musings, magical spells, and the details of romantic interest and sexual involvement (this list is by no means exhaustive).

Confronted by the wild heterogeneity of the notebooks, Druskin was initially puzzled that they recorded and preserved so much that seemed trivial or ephemeral: "Among them I found notes on money spent, lists of groceries that needed to be bought. But if money has been spent and the groceries bought, why preserve the notes?" Druskin contemplates the question and arrives at a tentative answer: "It seems to me that Kharms had, perhaps, an unconscious sense of responsibility for every deed done and for every word written or spoken, even if only in thought: 'For every idle word you shall give answer at the Judgment'."[24]

To follow Druskin's lead: if, as can be argued, the notebooks are some version of the self for which one is responsible, then not to include the "trivial" along with the "important" is to falsify that self, either before one's own conscience or, as Druskin suggests, before God. Moreover, it was from that self that all the other points in Kharms's universe were mapped, so if that universe were to be known, the self had to be known—completely.

But still, those shopping lists? Here, perhaps, we can turn to the insight that Marina Tsvetaeva recalls having had at age three, when she first became aware of the circumstances surrounding Pushkin's death:

> The first thing I found out about Pushkin was that they killed him. Then I found out that Pushkin was a poet, and that Dantes was a Frenchman. Dantes took to hating Pushkin because he couldn't write poems himself, called him out for a duel, that is lured him out onto the snow and killed him there from a pistol in the stomach. So at three years I found out for sure that a poet has a stomach and—I have now in mind all the poets I've ever met—and for that poet's *stomach*, which so often goes hungry and in which Pushkin was killed, I have had no less concern than for his soul.[25]

Kharms may have had something similar in the back of his mind when he recorded those shopping lists. The notebooks bear witness not only to the joys of a well-filled stomach and feasting with friends, but, as the years wear on, to the hunger and privation he and those close to him would have to endure.

* * *

Another thing to remember about Kharms's notebooks was that they were only semi-private documents. Unlike a diary, which by tradition is written when one is alone in one's room and then, perhaps, locked away in a drawer to keep it safe from prying eyes, a notebook is, in the first instance, carried to class and filled with other people present. Indeed, the first thirty pages of "Notebook 1" (Fall 1924-April 1925) contain lecture notes from Kharms's first year at the Electro-Technical College (not translated for this edition).

To judge from evidence in the notebooks themselves, a notebook was Kharms's constant companion as he went about his daily rounds. He would take one to lectures, meetings, talks, poetry readings, and performances; to the park, to the beach. He would write on the tram, in a sauna, at concerts, while visiting friends, visiting his aunt, or in the middle of a fight with his wife. Friends would write their own comments in his notebooks; back-and-forth conversations would be carried on; tongue-in-cheek contracts could be drawn up with both parties solemnly affixing their signatures.

It is precisely because of their semi-public nature that Kharms invented a code to keep certain passages secret from anyone who might happen to look into his notebooks. Fortunately, it is a simple substitution code, wherein one set of symbols stands for another (here: an elaborate set of symbols of Kharms's own devising for the letters of the Cyrillic alphabet), and it has been cracked quite handily by Russian researcher Aleksandr Nikitaev.[26] For the most part the coded passages contain material of romantic, sexual, or similarly intimate nature, and in many cases it is quite clear that Kharms employs the code to keep his infidelities secret from his wife and, perhaps, from cuckolded husbands.

As they have come down to us, the notebooks do not contain anything, coded or otherwise, that smacks of oppositionist politics. Kharms, by temperament an aristocrat to the core, makes no secret of his distaste for the proletarian vulgarity of Soviet life, and in any number of places he records a feeling of profound and even desperate alienation from the world that has taken shape around him. However, next to nothing in the notebooks indicates any real interest in politics or "current events": there is only one tantalizing reference to Bukharin, a brief mention of Kirov's funeral,[27] and some apprehension expressed about the prospect of war on the horizon— that is all. Whether there was ever anything more on pages that were torn out, or in notebooks that were confiscated or lost, we simply do not know.

Life and Art, Art and Life: 1924–1941

In the years covered by the notebooks, the trajectory of Kharms's career between 1924 and 1931 can be said to roughly describe an ascending arc. He begins as a young poet in his early twenties, at the tail end of the extraordinary moment of cultural revolution that begins in Petersburg at the end of the first decade of the twentieth century and continues through the revolutionary years into the Leningrad of the 1920s.[28] He develops ties with the older generation of avant-garde poets and artists, and himself becomes a leader in several groups of radically innovative young writers and artists who are making their presence felt through public readings, performances, and attention-grabbing conduct perhaps best described as a personalized form of "guerrilla theater."[29] Although he will have almost no success getting his work into print as the boundaries of the acceptable narrow after mid-decade, he will find a place for himself in the burgeoning field of children's literature, where he will make both a name for himself and a living.

* * *

By the time Kharms enrolls in the Electro-Technical College in September 1924, he is already writing poetry: one of his first original poems to have come down to us is dated June 12, 1924.[30] He is also memorizing poems by contemporaries (a detailed list of poems "I know by heart" is recorded in the notebooks) and reciting them at public readings wherever he can find the space and an audience: at the Electro-Technical College, the Turgenev Library, the Institute for the History of the Arts, even the hall of the State Steamship Line.[31] He befriends and is befriended by older poets like Nikolai Kliuev, Mikhail Kuzmin, and Aleksandr Tufanov. The last would become an early master and collaborator in the practice of *zaum* ("trans-sense" or "trans-rational") poetry, which in the radical version Tufanov championed was built on sound associations freed from conventional semantic content.

His increasing commitment to literature, combined with the school administration's disapproval of his work habits and social origins, lead to his expulsion from the Electro-Technical College in February 1926: the notebooks preserve a draft of a statement from June 1925 in which Kharms defends himself against charges of "poor attendance," "not participating

On the balcony of the Children's Publishing building in Leningrad (Dom Knigi).

in community service," and "not fitting into the class physiologically." This last could have meant that he simply did not fit in with the rest of his classmates, or that he had been somehow identified as a "foreign element," perhaps because his mother was a member of the "former nobility." Or both.

Sometime in the spring or summer of 1925, Kharms meets Aleksandr Vvedensky, another young and ambitious poet, who would become his closest friend and artistic comrade-in-arms. At the same time he meets Yakov Druskin and philosopher Leonid Lipavsky. With poet Nikolai Oleinikov, they form the core of the *Chinari* (singular: *chinar'*),[32] essentially an affinity group of radically original writers and thinkers who came of age and into their own in the 1920's. The *Chinari* would continue to meet into the 1930s and remain friends until the ends of their lives: indeed, it was Druskin's steadfast *chinar'* loyalty that saved Kharms's work from oblivion.

Kharms and Vvedensky were obsessed with the idea of uniting the radically innovative "left" writers and critics of Leningrad into one "truly revolutionary" grouping under whose banner they would publish their works. That things did not go quite as planned can be seen in a letter

Kharms and Vvedensky wrote to "Boris Leontievich" Pasternak on April 3, 1926. In it they complain that they were having no success finding an outlet for their work in Leningrad, and ask for his help in placing their work in Moscow publications. (Pasternak was fifteen years their senior and at the time was well established as a major presence on the Russian literary scene.) Whether they deliberately mistook his patronymic (he was *Leonidovich* not "Leontievich"), intending it as a demonstrative flouting of polite convention, or it was a simply a boneheaded mistake, is not at all certain. In any case, Pasternak never answered, something that Kharms, judging from later comments in his notebooks, never quite forgave.

From the second half of 1926 to 1928 Kharms and Vvedensky, while continuing to identify themselves as *Chinari,* were participants and organizers in an overlapping and rapidly evolving series of literary-artistic groupings: the experimental theater company the "Left Flank," "Radiks," the "Flank of the Left," and the "Academy of Left Classics." None of these groups survived very long. Plans by "Radiks" for staging a play jointly written by Kharms and Vvedensky called "My Mama's All in Watches" *("Moia mama vsia v chasakh")* fell through after rehearsals had begun. Unhappy with the progress of the text (now lost), the directors refused to show up, and the actors simply wandered off.[33] Throughout 1927, Kharms and Vvedensky continued their search for another organizational solution, but the ambitious plans for anthologies of poetry and prose and the elaborate organizational schemes Kharms outlines in his notebooks mostly went unrealized.

Undaunted by their inability to get their work into print, Kharms, Vvedensky and like-minded comrades pressed their case in public readings. As was fitting for poets who saw themselves as the successors to the Futurists, they quickly became notorious for their scandalous performances: Kharms would stroll down Leningrad's Nevsky Prospect in mismatched clothing and bedroom slippers, clutching a butterfly net; during his reading at a lecture hall, he might announce that another member of his group was simultaneously reading poetry out on the street; literary evenings could culminate in the reading of an outré critical statement, a nonsensical debate, or, just as frequently, a hostile argument with an outraged audience. (By the 1920s, it was a well-established tradition in Russian literature that the younger generation of writers would generate interest and notoriety by public demonstrations of non-conformity, and Kharms and his friend were not about to be outdone.)

However it is with the OBERIU, the "Association for Real Art," that Kharms and Vvedensky achieved their greatest organizational success and notoriety. In existence from the end of 1927 to 1930, the OBERIU included established young poets Konstantin Vaginov and Nikolai Zabolotsky, writer and artist Igor Bakhterev, prose writers Boris Levin and Yury Vladimirov, and two young filmmakers, Aleksandr Razumovsky and Klementy Mints. The wide-ranging ambition of the group can be seen not only in its published declaration, which speaks of "literary," "theatrical," and "cinematic" sections, and still-yet-to-be-organized "music and art" sections,[34] but even more so in its most elaborate public performance, the by-now legendary "Three Left Hours."

Presented on the evening of January 24, 1928, on the stage of Leningrad's Press House (*Dom pechati*), the feverish preparations for this event occupy an important place in Kharms's notebooks from 1927-28. Here, as elsewhere, he seems to revel in organizational detail and, quite simply, the sheer joy of making numbered lists: he records plans for a poster design, poster distribution, props lists, cast lists, expense accounts, invitations, etc. The first hour began with a "choral" reading of the group declaration, after which OBERIU poets read from their works: Vaginov read his poems as a ballerina twirled around him; Kharms read his work perched atop a wardrobe festooned with slogans: "We are not meatpies!" and "Art is a wardrobe!" The second hour was devoted to a performance of Kharms's only full-length play, *Elizaveta Bam*, an existential murder mystery about a woman arrested by agents of the secret police and accused of being responsible for the death of one of the arresting officers. (In its depiction of a hapless individual destroyed by arbitrary governmental authority, *Elizaveta Bam* anticipates Kafka's *Trial*[35] and Nabokov's *Invitation to a Beheading*.) Kharms's play was also meant to put into practice the theory of an OBERIU theater. The play's "dramatic plot" is deliberatively subordinated to its "scenic plot," which the OBERIU declaration presents as arising spontaneously from the play's "theatrical elements"—scenery, staging, language, music, performance—everything that made up the experience of the play and its production. *Elizaveta Bam* presents a constantly changing kaleidoscope in which characters, settings, themes, and verbal styles continually transform and contradict themselves, undercutting any attempts at a straightforward narrative reading of the play. The evening's third hour was devoted to a screening of the first (and last) OBERIU film, *Meatgrinder No. 1*. Now lost, it was apparently composed of reedited, "found" footage.[36]

Poster with the announcement of *Elizaveta Bam* performance, 1928.

One reviewer was so affronted by the trans-sense poems and the on-stage antics that she declared the proceedings "chaos, unvarnished-to-the-point-of-cynicism" and briskly dismissed the whole thing as warmed-over Futurist-style *épatage*. Worse was yet to come. As the twenties drew to a close, it was apparent that there would no longer be room in Soviet literature for a poetics that abandoned norms of logic, grammar and syntax in favor of "collisions of verbal meanings," or for a theater that replaced traditional lines of dramatic plot with a swirling combination of theatrical elements.

Public performances by the OBERIU came to an end after a disastrous performance at Leningrad University in the spring of 1930. The country was by then well into the second year of the "First Five-Year Plan," the crash program initiated by Stalin that was intended to transform the Soviet Union from a backward agrarian state into a modern industrial power—whatever the cost. No one was allowed to remain on the sidelines, much less pursue an idiosyncratic vision of art that was anything but committed, didactic, and devoted to the cause of what was then called "socialist construction." The

Kharms with Alisa Poret.

review of the Leningrad University performance was dated April 9, 1930, and it appeared in the student newspaper *Smena.* Signed "L. Nilvich,"[37] it was titled "A Reactionary Circus Act: (Concerning a Recent Sortie by Literary Hooligans)." The title alone was enough to condemn them. "Reactionary" would have been damning enough, but "hooligans" made it even worse by associating Kharms and company with "hooliganism," something that in the Soviet Union was not only stigmatized as the essence of anti-social (and therefore anti-socialist) pathology, but since 1922 had been listed as a crime. After accusing the members of OBERIU of standing "outside the social reality of the Soviet Union" and characterizing their poetry as "the poetry of the class enemy," the article concluded its dirty work by asking: "By the way, why is it that the Union of Writers tolerates in its midst such scum, such . . . OBERIUTs? After all, the Union is supposed to unite *Soviet* writers." Both the threat implicit in the question and the presumed answer were quite clear.

At the same time as the opportunities for the avant-gardists to either publish or perform their works were closing down, new avenues for literary work were opening up. At the end of 1927, Samuel Marshak, the noted Leningrad poet, translator, and editor, invited Kharms and several of his closest friends and allies (including Vvedensky, Zabolotsky, and Shvarts) to work in the burgeoning field of children's literature. Marshak was the first to realize that, despite Kharms's avowed and demonstrative aversion for children, the whimsy, strong rhythmical propulsion, and clever rhymes of his poems were well suited for children's poetry. Under his gentle tutorship, Kharms quickly became a successful and popular writer for children, a regular contributor to Leningrad's most important children's journals, *Hedgehog (Ezh)* and *Siskin (Chiz)*, as well as the author of numerous illustrated children's books.[38] Although Kharms claimed he never took this writing seriously, without the money he earned writing for children he would never have survived the 1930s.

Still, not even the world of children's literature was immune to the dangers of Stalinist literary politics. As the demands for ideological orthodoxy in children's literature became more strident, the whimsical and fanciful works by the OBERIU poets, despite their popularity with editors and readers, increasingly became targets of attack. In conjunction with a larger campaign of hostile speeches and articles in the press "unmasking" them as a band of "bohemianizing bourgeois holdovers" who had managed to worm their way into the ranks of Soviet children's authors,[39] Kharms and

Ester Rusakova.

several of his closest literary friends were arrested and charged with anti-Soviet activities in the field of children's literature on December 10, 1931. Thus, interrogating officers from the NKVD were far more interested in them as children's writers than as non-conforming avant-gardists. During his interrogations, Kharms confessed to being the leader of an anti-Soviet group of writers who sought to pervert the younger generation by ignoring "Soviet reality" and consciously introducing subversive themes and ideas into their works. In a display of tautological fantasy in no way inferior to those contained in his poems or stories, Kharms admitted his guilt and, in the wooden language customary on such occasions, described the crimes implicit in *What One Must Prepare for Winter*, a book for children detailing the quite necessary preparations that sensible Russians had made for winter from time immemorial: "In the book *What One Must Prepare for Winter*, I substituted a science lesson for the theme of the pioneer camp, and shifted the child's attention to those things which absolutely need to be prepared for winter." He added in a subsequent session: "In this way, the child's attention is redirected and torn away from the actively social elements of Soviet life." For this and similar crimes, Kharms was sentenced to three years in prison camp. Thanks in no small part to the efforts of his father, who activated his network of old revolutionary comrades, his sentence was soon afterwards commuted to a lesser period of exile.

After somewhat more than 6 months in preliminary detention, Kharms served several additional months of exile in Kursk, a drab and dreary provincial city located about 500 kilometers southwest of Moscow. Filled with obsessive complaints of ill health, loneliness, poverty, and hunger, Kharms's notebook and diary entries from the period focus on the thoughts, feelings, fears, and hopes of a tired, sick, and frightened man. Though Kharms was by no means alone in the city—several colleagues from *Hedgehog* and *Siskin* had also been exiled to Kursk, and he shared a house there with Vvedensky—he nevertheless felt himself isolated and alone. If in *Elizaveta Bam* he had imagined the powerlessness and vulnerability of the individual caught in the grip of a powerful, impersonal, and unaccountable political order, he now found himself living in that very position. Kharms never fully recovered from the trauma of his arrest and exile, and experienced an intense and growing awareness of his vulnerability within a system he could neither understand nor ignore.

In mid-November of 1932, Kharms returned to his beloved Leningrad. He would spend the last years of his life there, devoting most of his creative energy to prose in which black humor and grotesque violence combine to create a universe in which nothing seems solid, the absurd is the norm, and death and dismemberment are commonplace. The notebooks for these years record a life that travelled in a mostly descending arc: after the initial relief of returning home and his reinstatement in the Writers' Union, Kharms saw his income from children's literature (his only real source of income) dry up as it became increasingly difficult for him to place his work. The nadir of his fortunes seemed to have been reached in 1937, the same year that Stalin's "Great Terror" was at its height in the city of Leningrad.[40] A notebook entry dated June 1 (there are others like it for the same year) records:

> An even more terrible time has begun for me. At Children's Publishing they've made an issue of some of my poems and have got their claws in me. They've stopped publishing me, and say they can't pay me because of some accidental glitches. I feel that some secret evil is taking place there. We have nothing to eat. We're starving.

Although there is an uptick in the publication of his work after 1937, the shadow of imprisonment and exile resurfaces: in 1939, he is hospitalized briefly at a local psycho-neurological hospital. In the same year he finished his prose masterpiece "The Old Woman" (*Starukha*) and assembled

Kharms in the 1930s.

the cycle of stories called "Incidents" (*Sluchai*). Throughout the 1930s, he spent a significant amount of time listening to and playing music, meeting with his friends from the *Chinari*, and writing prose miniatures and quasi-philosophical texts (most never completed), but writing almost no poems.

Two months after the Nazi invasion of the Soviet Union, on August 23, 1941, agents of the NKVD arrested Kharms at his apartment, and he was accused of disseminating "slanderous and defeatist sentiments, in an attempt to cause panic and create dissatisfaction with the Soviet government." During his initial interrogation, he exhibited signs of mental derangement and was accordingly sent to the psychiatric division of the prison hospital for examination. Over the next several weeks he was examined by prison psychiatrists, who concluded on September 10 that he suffered from schizophrenia and therefore should not be held culpable for those crimes of which he stood accused. It was recommended that he be confined to the prison psychiatric unit for treatment.

* * *

On February 7, 1941, Marina Malich made her way through a frozen and starving Leningrad to one of the city's prisons to drop off a packet of food for her husband. It was, she recalled many years later, perhaps the third time she had made the same trip for the same purpose. The previous two times her parcels had been accepted: a good sign. This time the clerk manning the window asked her to wait, and then the window was slammed shut. Several minutes later, it reopened, and she was told: "Passed away on the second of February." The packet was thrown out back at her.[41]

* * *

Kharms's fate was officially confirmed in 1960 when, at the urging of his sister Elizaveta, his case was reopened. His family received news of his posthumous rehabilitation on July 25, 1960, nineteen years after his final arrest. No official cause of death was given. His place of burial remains unknown.

* * *

RECOVERY AND RETURN

Following his "posthumous rehabilitation," the long process of returning Kharms to Russian literature began. His poems for children were gradually republished in the 1960s and 1970s, and today are considered classics of the genre, read to and loved by millions of Russian children.[42] His rediscovery (really, discovery) as the author of poems, plays and stories intended for adults took longer.

In the late 1960s, Yakov Druskin was befriended by a number of young and talented literary scholars in Leningrad (Mikhail Meilakh, Anatoly Aleksandrov, Vladimir Glotser, Vladimir Earl) who saw him as a living link to a mostly forgotten period of Russian literature and history. Thanks to their tireless efforts, Kharms's works for adults began to seep into publication in the USSR beginning in 1965, with individual poems and stories appearing in anthologies, newspapers, and otherwise obscure scholarly journals,[43] and later in "*tamizdat*" collections published in Germany.[44] The first book-length publication of his works in the Soviet Union would have to wait until 1988, midway through Gorbachev's Glasnost.[45] Since then, works by and about Kharms have been published in Russia at an astonishing rate: there have been multiple editions for scholars and general readers in every possible format, works of scholarship, memoirs, a book of his drawings and sketches, and two full biographies.[46] Between 1997 and 2004, the Saint Petersburg publishing house Academic Project published a 6-volume edition of Kharms's complete works that included all of his then-known poems, plays, stories, essays, notebooks, diaries and letters.[47] Although new materials are still coming to light, Russian readers and scholars now have access to essentially all the surviving materials. Acknowledged as a pioneering poet whose difficult "trans-sense" poems represent a heroic, if doomed, attempt to continue the traditions of the pre-revolutionary avant-garde in the early Soviet period, Kharms has been a major influence on much of the most vibrant literature and theater produced in Saint Petersburg over the last few decades. He is also much honored as the creator of a new genre of mini-stories which use a special brand of grotesque metaphysical humor to reveal the dark truth about not only the world of Stalinism, but the world at large.

Marina Malich (playing Harmonium).

Nor has the Kharms revival been an exclusively Russian affair. In Europe and America over the last several decades, scholars have written dissertations and produced numerous studies of his writings, while filmmakers and theater directors have staged his dramatic works.

Kharms began to make his way into English with pioneering translations by George Gibian (1971) and Neil Cornwell (1989).[48] Over the last decade, a talented group of young Russian-American translators (including Ilya Bernstein, Eugene Ostashevsky, and Matvei Yankelevich) have introduced Kharms to a new generation of readers. Thanks to this small group of dedicated translators, Anglophone readers interested in the Russian avant-garde now have access to excellent translations of most of his stories and many of his poems. A growing audience recognizes Kharms as the creator of anarchically funny and shocking "microstories" that anticipate much that would follow, from the literature of the absurd to contemporary flash fiction.

A Life in Documents

Thus Daniil Kharms has been assimilated to the history of Russian and European literature as well as to the historical and political context of Stalinism. And yet, even as his works have become better known to general readers, the details of his private life and thought have remained largely unknown. Thanks to the publication in Russia of Kharms's notebooks, diaries and letters, a more complete version of the man and his work has become available to Russian readers in the last decade.

With the present translation of Kharms's notebooks, diaries, and letters, Anglophone readers without Russian will, for the first time, have access to the "inner" Kharms, the access that led Druskin to conclude that his work could not be understood apart from his life: it is our hope they will thereby be empowered to draw their own conclusions. In the documents collected and translated into English here for the first time, not only can readers observe Kharms writing, editing, and revising his stories and poems, but they have access as well to the private life, the love affairs, sexual obsessions, intense religiosity, fascinations with the occult, and the psychological oddities of an extraordinary and unusual man caught in the meatgrinder of Russian history and life in the first half of the twentieth century.

Readers can not only discover for themselves how Kharms spent his days and nights, who his friends were, and what books he read, but can enter into the writer's creative laboratory, following along as he revises poems and stories, some familiar from previous translations, many translated here for the first time. They can follow his development from a writer of experimental poems, where the center of attention is on expanding the etymological, semantic, and grammatical range of traditional Russian poetry, to the creator of the grotesque and tragic prose miniatures that, by continuing the comic tradition of Gogol, confirm the lessons that the absurd and the fantastic are, under certain circumstances, the best and only way to describe reality, and that beneath the apparent solidity and order of the world another order, sometimes frightening, sometimes beautiful, can be discovered.

In addition to seeing Kharms the writer at work, readers of the notebooks will discover the broad range of his intellectual interests and personal obsessions: women, sex, sexology, religion, psychology, philosophy, classical music, Eastern mysticism and occultism, nonsense, fashion, chess, smoking, his health, and an abiding desire to be recognized as a poetic ge-

С. С. С. Р.

НАРОДНЫЙ КОМИССАРИАТ ВНУТРЕННИХ ДЕЛ

АВЛЕНИЕ НКВД по ЛЕНИНГРАДСКОЙ ОБЛАСТИ

ОРДЕР № 550

Августа „ 23 " дня 194 1 г.

дан сотруднику Государственной Безопасности тов. _____

изводство: _____ *ареста и обыска* _____

Ювачева - Харм

Даниила Ивановича

ул. *Маяковского 11/1, кв. 8. -*

Начальник Управления
НКВД по ЛО

Начальник третьего
спецотдела УНКВД по ЛО

РАВКА: *арест санкционирован зам. прокурора*
гор. Ленинграда тов. Грибановым.

Место
для
печати

ши род занятий до ареста

в) звание _____

г) если не работает—когда и откуда уволен _____

Yuvachev-Kharms arrest order, 1941.

nius. More than simply a talented writer, an ambitious organizer of the literary left, or a symbol of the revolutionary artist in a totalitarian system, Kharms emerges from the pages of his notebooks as a man with a real biography, with all his personal idiosyncrasies and character flaws intact.

Seeing Kharms as he presents himself in these texts cannot but transform the way we read him. For example, while Kharms is often seen as a religious believer, the notebooks offer a much more nuanced image of his sense of the structure of the cosmos and his place within it. He will pray to God and the archangels on one page, while on the next, he will dictate summoning spells culled from books of magic without any sense that the two approaches should not be mixed. In one paradoxical entry from December 1929, Kharms examines faith in connection with what he calls "the positive action of reverse thinking" (i.e., whatever you want to happen will fail to do so as a result of your wanting it) and concludes that "faith is not necessary." Judging from our reading of the notebooks, Kharms combined superstition, a desire for miracle, and a belief in magic with interest in Eastern mysticism, occult thought, and the Kabbalah so haphazardly that he entirely lacked the ability to see the world in religious or ethical terms.

Other than literature itself, the central issue of Kharms's life, and one that occupies an important place in the notebooks, was his long and tortured relationship with his first wife. While still a student at the Electro-Technical College, Kharms met and fell in love with Esther Rusakova, the daughter of revolutionaries, sister of the composer Paul Marcel and sister-in-law of the well-known writer and revolutionary, Victor Serge. The notebooks tell the story of an obsessive love-hate relationship that dominated Kharms's life and thoughts between 1925 and 1932. Kharms records in great detail their disagreements, fights, reconciliations, and lovemaking; sometimes the effect is excruciating, sometimes hilarious. As noted previously, some of Kharms's entries were written during the episodes he is describing: Kharms sits stewing in one corner of a room, writing about Esther, who at that very moment is sitting and chatting amiably with his mother in another corner of the same room. (The intensity of such passages is reminiscent of Dostoevsky, the master of drawing-room scandal scenes in Russian literature.) Kharms claimed to have loved Esther "for seven years," but when he writes about her, it is clear things were not so simple: he protests his undying love for her or lambastes her for being superficial; he rages at her infidelity or grovels at her feet; he asks God to make her love him or to free him from her hold.

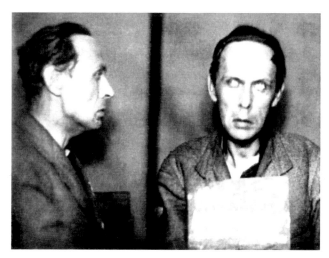

Last photograph
of Kharms,
NKVD file, 1941.

Although he dedicated several works to her, their relationship was so violent and stormy that she was a poor candidate for a muse.

The situation is almost exactly the opposite with Tamara Aleksandrovna Meier-Lipavskaya. "TAM," as he often referred to her in the notebooks, had been romantically involved with Vvedensky (she is sometimes referred to as his "first wife") before eventually marrying another charter member of the *Chinari*, Leonid Lipavsky. While it is unclear if she was ever Kharms's mistress, she inspired some of his most brilliant writing: during the four months he spent in Kursk, Kharms was able to transform the boredom and despair of exile into several sparkling and astonishing letters addressed to her. Reading the funny, touching, and absurd letters today, one senses how, by resurrecting the comic style of the former Leningrad dandy, Kharms was able to preserve his sanity.

In letters and notebook entries, Kharms describes his many love affairs, both during and after his marriage to Esther. He also describes his sexual routines, obsessions and dysfunctions with a frankness that will come as a surprise to those who remember the famous claim that "in the USSR we have no sex." Whether fantasizing about the women sunbathing next to him on the beach at the Peter-Paul Fortress, spying on the woman in the apartment opposite his window, or detailing his sexual needs, Kharms was always brutally honest in his private notebook entries, although he would resort to his code to hide his most dangerous thoughts and feelings from prying eyes.

By comparing his notebook entries with his surviving letters to female friends and lovers, the reader will readily comprehend the complexity of Kharms's relations with women. His letters to lovers run the gamut from sincere statements of attachment to hilarious spoofs of a jealous or sentimental lover blind to everything but the attention of his beloved, and everything in between. The care with which Kharms composed his letters suggests that he considered them works of art on the same level as his poems or stories. In fact, letters represent one of the ways that Kharms combined his life and art in his writing: in many of the notebook entries and "quasi-autobiographical" prose texts (some of which are included here), Kharms erased the once clear-cut boundary between art and non-art and created a new genre that has yet to be named.[49] It is for this reason that we have decided to include a translation of the so-called "Blue Notebook" (*Golubaia tetrad'*) in this collection. Although translated before and usually considered a part of Kharms's "artistic legacy" (as opposed to what Druskin would have called his "personal papers"), the "Blue Notebook" is in form and content so similar to the actual notebooks that we though worthwhile to include it here, if only to put it into a dialogue with the other notebooks. By doing so, we again hope to empower readers to draw their own conclusions about the problem Druskin posed.

Although it may be impossible to see any writer whole, the translators are confident that the Daniil Kharms who emerges from these pages presents a more complex, lifelike, and complete image than has previously been possible for readers without Russian. The documentary portrait of Kharms's life, public, private, and secret, contained in *I am a phenomenon quite out of the ordinary* will, we believe, prove essential reading to all those who know and love Kharms's writings and are interested in the extraordinary and tragic history of Russian literature in the twentieth century. It is our hope that this book will contribute to the work of introducing a major Russian writer of the twentieth century to a generation of new readers.

Anthony Anemone and Peter Scotto
Pound Ridge, New York;
South Hadley, Massachusetts;
Surry, Maine

Endnotes

1 Pushkin died on February 10, 1837 (new style), January 29, 1837 (old style). Although replaced in Western countries by the more accurate Gregorian calendar beginning as early as 1582, the Julian calendar was retained in Russia through 1918. The Julian ("old style') calendar was 12 days behind the Gregorian ("new style") calendar beginning in 1800, and 13 days behind beginning in 1901. The Julian calendar is still used by most branches of the Orthodox Church, including the Russian Orthodox Church.

2 A sampling of various editions and their press runs:

Polet v nebesa (1988)	50,000;
Vanna Arkhimeda: Sbornik (1991) [includes other OBERIU/Chinari writers]	100,000;
Igra: Sbornik stikhov (1993) [children's poetry with other OBERIU writers]	100,000;
Dnei katybr: izbrannye stikhotvoreniia, poemy, dramaticheskie proizvedeniia (1999)	3000;
Povest'. Rasskazy. Molitvy. Tseny. Vodevili. Dramy. Stat'i. Traktaty. Kvazitraktaty (2000)	10,000;
Polnoe sobranie sochinenii	5000-3000 depending on the particular volume.

On the other end of the publishing spectrum there is *Chetyre sluchaia i Aviatsiia prevrashchenii* (Leningrad: Kharmsizdat: 1990-91), a beautifully illustrated set of five lithographed books in a signed and numbered limited edition of 33. Illustrations are by artist Mikhail Karasik.

3 "Sluchai na zheleznoi doroge" in 1926 and "Stikh Petra Iashkina," in 1927, the latter only with a significant cut by the censor.

4 Iakov Druskin, "Kharms" in Daniil Kharms, *O iavleniiakh i sushchestvovaniiakh* (St. Petersburg: Avrora, Azbuka, 1989); for a version of this essay see: "On Daniil Kharms in Neil Cornwell ed., *Daniil Kharms and the Poetics of the Absurd: Essays and Materials* (London and Basingstoke: Macmillan, 1991), 22-31.

5 Based on various accounts. Lydia Druskina (Yakov Druskin's sister) offers a more or less consistent version of this story in three places of which we are aware: "Bylo takoe sodruzhestvo," *Avrora* No. 6 (1989): 102; Iakov Druskin, *Dnevniki* (St. Petersburg: Akademicheskii proekt, 1999), 506; *Lestnitsa Iakova; esse, traktaty, pis'ma* (St. Petersburg: Akademicheskii proekt, 2004), 15. In 1999 and 2004, however, the events are placed in October rather than September 1941, with no explanation given for this change.

In her published memories of Kharms (*Teatr* 11 [1991]: 38-45), Elizaveta Gritsyna (Kharms's younger sister) gives, in outline, essentially the same account as Druskina:

> ...one of the first bombs hit our building, but it was the other half of the building that was destroyed (*razbita*), while ours was only damaged (*razrushena)* by the shock wave. This was already after Danya's arrest. None of his personal things were preserved, only the manuscripts that Marina gave in a suitcase to Druskin. (44)

Artillery bombardment of Leningrad began on September 4, 1941. Large-scale air raids began four days later.

Although he does not indicate a month, Mikhail Meilakh offers essentially the same version of the story in the foreword to his second edition of Vvedensky's *Complete Works* (Aleksandr Vvedensky, *Polnoe sobranie proizvedenii v dvukh tomakh* [Moscow: Hylea, 1993], 38). However, in a 2006 account he places the event in October 1941 ("Vvedenie v istoriiu oberiutovedeniia," *Tynianovskii sbornik* [Moscow: 2006]).

Gritsyna also recalled a second rescue operation on Druskin's part. She says that after she returned to Leningrad following her wartime evacuation from the city, Druskin came to the damaged apartment and, together with Gritsyna, recovered whatever remained of Kharm's manuscripts (44).

6 Druskin says that because he considered them to be a part of Kharms's "personal papers" (as distinct from his artistic legacy), he did not read Kharms's notebooks and diary until the second half of the 1950s. He also says that he was nurturing the hope that, somehow, his friend would return and that he could hand the notebooks over to him; see Iakov Druskin, "Chinari: Avtoritet bessmyslitsy," in *"Sborishche druzei, ostavlennykh sud'boiu": A. Vvedenskii, L. Lipavskii, Ia. Druskin, D. Kharms, N. Oleinikov: "Chinari" v tekstakh, dokumentakh i issledovaniiakh*, 2 vols. (1998), 1: 53-4.

7 On Sakhalin, Ivan Yuvachev met and favorably impressed Anton Chekhov, who was then (August 1890) investigating the local conditions for prisoners and exiles.

8 See Valerii Shubinskii, *Daniil Kharms: Zhizn' cheloveka na vetru* (St. Petersburg: Vita Nova, 2008), 18-35. Useful summaries of Ivan Yuvachev's life and career can be found in: A. A. Aleksandrov, "Charodei," introduction to *Polet v nebesa* (Leningrad: Sovetskii pistatel', 1988), 8-11, and: A. Aleksandrov, "Materialy o Daniile Kharmse i stikhi ego v fonde V. N. Petrova," in *Ezhegodnik rukopisnogo otdela Pushkinskogo Doma na 1990 god* (Leningrad: Nauka, 1990), 208-13. See also: E. M. Sakharova, "A.P. Chekhov i avtor knigi 'Vosem' let na Sakhaline' I.P. Iuvachev," in *A. P. Chekhov i Sakhalin: Doklady i soobshcheniia mezhdunarodnoi nauchnoi konferentsii, 28-29 oktiabria 1995 g.* (Iuzhno-Sakhalinsk: Upravlenie kul'tury i turizma Administratsii Sakhalinskoi oblasti, 1996), 203-11. A very revealing group of letters written by the elder Yuvachev in exile can be found in: E. N. Stroganova and A. I Novikova, "'Mne kazhetsia, ia liubliu ee i liubil iskrenno': Epistoliarnyi dnevnik Ivana Iuvacheva," *Novyi Mir* 6 (2001): 128-58.

9 Biographical information on Kharms's mother is comparatively scarce. A good outline of her life is available in Shubinskii, 11-16; Kharms's childhood letters to his father and touching excerpts from his mother's letters to his father reporting on their son are available in: E. N. Stroganova, "Iz rannikh let Daniila Kharmsa: Arkhivnye materialy," *Novoe Literaturnoe Obozrenie* 6 (1993/94): 67-80. For a fascinating set of letters between his parents in the year prior to their wedding, see Stroganova, "K biografii Daniila Kharmsa: predystoriia sem'i v pis'makh roditelei," *Fol'klor, postfol'klor, byt, literatura: sbornik statei k 60-letiiu Aleksandra Fedorovicha Belousova* (St. Petersburg: Sankt-Peterburgskii gos. universitet kul'tury i iskusstv, 2006), 308-18. A well-researched genealogy of the Koliubakin family is available in M. N. Marov, *Rod Koliubakinykh v Russkoi istorii*, at http://admin.cherlib.ru/files/133321112011Marov.pdf.

10　Our account of Kharms's schooling follows that of Shubinskii. This fine biography contains the most careful and meticulously documented account of Kharms's life published to date.

11　Shubinskii, 59.

12　This suggestion belongs to Shubinskii, 60.

13　In accordance with a decree of the All-Russian Central Executive Committee (VTsIK) of October 16, 1918. This same decree mandated co-education in all Soviet schools, hence the "unified" in the new names.

14　Shubinskii, 67.

15　On the actual sources of this poem, which had previously been attributed to Kharms, see A. L. Dmitrenko "Mnimyi Kharms," *Avangard i ideologiia: Russkie primery*, ed. K. Icin (Belgrad: Filologicheskii fakul'tet Belgradskogo universiteta, 2009).

16　Kharms's father may have suspected something of the sort. In a notebook entry dated Dec 23, 1936, and signed "Daniel Charms" (*PSS* 5:2, 190) Kharms records a remark by his father: "Yesterday Papa said to me that as long as I'm Kharms, I'll be hounded by harms."

17　For some recent contributions on the subject of Kharms's naming and summaries of previous conjectures, see F. Kuvshinov and E. Ostroukhova, "O psevdonimakh Daniila Kharmsa," *"Strannaia" poeziia i "strannaia" proza: Filologicheskii sbornik posviashchennyi 100-letiiu N. A. Zabolotoskogo* (Moscow: 2003): 203-45, Mikhail Meilakh, "Kharms/Charms: Istochniki i znacheniia psevdonima," in *Avangard i ideologiia: Russkie primery,* 399-412, and M. N. Nechaeva, " '…poka ia budu Kharms menia budut presledovat' nuzhdy' (psevdonim kak biografiia)," *Russkaia literatura* No. 1 (2010): 220-226. See also Aleksandr Kobrinskii, *Danill Kharms,* in the series *Zhizn' zamechatel'nykh liudei* (Moscow: Molodaia Gvardiia, 2009), 17-18, and Shubinskii, 70.

18　In an official history of the Institute of Linguistic Research of the Russian Academy of Sciences, she is listed as a "junior researcher" ("*mladshii nauchnyi sotrudnik*") working on a "Dictionary of Modern Russian" in the years prior to the Second World War. See A. N. Anfert'eva, *Institut iazyka i myshleniia im. N. Ia. Marra AN SSSR (nyne Institut lingvisticheskikh issledovanii RAN) vo vremia voiny i blokady* (section 2: Institut iazyka i myshleniia pered voinoi, Slovar' sovremennogo russkogo iazyka, 15) at http://iling.spb.ru/history/anfer.html. This confirms Elizaveta Gritsyna's report that "[…] before the war […] she was working with Academician Marr on the compilation of some dictionary or another, as a researcher" (Gritsyna, 40).

19　See Gritsyna, 40; and "Pokrovskoe kladbishche. Slava i zabvenie: Natal'ia Ivanovna Koliubakina (1868-1945)" at http://www.russkije.lv/ru/pub/read/pokrovskoe-ceme-try/lica-28.html, a reminiscence by Olga Viktorovna Chernobaeva-Saldon recorded by S. Vidyakina. She and her father Professor V. G. Chernobaev (1891-1947) occupied the same house as Natal'ia Ivanovna in Detskoe Selo (Pushkin) before and during the Second World War. Viktor Chernobaev worked together with Natalia Ivanovna as a senior researcher at the Institute of Linguistic Research (see Anfert'eva, section 2: Institut iazyka i myshleniia pered voinoi, Kabinet sovremennogo russkogo iazyka: 15). Chernobaeva's reminiscence provides important details about Natalia Ivanovna's death from a heart attack in Riga on June 21, 1945. For reminiscences of Kharms by a classmate from his school years at Detskoe selo, see: Aleksei Dmitrenko and Aleksandr Kobrinskii, "Vospominaniia Natalii Zegzhdy, souchenitsy Kharmsa," *Avangard i ideologiia: Russkie primery,* 452-459.

20 *I Leningradskii èlektrotekhnikum*: located on the 10th Line of Vasilevsky Island, No. 3 following the flood of September 1924 (Shubinskii, 77); not to be confused with the more prestigious (and harder to get into) Leningrad Electro-Technical Institute (LETI) located at No. 5 Professor Popov Street.

21 A crucial functional distinction between a *tetrad'* and a *bloknot* is that you can tear a page from a *bloknot* without destroying its integrity. As every American schoolchild of a certain generation knows, you can't tear a page out of a true composition book (*tetrad'*) without running the risk of another falling out somewhere. Therefore what in American English would be called a "spiral notebook" is still a *bloknot* in Russian.

22 *PSS*, 5:1, 5.

23 This surmise concerning the source of the ledger (entirely probable in our view) belongs to Sazhin, *PSS*, 5:2, 315.

24 A version of Matthew 12:36: "But I say unto you, for every idle word that men shall speak, they shall give account thereof in the Day of Judgment."

25 Marina Tsvetaeva, "Moi Pushkin," in *Izbrannaia proza v dvukh tomakh 1917-1937*, vol. 2, ed. A. Sumerkin (New York: Russica Publishers, 1979), 249.

26 On Kharm's code, see Aleksandr Nikitaev, "Tainopis' Daniila Kharmsa: Opyt deshifrovki," *Daugava*. 1989, No. 8, 95-99; reprinted in *Risunki Kharmsa*, ed. Iu. S. Aleksandrov (St. Petersburg: Izdatel'stvo Ivana Limbakha, 2006), 237-247.

27 Nikolai Bukharin (1888-1938); was a prominent Soviet politician and intellectual whose opposition to Stalin's policies led to his fall from favor. He was later arrested (1937) and subsequently tried, convicted, and executed (1938); Sergei Kirov (1886-1934) was a Leningrad Communist Party Secretary whose murder on December 1, 1934, set in motion a wave of investigations, arrests, reprisals, and executions that peaked in 1937-38 in a massive purge that would come to be known as "The Great Terror." The classic history of this period is Robert Conquest's book *The Great Terror* (1968; revised 1990), whose title gives the period its name.

28 From the point of view of Saint Petersburg, the Revolutions of 1917 (the first of which topples the autocracy in February and the second of which brings the Bolsheviks to power in October) could be seen as waypoints in a much larger process of renovation and renewal.

One of the best accounts of this moment in Russian culture is Katerina Clark, *Petersburg: Crucible of Cultural Revolution* (Cambridge, MA: Harvard University Press, 1995). Clark begins with 1913. One of the best discussions of Kharms's place in the era remains Jean-Philippe Jaccard, *Daniil Harms et la fin de l'avant-garde russe* (Bern: Peter Lang, 1991).

29 See Tatiana Nikolskaia, "The Oberiuty and the Theatricalisation of Life," in Cornwell, 195-99.

30 "Mednaia," see A. A. Aleksandrov, "O pervykh literaturnykh opytakh Daniila Kharmsa," *Russkaia literatura* 2 (1992): 150; also Shubinskii, 81; Kobrinskii, *Danill Kharms*, 20.

31 A. A. Aleksandrov, "Kratkaia khronika zhizni i tvorchestva Daniila Kharmsa," in Kharms, *Polet* , 540.

32 Yakov Druskin, one of the founders of the *Chinari*, described the word, a neologism that combines the Russian word for "rank" or "ceremony" (*chin*), to refer to both military and spiritual authority (e.g., the rank of General or the ranks of angels) with the verb *chinit'*, which can mean "to carry out, do, create, cause." The term was originally coined by Vvedensky for a group of friends (specifically Leonid Lipavsky,

Yakov Druskin, Vvedensky, and Nikolai Oleinikov) who met to discuss art, literature, and philosophy starting in 1922. Kharms was invited to join the *Chinari* in 1925. For a time, the term was used as a substitute for *zaumnik* ("trans-sense poet"): both Kharms and Vvedensky used the term for a while under their signatures: Vvedensky called himself a "chinar, authority on nonsense" (*Chinar' avto-ritet bessmyslitsy*), while Kharms was a "chinar-observer" (*chinar'-vziral'nik*). See Yakov Druskin, "Chinari," in *Avrora* 6 (1989): 103-115. Transcripts of their discussion were kept by Lipavsky and eventually published as Leonid Lipavsky, "Razgovory" ("Conversations"), *Logos* 4 (1993): 7-75.

33   In a notebook entry for November 4, 1926, Kharms recorded: "Directors didn't show up and performers left soon after," and for November 10: "Radiks has collapsed"; see also I. V. Bakhterev, [Interview given to Mikhail Meilakh], in *Aleksandr Vvedenskii: Polnoe sobranie sochinenii v dvukh tomakh,* vol. 2, ed. M. Meilakh and V. Erl' (Moscow: Gileia, 1993), 127-31.

34   *Afishi Doma pechati* (Leningrad, 1928): reprinted in *Vanna Arkhimeda: Sbornik*, ed. A. A. Aleksandrov (Leningrad: Khudozhestvennaia literatura, 1991), 456-62.

35   According to Shubinsky, when introduced to some of Kafka's works in 1940, Kharms criticized them for lacking humor. Shubinskii, 457. There is no evidence that Kharms knew Nabokov's works.

36   For a reconstruction of this performance, see Mikhail Meilakh, "Kharms's Play *Elizaveta Bam*," in Cornwell, 200-19; this article appeared originally as "O *Elizavete Bame*" Daniila Kharmsa (predystoriia, istoriia postanovki, p'esa, tekst)," in *Stanford Slavic Studies,* Vol. 1, ed. Fleishman et. al. (Stanford, CA: Stanford University Department of Slavic, 1987), 163-246.

37   Speculation on the identity of "L. Nilvich" centers on two candidates: Evgeny Evgenevich Sno (1901-38), a sociologist, later identified as an employee of the OGPU, who was eager to make the acquaintance of Kharms and his circle sometime after April 1930; and Lev Nikolsky, a young journalist who, according to a co-worker, was notable for his "Robespierrian intransigence." See Shubinskii, 229-31.

38   For a listing of Kharms's publications for children in the 1920s and 1930s, see Jean-Philippe Jaccard, "Bibliographie," in *Daniil Harms et la fin de l'avant-garde russe*, 514-16.

39   A. Serebriannikov "Zolotye zaichiki na poliakh detskoi literartury," *Smena*, No. 270 (15 November, 1931); An excellent account of the campaign to purge children's literature (which had Marshak as its larger target) can be found in Shubinskii, 302-11. See also: A.B. Ustinov, "Delo destskogo sektora Gosizdata," *Mikhail Kuzmin i russkaia kul'tura XX veka* (Leningrad: Sovet po mirovoi kul'ture AN USSR, 1990), 125-35. Other articles that targeted the Oberiuty as part of this campaign include N. N. Aseev, "Segodniashnii den' sovetskoi poezii," *Krasnaia nov'* 2 (1932): 159-72 (originally presented as a speech on December 16, 1931) and O. F. Berggol'ts, "Kniga, kotoruiu ne razoblachili," *Nastuplenie: Leningradskaia gazeta* No. 2 (16 March, 1931): 2; and No. 3 (22 March, 1931): 3.

40   See also note 25; the wave of arrests, imprisonments, exiles and executions in 1937-38 hit Leningrad's *intelligentsia* with a special ferocity. Outstanding literary accounts of this dark period in the city's history include Anna Akhmatova's poem-cycle *Requiem* (various translations available) and Lidia Chukovskaya's novella *Sofia Petrovna* (available in a fine translation by Aline Werth with emendations by Eliza Kellog Klose).

[41] V. I. Glotser, *Marina Durnovo: Moi muzh Daniil Kharms* (Moscow: B.S.G-Press, 2000), 121-22.

[42] Kharms reemerges in print as a children's author after a 21-year hiatus beginning in 1962 with the publication of *Igra*, a collection of 10 poems (Moscow: Detskii mir). It was quickly followed by a second edition in 1963. See Jaccard, "Bibliographie," 516-18, for publications of Kharms's works for children in the Soviet Union between 1962 and 1989.

[43] "Vykhodit Mariia otvesiv poklon," published by A. Aleksandrov in *Den'poezii 1965*, 291; "V al'bom," published by A. Aleksandrov and M. Meilakh, in *Materialy nauchnoi studencheskoi konferentsii*, Tartu, XXI; "Skazka," "Tiuk," "Anekdoty iz zhizni Pushkina," in *Literaturnaia gazeta,* November 22, 1967, 4 (with an introduction by Viktor Shklovsky); see Jaccard, "Bibliographie," 506.

[44] Notable Russian-language editions published abroad during the Soviet period ("*tamizdat*") include *Izbrannoe* (Würzburg: Jal-Verlag, 1974), edited by George Gibian and *Sobranie proizvedenii*, 3 vols. (Bremen: K-presse, 1978; 1980), edited by Mikhail Meilakh and Vladimir Erl'; see Jaccard, "Bibliographie," 505.

[45] Kharms, *Polet*.

[46] Valerii Shubinskii, *Daniil Kharms: Zhizn'cheloveka na vetru* (SPb: Vita Nova, 2008) and Aleksandr Kobrinskii, *Danill Kharms* (Moscow: Molodaia Gvardiia, 2009).

[47] D. I. Kharms, *Polnoe sobranie sochinenii*, ed. Valery Sazhin (SPb: Akademicheskii proekt, 1997-2002).

[48] See the bibliography in this edition.

[49] Another Kharmsian text that exists on the border between life and art is the "Statutes of the State Publishing Roof Watch" (May 22, 1929), in which Kharms combines his taste for the comic grotesque with a parody of the national obsession with rules (see, for example, http://mosmetro.ru/info/regulations/).

About This Translation

From the foregoing we hope it is clear that this translation is intended as a "creative biography in documents."[1] While the surviving notebooks form the core of our work, we have also included Kharms's letters and his "quasi-autobiographical prose" in the mix: such texts fill out the picture we have worked to create, particularly for those years when notebook entries are either sparse or non-existent. To sketch in the historical and literary-historical contexts of the life, we have included contemporary reviews of *Chinari* and OBERIU performances, OBERIU performance programs and invitations, the OBERIU declaration, and the protocols of Kharms's interrogations following his arrest in 1931 and again in 1941.

In doing so, we believe that we have remained true to the spirit of the notebooks. They were, in practice, permeable objects: in addition to writing entries on the pages, Kharms would insert tickets, notes, and various scraps of other things printed or written between them. In effect, we have done likewise.

Translating the Notebooks

As Matvei Yankelevich has shrewdly observed: "The very impossibility of fully reproducing Kharms's notebooks and scraps of paper, with their intricate, playful, sometimes hieroglyphic or cipher-like writing and drawings (and writings and drawings) makes this marginal *oeuvre* a challenge to the standardizing mechanism of assimilation."[2] And, we might add, to translation.

---

[1] In making this choice we hope to stand in the tradition of Veresaev, whose documentary compendium, *Pushkin v zhizni* (*Pushkin in Life*), though sometimes taken to task by scholars, has more often than not provided insight and inspiration to poets, Aleksandr Vvedensky among them. See Anna Gerasimova, "Ob Aleksandre Vvedenskom," *Vse* (M.: OGI, 2011), 15.

[2] Matvei Yankelevich, "Introduction: The Real Kharms," in his *Today I Wrote Nothing: The Selected Writings of Daniil Kharms* (New York: Ardis/Overlook Duckworth, 2009), 40.

Therefore it has never been our purpose to either reproduce the notebooks (impossible), or transcribe them (more about this below), but to *represent* them, always with the clear—and sometimes painful—understanding that our representation is only partial and not adequate to the thing itself. Moreover, the inevitable limitations on time and space available have made it impossible to translate the notebooks in their entirety, but we offer a substantial selection of what is contained within them.

Although we have had the opportunity to inspect the original documents, we have not, perforce, had continuous or complete access to the notebooks. Our main source, therefore, has been the transcription of the notebooks offered in volume 5 (parts 1 and 2), of the *Complete Works (Polnoe sobranie sochinenii)* published in 2002 by Akademicheskii Proekt, as compiled and edited by Jean-Philippe Jaccard and Valery Sazhin. As Sazhin notes in prefatory remarks to his commentary, "The main goal of this edition is the publication of the notebooks and diary of Daniil Kharms in a form that is as close as possible to their original form [*podlinnyi vid*] and content."[3] To that end, Sazhin and Jaccard offer a notebook-by-notebook, page-by-page transcription, presenting entries within notebooks whenever possible, in the same order in which they appear in the originals. They reproduce essentially all of Kharms's drawings, as well as the coded passages in Kharms's own handwriting.

Nevertheless, as valuable as this transcription is, the version of the notebooks Sazhin and Jaccard offers looks and feels nothing like the notebooks themselves. It could not have been expected to. In a standard-format edition like the *Complete Works*, torn-out pages cannot be reproduced, scraps of writing cannot be folded in, variations in handwriting have not been registered by type fonts, color is not available; the coded passages have been decoded in boldface. To frame the problem in terms suggested by Yankelevich: the best intentions on the part of the editors are defeated by the standardizing mechanisms of assimilation.

We have, therefore, chosen to represent the notebooks consistent only with the purposes of our project. Our claims for this translation extend no further than that. To the extent that those purposes are biographical, we have re-arranged notebook entries by year in chronological order as far as can

---

3 *PSS* [*Complete Works*], 5:2, 221; "*podlinnyi vid*" could also be translated as "genuine look."

be determined from those entries that are dated.[4] To represent something of the graphic aspect of the notebooks, we have included a sampling of drawings we think are essential to understanding a particular passage, or simply interesting in and of themselves. To convey the sheer variety of Kharms's interests and obsessions as they are recorded in the notebooks, we have included a great deal of material (including chess problems, addresses, phone numbers, shopping lists, lists of debts, to-do lists, etc.) that may on first impression strike a reader as marginal even within this "marginal oeuvre."

Regarding passages that may not seem to be of inherent interest and might, perhaps, be regarded by some readers as boring: we can say that we wanted to represent the notebooks, quirks, warts, *byt*,[5] and all, and that we want our readers to have at least an inkling of what it might be like to confront the notebooks in their wild heterogeneity. But beyond that, there are larger connections to be drawn. A few examples: we chose to include the chess problems because, like many young Russians of his generation, Vladimir Nabokov prominent among them, Kharms was caught up in the fad for chess-playing that took the country by storm in the 1920s.[6] To leave these out would be tantamount to leaving out crossword puzzles from a biography of Nabokov. In any case, they are compact enough that a reader with no interest can skip right over them, while readers with an interest in chess may find yet another avenue into Kharms's creative imagination.

The shopping lists, lists of debts, etc., belong, of course, to the category of *byt,* but we believe they are revelatory in their own way. They set up patterns that can be discovered by an alert reader and can be contemplated in relation to Kharms's works by a reader familiar with them. The transition from the abundance recorded in the earlier notebooks to the destitution to

---

4 This "biographical" approach, including letters, drafts of poems and stories, contemporary articles from the press, in the body of the text, was first used by Ustinov and Kobrinskii in their publication of a selection of Kharms's notebooks in *Minuvshee: Istoricheskii almanakh*, 11, 1991: 417-583.

5 "*Byt*" (derived from the verb *byt'*—"to be") is a nearly untranslatable Russian word that designates quotidian reality, the daily round, the stuff of everyday life.

6 Various aspects of the Russian mania for chess in the 1920s can be seen in Vsevolod Pudovkin's film *Chess Fever* (*Shakhmatnaia goriachka, 1925*), Ilf and Petrov's comic masterpiece, *The Twelve Chairs* (*Dvenadtsat' stul'ev*, 1928) in a chapter entitled "The Interplanetary Chess Congress," and very differently in Vladimir Nabokov's 1930 novel *The Luzhin Defense* (*Zashchita Luzhina*).

the point of starvation that makes itself felt ever more strongly as the years go on not only speaks eloquently about the material conditions Kharms had to labor under, but can be profitably considered in relation to a "poetics of eating and hunger" in Kharms's works. His smoking schedules and his listing of tobacco brands are all bound up with his iconic pipe and his idiosyncratic meditations on the meaning of smoking that occur elsewhere in the notebooks; the loving lists of stationery and writing implements exist in a dialogic relation with the impossibility of writing and the horror before the blank page that are the themes of so many of Kharms's works, some of which are included in our translation; the elaborate wish lists of clothing that he would never be able to purchase connect with other meditations in the notebooks on the art of dressing, his affected dandyism in the 1920s, and his painful awareness of his shabby appearance recorded in the diary as he moves into the 1930s, all of which are connected to his concern for self-presentation and self-creation on the deepest level.

Our hope is that we can prod our readers to pay attention to these manifold connections that underlie what may seem to be trivial on the surface, and that by paying that attention they will discover for themselves things that we have failed to notice or do not fully understand ourselves.

Translating the Poetry

Translating poetry is always challenging, and with a poet like Kharms it becomes all the more so. This, however, is not the place to offer a full-scale account of his development as a poet or our own theory of poetic translation, so we will simply confine ourselves to a few practical remarks.

Poems and poetry in the notebooks span a range from early *zaum* works to at least several examples of the so-called "exercises in classical meters" that make their appearance beginning in the mid-1930s, with just about everything else in between. As far as we know, Kharms was never quite comfortable with the radical version of *zaum* advocated by Tufanov (called "abstract *zaum*" in the notebooks), and his earliest works as represented here rely more on morphological and lexical wordplay than on the "semanticization of the phonemic" that characterizes Tufanov.[7] As he

---

7 On Kharms's early *zaum* poetry, see Zhakkar (Jaccard) and Ustinov, "Zaumnik Daniil Kharms. Nachalo puti," *Wiener Slavistischer Almanach*, 1991, Bd. 27.

went on, he relied more on grammatical, syntactical, semantic, and logical "displacements" ("*sdvigi*") to free language from its established protocols, set it in motion, and thus create a version of that "new poetic language" of the "real" that was collectively sought by the OBERIU.

Moreover, the OBERIU Declaration notes that in Kharms's work "action […] retains in itself its 'classical' imprint." One of the things this could mean is that Kharms never abandoned meter and rhyme in his poetry, and, therefore, we have chosen to follow him in this. Again, we do not claim to reproduce these features of the Kharmsian text precisely, only to represent, suggest, or otherwise simulate them as best we can so that, to our ears at least, our translations sound like Kharms as best we hear him. Besides, Kharms believed human beings were quite literally moved by the prosody of a poetic text,[8] and everything in the notebooks indicates that he took a visceral delight in rhythm and rhyme. That, surely, is why his poems for children were so successful (whatever he claims to have thought of them). Rhythm and rhyme were also an outlet for him, a way he interacted with the world: in a fit of jealous rage over Ester he dashes off a series of rhymed quatrains to give vent to his anger; stimulated by the presence of nude young women on a Petersburg beach, he reacts with an erotic poem that looks as if it might be working its way toward a sonnet. Further examples abound.

There is also another way to understand the choice we have made. Speaking only in our capacity as translators, rather than as verse theoreticians or historians, we can say that our practical experience with Kharms's poetry has led us to the conclusion that in a typical Kharms poem (assuming there even is such a thing) "disorganizing forces" are counterbalanced by "organizing forces," i.e. forces that pull language apart and forces that pull it back together. The former can be understood as the the various "displacements" (*sdvigi*) which (to borrow language from the OBERIU declaration) put language in motion, thereby allowing "objects" to "collide" and "interact," while the latter can be understood as the structuring functions of meter, rhythm and rhyme. The tension between the two creates the dynamics of a Kharms poem: without the one and the other, you really

---

[8] See notebook entry: "The power latent in words must be set free . . ." *PSS* [*Complete Works*], 5:2, 174; pages 289-290 in this edition.

don't have a poem by Kharms. At least that's what we think. Our goal, therefore, has been to translate the poem and not just the words.

A Note on Spelling and Punctuation

For some time now, Kharms's various Russian editors have been embroiled in controversy over the extent to which punctuation should be added to texts which exist only in unpunctuated or erratically punctuated versions, and whether or not Kharms's idiosyncratic spelling (or misspelling) should be incorporated into published versions of the texts. We have no dog in that fight. As translators, our approach has been purely pragmatic: we have added punctuation (and capitalization) when and where we thought it would aid our readers in comprehending a text, and have chosen not to represent Kharms's non-standard spellings in this translation.

In the Interest of Full Disclosure (What's been Left Out)

Since our translation is intended to include only a selection of the materials contained in the notebooks, it necessarily omits much material that would otherwise be of considerable interest to literary critics, scholars, and historians working in Russian. We did not include a translation of notebook 7 (the weekly planner), because much of the material recorded there is repeated in sufficient detail in notebook 8. Because of limitations on space, we have not translated the "Egyptian notebook" (notebook 36), which contains notes that Kharms made from his reading in Egyptological literature. As a general rule, we have not included translations of the poetry by other poets that Kharms recorded in the notebooks, including Polonsky, Vvedensky, Inber, Oleinikov, Kuzmin and Pasternak.

We have largely omitted *zaum* wordlists, Kharms's notes on poetry readings he attended (which don't add much without knowledge of the poems read)—in general anything we felt did not contribute to the overarching purpose of this project or would make little or no sense to a reader without Russian. Finally, as much as we might have liked to, we have not included translations of all of Kharms's poetry contained in the notebooks: here, more than anywhere, we ran into limitations on time and space.

Apparatus

This translation includes two sets of apparatus: a page-by-page running commentary that follows the text and a glossary listing in alphabetical order the people, places, institutions and concepts that appear repeatedly in the text and providing brief information about them. In preparing these, we did not simply translate commentary or notes from the *Collected Works*, but did our own research and fact checking. In order to allow Kharms to speak for himself to the extent that it is possible to do so in a translation, we have chosen not to interrupt the texts with superscript numbers directing readers' attention to the commentary.

* * *

SOME CONVENTIONS USED IN THIS TRANSLATION

Times New Roman: Used for text that appears in the notebooks written in the Russian Cyrillic alphabet.

Times New Roman (Bold): Used for text that appears in the notebooks written in a code of Kharms's own devising (a simple substitution code for the letters of the Russian Cyrillic alphabet).

Calibri: Used for text that appears in the notebooks written in the Latin alphabet, *except* when a text is reproduced in an original language (French, German) other than English. Texts that originally appear in the notebooks written in English are given in Calibri in order to distinguish them from texts translated from Russian into English.

Italics: Used where there is a portion of the text written in a language other than Russian. The original language is first reproduced, and then a translation appears in italics.

A note on the spelling of the name Ester (Esther): Kharms spelled the first name of his first wife both in Cyrillic as "Эстер", and in Latin letters as "Esther." We know that this was an important and meaningful distinction to him (see: letter to Poliakovskaya, pages 285-287 in this edition). To maintain this distinction, we translate the first as "Ester" (Times New Roman) and the second as "Esther" (Calibri).

ȷ stands for *Jucunditas* (or *iucunditas*), Latin for "pleasure," is used in the notebooks and diary to refer to masturbation.

A note on the spelling of Russian names and the transliteration of sources: for translating Russian names we have adopted pragmatic spellings that we think will be most natural for English-speaking readers.

For citations in endnotes and the glossary we have employed Library of Congress transliteration.

Preliminaries

"And So They Put Me Into The Incubator . . ."

Now I'll tell you how I was born, how I grew, and how the first signs of genius came to light in me. I was born twice. Here's how it happened.

My papa married my mama in 1902, but my parents brought me into the world only at the end of 1905, because it was papa's desire that I be born without fail upon the New Year. Papa calculated that the conception had to take place on the first of April, and only on this day would he come around to mama with a proposition to conceive a child.

The first time papa came around to mama was on the first of April in 1903. Mama had long waited for this moment and was terribly happy. But papa, as you see, was in quite a playful mood, and he could not contain himself and said to mama: "April Fool's!"

Mama was terribly insulted and did not allow papa to come near her on that day. So it had to wait until the following year.

On the first of April of 1904, papa again began to come around to mama with the very same proposition. But mama, remembering the incident of the year past, said that this time she had no desire to be left in a foolish position and once again she did not allow papa to come near her. No matter how papa raged, nothing helped.

And it was only after another year had passed that my papa succeeded in bringing my mother around and conceiving me.

And so my conception took place on the first of April of 1905.

Nonetheless all of papa's calculations collapsed because I turned out to be premature and was born four months before I was due.

Papa flew into such a rage that the midwife receiving me got flustered and began to cram me back in from where I had just come out.

A student from the Military-Medical academy whom they knew was present and he stated that it would not be possible to cram me back in.

Nonetheless, regardless of the student's words, they just kept on cramming and cramming me back in, but in their haste not into the right place.

And that's when a terrible turmoil began.

The mother shouts: "Hand me my child!" But they answer her: "Your," they say, "child is to be found inside of you." "What!" shouts the mother, "How can my child be inside of me when I just gave him birth!" "But," they say to the mother, "perhaps you are mistaken?" "What," shouts the mother, "do you mean 'mistaken'? How can I be mistaken? I saw for myself he was just lying here on the sheet!" "That's correct," they say to the mother, "but perhaps he's crawled back in somewhere." In a word, they themselves didn't know what to tell the mother.

But the mother makes a fuss and demands her child.

An experienced doctor had to be called. The experienced doctor examined the mother and shook his head, but nonetheless still kept his wits and gave the mother a good dose of Epsom salts. The mother's bowels moved and, in this way, I came into the world for a second time.

And here again papa flew into a rage: "you can't," he says, "even call this a birth, and this is, so to say, not even a person, but rather halfway a foetus, and he either has to be crammed back in or put into the incubator."

And so they put me into the incubator.

September 25, 1935

Incubation Period

I stayed in the incubator four months. All I remember is that the incubator was made of glass, was transparent and had a thermometer. I sat inside the incubator on cotton. More than that I don't remember.

After four months they took me out of the incubator. They did that right on the first of January of 1906. In this way I was born as if for a third time. And so they started to consider the first of January the day of my birth.

September 1935

EARLIEST SURVIVING LETTERS

[Letters to Ivan Yuvachev]

St. Petersburg. September 25, 1910

Sweet Papa!

I send all my love. And thank you for the photograph.

Danya

* * *

St. Petersburg. March 1911

sweet papa how's your health I'm writing myself can't write very much I'm tired.

DANYA

* * *

Village of Tarkhovka, St. Petersburg district. June 29, 1912

sweet papa. I'm learning to read.

* * *

Village of Tarkhovka, St. Petersburg district. July 13, 1912

sweet papa,

first I put together the words with blocks, and then I write them to you; I ride horseback on mushka, kisses,

your danya

* * *

Village of Tarkhovka, St. Petersburg district. June 7, 1914

Dear papa! It's nice here at the dacha, we're all healthy, we run, play, ride on the donkey, it's lots of fun. In the morning I study with Masha. Olya says hello to you, she's been living with us for two months. Grandmother says hello. Nastya thanks you for the blouse. We all love you. Come see us soon. Your Danya

* * *

Petrograd, February 6, 1917

Sweet Papa,

I found out that you are sick and asked Mama to send you a box of cough drops and other medicines. You should take them when you cough. The children are healthy. Liza and I were sick but now we're also healthy. I have a slight cough. Mama is also all right.

Danya

^{oo}7 or 19 6/II 17
I've been writing it this way for 1 year. I already showed you.
Be healthy.

* * *

[From notebook 1]

Daniel Charms
1924 E—z

* * *

Boole discovered pure mathematics in his *Laws of Thought* 1854.
Pure mathematics: this = that, something else = that.
The Italian professor Peano introduces logical symbols into mathematics.
Three symbols.
Georg Kantor

* * *

Read sitting at your desk and have pencil and paper at hand. Jot down thoughts from the book, as well as your own thoughts that pop up from reading or for any other reason. (Papa)

Often a woman will deny you that which she desires most passionately. (Kuprin)

* * *

$$\frac{+A}{B+C+D} > 1; \quad A > B+C+D$$

$$\lim \frac{+A}{B+C+D} = 1; \quad A = \lim B+C+D$$

$$\frac{A}{B+C+D} < 1; \quad A < B+C+D$$

$$\frac{A}{B} < 1; \quad A < B!$$

$$\lim k = \infty$$

$$|\lim| \beta = k(C+D)$$

$$A < B \qquad \alpha + j = H.$$

$$H = kH'$$

$$\frac{\alpha+j}{k} = H' \qquad \frac{\alpha+j}{\beta+j'} = \frac{H}{H'}$$

* * *

$$\lim t = 0 \qquad \frac{\alpha + \gamma}{\beta + j}' = t$$

$$\alpha + j = tH. \qquad \beta + (tH - \alpha) = ktH.$$

$$\beta + j = ktH. \qquad \beta = ktH - (tH - \alpha)$$

$$j + tH - \alpha$$

Individuality is represented by S

$$H = \frac{A}{S} \qquad [\beta = kt\frac{A}{S} - t\frac{A}{S} - ktH]$$

$$\beta = kt\frac{A}{S} - t\frac{A}{S} + \alpha$$

$$\beta = \frac{A}{S}(kt - t) + \alpha$$

$$\beta = \frac{A}{S}[t(k - 1)] + \alpha$$

$$\lim t = 0$$

$$\alpha = \beta$$

$$\alpha^2 = \beta^2$$

$$(tH - j)^2 = \beta$$

$$t^2H^2 - 2tj + j^2 = \beta$$

$$t < 1 \qquad \lim t = 0$$

$$H^2 = t$$

* * *

$\alpha > \beta$. I know this purely from observation. Moreover, α is a very large quantity, while β is infinitely small, though variable. It varies from some significant part of α to an infinitely small segment.

DCH 8 nov. 1924.

* * *

Nov. 8, 9 o'clock 17 minutes. β was completely unknown to me. I didn't concern myself with the observation of a. N – a is of no concern. I think that b (A) has achieved velocity C and has ceased to exist in relation to me as matter.

The fundamental ratio:

$$\frac{+A}{B+C+D}$$

Today on the 9th of November, b changes place from the numerator to the denominator. When the numerator equals zero, the entire fraction will cease to be material. This means that ES is lost.

The loss of ES equals death, which is impossible.* Consequently, in place of A, another quantity must arise. I have insufficient data to determine this value precisely. My goal is to reduce it to the form (A)β. In other words B+C+D must equal zero.

Therefore

$$\frac{+A}{B+C+D} = \frac{+A}{0} = +\infty$$

$$t = +\infty \qquad (A)\beta = +\infty$$

$$\beta = \frac{+\infty}{A} \; ; \quad \beta = +\infty$$

For any ES known to me.
B+C+D cannot = 0!!!

*I have said that the loss of ES equals death. This is not entirely true. S is individuality, consequently, the loss of ES, and of S in general, is the complete deindividualization of a given person.

* * *

I am, as they say,
ready to bray.

* * *

Phrenology
Physiognomy
Cheiromancy
Montgristics (by the fingers)
Cheirosofia (by the nails)
Graphology

* * *

The fool cannot distinguish the essential from the accidental.

The boasting of a fool is sincere; the boasting of an intelligent man is always malicious and unattractive.

* * *

Preludes
1) Miniature
2) Prelude of Death
3) from "The Bell"
4) Fiery Snow
5) Oriental
6) Fugue
7) Military
8) New

* * *

Sacher Mädchen, doch liebe ich dich noch, wen du wilst mit mir wieder sein so komm zu mir und wert dein Breutigam Siest und doch wer war recht, du oder ich? Ich sagte dir, dass du wirst früher mich werfen, als ich dich. So ist es auch gescheen. Weren wir noch zusammen, so hätten wir so rein gewesen, noch so immer jung. Aber jetzt, weil du so sarkastisch bist mit mir, sprech ich mit dir nicht, du bist jetzt grob geworden. Doch versuch (wenn du mich noch liebst) wieder mit mir zahrt sein und vieleich werden wir, wieder Freunden. Ich kan dir sagen wie es machen, komm zu mir. Sah, mit Sinaida Nikolavna und frage etwas von Relitivitastheorie. Es wird alles schön gehen. Dieser Tag wird uns alles zeigen. 1 April 1925.

Lies meine liebste gedichte alle des ich dir einmal gelesen habe. Fedor Sologub. Treumenlied. Z.b.

> *Sweet Girl, I love you still, and if you still want to be with me, then come to me and see what your fiancé is worth: so who was right, you or me? I told you that you would drop me before I dropped you. And that's just how it happened. Were we still together, we would have been so pure, so young forever. But now, since you're so sarcastic with me, I'm not speaking with you, you've become rude. So try (if you still love me) to be nice to me and perhaps we'll*

be friends again. I can tell you how to do this: come see me. Go see Zinaida Nikolaevna and ask her something about the theory of relativity. It will all go well. This day will show us everything. April 1, 1925.

Read my favorite poems, all those I once read to you. Fyodor Sologub. "Dreamsong," for example.

* * *

Tel. 5-37-35. Fontanka 38, apt. 13. Lev Nikolaevich Levkovsky.

Got to get down to work.

* * *

[From notebook 2]

H.G. Wells
"Armageddon."
Tales of Time and Space.
The Passionate Friends.

Chesterton, *The Club of Queer Trades.*

* * *

Lesgaft, 571 – 90
Nikolai Aleksandrovich Morozov.
The Society of Political Prisoners.
N. A. Morozov, 25 Torgovy Lane, apt. 31.
At the office around 2 o'clock.

* * *

Rusakov, Alesksandr Ivanovich. Zhelyabov St. 19/8 213—58.
571—90—P. F. Lesgaft Institute of Physical Education.
34 Maklin Prospect.
3rd of July Street to Ekaterinhofsky Prospect.
Tram №№ 7, 13, 21. From 25 October Prospect. One stop.

Tuesday 8:00 at Tufanov's. DSO
Friday 7:00 Chemistry
        9:00 House of the Arts.

On Thursday, March 19, 1925 at 8:00 p.m. be at Marcel's. He's going to play Kruchinin's "Vampire Tango."

March 16. Sold Viktor bicycle and jacket for 25 rubles. 6 rubles for home.

* * *

Today is March 18, 1925.

Baba-Yaga.
Broken Lily.
trrash!

Not a word about the "Thief of Baghdad."
Shush!

But on the way, I (don't know about you) thought about it the whole time and it was funny. Damn you, all because of your ugly little mug and Rita, I've got to waste my time on this idiotic letter. Varshavsky, quite clearly, has vanished, and, may you get stuffed and burst, I'm condemned to writing.

The situation is hopeless! I, as an honest man and a friend in pursuit of the honor of a blowjob, unadulterated by any other perversions, am not going out into the hall to get my coat, but I'm sitting on your bed and praising myself for my honesty.
So it turns out you're inviting me, but I've already gotten excited and now I want to keep writing on and on. Some sort of coarse cardboard bends in hymn and theme, even gluckerlets

string on soffets.
Thusmight gluve
the winding sticks
of steenery. Weightup
northerlies' endeavorous

pensail, knit it up
shiftdriven blowspast
some fur. Doubleup
occufolia debutchers
for a second call yourself
naïve phreak.
Facet up outofwalled
a flamelet not in walls,
crumbly and
dreary
ornamental suddenly.

Billets dance
ballet there
in heady change
and winks twinkle
blow me. Dewdrops
are poison and gluggings
do you harm. You toss out
a guestgift: debauchery, a gun.
Naturejoy smelts
And it's versing like viols,
Let's all caper merrymaid
in dance polonaise.
They'll all them fall in love,
Dovebluely like a wall
style started sliding shut
hey sing donny
hey doony, hey dee.

Clayily glacially,
So hobbletrilegedly
Barefootbaby of the boobybells.
Bobies are strumming out
songing nearby,
twice and thrice
and lots and blue.

slatternly fanciful
to your legs and closer.
Pull out rudely opening wide.
Boombola vimbola
in bolo blubbings
Style—hey sing donny
hey doony, hey dee.

* * *

Andrei Bely.
Star
The Princess and Her Knights.
Ashes.
The First Encounter. A poem.
After Parting.
Urn.

H.G. Wells
The Island of Doctor Moreau.
A Life's Morning.

G. Chesterton
The Man Who Was Thursday.

* * *

[From notebook 3]

Books from "The Library of New Books"

Aristophanes, *On the Art of Poetry.*
W. Barret, *Enigmatic Aspects of the Human Psyche.*
H.O.T.
F. Baumgarten, *Psychotechnica*, part 1

H. Bergson. *Introduction to Metaphysics*, vol. V.
1) Psychophysical Parallelism and Positive Metaphysics.
2) Laughter
vol. IV.
-*Questions of Philosophy and Psychology.*

-*Time and Free Will.*
-*Duration and Simultaneity.*
H. Bergson
Matter and Memory: An Essay on the Relation of Body and Spirit.
The Immediate Data of Consciousness, vol. II.
Creative Evolution.
Bergson. *Laughter in Life and on Stage.*

Bernstein, A. *Clinical Methods for the Psychological Study of the Mentally Ill.*
V. M. Bekhterev, *Collective Reflexology.*
The Objective Study of Personalities
On Hypnotism.
Fundamentals of the Study of Brain Functions,

* * *

The Sexual Question:

Beard and Rockwell, *Sexual Exhaustion as a Type of Neurasthenia.*
Iwan Bloch. *The Sexual Life of our Time.*
L. M. Vasilevsky, *Towards a Healthy Sex Life.*
Vasilevsky, *Sexual Deviance.*

Otto Weininger, *On Henrik Ibsen and his Works.*
Weininger, *Sex and Character.*
Weininger. *Last Words.*

Afanasiev, *Erotic Folktales* "The Bashful Noblewoman."
A. Hegar, *The Sex Drive*
Professor Gertsegi, *Woman in her Physiological, Pathological and Moral Aspects.*
L. Levenfeld, *Sexual Problems.*
A. K. Lentz, *Shame and its Meaning for Sexual Feeling.*
A. Meyer, *Hygiene of the Childless Marriage.*
Freud, *Theory of the Sex Drive.*
Kovalevsky. *Sexual Psychology.*

* * *

Havelock Ellis, *Geschlechtstrieb und Schamgefühl*.
Chekhov, "Untitled."
Engineer F. G. Narli.
A course in Trigonometry with Supplementary Materials.
2nd Ed. Petrograd 1916.

* * *

Anton Shvarts read poems.
Tiutchev.

* * *

Soon my steeds shall take a piss—
Surely they all wanted this.
(Arabia)

* * *

Stops from the Embankment and 8th line:

to Haymarket 12:48-1:00		12 min.
to Nevsky	6 min.	18 min.
to Nikolaevsky Station	14 min.	26 min.
to Zoo	19 min.	31 min.

Legs:

From Embankment and 8th line to Haymarket	12 min.
From Haymarket to Nevsky	6 min.
From Nevsky to Nik. Stat.	8 min.
From Nik. Stat. to Zoo.	5 min.

* * *

1.
Resembling pinion wheels and cogs
Passing they march on and on
And their echo crashes
And step gnashes step

2.

Beat out the trumpets rumbling then
Beat up the hooves with thumping then
Past wall top
A' gallop
The cobbles beat their brains

3.

But you don't seem to understand,
And I'm your own Ionia
And all our life
Is struggle.

4.

Pour out yourself resplendent night;
I'm under banner red (not white)
and marching
and arching
and eyes going blind.

My dear ones . . . my dear ones . . . my very very best
And all our life is struggle!

* * *

~~Holy Mary Cross and Mary Cross and Mary~~
~~Help me~~.

Ich fuhlte mich schlecht. Aber G. hilf mir. Das Konst Du mir helfen. Lass auch alles mich Technikum gut umstehen.

Liber G. Hilf mir heute examen aushalten. Las mich gesund sein.

An. G.–↑

> *I don't feel well. But God help me. You can help me. Let everything go well with the Electro-Technical College.*

> *Dear God, Help me pass the exam today. Keep me well.*

> *To God– ↑*

* * *

Shakyamuni, Dhanwantari and Maitreya

Chakravartin (rulers of the world)
Akshobhya
Muchalinda Buddha
Dzo-bo
Zandanzu
Amitabha

Dalkha (God of War) Dakini (Erotica)
Hanuman (with member)
Khora-Khoto

Tsam

Sitatapatra
Saraswati
Pancharaksha
Vajravarahi
Kurukulla (fiery dance)

Ushnishavijaya
Amitayus
Avalokiteshvara
Amagopacha
Maitreya
Saptapadi Mangalsutra
Virudhaka
Gessar-Khan

* * *

In a bag full of holes
milk well
milg keeps.

* * *

Thomas Mann, *Herr und Hund* etc. 1919. Berlin.
Wilhelm Hegler, *Der verschüttete Mensch.* 1924. Berlin.

Vera Inber, *The Goal and The Path.*
Anatoly Mariengof, *Imaginists.* 1925.

Ushkuiniki. River Pirates.

* * *

Wartete sehr lange sibente Nummer. Fick seine Mutter. Ich bin böse. 7 čþíÿ.

9 Iuni. G.H. m in Technikum bleiben. Gott mach das ich hir lernen. Weiter werde Hoffnung, Kreutz und Marie, Kreutz und Marie, Kreutz und Marie. Daniel Charms.

1925. Hilf.

> *Waited very long for number 7. Fuck its mother. I am bad. 7 June.*
>
> *June 9. God Help me stay at the Technical College. God grant that I be allowed to study here. Then there will be hope. Cross and Mary, Cross and Mary, Cross and Mary. Daniel Charms.*
>
> *1925 Help!*

* * *

[Entry in Semyon Polotsky's handwriting]

Dear friend,
Here's my handwriting for you. Write something amusing about what's going on behind the scenes of the soul of your most obedient servant. Wear your trousers softly.

Semyon Polotsky

[Entry in Kharms's handwriting]

S.P.

Sentimental, logically frank. There is self-esteem, but not as it seems from the outside, not showy but secret. You won't be an innovator in anything. I suppose that by conviction you're now a Bolshevik Communist. You've also got, perhaps, some higher education. But somehow it's either unsystematic or not.

* * *

Mugface calico
grabfork for the fob
Pecked out scarfed up
in figure of a pony
like asparagus and wintergusts
suspenders on now
cardboard branches
a lilac by the House.
overhatted stuckround hat
wallpaper spurk to indicate
grab vargoon kare
quiver
skeet
a skew skews
khaliazins softyolk
isked

* * *

Semyon Anatolievich Polotsky, Petrograd Side, 74 Bolshoy Prospect, apt. 8.

* * *

Thursday	Geometry.
Friday	Math Test
Tues.	Literature
	Physics
	Chem.
Thursday	Drafting

* * *

From home:
Paper
Food
Draft of sketches
Smokes
Physical work. Book.
The Dog Train.
Zaum, Kruchenykh and Khlebnikov.

* * *

The phrase "let's be friends."
The difference?
Similar in being shortchanged.

Another time there could be a quarrel, but here there's courtesy.
No argument.
You don't respect the least bit of talent in her, nor she in you.
Obsessed with thoughts of making her a comrade.
Wondering how she'll do.

* * *

At first you can be with other women. Physically zero. Utopian marriage.
She's not a comrade, because you come to her not as a counselor, but as a teacher.
You're not in love with Maro, but with her description.
You're not in love because from the very first day you started bragging.

It all came down to you, not to Maro: how well you know life and how you found it. The debt and the debtor. Disdain. Trivial mistakes, fencing.
You love aphorisms and see in them thoughts too great, and you want to pack too much life into an aphorism.

* * *

Several accusations have come down on me for which I may have to leave the Electro-Technical College. As far as I know, these accusations amount to:
1) Poor attendance,
2) Not participating in community service,
3) I don't fit into the class physiologically.

In response to these accusations, I can say the following:
The College is supposed to produce electrical technicians. Indeed that much seems clear. In order for that to happen, the students must be good workers so they do not get in the way of others. People's capacity for work is judged either directly from their work or by way of psychological analysis. I call your attention to the second.

* * *

A complement to Lermontov.
The cliff as a way of describing the "Demon."
A discussion of the artist.
About hyperbole, supposed to enhance artistic quality.
Psychological significance of the "Demon."

Nothing about *Hero of Our Time*.
That came earlier. Psychologism.

About Lermontov and Pushkin.
For some reason about society in a short speech. The end is closer to my theme.

* * *

Harald Høffding, *Essays in Empirical Psychology*.
S. Gruzenberg, *The Psychology of Creativity*.
V. Danilovsky. *Hypnotism*.

* * *

With her eyes she raised an arrow up.
Wipe that smile from your face.
While the heart hankers for a bullet.
While the throat raves razors.

* * *

P. Dubois. *Self Education*.
Bonch-Tomashevsky. *A Book about the Tango: Art and Sexuality*.
K. Bücher. *Work and Rhythm*.
Volkov-Davidov. *A Brief Guide to Melodeclamation*.
The Art of Declamation.
A Theory of Russian Speech Intonation.
A. Gastex. *Vocal Hygiene*.

* * *

Poems by heart by me:

Kamensky: Myne Hearte. Persia. U. Seasong. Lullabye. Juggler. The Surf in Sukhumi. Sunburne-Springburne. The Seasons.   9

Severianin: Ingrid. Predeath. Beauty. Poesy of Refusal. Flash. Cinquefoil II. Poesy about Kharkov. Your Morning. Quenzelles. It Happened By the Sea. Spring Day. Woodnymph. *Victoria regia*. Habanera III. Champagne Polonaise. My Funeral. His Thirteenth Princess. Russian Girl.   18

Blok: The Twelve. The Stranger. "You pass by without a smile." Tinsel Angel. "The hallways darkened and faded." In a Restaurant. "In a far blue bedroom."   6

Inber: Centipede. Romance I.   2

Gumilev: Master of Cardboard. Baby Elephant. Streetcar. A Children's Song. The Wanderer. The Mandarin's Three Wives.   6

Sologub: Lullaby I. Lullaby II. "Everything was restless and orderly, as always." A Simple Song.   4

Bely: Merrymaking in Old Russia. The Priest's Wife.   2

Akhmatova: "Of flowers and of lifeless things." "The twenty-first."   2

Mayakovsky: Left March. Our March. A Cloud in Pants. From Street to Street. Port. In an Auto. Petersburg Again. They Don't Understand a Thing. And Could You? Old Man with Cats. Naval Love. Streetways. About Old Woman Vrangel.   14

Aseev. Funeral March. Dog Train. Day.   3

Esenin. "So now it's been decided. . . ." Pugachev's first aria.   2

Khlebnikov. Razin's Barque (excerpt). Opus 13.   2

Tufanov. Spring. The Nen.   2

Vigiliansky. A Poem about Horses. At Moonlit Noon. Minuet. Cornflowers. Incantation. Tango.   6

Mart. The Black House. The Ball in the Black House. White Devil. 3 Tanks.   4

Markov. March. Romance.   2

* * *

Pushkin *500 New Jokes and Puns*. Collected by A. Kruchenykh.
E. P. Radin, *Futurism and Insanity*.

Collections on the theory of poetic language:
Literary Encyclopedia.
Lvov-Rogachevsky. *Current Russian Literature.*
Tomashevsky. *Russian Versification. Metrics.*
Tynianov, Yu. *Problems of Poetic Language.*
Shklovsky. *The Unfolding of Plot.*
A. M. Peshkovsky. *Russian Syntax Considered Scientifically.*
Eikhenbaum. *The Melodics of Verse.*

* * *

Saw Tufanov June 15, 1925.
Arrived. Saw him on № 12 tram at 11:30 a.m. corner of Liteiny.

* * *

A nasal ananas or a perennial pineapple.

Kerosene. Beth in the bath.

In the end the maid will sit on an end.

* * *

I. Bloch, *The Sexual Life of Our Time*
H. Ellis. *Man and Woman.*

That babe with you ain't bad

* * *

On the subject of Naming:
Should do a survey: what associations come up with the names of certain streets?
2 Mud [Gryaznaya] Street, apt. 15.

* * *

8th line near Sredny. Pharmacy 3rd floor, apt. 19.
Housing assistance.

* * *

"Distcom"—the devil only knows what that means!

[From notebook 4]

ESTHER
1925

* * *

ESTHER

* * *

Leningrad
Daniil Kharms
3/4 Mirgorodskaya Street, apt. 25
is the Owner of this notebook.
1925
August 18.

* * *

Schedule for August 19.

Get up at 10:00:	Be ready by 10:30.
10:30 – 12:00:	Read Chekhov's notebook.
12:00 - tea time:	Call Vvedensky.
1:00:	Go see Fedya. If I get the money from Fedya, go to Library of New Books. If not, then to Semyon Polotsky. If I'm at the Library, drop in on Tufanov, and then Polotsky.
5:00:	Home. Dinner. After dinner, from 6:30 or 7, read library books or Kropotkin.
10:00:	Tea. After tea, read German.
2:00:	Go to sleep.

* * *

572 Kharms. Card Number, Library of New Books.

* * *

The fourth Michael is stupid. He comes into the room shuffling his feet and swaying: "sail out sharp-prowed barques bright painted" he says, and listens off to the side and bugs the muscles out around his eyes. In quiet moments he thinks for a long time and then asks someone an official question he doesn't even need. He has a conversation with someone whose mother is dying to the tapping of a typewriter

* * *

When I get back to Leningrad, take a look at the following books:

Prof. A.I. Vvedensky, *Psychology without the Metaphysics*, 1917.
Popov, *Popular Timetables in the History of Philosophy*, parts 1 & 2.
Prof. N. O. Lossky, "_____"
Brentano, 1874
The Psychology of William James. Trans. by I. I. Lapshin. 1911.
Aristotle, *On the Soul*. Snegirev translation. 1885.
Grot, *The Psychology of Sensations*. 1880.
Prof. Kozlov, *A Critical Sketch on the Subject of Grot's The Psychology of Sensations*, 1881.
Windelband, *Preludes. A System of Categories.*
Falckenberg, *History of Modern Philosophy*. Translation by Viktorov. 1910.
Shpet, *Appearance and Sense*. 1914.

* * *

Never look for a fool—he'll find you; look for a wise man—you won't find him anywhere. (Papa)
The fool looks for a wise man among fools, but the wise man finds him. (me)

* * *

I. S. Breslau, *The Human Factory*, Gomel, 1925. Pg. 136.

* * *

M. G. Es ist doch logisch mich einladen Gedichte zu lesen.
Mach es M. G. da sind Menschen die Literatur lieben, es wird ihnen
interessand sein doss zu hören. Lass Natasche hofliches sein zu meine
Gedichte. G. mache doch das un ich bitte dich. Mach es liebe G.

> *Dear God. It's surely logical to invite me to read some poems.
> May there be people there who love literature and are interested
> in listening. And please let Natasha be more polite about my
> poems. God, grant that which I ask of you. Grant this, my dear
> God.*

* * *

Epigram for Papa

The awl-like answer of a sovereign
Like a prickly vampire of the drawing room
Mustaches slanting behind a beard
Papa and Papa's son.

The years are just such a roller
Listen to me by the button
How foolish in the year 2000
~~To cry to the wind~~
To shoot and think I'll hit the mark.

Epigram No. 2

My poems for you, my dearest papa
Seem little better than cold kasha,
Though yours attain the highest peak still
For me they trickle out like treacle.

* * *

Aleksandr Ivanovich Vvedensky, 37 Syezzhinskaya, apt. 4.

Evgeny Ivanovich Vigiliansky, 41 6th line (Vasilievsky Island), apt. 9.

* * *

From Leningrad

Zangezi
Socks
2 shirts for daytime
1 for 4 nights
Tobacco and cigarettes
Vvedensky's poems
Notebook with addresses

In Leningrad

Call Vvedensky.
Call Tufanov and Vigiliansky.
Tell Tufanov that I won't see him today.

* * *

II Spiritualist séance,
August 31 ~~23:58~~ (24) (0:00)
Left hand moved. Had the sense I helped it. In general very disorganized.
The following letters were indicated: prasheshiparshyaye. Then:
Goodbye. 0:30.

* * *

He speaks six known and six unknown languages.

* * *

Nikolai Andreevich Nikitin, 30 Revolution Street, apt. 7.
Pornographic pictures.
Pavel Andreevich Mansurov.

* * *

About abstract *zaum*.
If the national can be required from a thing not in *zaum*, then even more
can be asked from *zaum*.
Develop my own theory about the beauty of the national word.

* * *

Now the factory wakes up
Starts its singing, calls and huffs
Time to rise and shine now brothers
To get down to work together
And the night flees
                the
                      day
And the shadows
              go
                  away
And He makes them hurry hurry
Out to meet him on the fly
Come the workers, all the workers
        all the workers marching by.

        2.

Come and see the Leninist
Leninists don't laze a bit.
With a squad of workers he
Steps off for the factory
Out to meet them at the threshold
—model for all bosses here—
Quite politely, quite correctly
Comes the senior engineer
Makes a bow to Nastya, Mitya
Says to all
        I'm pleased to meet ya'
Glad to meet you each and every . . .
then he takes them up the stairway.

        3.

What goes on here
              light
                  flash
What a racket
            noise
              crash
Hustle bustles roaring and
Guests head backwards, doorwards then

Fires flare and flame like suns
Everywhere the hot sparks run
Like small candles dancing
                         burning
Sparks come flying out the furnace
And the furnace churns churns
She just wants to burn-burn
Flames lick the walls and writhe
Let's take a closer look inside.

                4.

Furnace breathing fire
Day and night respires.
Fall in her fell maw:
Fall and rise no more.
Furnace opens wide
Folks run to her side
Folks in soot and grime
"What is it you'd like?"
Time for her to eat
Furnace wants a treat
Meat's not her demand
But just simple sand
So that it be white
Like good chalk, and bright.
Put it down below
Where lime and soda go
Mix it in a lump
Scoop it up and dump
Shovels-full right in the furnace
That's it Mistress eat in earnest!

* * *

72 Moika Canal, Pawnshop 10:30

I bought "Jim" boots on September 26, 1925 at Gostinny Dvor, on the
Nevsky side, store number 28.

* * *

Lord, I made so bold as to demand of thee a blwjb from ⊟, and am
punished for it. No, Lord, guide us, so that it's normal and easy for us
together. Amen.
September 30, 1925.

* * *

For September 30, 1925.

I thought: if Esther and I were to quarrel today, we were doomed to part.
The horrible thing is it's just what happened.
We quarreled. And now we'll part.
This might have been expected.
Lord, I wanted a blwjb today, but this is the death of love. Oh Lord, be with
us. Do not forget us. My sweet little girl Ester was lost to me today. I know
that.
It's beyond all doubt.
She's calling to me now, but I know it won't be for long. What can you do?
Surely it's just the way I am. She's got nothing to do with it: she's a woman
like any other, while I'm some kind of degenerate.
Lord, Thy will be done.
No, either I get a blwjb today or it's all over with Esther.
Ester for ever.

* * *

[From notebook 5]

Daniil Kharms
1925

* * *

Daniil Kharms
October 8, 1925

* * *

Evgeny Vigiliansky
Vasilievsky Island, 41 6th Line, apt. 9
Tel. 134-11.

* * *

79

Cinetechnicum
Kabinetskaya Street
tel. 611—96

Society of the Friends of Radio.
29 Herzen Street, apt 4
tel. 157-89.

* * *

Paul Marcel
—ESTHER
19 Zhelyabov Street, apt 4
tel. 213-58.

* * *

545-26
Aleksandr Iv. Vvedensky
37 Syezzhinskaya, corner of Kronverk Prospekt
2nd entrance, apt. 14

* * *

Tamara Romanovna Rappoport (Maro)
209-69.

5-57-32
Boris Konstantinovich Cherny

* * *

[Entries in other handwritings]

It's not like I have any grub. I don't even want to eat. Afterwards I can always get away from Cherny.

If I'm with Cherny, then I'll go to your place, if not, I'll go home.

That's not right, I don't want to walk down the street with him.

What do you think?

Your fly is unbuttoned.

* * *

S. O. Gruzenberg, *Genius and Creativity.*
Hoffding, *Jean-Jacques Rousseau and his Philosophy.*

W. Windelband, *On Free Will*, Lectures.
W. Wund.
1. Introduction to Psychology
2. Introduction to Philosophy
3. The Soul of Man and Animals. I and II.
4. Myth and Religion
5. Fantasy as the Foundation of Art

* * *

[Entry in another handwriting]

Your right ear is itching.

* * *

Nonsensists
Tuesday 8:00.

* * *

Verbal art is temporal. Emotion theme meaning. Perception of time changes, emotion, meaning, themes change. We're the ones who have to bring together those most left, that is, the most fluid, and if someone doesn't understand Vvedensky and me, he's mistaken in his definition. He's not fluid. When the futurists shout that they're in the future and that they're fluid, then we see them for what they are. Stop! (they say) we're fluid. This cannot be, you're either fluid or not fluid. Not completely fluid simply isn't possible.

* * *

[Record of a poetry reading, October 17, 1925]

An Evening of the *Zaumniki*

On October 17 an evening of Leningrad *Zaumniki* ("trans-sense poets") took place at the Poets' Union (Fontanka 50). An announcement was made about the "Order of *Zaumniki* DSO" and a "Manifesto" was promulgated by Aleksandr *Tufanov. Ivi* read a report entitled "The

Tournament of the *Zaumniki*" and Tinvin made some introductory remarks on art.

On the basis of their theory of an "expanded perception of the world" and an "immediate perception of time," A. Tufanov proposed a trans-sense classification of poets along a circle. Poets at an angle of 1-40° *correct* the world, still others between 41-89° reproduce it, and a third group from 90-179° ornament it. Only the *zaumniki* and the expressionists who perceive at an angle from 180-360°, by *distorting* or transforming the world, are revolutionary. That's why the evening's program was subsequently taken up with: at 180°: a choral reading of an excerpt from a long poem by Tufanov, "The Michaels" by Kharms, and then: Ivi, Tufanov and Kharms offered examples of "abstract *zaum*" (at 360°).

In addition, A. Vvedensky presented his prose, declaring himself the representative of the "Nonsense Authority." The combative atmosphere the *zaumniki* created, the large number of participants, the invitation extended by the President of the *Zaumniki* to a performance the following evening, and the demand for trans-sense literature—all of it indicated that the evening had gone off successfully.

The audience was not prepared for the debate that followed, and the presentations had a curious character which led A. Tufanov in closing to remark on a "speech impediment" on the part of the orators and on the unconvincing prophesies by the would-be "Pythians."

There will be a reading of A. Tufanov's "Home to the Zavolochye" at the Institute of Artistic Culture.

* * *

[From notebook 5]

How stupid we are, we want to read everything that has been written. Little boys are what we are.
November 1, 1925. With Boris Cherny.

[*From notebook 38*]

It's just Me.

Left Flank meeting.
January 5, 1926.

Order of presentations:
1. Vvedensky, Kharms, Dzhemla, Cherny, Tufanov, Markov, Solovyov.
2. Solovyov, Markov, Tufanov, Cherny, Dzhemla, Kharms, Vvedensky.
About Bogaevsky. We're building a free organization while relying on
the old.

* * *

[Letter to Boris Pasternak]

April 3, 1926

Honored Boris Leontievich,
We've heard from Mikhail Kuzmin about the existence in Moscow
of "Knot" publishers.
We are the only real left-wing poets in Petrograd, however we
cannot publish our work here.
We append to this letter several poems as examples of our work,
and ask you to inform us about the possibility of publishing them in
the "Knot" anthology or as a separate book. In the latter instance,
we can send you additional materials (poetry and prose).

Daniil Kharms
aleksandrvvedensky
April 3, 1926. Petersburg

* * *

[From notebook 6]

On Friday, May 7, take payment to Library of New Books.
№ 248

A. Binet and T. Simon. *A Method for Measuring Mental Endowment.*

Chinar   1926
Daniil   Kharms

* * *

Dear young maidens, don't be dumb
they might stick you with a drum.
Drums don't scare us as you know
we'll get married even so.

* * *

In all likelihood my life will pass in terrible poverty, and I'll live well only
when I'm at Home, and then maybe if I live to be 35 or 40 . . .

Missed it. So there!

* * *

Lips were burning on a birchtree
An udder wandered through the hills
And bluebells et cetera.

For May 12, 1926

7pm – 10:   Read Dostoevsky *The Village of Stepanchikovo.*
After dinner: Memory exercises.
12 midnight: Lights out.

Lyonka came by and the plan changed.

* * *

Tamara Aleksandrovna Meier's name day is May 14.
At the same time there's also something happening at Amalia Yakovlevna
Goldfarb's.

Dina's birthday: 20 June.
Lina's wedding: 20 August.
Lina's birthday: 31 December
Tamara's birthday: 17 May

* * *

May 13, 1926
Drank to FRIENDSHIP

May 13. Drinking at Markov's. Tufanov got so drunk that they beat him with a cane when he came home.

I was too, and barely knew what to do. Maybe it seemed that way because I was so drunk.

* * *

Pens: 1. F. Soennenken III p. Bonn.
          2. Universelles. D. Leonardt & Co. extra A.
          3. Copier pen N. 404.
          4. Toyoseiko & Co. NIKKO PEN. N1.
                    Tokyo Japan.

Zabolotsky. Tuesday, May 18. 4:30 pm.
Saturday May 15: morning at the Markovs.
Saturday night to Sunday: blowout at Zhenka's.

* * *

Nikolai Aleksandrovich Zabolotsky, 73/75 Krasnykh Zor' Street, mansard, room 5.

Institute of Artistic Culture. 585-72
9 Vorovsky Square.

Mikhail Alekseevich Kuzmin. 613-84
17 Spasskaya Street, apt. 9.

Sergei Mitrofanovich Gorodetsky.
Moscow, 1 Red Square, apt. 3.

Boris Konstantinovich Cherny.
Moscow. 351-37.

Sofia Grigorievna Vysheslavtseva.
4 Petropavlovskaya Street, apt. 58.
tel. 124-08.

Ilya Ivanovich Sadofiev. 152-43.
29 Rakov Street.

* * *

Tamara Romanovna Rappoport. 209-69.

Semyon Anatolievich Polotsky. 110-26.

Mikhail Ginzburg. 131- 23.

Union of Writers. 50 Fontanka, apt. 25.
tel. 79-98.

Tamara Aleksandrovna Meier.
23 Kronverk Street, apt. 71.
5th entrance, 6th floor. Don't ask for Sofia
but for Tamara Aleksandrovna.
Work phone 50-20.

* * *

K. K. Olimpov (Fofanov).
39 Lenin Street, apt. 12 (formerly Shirokaya Street).

Sergei Evgenievich Neldikhen.
19 Preobrazhenskaya Street, apt. 3.
106-26.

Yashka Druskin. 199-44.

Benedikt Konstantinovich Livshits.
3 Mokhovaya Street, apt. 43.

* * *

On June 15 at the Markovs' a large mirror shattered. Jinx!
Jinx! God help us!
That's how you ward off the bad luck.

* * *

Müde, immer auf dem Wege.
So soll es schon gehen. So binn ich. Mir ist er wiederlich. Ich will es mehr
nicht. Geht ihr alle zum Teufel. Kameraden!
Das ist das schlimmste. Warscheinlich doch alle Menschen sind so eben.
Und weil du siehst einige ofter, deshalb findest du da allerei schlimmes.
Und doch in allen Fällen sind immer Weiber schuld. Jetzt ich nur
niemanden stosse. Nur vorsichtig sollst du sein. Halt dein Weg.

    May 26.

    *Tired, always on my way. That's how it is. That's how I am. I'm
    used to it. I don't want it anymore. You can all go to hell, comrades!
    That's the worst. Apparently people have always been like this.
    And the more you see them, the worse you find them. And whatever
    happens, the women are always to blame. So now I'm not going
    to bother anyone. Only you have to be more careful. Keep to
    your path.*

    May 26.

* * *

46 Basseinaya Street, apt. 9. Druzin. The poetics of *chastushki*.

* * *

Iretám enébek
Iretém inébek
iretám enébeik

Vladimir Balnis. Detskoe Selo. 7 Malaya Street, apt. 1.

217-81, Press House.

* * *

Yury Ivanovich Yurkun.
The thing smells of bedbugs.

What's this you've served up?

There are personas and there are persons . . . and also personality, but then there's also: the writer Yurkun.
As if there isn't already enough garbage in the world!

Close in spirit to Aleksandr Ivanovich.

* * *

A terribly modern novel. On sheets of toilet paper.

Went to the bakery or better yet the pastry shop. And what do I see above the counter? A little fop.

* * *

108 Griboedov Canal, apt. 12. Entrance from the lane across from the Conservatory. K. K. Vaginov.
Friday, 8 pm.

* * *

[Entry in another handwriting]

Although I don't have anything against it, should we wait for Igor?
What do you think?
Naw.

* * *

Let's not look at anything. Rivals. Got to pay attention to the stomachs. Let the heads turn red. I'll lie here like a knout.
No jealousy. This is either an accomplishment or not getting enough sleep. Peace to you all. Digestion ruined somehow unexpectedly.
Two will remain. I'll stay home a few days as promised. They showed up here and at once became organs; my ribs can be seen from under

my vest. Going to be gossip, you can bet. Time to go home. Love or a three-way handshake.
Dogs. Khamalans!
Pf.

* * *

Badmaev's memoirs.
Rasputin is there as well.

* * *

[From notebook 8]

Daniil Ivanovich Kharms
SPb. 11 Nadezhdinskaya Street, apt 9.
Tel. 90-24
1926. November 2.
Anyone who finds this book is asked to please call me immediately by telephone. D. Kh.
Z. B. 1926/27 Vvedensky
Press House card number № 684.
Member card, Union of Enlightenment Workers 60157
Labor registry book 5146
Number of my union book, All-Russian Union of Poets 7−1927
Subscription number Library of New Books 967.

* * *

Tues.   12−2. Chess.
        2−3. read German
        3−6. 1) ~~Free~~ Walk. 2) Light reading
        7−9. Study.
        9−11. Read.

Weds.   12−2. Chess.
        2−5. 1) Walk 2) Read.
        7−8. Write.
        8−9. Chess.
        9−11. Read.

* * *

	5-6:30	6:30-8	8-9:30
Monday		Trauberg, Contemp. cinema	Radetsky, Tech. found. of cinema
Tuesday	Gushchin. Theory & sociol. of art.	Eikhenbaum	
Wednesday		Derzhavin, Intro. To cinema	Izvekov, Theory of spectacle
Thursday	~~Tynianov, Plot~~	Radetsky	Kozintsev, Genre cinema and cinema actors
Friday			Leonidov, Screenplay
Saturday		Gvozdev. Euro. Theater 19th & 20th cent.	Trauberg, Seminar contemp. cinema

* * *

Tuesday.   7–12. Foxtrot at Igor Bakhterev's

Friday.   8–9. Union of Poets

* * *

On Friday, November 5, six poets are reading, of which these are: Froman, Ehrlich, Botova, Braun, etc. One of the discussants is Sayanov.

The other day Ester called me and asked if I would be reading this Friday. She's leaving soon for Petrozavodsk. By the way, of all the women I've ever seen, she is, perhaps, the very best.

* * *

Marcel Berger, *The Gods Tremble.*

S. L. Tsimbal is currently writing a play on this topic. From what I know of it so far, it's not to my taste.

Some have called Hermes the god of tricksters.

More than a few recipes for the ointment witches and warlocks rub on themselves before flying to the Sabbath have been preserved. Here is one such recipe as reported by Hieronymus Cardanus (1501-1576): rendered fat of an infant, juice of poppy (opium), wolfsbane (aconitum), cinquefoil (potentilla reptans), nightshade (solanum), soot (Hieronymus Cardanus. *De Subtilitate*. Lib. XVIII).

Ulrich Zell is honored as the oldest of the Cologne printers; his publications are in the greater part marked "apud Lyskirchen," and are known to us beginning in 1466. There is also the printer Johann Soter. Also widely known are the names of Aldo Manuzio, the inventor of the "Aldine" font, active in Venice (from 1495) and of Henricus Stephanus or Estienne (1460-1520).

* * *

Books related to magic

Opusculum, printed in Cologne Köln 1506:
"Das Geheimniss der heiligen Gertrudis zur Erlangung zeitlicher Schätzer u. Güter."
"Buch Mosis und dreifacher Hollenzwang."
"Mächtige Beschwörungen der höllischen Geister."*
"Hauptzwang der Geister zu menschlichen Dienster."

The works of Albert the Great, Arnold de Villanova, Roger Bacon, Robert of England, Anselm of Parma, Picatrix of Spain.
Abbot Trithemius "Philosophia naturalis" and "Antipalus maleficiorum."
Peter Abonensis: "Elementa magica."
Henrici Cornelli Agrippa ab Nettesheym,
"De Occulta Philosophia libri tres."

1506-1576

Hieronymus Cardanus. *De Subtilitate*. Lib. XVIII.

De l'Ancre. *Tableau de l'inconstance de mauvais anges et démons*.
Paris, 1612.

M. N. Speransky. *Witches and Witchcraft*.

Dictionnaire Infernal, par M. Colin de Plancy. 2 éd. Paris. 1825.

Roskoff. *Geschichte des Teufels* 1869.

_____

* published according to monastic manuscripts of the XV and
XVI centuries, in *Bibliotheca Magica*. Köln, 1810.

* * *

Books considered authorities on magic of the XVI century.
A listing by Johannes Wierus:

"Apion le Grammarien, Julian l'Apostat, Artephie, Robert l'Anglois qui
mourut miserablement en Suisse, Roger Bachon, Pierre d'Apone, nommé le
Concilateur, Albert Teutonique, Arnault de Villeneufe, Anselme de Parme,
Picatrix Espangnol, ou bien l'autheur du livre envoyé a Alphonse sous
le nom de Picatrix: Cicchio d'Ascule Florentin, et plusiers autre moins
conus, hommes de malhereux ésprit, ont enseigné sotement les folies
et bastelleries des premiers magiciens." *Des illusions et impostures des
diables*, Livre II, ch. IV.

The works of Albert the Great (1195-1280) were published more or less
in their entirety only in 1651, but individual works of his were widely
distributed at the end of the Middle Ages. Among the magical treatises
of Arnold de Villeneuve (died 1314) considered to be of special value
were: "De phisicis ligaturis" and "De sigillis duodecim signorum."
Of Roger Bacon's magical works: "De mirabilis potestate, artis et naturae."
Of works on magic by Abbot Johannes Trithemius (1462-1516) besides
the "Philosophia naturalis" and the "Antipalus maleficiorum" we know
several others, among which are "Steganographia" (on cabbalistics)
and "Quaestiones VIII ad Maximillian" (with chapters "De reprobis
et maleficis," "De potestate maleficarum," etc). The works of Peter
Aponensis (or Abonensis 1250-1316) were often ascribed to Agrippa*;
of them the best known are the "Geomantia" and the "Heptameron sive

Elementa magica." The first printed edition of Agrippa's work "De Occulta Philosophia" is dated: anno MDXXXIII mense Julio.

De Natura Daemonum Io. L. Ananiae Tabernatis Theologi.
Libri IIII. Venetis MDLXXXI.
Petri de Abano.* "Heptameron sive elementa magica."

*Agrippa of Nottheim
*Peter Aponensis

* * *

To call up a thunderstorm. In a field where the herb nightshade grows, dig a hole in the ground, squat above it, and water it saying: "In the name of the Devil, Let there be Rain!" and at once a stormcloud will come up and there will be rain.

* * *

The Library of Occult Sciences. *Ancient high magic. Theory and practical formulas.* (P. Piobb. *Formulaire de haute magie*). Translated by I. Antoshevsky and edited by I. Sveshoten. Published by I. Kuprianov and A. Laptev. SPb. 80k.

Gustav Meyrink. *The Golem.* 1868.

On the Life of Gotama Buddha. G. M.

A very good way to get a quick rest is to lie there reading a good book and eating black bread sandwiches with onions.

* * *

Chess Bibliography. Library of New Books.

I. Berger. *The Game of Chess.*
N. Grekov and V. Nenarokov. *A Guide to Learning Chess.*
Capablanca. *Chess Fundamentals.*
Lasker. *Common Sense in Chess.*
Levenfish. *A First Book for the Chess-Player.*
Schiffers. *Chess Self-Taught.*

<u>some books I need to get</u>:

Madwig's *Latin Grammar*, or other.
The Big Latin-Russian Dictionary and a shorter self-taught Latin.

* * *

I. Solomonov's genuine "Quickshine" cream. (red and black box)
also in black and yellow box. Leningrad. tel. 527-42

Gaga says 62 is too little while 78 is too much.

* * *

"RADIKS" rehearsals at the Institute of Artistic Culture (INAC) in Kazimir Malevich's studio:

I (10)	Oct. 18.
II (11)	Oct. 20.
III (12)	Oct. 21. for *Les Six*
IV (13)	Oct. 22.
V (14)	Oct. 26. Antonio. Borodina's dance.
	November 3. *My Mama's all in Watches* taken to the censor. Spoke with Voskresensky. Agreed to his seeing the show without reading the thing beforehand.
VI (15)	November 4. Directors didn't show up and performers left soon after.
VII (16)	November 10. Radiks has collapsed. Daniil Kharms Georgy Katzman

* * *

Principle roles in "My Mama's all in Watches."

Etinger	general	Afanasy
Mikhailovsky	spouse	
Shumov	Epops	
Goldfarb	Elizaveta	
Vigiliansky	Papa	

Ratur	Lohengrin	Nanny
Babaeva	Mother	
Solntseva	ballerina	

Quartet—Chugunov, ~~Shum~~, Ermakov, Borodina.

* * *

<u>Gymnastics</u>:

    1) Ju-Jitsu hand movements. 5 x 5 reps.
    2) Isometric arm exercises (resistance) 3 reps.
    3) Grip 50 reps.
    4) Body twisters, both sides 8 x 2 reps.
    5) Head turns, both sides 10 x 2 reps.

<u>To develop will power</u>:

    1) [illegible]
    2) Head massage 1½ min.

* * *

Using ether, some people can attain to mysteries of a higher order, but only in an extremely narrow aspect, as for example:

If the entire truth extends along line *ab,* then man can see only a part, no further than (*c*) at the very limit of the possible. Using ether, it is possible to extend perception to a different part of the universal truth, for example to *d*, but it is hardly possible that man can have any real understanding of what has been "seen," because he will know only two parts of the world, one unconnected with the other: that is *ac* and *d*. Genuine understanding can only come from the growth of truth from *a* through *b*. However, in the instance given here, sequentiality is disrupted by segment *cd*. I believe that there are possibilities, albeit occult, to grasp the truth, not by carving out its separate parts, but by moving smoothly beyond the bounds of the possible (*c*), comprehending the distance covered in its entirety.

    After Shurka's sniffing, Nov. 2.

* * *

Light on the path. M.C. (Mabel Collins)

November 6, 1926. Began reading Ramacharaka's *Paths of Enlightenment of the Indian Yogis.*

S. Tukholka. *Occultism and Magic.* Published by A. S. Suvorin. SPb. 1907. Price 1 r.

Papus. *Basics of Occultism.*

* * *

In April of this year I read Ramacharaka's first book, *Fundamentals of the Yogi Philosophy.* No sooner had I read it than Shurka came by and tempted me. I gave in to temptation and burned the book. Then I repented. A few months passed and I reached the point where I felt an unhealthy urge to take up the study of black magic. And I was just about to go into action when I suddenly came across the book *Paths of Enlightenment of the Indian Yogis,* Ramacharaka's second book. And now I'm planning to study occultism again, true occultism.
November 6.

* * *

Checkers
white c3, f4. black a3, h8 white begins and wins.

Chess
White. Kh2, Rf2, Rh5, Nc2 (4)   Draw.
Black. Kf6, Qb3, Bc3, Bf3, Nf5 (5)

* * *

Foxtrots
Matador
Barcelona
Hoody hoo
Voici le garçon (tango)
In my gondola (foxtrot)
Yearning

* * *

Cigarettes—Carolina
Cigars—Cuba Nova 50 for 25 rubles

* * *

Malleus maleficarum. The Hammer of Witches.
by Jacob Sprenger and Institorus. A guide to witch trials for inquisitorial
courts. First published in 1487. Translated by A. Briusov and V.
Khodasevich. Introduction and notes by A. Briusov.

On Friday, November 12, I want to read: *A Comedy of the City of
Petersburg*, part 1, "Whaleslayer," "A Cossack's Death" and, for an encore,
"The History of a War."

I advise Shura to read: "Education of the Soul," excerpts from "Russian
Reading." As an encore, "Tempest and Uncle."

* * *

Speransky. *The Gates of Aristotle or, the Secret of Secrets.*
[ibid.] *Fortune-telling on the Psalter.*

* * *

What should I do! What should I do! How am I supposed to write?
Meaning is pressing itself upon me. I feel a need for it. But is it necessary?
God help me. And the same to you too.
November 9.

There are two people, Vvedensky and Zabolotsky, whose opinions are
dear to me. But who's right, I don't know. It's possible the poem they both
approve of is, in fact, the right one. For now, that's *A Comedy of the City
of Petersburg*. Personally I stand behind "A Cossack's Death." If that one's
vindicated in its entirety, I'll be happy.

Dostoevsky "Uncle's Dream." Adapted for stage as a comedy.

Write a "Golden Ass." The beginning something like Apuleius, and then,
after his transformation, the ass keeps losing more and more meaning and
turns into an abstraction.

Write a poem: a husband throws his wife's lover out of the sixth-floor window. He flies down, reciting a monologue. Then, having fallen, he lies there. Again, he lies there. Then he curses and lies there again. Dialog with passersby. Then again he lies there. I don't know what comes next, but he shouldn't just die and he shouldn't just get up and leave. He shouldn't do that either. The reader must maintain the clear impression that he's alive. My next work.

* * *

Gaga said: 68 is too little while 72 is too much. One time in the home of a respectable family, he was talking about his adventures in the churches of the Aleksandr Nevsky monastery, and finally he left, explaining his departure by saying that at home there were some nine virgins who were supposed to wash off his feet. That's good.

For this Friday, November 12, I want to set out our orders of battle, of which there are the following: After our reading, Igor Bakhterev will come out and make a speech that makes no sense, quoting from unknown poets, etc. Then Tsimbal will come out and will also deliver a speech, but with a Marxist slant. In this speech he'll defend us, vindicating our works in the eyes of all sorts of scum. Finally, two unknown personages holding each other's hands will come up to the table and declare: "We can't say much on the subject of what's been read here, but we shall sing a song." And then they'll sing something. Lastly Gaga Katsman will come out and recount something from the lives of the saints.
<u>This is going to be good.</u>

* * *

~~Marusia~~ About how Marusia looked for her mama

Marusia's walking with the wind
the bathhouse on her way
just four more steps to go now
not very far away.
Seems you're not rushing to your mom
your mama in her sandals

just ran off for the train.
Marusia answered asking:
where has my mama run?
then turned into the bathhouse
they answered her as one:
your mama ran away dear
to the pantheon she's run
they let her in
but out no way
~~your mama's now~~ and now she is Svetlana
the fourteen mushrooms too.
Marusia became Zhenya
and got onto the bus.
Take me, handsome busman,
take me around the world
and four times to the sea.
I'll buy myself a tiger
and mama a giraffe
and for my aunties' namedays
all Africa I'll buy!
And look a palm tree's growing
beneath that palm an elephant.
On the elephant sits a monkey
the river flows past by.
On the river people sailing
they've opened their mouths wide
they've opened something else too
but what I will not say.
What is this a grubshop?
open up the gates!
Oh mama please be well
and papa please don't swear!
        I'm not the one to blame!
Cutlets for me cutlets
they bring from far away
the shaggy conversations
and uncle's pistolet.

(Marusia's found her mama)
Hello bathhouse!
Hello priest!
Hello nanny!
Hello P!

THAT'S ALL.

* * *

I am a sad butcher.

A remedy for hair loss:
5 grams Balsam of Peru
5 grams castor oil
Rub into scalp 3 days, on 4th day wash.

Sukhovo-Kobylin. *The Death of Tarelkin*.

November 13, listened to a certain person tell a story of her mystical experience. The style of their conversation is always the same. <u>Bad</u>.

I.D.
Registration certificate (pink).
Certification from house committee concerning my own social status and that of my parents.
Certification from the Institute of the History of the Arts.

I don't envy Shurka.

* * *

Lucius Apuleius of Madaurus.
Platonist Philosopher
Eleven books of *The Metamorphoses or The Golden Ass*.
2nd century A.D.

Endymion is the beloved of Selene, goddess of the Moon.

* * *

Reply of Nikolai Zabolotsky and Evgeny Vigiliansky. November 15.

We now hasten to this call
to these groans of owls and all
these obedient youths so peerless
in helmets memorable and airless.
So as far as autumn's keeping
we won't trade our caps for sleeping
for a cap with pointed end
with a star across it, friend,
with the crimson star five-rayed
with a cavalry cockade.
The two warriors took a peek:
"wait for us at end of week
when they pour out morning tea
we'll turn out for reveille."
      D. Kh.

Albert Erland. *Crime and its justification.* Translated by G.A. Duperron.

Smoking tobacco, 1st quality A. "Lion" brand.
"SAMSON" tobacco factory. Theodosia.
Turkish tobacco № 100. Price for 100 grams, 1 r. 15 k.

Crimean Tobacco Factory. "OTTOMAN." Simferopol.
Smoking tobacco, 2nd quality A. № 150.
"Dubek-Mursal" 100 grams, 70 k.

* * *

That poet Kuzmin from Rostov. Altogether trash.
Swept up the Hermitage, better yet the Swarmitage

Werfel. *The Mirror-man.*

* * *

Shura's ~~pain~~ danger on the night of November 15-16 from Ermolaeva.

* * *

16 November, beerhall at the corner of Vvedenskaya Street.
XV cent. ZEIR ANPIN

ZOHAR—Radiance. XII.

Gustav Meyrink (Austrian) born in Vienna 1868. He first appeared in print 1902.
The Golem 1915.
I am Athanasius Pernath.
Laponder with the face of the Buddha.
The book "Ibbur," pregnancy of the soul.
Archivarius Schemajah Hillel.
Playing Cards, the Pagad. 78 cards.
A true double: "Habel de Garmin," that is, the "breath of bones."
Pagad ultimo.
The taro game (of cards) *tarok* or also *tarot* is the same as the Hebrew *Torah*, that is, "the law" or the ancient Egyptian *tarut*, "the enquired of," or the Zend word *tarisk*: "I require an answer."
Pagad: the first card of the deck.

Rabbi ben Akiba once ran into himself.

* * *

Vomit forth the fruit of the knowledge of good and evil and the sword of the archangel shall be extinguished and thou shalt taste of the fruit of life.

The age of the creation of the Talmud can be divided into three periods:
the soferim (scribes),
the tannaim (teachers) and
the amoraim (interpreters).

There exist two Talmuds: the Palestinian and the Babylonian.
Chasidism.
Rabbi Yisroel Baal Shem: master of the good name.

Rabbi Nachman of Bratslav.

His fingernail is sharp.
That seventh cat of yours (capital city oink).

* * *

Prof. N. I. Nikolsky, *Vestiges of Magical Literature in the Book of Psalms.*
Aggadah: Legends, Parables and Sayings of the Talmud and the Sages.
N. Rubakin, *Amid Signs and Wonders.*
I. Stepanov, *Pious Reflections.*
Fielding Hall, *The Soul of a People.*
Gaston Ranseau, *Scientists and Philosophy.*

* * *

Essays on Kabbalah. E. Trubik. 1886.
Occultism by Doctor Yanovsky.
Vladimir Soloviev. vol. VIII or IX: *On the Kabbalah.*
The Synagogue of Satan. Przybyszewski.

The Talmudic Schism
1) Mishnaists   rationalists
2) Chasids.

November 22. Help me, God, through Thy hope that I may know what to do. Grant me inspiration today that I might write some thing. This will be a sign to my lowly reason that my path is correct.

Can visit the short-termers on Wednesday and on Sun. between 6:30 and 8 or 9.

* * *

Thy Name is Woman, a melodrama.
Brood of Pirates, a grotesque.
Typical American-produced films are adaptations of theatrical plays.

First law of cinematography is that by using close-ups it can get closer to the emotions of the author.
Second law. Montage endows the play with great possibilities.

Fred Niblo is the director of *Thy Name is Woman*. Gave us the device of fading-out on a pose (static fadeout).

To me as a dilettante, all the achievements of these directors seem pathetic. *The Brood of Pirates* is built around surprises and rapid pacing. *Thy Name is Woman* (just the opposite) builds on decelerated, extended pacing. Fred Niblo's tendency toward the grotesque. Niblo is a formalist.

* * *

The Gospel is the key to the Bible.

Among Christians, there is the belief that while on earth we must live by Biblical law, in heaven by the Gospel.

* * *

Tuesday, November 23, 1926.
I, Daniil Kharms, am hereby obligated to appear before Aleksandr Ivanovich Vvedensky, on or before this Saturday in the matter of drinking bouts and overnights.

Note: If the drinking is not such as Vvedensky deems sufficient, the terms of this agreement are carried over.

> Daniil Kharms
> A. Vvedensky

I swear to faithfully execute the above by all that is most holy to me on this earth.
> D.

Done. D. Kh.

* * *

November 24. Sat with Gaga on the desk.

* * *

Jacob Leibus, he's a painter
was in a bar, and I was there,
Said to me: you're just a baker
I answered him: let's split a beer.
November 24.

I never wanted a drink as badly as I did on November 24.

Things prophetic have no author.

What do I have to do to write more often?

Make up a little anthology for 1926 into which four of my works will go:
A Comedy of the City of Petersburg
"Johnny Jump-up"
"The End of the Hero"
"A Cossack's Death"

Made it and presented it to Natasha.

* * *

I was sitting at the Poets' Union feeling bad. Head was spinning. Nov. 26.

Night of November 26 to morning of November 27.
We got ether with some additives. At home, the smell made mama feel bad.
I sniffed for the first time.

An anonymous work with the title *Philokalia*.
Gregory the Theologian
The Monk Nikita, Gregory of Sinai.
Discourses of Symeon the New Theologian. "On the Three Methods of Prayer" and "Sermon on Faith."
Works by Patriarch Kallistos and his comrade in faith Ignatius Xanthopouloses.

* * *

Program. "Casting-Off" Ritual.*
1) Silence, 10 min.
2) Dogs, 8 min.
3) Driving in nails, 3 min.
4) Sitting under the table holding the Bible, 5 min.
5) Enumeration of the saints,
6) Gazing upon the egg, 7 min.

Pilgrimage to the icon. 7=3+1+3 (33 + x)
Chinar Aleksandr Vvedensky I hereby obligate myself to fulfill this.
Chinar Daniil Ivanovich Kharms I do not pass by in vain.

---

* Ritual conducted in tulle masks.

* * *

Sokolsky's Daughter

the hunters drive the hounds
the hunt goes onward swiftly
the faces without whiskers glow
the parquet floors are slippery.
the master wanders here at nights
the master's called Sokolsky.
his daughter the ungrateful girl
has run off with a Frenchman
and when the mother heard the tale
the grandma cried and wept then
and gulped some sugar water down
and tried to tear out all her nails
and fell into ecstatic swoon
and hoped towards night to catch them.
the letters travelled on the clouds
from town to tavern and nearer
the grandma fallen on her knees
the daughter pines in Paris.
a ball: the revelers spin around
but the daughter's absent: autumn
waits beyond the gates
the grandmother weeps by the sea,
she's helped by generals eight.
and now the maddened ocean-sea
twirls whirlwinds on a leash
the husband, the late Lucian he
roasts modestly in hell.
where's my daughter tell me where?
cast your horns across here.
the woman cries and trembles then
she stands up straight and stern.

---

the hunters come into the woods
upon the boar with power
Sokolsky trumpets on his steeds
the hounds are dreaming on the mead

the night comes jumping through the trees
and grandma seeks the daughter.
Where are you now o wayward lass?
the Frenchmen guard you as they should
come back here now o dark-skinned lass
and papa will say *verry gud.*
he throws the herb upon the flames
bending down and bowing.
old woman drive the fiend away
and say your prayers howling.

above his chamber raindrops dance
Lucian seeks his bride;
then he flies to fairest France
just resting on the cliff
then on a table he's laid out
he lies there cold and stiff.

Sokolsky trumpets on his steeds
galloping on the brink.
he speeds through heaven on his sleigh
and sneezes rearing backsome
he grabs the Frenchman by his birthmark
and takes him to the window.
the collar rises in the air
the Frenchman begs *diable*
he flaps his arms on both his sides
and like a bird above the tide
he smiles to the gods,
the poor young Frenchman.
the sinful river flashed and gleamed
it's now bereft of water
the useless arm is broken now
she's free Sokolsky's daughter.
her husband out the window killed
she hurried back to home
went to the seamstress, she's asleep
and hasn't sewn the jacket.

oh how can I come to the ball
thus treated by my father?
my husband through the transom fell
and he was like no other.
the birds are saying that quite soon
the ocean-sea will dry up.
I'll go down to the hottest hell
where my dear Lucian's waiting:
but with your love all's well in hell!
Farewell now father, mother
To the world beyond the grave
I go (and you won't catch me).

       THAT'S ALL. D. KH. 1926
       November 27

A Night at the Dacha.
A feuilleton.

The elephant takes a bath and snuffs
holding worlds up with his trunk,
the wolves are wandering by the creek
and climbing through the window—thieves!
a candle's lit to meet them there
they clamber down with knife in teeth,
run through the garden skirting past
the watchtower in just three leaps.
and there's a fence across their path
much higher than the drying barn,
swiftly the first thief climbs in
the rest come in right after him.
BANG! the rifle's roar resounds
a bullet ploughs into a tree,
the guests are on the ferry now
heading off for sleep.
Lilia dozes upside down
but still her face looks mad,

mother shakes her head and frowns
dreaming of a naked lad,
and turns her eyes afar around
somewhere there a train car bumps
lighting up the gloom inside
auntie Vera sends her best
Kolya without epaulettes
rides to infantry div. 35.
they need a doctor urgent rush
someone ate one *blin* too much
the doctor shows up in a huff
the elephant takes a bath and snuffs
there by the lazy shores.

THAT'S ALL

November 27, 1926

* * *

Shmakov. *The Great Arcana.* "Pneumology."
P. I. Karpov. *Art of the Mentally Ill.*
Khlebnikov. "Night in a Trench."
John Damascene. Book 4, ch. 27, p. 56.

Sefer Raziel   Sefer Yetzirah
Mekhavia [Merkhaba]   Sefer Ha-Bahir
          Pardes Rimonim

* * *

Hoffman, "The Golden Pot."
Aronson, *Marc Chagall.*
Annie Besant

Academy of Arts, 74-81.
Red Vyborg Barracks.
Short-term Company, 70-0.

* * *

UNOVIS, "The Champions of the New Art," K. S. Malevich's group in 1922-23.

* * *

Saturn	Sn	black	Sulfur
Jupiter	Pb	blue	Aloe
Mars	Fe	red	Frankincense
Sun	Au	yellow	Laurel
Venus	Cu	green	Musk
Mercury	Hg	varicolored	Juniper
Moon	Ag	white	Magnet

* * *

Planetary or magical hours

Michael, Gabriel, Raphael, Uriel, Salathiel, Jegudiel, Barachiel

Michael	Who is like God.
Gabriel	Courage of God.
Rafael	Healer of God.
Uriel	Fire of God.
Jegudiel	Praise of God.
Barachiel	Blessing of God.

* * *

<u>Words characterizing organic mass</u>

Collective, Union, Club, Meeting, society, class, clan, family, apartment, institute, university, school, academy, dump, collection, panopticon, archive, museum, exhibition, cabinet of curiosities, park, crematorium, cemetery, garden.

<u>Words, characterizing extremity</u>

Leftists, rearguard, *zaumniki*, extremists, the heaven-born, the advanced.

* * *

Dec. 8. There's an expression: "birth pangs of creativity." Creation is grace, but in the meantime you can't create the pangs. God Cross Mary, C. M. C. M., I want 1927—I don't dare to want—I ask, I pray, please send me a 1927 that's creative and fresh. Grant that in the coming year, I may write 5 times more and 1000 times better than in 1926.
    D. Kh.

December 9. Submitted an application to the Friends of Chamber Music for permission for a morning performance of left literature.

Agreement with House of the Arts for evening performances of Left Flank and then for the entire Poets' Union.

* * *

Jean de Pavly. *Le Zogar.* Several volumes.

December 11. Opening of exhibit "Old Russian Painting" at Russian Museum.

In every person there are some things that you don't like, and perhaps you've got nothing comparable to those things in yourself, so you have a falling out with that person.
That's how I fell out with Igor Bakhterev.
    D. Kh. December 16.

December 17. Beat up on a certain Ginzburg. I repent.

* * *

Proposed members for a future "Left Flank":

A. I. Vvedensky   K. S. Malevich
N. A. Zabolotsky   N. Dmitriev
I. V. Bakhterev   S. L. Tsimbal
D. I. Kharms

Sinelnikov
A.V. Tufanov
E. I. Vigiliansky
Matveev from the University
G. N. Matveev from Vladivostok

A list of names for the "Left Flank."

According to Jules Bois, occultism is an esoteric philosophy usually set forth as a series of symbols: to grasp it in its fullness requires direct oral instruction from a special type of teacher, as the Hindus call him, a "Guru."

* * *

December 23. Academic Opera House: *Prince Igor*. Academic Dramatic Theater: *The End of Crookedface*. Little Opera House: *Grooms on Wheels*. Greater Dramatic: *The Time Will Come*.

Colossus. *Miss Mend*, 3 reels 8:45 and 10:30 pm.
Titan. *Two Smokes*.

The Vaginov Question

Need to put together a meeting with:
Malevich   by December 28.
Vvedensky   1) Rewrite questionnaire
Zabolotsky   2)
Bakhterev
Kharms 465-06. Local committee Union of Poets.
Vaginov.

Decided without Vaginov.

In Finnish "Citizen" or "Citizeness" is *kansalainen*.

* * *

Eliphas Levi. *The Doctrine and Ritual of High Magic.*

* * *

<u>Conversation with K. S. Malevich</u>

1) Absolute agreement by K. S. to joining our organization.
2) How many activists is he providing for category I? (we provide 4).
3) How many in category II? (we provide 7).
4) Is he giving us space? (for ~~closed~~ smaller meetings we've been provided a room).
5) Affiliation with Institute of Artistic Culture.
6) How many points per rabbit? (we say: a gramophone swims gracelessly).
7) On the name (impossibility of "UNOVIS").

    1) Oblique fame.

    2) We will not sanction its original existence.

    3) Rebirth of the ephemeral.

8) What about the supreme authority?
(We propose   Malevich

                  Vvedensky

                  Bakhterev

                  Kharms)
9) Principle of Unification? (We, the basic core, provide four supreme members, and perhaps, the entire group for category I).
10) Length of first meeting?
11) How many people in category III? (We provide 20).
13) On what basis do members of category III join?

* * *

December 29. At K. K. Olimpov's around 6:00.

For December 31, 1926.
27 r.
Boots   18
Shoes   <u>4</u>
Galoshes   22
Shirt

* * *

Merry, interesting and sad stories.

Merry ones suitable for all ages. Lacking almost all sense. Chatty, with a clear outline or where the ending is cut off. You get the sound of a little boy blowing bubbles of saliva. He blows it up till it bursts like a soap bubble. More precisely, in its outline the thing seems completely finished but there's no ending because there's no middle. The plot of something like this should be distinguished by the absence of the connections which make a plot a plot.

[From notebook 8]

Here's a puzzle for you, how did my gloves end up in Papa's coat at New Year's???

Answer. They weren't there, but under my mattress there were someone else's gloves put there by the maid. (Polya).

* * *

Buy a notebook just like this one	+65 k.*
Buy a small address book	+29 k.
Buy 5 small brass caps	15 k. +
Buy deep black ink	15 k. +
Buy shoelaces for boots	
(Buy a pen knife)	
Buy toothpaste	50 k. +
Ball (arabian)	40 k. +

---

*presented to Zabolotsky

* * *

For the night of January 3-4, 1927.
  1) Rewrite poems.
  2) Compose a letter to a billionaire.
  3) Put together theses for tomorrow.
  4) Go to bed no later than 3 o'clock.

For January 4.
  1) Hang poster up on Nevsky.
  2) Be at INAC by 1 o'clock.
  3) After INAC stop in at Friends of Chamber Music.
  4) Drop in on Kliuev.

Performance of Left Flank of Poets at the Friends of Chamber Music on January 9, 1927. Not happy with myself.

* * *

Gaga said I have a forehead like a skating rink.

I've got to really hurry to get the next thing written.
How to speed that up?
                    Jan. 10.

I want to write something called "The Directorate of Things."

* * *

A collection of poems by Daniil Ivanovich Kharms. On the front cover:

CHINAR
Daniil Ivanovich
KHARMS

the
DIRECTORATE
of
THINGS

Hard-to-get Poems

Foreword.
                    To the reader.
Reader, I'm afraid you won't understand my poems. You might have understood them if you had gotten to know them gradually, even if only in various journals and magazines. But you didn't have the opportunity to do that and it is with pain in my heart that I am publishing my first book of poems.

                    To the reviewer.
First, before you say anything about the formal deficiencies of my poems, read *The Directorate of Things* from cover to cover. Second, before

lumping me together with the Futurists of the last decade, read them, and then me <u>a second time</u>.
D. Kh.

Money: by Wednesday get 50 k. By Friday get 2 r.

Perhaps up to now I still love ⊟. That's more than great.
Jan. 11, 1927.

* * *

For January 11.
>Phone Bluma.
>Evening, dance the foxtrot.
>Call Froman.

For January 13.
>See Froman to pick up Union card.
>Go to Library of New Books to get deposit.
>Go see Bakhterev around 4 o'clock.

For Jan. 14.
>Starting at 0 hours, "Radiks" performance.

* * *

We danced the foxtrot. Moved the tables back. Music was playing.

Gaga said: when people go out of their minds, it's very good because it proves they had one to begin with.

Igor has 12 salt-cellars: 6 pink, 6 green; 8 cups, I've probably forgotten the rest.

Kolya's good at tap dancing.

Lit up a cigarette.

Kolya gets it with his feet.

we've gone and danced the floors right through
got to dance away the blues
nothing more to do, you say
well now we'll dance the coat away

Neldikhen's dictum:
It's not important what's said or how: it's important who says it.

* * *

Vodka 2 btls.	3 20	
Liqueurs	2btls.	4 40
Port	2btls	5 r.
Vodka	1 ½ btls.	2 20
Red	1 liter 1 30	
Sausages		3 r.
Wieners		3 r. + 1 r.
Cheese	1 20	
Herring	1 50	
Halvah		1 r.
Cookies		1 r.
Candy		2 r.
Mineral water	3 r.	

* * *

<u>Material for publication</u>
Vvedensky.   People riding on an ass
                                          A nymph is riding, not a prince

Kharms
Zabolotsky
Vaginov
Bakhterev
Dimitriev
Koch-Boot   articles: "Music Hall." "Ballet without Plot"
Malevich
Bakhterev   articles: Painting article

* * *

January 12. Saw *Enforming Reality* at the "Crooked Mirror." The beginning's better than the end. The acting's better than in other things they've done. For example, their "Deaf Mute" (from the *Decameron*) is an example of bad acting and bad production. Kugelem's production of *Reality* isn't so bad, but the acting's simply unbearable.

The actress who sings the intimate songs has a rich range of expressivity and a complete absence of voice. Watching her is more interesting than listening. Now the pederast* in the skirt didn't dance badly. The theater itself is one of the most sophisticated we have in Petersburg. And the buffet's conveniently located. The audiences aren't that big and that's nice.

D. Kh.

---

*Poluianov

* * *

I've almost fallen in love with the young lady who was sitting behind me at one of the Poets' Union Fridays on Jan. 14, 1927. She reminds me of Ester. There was a scruffy-looking type with her. Maybe her [illegible]?

In that case I'll give up. But no, he's just that, an acquaintance, so at the next Friday I've got to get to know her. She's really good looking. I need to fall in love. I've become painfully stale of late and have ceased to resemble a human being. I don't know how you're supposed to meet women. How do you approach them? Maybe she'll notice me herself. If that works, I'll go up to her at the next Friday. Will she be there at the next Friday?

I'll tell my fortune on the Bible. Whatever it says, I'll do. I'll open the Bible to a random page and whatever's in the right-hand column in line 10 or 11, I'll consider the absolutely correct answer to the question of whether I have the right to start up a romance with this young lady, and if yes, then will anything come of it?

The answer was: "And he carried out thence all the treasures of the house of the Lord, and the treasures of the king's house." 2 Kings, 24:13. I'll try again for clarity. Pg. 401, line 17 from the bottom in the second column: "As Mordecai had written to them." Incomprehensible answers.

* * *

Verochka, you could stand a shave.

Today we can drink some beer, not too much it's true, two bottles each. They'll give me money for socks.

I need 7 kopecks for the tram, now!

* * *

Sherwood Anderson, *The Triumph of the Egg.*

Playing cards is just the same as not walking through the door.

a b c d f g h i j k l m n o p q r s t u v w x y z
I left out the e. Strange. W−H−Y?
for many reasons.

* * *

Now I realize: I am a phenomenon quite out of the ordinary.
                    Jan. 16, 1927

Ask papa about Morozov.

Jan. 18, 1927. We cut our hair off.

* * *

A. I. Vvedensky sniffs ether. At the moment he simply disgusts me. Maybe I haven't grown enough to reach him yet. He sounds good, like a trumpet. Everything he does offends me. Why is this? I made a firm decision that he not sniff in my presence, but he demanded this sacrifice from me and I gave in. It is possible that he really does comprehend something higher, but I don't especially believe that.

I'm clicking my teeth in front of the mirror.

"Danka, write down word-for-word what I tell you: that's your answer."
I've heard that twice already.

You can tie yourself up in knots, but here's something for you to remember: Once certain things get established, there's no way of refuting them.

Let me shake your hand, Shura. Ether's the chicken in reverse.
I expected miracles and rightly so.
Whatever's worrying you, that's what you see.

That night was bad. I sniffed ether for the first time. It was remarkable.
I don't remember when. It must have been in January 1927.

Ether. Like at an electric power station.
Ether is the same for everyone.
Everyone experiences the same things.

These experiences are like islets. You have to sniff ether by yourself and
in half-light, and even so it's all in vain, since you won't remember the
essence of what you need to, and so it's just self-indulgence.

* * *

Subject for a drawing by Igor Bakhterev: A pharmacist: a man made from
various ampoules and little bottles.
Jan. 29, 1927

* * *

For January 31, 1927
    Study ~~occultism~~ from 2:30 to dinnertime.
    After dinner phone Igor and maybe go to INAC.

Culture, ah! People oh ho ho!

[From notebook 38]

For February 2, 1927
1. Sit down in a rocking chair and concentrate to the point of losing
   yourself; imagine a piece of paper with a figure drawn on it.
2. Copy out Aseev's "Song about an object of luxury."
3. Have a smoke only after dinner.
Then you are free for February 2.

* * *

[From notebook 8]

Ich gebe das Wort bis 14 Februar nicht riechen.
7 Februar 1927 Jahr.

I give my word not to sniff until February 14 .
February 7, 1927

D	a	n	i	i	l	Kh	a	r
m	s	(ъ)	Yu	v	a	ch	e	v
5,	1,	13,	9,	9,	11;	21,	1	16,
12,	17;		21,	3,	1,	23,	6,	3
	37	;	67	63=9				
	10	13	9					
	1	4						

Aleksandr—1, 11, 6, 10, 17, 1, 13, 5, 16 = 80 = 8
Vvedenskii—3 + 3 + 6 + 5 + 6 + 17 + 10 + 9 + 9 = 80 = 8
Pushkin – 15 +19 + 24 + 10 + 9 + 13 = 90 = 9
Blok 2 + 11 + 14 + 10 = 37 = 1

* * *

Feb. 7. Put out the lights at exactly 3:00.

February 8.
    1) Get up at 12:00.
    2) Make bed and do exercises.
    3) Go outside and walk for a half hour.
    4) Evening, wash head.
    5) Without great inspiration, don't write any poems the whole day.
    6) *nicht riechen* all day.
    7) Go to bed at 12 h. 30 min.
    8) Put out the lights at exactly 1 am.

* * *

To smoke Feb. 8.

       1st cigarette in bed.
       2nd " "   after tea.
       3rd " "   on walk.
       4th " "   back home.
       5th " "   before dinner.
       6th " "   after dinner.

White: a4, b5, c3, f2, g2, h3; Nb6, Re1, Kg1.
Black: e6, g7, h7; Nf5, Rd8, Be7, N8.

       Black's move.

* * *

Saturday evening at Zabolotsky's, Feb. 12, beginning at 8 o'clock.

Anacreon—Pederast.
Sappho—Lesbos.

* * *

Is it nerves or something else? My head was spinning horribly, everything was shuddering inside, something monstrous in my thoughts. Maybe I'm sick? But how can I get treatment without a doctor? I want to treat myself on my own somehow.
Whatever's happening to me tonight, it's the first time. So what is it?
Is there any way to find out?
I need to sleep, but I literally can't shut my eyes because just as soon as I do, everything I see looks impossibly distorted and deformed.
If I'm feeling this bad tomorrow, I won't go to Lipavsky's.
Now my head is spinning and sexual. . .

I feel better now. I woke mama up and took some Valerian.
There was a minute there when I was afraid I was losing my mind.
I hope it will be better now. Cross and Mary C. and M. C. and M.
Feb. 14–15, 1927.
6:30 am.

* * *

White: g6, Kh7, Rg8.
Black: Kg5, Bd6
White wins

Gaga said: An autumnal brick is born.

February 19, call Zabolotsky at 6:00.

For February 20.
    Be at Bakhterev's by 3 o'clock, by 9 o'clock at Nikolaevsky
    Station.
    Then at 4 or 5 call Zabolotsky.

* * *

Feb. 26. I've begun writing in my notebook every day. Dangerous, might
stop living.

* * *

Material for a Collection of Poems, All-Russian Union of Poets.
Combinations to which I agree:
    I. A Cossack's Death. The Poem of Peter-Yashkin-Communist
    (114 lines).
    II. Poem of P-Y-C. Stinginess. Whaleslayer (92 lines).
    III. The End of the Hero. Poem of P-Y-C. (106).
    IV. Poem of P-Y-C. Unfinished poem. Whaleslayer (92).
    V. from *A Comedy of the City of Petersburg*. Poem of P-Y-C.
    (81 lines).
    VI. – Nothing. (0 lines).

Chest, 91 cm.
Waist, 87.
Biceps, right arm 33.
Biceps, left arm 31.
Chest, breath out, 86.
Chest, breath in, 98.

* * *

Sat. Feb. 26. Shurka spent the night. We called Froman. My 24 lines.
Evening at Lina's, that night at Shurka's. Spoke about birth (higher).

Sun. 27. With Shurka at Igor's, then at Gaga's. Evening at TAM's. Shurka
spent the night at my place.

* * *

Warszawa Senatorska 38-13. "Kwartalnik Modernistov." Praesens.
Toward of Theory of Dead Ends
The perception of any phenomenon and its evaluation.

Malewitsh.

* * *

V. K. Zapriagaev. *Fundamentals of Astrology.*
Doctor Papus. *The Genesis and Development of Masonic Symbols.* A
translation from the French by V.V.V. SPb. 1911. (33rd, 90th, 96th degrees).
Eliphas Levi, *Doctrine and Ritual of High Magic."* Translation by A.
Aleksandrov. Vol. 1.

Russia—Horse Land (Ross-Land)
Poland—(Poll-Land)
Boundary of souls (D'AHN-Mark)
Western Land—(Holl-Land, Choll-Land, la Gaule, Gallia)

Völuspa—the woman who acts upon whites.

Uroboros (ούροβορος)

* * *

Some part of the Celts, in order to save themselves from the *Druidesses,*
migrated from their homeland (around 10,000 years before the birth of
Christ) and made their way through countries inhabited by blacks to those
places now called Arabia. These were the nomadic Celts or *Bodonoi,* a part
of which later, after thousands of vicissitudes, came to constitute the Jewish
people.

* * *

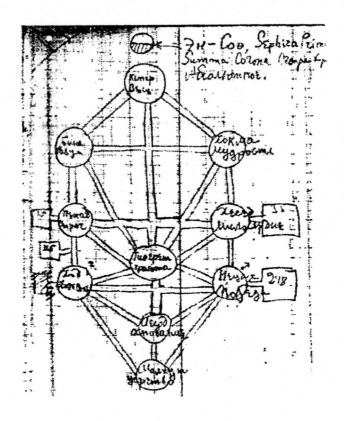

"Tree of Life" after Athanasius Kircher *Oedipus Aegypticus* (1562).
(Translators' attribution).

* * *

To A. I. Vvedensky

Into a funny bath a friend fell down
The wall went whirling round and round
A wondrous cow came floating now
There was a street above the house.
And flashing on the sand my friend
Around the rooms in socks he went
Twirling his hand magician-like
First the left one, then the right

126

Then threw himself upon the bed
while in the swamps a corncrake red
Chirped like a cap and wailed in woe
My friend was in the bath no more.

March 5

* * *

From above with a crash
you fell into the bath.
Too brief
is the life
of the poet.

"Enclosuration"—from the word "to enclose."
"Subjectrix"—feminine from "subject."
From a Cossack letter of grievance.
(Collection of Yu. Yu. Yurkun)

* * *

March 12 at 11:00 pm. There's a show at Press House. How can I get the money commensurate for this? Need no less than 1½ rubles.
Was there. Not good (weak).

Jozef-Emil Kreichik. *Thirteen Children of Caissa: Chess Humoresques.* 1926.

Akhókhm, a wit.
Akhósm, a bridegroom.
Azókhm, waft.

* * *

You can die from ether. I've sniffed too much as it is. I was warned. Don't sniff anymore!

The Numeration of Jerome Cardan.
"To ascertain the fortune of a given year, he sums up the events of those which have preceded it by 4, 8, 12, 19, and 30; 4 is the number of realization, 8 is of Venus or things natural; 12 is the

number of Jupiter and corresponds to successes; to the number 19 correspond the cycles of the Moon and Mars; 30 is the number of Saturn or Fatality."

Alliet or Etteila, the father of modern soothsayers.

It somehow seems to me that Bondi isn't nearly the performer Gibshman is. The latter is a wonderful master of ceremonies: it's possible that Bondi is also though I haven't heard him as a master of ceremonies.

* * *

Froman will say: "I'll talk to you, Vvedensky, but to hell with Kharms!"

They say I'm reproaching the Board, i.e. 5 people, however it's not a personal affront. But thanks to my presentation, which must have been pretty bad, or thanks to something inadvertent, I felt as if I were slandering and insulting M. A. Froman.

* * *

A chin that looks like a boot heel.
Chekhov's expression.
Kolya Nikitin's got a chin like that.

* * *

When Rozhdestvensky's going to read, don't say "for our next number we have Vsevolod Rozhdestvensky," but "for our next stunt we have Vsevolod Rozhdestvensky."

* * *

The postman's brought a letter here
And oh! we're so delighted.
We opened it and phoo! oh dear!
what awful filth inside it!

I'm sitting and drinking tea. Mama's talking about Leikin's biography.
For dinner we had meat-and-pickle-brine soup with multicolored garnish.

* * *

I'm sitting on a bench. Across from me is the Summer Garden. It's great. The servant girls are out there for a walk. They're always out walking.

The Summer Garden's closed. And I had wanted to take a nice little stroll through the garden (someday they'll read my book and delight in my diction).

* * *

I had a terrifying dream that mama was dying. I got very frightened and woke up. Now I'm anxious all the time. March 21.

Night of March 21-22.
Shurka's coming here.

> 1) I propose that tonight we analyze Gunsberg's chess game.
> 2) Write some poetry.
> 3) Eat some radishes.
> 4) Play chess.
> 5) Have Shurka read me his "Palm of a Kievan" and "I'm in an overcoat too."

* * *

Material for the first Radiks collection:

<u>Theoretical section</u>

1) Shklovsky	On Khlebnikov
2) Malevich	On Art (Western correspond.)
3) Lipavsky	On the *Chinari*
4) Kliukov	On the Left Flank (Radiks).
5) Bakhterev	On painting.
6) Koch-Boot	On theater.
7) Tsimbal	"Radiks" Information
8) Ostrovsky	Moscow LEF
9) Bukhshtab	Konstantin Vaginov
10) L. Ginzburg	
11) Gofman	
12) Stepanov	

Creative section
1) Vvedensky   Prose and poetry.
2) Kharms   Poetry and drama.
3) Zabolotsky   Poems.
4) Bakhterev   Poems.
5) Vaginov   Prose and poetry.
6) Khlebnikov   Poems.
7) Tufanov   Poems.

Painting
1) Bakhterev
2) Dimitriev
3) From INAC

Graphic Arts
1) Zabolotsky
2) Filonov

* * *

I gave a reading last Friday, i.e. March 18, at Press House at a meeting of the Leningrad Association of Proletarian Writers. I read a lot. I ran into Vanka Pribludny there. He hasn't written any poetry for some time now. He's taken up sports. His reading is significantly worse now. He's lost that singing quality.

* * *

Phillipus Theophrastus Bombastus (Aureolus Paracelsus "the divine").

On Saturday, March 19, I saw *The Game* at the Satire Theater. Really not good. The actors were terrible and the piece itself isn't all that good.

On Thursday, March 17, I saw *Seven Days that Did Not Shake Senka* at the Free Theatre. Very successful.

* * *

March 26, at Institute for the History of the Arts (IHA), An Evening of the Left Flank (Tsimbal).
March 28, at Literary Association of the IHA. An Evening of the Left Flank (Borozina).

"The Academy of Left Classics," that's what we've been calling ourselves since Friday, March 25, 1927. The name came to Gaga, Igor and me at the same time. It came to us at the Katsmans. We were there to write a manifesto, and then the name dawned on us. Everyone agrees. Except for Shurka. That lousy skeptic has no use for any name other than *Chinari*.

The long-awaited solution to this problem has finally arrived. The decision must be considered brilliant.

* * *

The struggle against hackwork.
Against conservatism in form and feeling.
New form is revolutionary.

Our most immediate tasks:
    1) Found a robust Academy of Left Classics.
    2) To this end, convene a conference and compose a manifesto.
    3) Enter Press House as a section of the Left Workers of Art.
    4) Secure an evening of dancing to obtain the sum of around 600 r. for the publication of our collection.
    5) Publish the collection.

Board
    Zabolotsky
    Vvedensky   Sadofiev.
    Tufanov
    Rozhdestvensky

Candidates
    Tikhonov
    Froman
    Braun
    Vvedensky
    Rozhdestvensky
    Kharms
    Tufanov
    Volpin

* * *

[Article by N. Ioffe and L. Zheleznov, Smena. April 3, 1927.]

The Literary Scene . . .
(About the "*Chinari*")

"*Chinar*": it's not a tropical butterfly or a tribe of African savages; it's not a particular species of bird that makes its home in mountain ravines.

It is, by your leave, a poet.

It is not our goal to get into a discussion of all the fine points of poetry: that's already been done and is being done by the "learned" critics. We're not about to take the bread out of their mouths! We just want to say a little bit about one modest variety of our poets, the "*chinari*."

The roots of these so called "poets" derive from "trans-sense" poetry—they also call themselves the "Left Flank" or "Left Classics." But the point here isn't in the names. The essence of their poetry is that meaning—the foundation of every work of art—is something that the "*chinari*" don't recognize in any way as obligatory. Their primary concern is the correlation of sound. They don't care in the least that their poems be put together in a human language. It's of no importance to them what effect their poems might have on a reader's limited time or on his nerves. It's not even important whether anyone reads them or not.

But we, as we said, agreed to leave it up to the critics to go into all the fine points. Our task is different.

. . . Do you remember the good old Russian swagger; do you remember the broad nature, the troika of drunken horses, drunken merchants, drunken drivers, and drunken poets?

Those were the days . . . lolling around in his sleigh, a drunken little merchant, whooping and hollering, flies down the street, bearing down on passersby, cursing a blue streak and won't calm down until he breaks someone's jaw.

Remember? The drunken fumes of Moscow taverns, bottles breaking, fistfights, cursing—now that's your broad Russian soul, is it not?!

. . . A "*chinar*" is a man too. A "*chinar*" keeps "on hand" his share of the besmirched old traditions too.

The "*chinari*" do write, but they don't just write: sometimes they even give performances that work their audience up into a fury.

…The other day a gathering of the literary circle at the Institute for the History of the Arts took a violent turn.

The "*chinari*" showed up and read their poetry. Everything was going well. The assembled students laughed or made witty remarks under their breath no more than a few times. Some even clapped.

Well, show a fool a finger and he'll laugh. The "*chinari*" decided that their success was guaranteed. After reading a few of his poems, one "*chinar*" decided to find out what affect they were having upon the audience.

"Should I read some more?" he inquired.

"No, it's not worth it," a voice rang out. That was Berlin, a young writer just starting out and president of Leningrad LEF.

The "*chinari*" took offense and demanded that Berlin be ejected from the meeting. The meeting unanimously objected.

Then, clambering up on a chair, "*chinar*" Kharms, a member of the Poets' Union, raised his arm (brandishing a cane) in a "magnificent" gesture, and declared:

—I do not read in stables or brothels!

The students categorically objected to hooliganish attacks of this sort on the part of persons appearing in the capacity of official representatives of a literary organization to student meetings. They are demanding the expulsion of Kharms from the Poets' Union since they consider that there is no place in a legally-constituted Soviet organization for someone who at a well-attended meeting would dare to compare a Soviet Institution of Higher Education to a brothel or a stable.

We too protest.

At first glance all this would seem to be a fact without much significance. Nevertheless it lets us see depicted in the most lurid colors the hooliganish aspect of certain representatives of literary groupings who are heirs to the old "glorious" traditions. And that's nothing but "vileness"—and it has to be fought.

* * *

[Response by Kharms and Vvedensky]

A statement to the Leningrad Union of Poets from the Academy of Left Classics:

The reason for the duly described scandal and its significance has been misinterpreted by *Smena*. Even before the evening began, we had heard warnings that the assembled public was to a not insignificant degree inclined toward hooliganism . . . The hall was ringing with whistling, shouts and argument. Orators would come out and no one even listened to them. This went on for about 5-7 minutes until *chinar* D. Kharms came out and pronounced his fatal phrase: "Comrades, please bear in mind, that I do not perform in either stables or whorehouses," after which he left the meeting. The uproar continued for a time and ended with a fistfight in the audience without our participation.

Pursuant to the abovementioned, we, the Academy of Left Classics, consider our behavior wholly appropriate to the reception we were given and we consider D. Kharms' incisive comparison, which concerned the meeting then taking place and not the Institution of Higher Education as a whole (as interpreted by comrades Ioffe and Zheleznov) to be entirely apt. *Chinar* A. Vvedensky, *chinar* D. Kharms.

* * *

[From notebook 8]

Wednesday, April 6, at Ermolaeva's. 8 o'clock.

I have definite tastes in women: I like women who remind me of Ester.

Smoke for April 6.
　　　　First cig. after breakfast.
　　　　Second, when I go outside.
　　　　Third, at Press House.

* * *

⊟ **called me.**
I'll go to her.
⊟ **I love you.**
⊟ **I want you to give me a blowjob.**

I love you, Daniel.

From drawing things, things are from drawing.
He speaks unexpectedly well and says what needs to be said. Wait!

~~I'm afraid I'll fart~~.

* * *

Chronicle

On Wednesday, March 30, 1927, Ivan Aleksandrovich Riazanovsky, whom I deeply respected, died in Kostroma.

Thursday Apr. 14, Major deal with Terentiev re: play *Love*.

Saturday Apr. 16, at 2:00 pm. Gaga K. arrested.

Friday, May 13. Found out about Esther's divorce from her husband and spoke to her for the first time.

* * *

[entry in another handwriting]

Love

Point of departure: Love is a social phenomenon, i.e. where the social resonators die out, love grows dim; where such resonators have been established (by the culture of class), love reaches Leotolstoyan proportions and "universal" dimensions. Our time is transformational: there is no love and it is perishing. Asexuality is the sign of the times! Eros is an anachronism. The future is love for your comrade, those close to you, love like that of a moth!

Modern relations between M and W are paradoxical and pointless in all their variants.

Because they are flowing! Not fixed. Phases of the approaching future.

The marital codex must be realized exhaustively:

1. He's alone.
2. She's alone.

1. He's married.
2. She's married.

1. He has a job.
2. She doesn't have a job.

1. She has a job.
2. He doesn't have a job.

1. He has a lover.
2. She doesn't.

1. She has a lover.
2. He doesn't.

1.
2. } Both of them have lovers.

1. Neither does.

1. He leaves her.
2. She doesn't want him to.

1. He stays.
2. She leaves.

1.
2. } Both go their separate ways.

1.
2. } Both stay.

etc.

All this for economic reasons.

* * *

After *A Comedy of the City of Petersburg,* arrange a reading and invite: Vvedensky, Zabolotsky, Vaginov, Bakhterev, Lipavsky, Shteinman, Terentiev, Dimitriev, Erbshstein.

* * *

Jearning just for you
That's all I do
my dear
Learning why I'm blue
I wish that you
were near
Smiles have turned to tears
Days have turned to years
Jearning just for you
I hope you're yearning
too.

* * *

Books I've read since October 28, 1926.

       Maurice LeBlanc. *The Crystal Stopper*.

       Luigi Pirandello. *The Turn*.   -

       Johan Bojer. *Northern Heroes*.   (+)

       V. Briusov. *The Fiery Angel*. Began Oct. 31—Nov. 2.

       F. I . Shalyapin. *Pages from my life*.

       Viacheslav Shishkov. *Funny Stories. (A Play in the Village Ogryzovo)*.

       Gustav Meyrink. *The Golem*. November 11.   +

       Dr. Magnus Riddell. *Personal Magnetism*.   -

       J. Galsworthy. *A Member of the Milltown Chamber*. -

       January 15, 1927. Chekhov. "A Dreary Story."   ++

       Daudistel. *Peter Gippel*.

       Elifas Levi. *Doctrine and Ritual of High Magic*.

       Karyshev.

       Carpenter. *Life and Death*.

       Morgenstern. *Psycho-graphology*.

* * *

[From notebook 9]

My chess problem № 1.
White: Ka4, Qf6, RRc8 and e1, BBa5 and e6, Nf3, p e5 and g2.
(-9-)
Black: Kd3, Qf1, Rc1, Be4, Nf7, p e7, f2 and g3
(-8-)
Mate in 3 moves.

Solution: 1. R e1−e3 +... ~
                 2. Q f6 –f4 +... ~
                 3. a. B a5−d2 #
                   b. Q f4 pins knight check and #

* * *

June 26.

    Spades: I won't see her anymore.

    Clubs: I'll see her, but nothing will come of it.

    Diamonds: In the end, I'll go to her.

    Hearts: She'll come to me and everything will be as I want it to be.

I drew a 10 of hearts.

    Spades—month

    Clubs—week

    Diamonds—days   Ace—1

    Hearts—hours   King—0

I drew a Three of Diamonds. That means that she'll come to me in 3 days.

* * *

For July 6, 1927.

    1. Call Shura.

    2. Call Igor and find out about the passes to Ernst Krenek.

    3. Clean up my room.

    4. ~~Get up at noon~~.

Send Gaga a postcard.

* * *

José-Maria de Heredia, *Trophies*, Gosizdat, 1925.

Owed to T.A.M.	75 k.
~~Light bulb~~	~~1 r. 25 k.~~
Notebook	65 k.
Sundries from stationary store	1 r. 00 k.
Anthology	60 k.

* * *

Daniil Ivanovich Kharms

Daniil Ivanovich Kharms

~~Est~~

* * *

Conjoining literary phases are related to each other by contrast. The development of each phase and its transition to the next phase can be expressed by the following scheme:

1. Contrast (to the previous stage).
2. The element of simplicity and living reality.
3. The emergence of devices.
4. The localization of devices.
5. Verbal abstraction.
6. Development of a style.
7. Complication.
8. Stylization.
9. Decadence.
10. Emergence of the Contrast, etc.

A triple example of literary pivots:

First pivot: of reality, simplicity and hiding the device: logic.
Second pivot: complexity, stylization and verbal abstraction.
Third pivot: specificity, simplification relative to the second pivot, at times the device is revealed, alogical motivation, disruption of ordered sequence of meaning.

Example:

I. A man sits in a room. He gets up and goes out the door. Motivation is given. The cause is either outside or inside the room.
II. A man sits in a room. He gets up and goes out the door. His movement toward the door is given, as is his feeling, his sense of both the tangible and intangible. No cause is given.
III. A man sits in a room. He gets up and goes out the door. The cause is omitted. An intrusion based on dissimilarity. Disruption of the ordered sequence of meaning. Concrete presentation.

One of the characteristic devices of the third instance is the "demonstrated phenomenon." A phenomenon of this sort, despite its abstractness and semantic remoteness, must be taken literally. Any action described in this way attains the maximum specificity. Description ceases to be description and becomes the action itself, to which one may attach a unitary label.

Hence also the name of the device: "Labeled action" (which is the same as a demonstrated action).

* * *

⊟ **you're my sweet
little girl**

* * *

"Encore" cigarettes
Ducat. Moscow. Mosselprom, 20 for 11 k. Weak.

A delicious evening

Malevich	limonade	~~12 b.~~ 6 b. ~~10 r.~~ 5 r.
Vaginov	à la vanille	~~2 b.~~ 1 b.
Vvedensky		
Bakhterev	Ice-crème—2 r.	
Kharms		
<u>Kotelnikov</u>	Petit four	

Fruit.
Apples and cherries

<u>Take with me to Shurka's</u>:
1. Shaving brush.
2. Khodorovskaya's book.
3. Stupid objects.

* * *

Take to Detskoe:
~~Chess set.~~
Manuscripts.
~~Bible.~~
Ramacharaka.
~~Blok — Correspondence.~~
~~Orthographic Dictionary.~~
Paper.
~~Ink.~~

~~Pens.~~
~~Pencils.~~

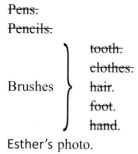

Brushes
~~tooth.~~
~~clothes.~~
~~hair.~~
~~foot.~~
~~hand.~~

Esther's photo.

* * *

A salty papa fell into a well-worn ditch,
Smooth children rushed to their tubercular father and grabbed at his
villanous hands.
Pock-marked faces.

* * *

To N. A. Zabolotsky

I look and see life's landmark vanished.
Myself quite happily, quite so,
Left all things back in Leningrad
And left for Detskoe Selo.

My friend, do send me an epistle!
While your pen's too hot to tame,
Your line will fly here like a deer,
And stand before me like a flame.

July 10, Detskoe Selo Station.

* * *

I've sent more letters to you than to Vvedensky. But even though he doesn't
like to answer, he already has. But you, you haven't. Goodbye. I don't
know you anymore. It's all over, Ester.
        D. Kh. July 14, 1927.
        Tsarskoe Selo.

* * *

What a cruel and empty girl Ester is. How many days has it been and I still can't get a letter out of her.

Even today I thought she'd come. But she WILL NOT COME. It's so hard for me that she cares so little. I won't write her again until I get a letter. Who needs a letter? I wanted her to come see me today, tomorrow's no good, tomorrow's Thursday, the Feast of the Annunciation.

Shurka will get here on Friday or Saturday, Lyonya on Sunday. That means that I can't expect her before Monday, July 18. Long and boring. I really do love her. And then again, it's so annoying: she used to belong to another man and wouldn't let me touch her. I want to go down on her. That's what I want.

> July 13.
> Detskoe Selo.

* * *

July 17, 1927. Absolute End with Ester.

Monday, July 18. Ester came to see me. I was pleased at first, but then . . . then . . . I'm finally convinced that we don't need each other. Completely different people. I'll say it straight out. It's too bad she came. I had made plans for this evening and all evening long she's been sitting there in the dining room. God, how different we are! She's not stupid, but her mind is as far from my understanding as mine is from hers. In her presence I feel so out of place that there's no way of talking to her.
Still, I'll have to go back into the dining room.

In the dining room, conversation about my poetry. Rather more pleasant than not. Soon she'll come to me, I know it. Not g-o-o-d. How can I adopt a tone that I'll be able to maintain all evening (especially if it turns out to be a long evening) that's at once pleasing both to me and to Esther?

What the fuck! I can't remember a worse evening. Now I understand that I can't bring Esther back. She's sitting all of 4 feet from me, but she's lost to me forever. Farewell, my beloved. May God bless you. Amen. D. Kh. July 18.

> At 1 am.

* * *

How it all turned out. Ugh. Well D. Kharms, shoulders back and be strong. Shout Hurrah so as not to lose heart. Be a Tsar.

Everything's for the best, remember that. That's all you've got to console yourself.

If she knew your thoughts right now, she would sit just as she's sitting now. That's what she's like. And if you knew her thoughts, you probably (shameful to admit) would start crying. Which of course will follow. (Shame!)

How could you have been so wrong! That's not who she is.

There are moments when you resemble a mountain.
That doesn't suit you, Danya.

* * *

Hand in application.
Give Union book to Esfir Borisovna to exchange.
Call Sorokin.
Find out about Spassky's arrival.
Pay membership dues.
Find out the latest news about Gaga.
Price of a duplicating machine, find out.
Negotiate with Golts.

* * *

You always want to condemn and revile her. Why? It doesn't make things any easier for you. You know this yourself! Think better and better of her. Then she will become a saint.

* * *

You came to Tsarskoe a complete witch. But now you're better than an angel. Let's go Ester! I beg you.
IT'S DISGRACEFUL!

Cruel people.

* * *

[Draft letter to Aleksandr Vvedensky]

Dear Al. Iv.,

Don't you hear the little note of sarcasm right there in the greeting? The sarcasm is not aimed at you, but at an unsuccessful life. Please try to feel this and understand it. The whole business started like this: I sent Ester an invitation for Monday. You were the one who brought back an answer in which she seemed to agree. Fine. I wait. I send a few more letters. I want to get an answer before Monday. No answer. I even got an answer from you, but not a damn thing from her. And then you write that she says, if she doesn't come on Monday, she'll maybe come on Tuesday, maybe on Wednesday. Right. On Sunday I go to the telephone and call to tell her that, no matter what, she's coming on Monday and no excuses whatsoever. And she has the nerve to announce to me on the phone that there's supposedly no way she can come before Thursday. Now I'm furious. I say: maybe it's better if you don't come at all.

I got home and immediately dashed off a letter. I write in it: "We are different people, we don't understand each other, and the best thing to do is go our separate ways." And so on. Then I went and threw the letter into the box and noted the exact time since it was a critical break in my life. Then, of course, as is only proper, I made all sorts of gestures known as "tearing the hair out of your head," and made everyone at home miserable with, as my sister terms it, my "unwashed mug." On Monday, to make things even worse, I woke up with an impacted tooth and with such a twisted and miserable look on my face that I didn't want to walk past the dining room and disturb people. So I wake up and get dressed. Suddenly the doorman comes in and announces that some young lady is asking for me. I panic, run to mommy and she catches sight of me and now she's also in a panic. What's the matter with you, she asks. I tell her that I'm fine but that some guests have come to see me. I ask her to go out and take a look. So mama comes back and tells me Ester has come. OK. She's shown into the dining room. I finish dressing and go there. Nothing particularly noteworthy happens. I say hello to Ester, and I say: did you get a letter? She says she got it. Did you read it? I say. I read it, she says. And did you like it? I say. Yes, she says, I liked it. I understood, as it happened But she wasn't talking about that letter. I realized that very quickly. But just in case, so she wouldn't get angry when she got home,

I told her quite casually which letter I had been talking about. I spoke to her a bit about this and, before you know it, there was nothing left for me to say. At that point I accidentally look in the mirror and think to myself: well, I'll describe my bad luck to her humorously. I began telling her about my tooth. I thought I was being witty (I was laughing myself) but not her. You won't get at her with that. I can't

I put myself in the hands of fate. Ester kept talking with mama and my sister, and looked at me as if I were an idiot. We sit like this for a while in the dining room, and then I invite her to my study. Again I said something funny, again she didn't get it. We both fell silent. Suddenly it dawned on me. In her letter she had written that she was itching to punch me. Now I think, begin with this and it'll all be good. Somehow I reminded her about her letter, even read it to her. She heard it out without saying a word. So then I say: since you, Ester, wanted to hit me, let's fight. But she just stared at me a bit, and let me have it right in the teeth! Right in my impacted tooth! Take that, she says, you ugly mug! Fuck. I couldn't believe it. I think, now I got what I deserved. It's all over now. But nothing: we sat, sat some more, and then went out for a walk.

We walk for a long time in silence, concentrating. She yawns, I take offense. I smile, she asks why I'm making a such a stupid face. In general, everything seemed ok. We walked up to a bench. Sat down. And I have no idea why a satanic courage came upon me then. I decided to have it out with her once and for all, bring it all out into the open. I began from afar. I talk and I talk, I see that she seems to understand. I immediately started to talk about love. She's listening and is even encouraging. I talk some more. She's even more encouraging. But as soon as I wanted to get to the bottom of everything, she ups and yawns. I jumped up and nearly cursed her out. Really flared up. We then calmed down a bit and went to have a beer.

What's the point of talking, that's how it was. After the beer, we got drowsy, felt sicker still. We went to have dinner. At dinner I sat silently, even majestically. Again Ester spoke mainly with mama and my sister. After dinner we went for a boat ride. We took Balnis along. But here I hadn't counted on one thing. He can swim, so what does he care? Ester is also thoughtless. So they start rocking the boat every which way for all it was worth. And worse, they start laughing at me. Of course they splashed water down my neck, humiliated me and, you could say, spit all over me.

I won't even begin to describe how I tried to persuade Ester to stay and spend the night; how she refused, dumping it all on her dear mother; how we made a call to her on the telephone and even how quickly she agreed to let her stay. It's not hard to imagine all this for yourself. But just think, how was I going to keep her busy till evening? There's a trick. I mulled it over all the way back to the house and decided to try to divert her, first with some light flirting, and if that failed, to resort to my sense of humor. The first didn't work for the simple reason that as soon as I sat down and snuggled up to her, she starts telling me some story. Either about Petrozavodsk and how the wires look there in the winter, or about going with Blumochka to see some Armenians and how much fun it was there. I didn't give up. I was thinking: she'll say everything and then shut up. I already knew that the only thing left to tell me was how Chernov drinks vodka and how she taught some commander to ride a horse. But she suddenly stopped talking before this. I rejoiced, moved in to kiss her, and she took a look out the window and says: I went with Misha to Gatchina once . . . I spat and walked into the other room. That evening, she again, of course, talked with mama and my sister and deigned to ask me just one question: were my teeth hurting?

It's time to put an end to all this. Today when she comes, I've got to make it clear. If she refuses to give me a blowjob *today*, then I am breaking with her for good. If she doesn't come before 4 o'clock, then I am also going to consider the entire affair finished. God will forgive me and my deeds on this Annunciation day.

Thursday, July 21, 1927. D. Kharms.

> (Today is January 31, 1928. Esther is sitting next to my sister.
> After two or three simply wonderful days, things have started to
> look again like July 21, 1927. Interesting to put these two notes
> together.)

* * *

Why must I suffer because of this girl?
I do many things that I'd rather not do, and don't do many things that
I would do just so as not to hurt her feelings.
But my patience is at an end. Why is she acting this way? She should just
say straight out: yes or no. All the same, she's been fucked backwards and

forwards. If she loves me, she herself should be willing to move toward sexual relations.

I don't understand her.

Still it would be better to tell her to fuck off.

Fuck you, whore and sovereign mistress.

I'm sick and tired of your behavior. Go where you want and shake your ass.

* * *

I finally broke up with Esther for good on July 21, 1927. I saw her for the last time at 8:56 in the evening of the same day in Tsarskoe Selo.

I can't remember another day like this one.

Now Esther is at the station and will be leaving on the first train so that she never has to see me again.

Esther, feel how much I love you and what anguish there is inside me.

My dear, beloved one, come back!!! Oh Lord!

* * *

Soh is schon alles geschehen. Ende. Oh Gott! Sei barmherzig. Vergis uns nich. Wir sind verloren. Segne, mein liebes Mädchen. Segne sie auf ein schönes Leben. Las sie glücklicher sein als jetzt, als bis her. Ich liebe sie ewiglich und bleibe ihr treu. Esther sol blümen auf ewige Tagen. Gott segne mein liebes, teures, schönes, kleines Mädchen.

Juli 21, 1927 Jahre.

Tsarkoe Selo.

Esther wird gleich sagen, das Sie soll abfaren. Und das wird heisen: Daniel sei ewig alein, ungeliebt.

Schwer ist mir.

> *Everything is over. The end. Oh God! Be merciful. Do not forget us. We are lost. Bless my beloved girl. Bless her for a better life. Make her happier than she is now, than she has been up to now. I love her eternally and remain true to her. May Esther thrive for all her days. God bless my beloved, dear, beautiful little girl.*
> *July 21, 1927.*
> *Tsarskoe Selo.*

> *Now* Esther *will say that she has to leave, and that means: Daniel,*
> *be always alone, unloved.*
> *This is hard for me.*

I wrote these lines when she was sitting in the next room for the last time.

* * *

Esther, if you ever think of me, never think I'm as bad as I seemed when you received my last note.

Lord, I don't need anything now. All those terms like: "a broken life," "lost youth," etc. are applicable to my present condition.

Oh God, preserve not me, but her.

No, I don't know what to write. But I can't just sit here like this. Lord, even if everything is for the best, not everything gets by unpunished, not by a long shot.

* * *

Any moment now I'll see the train on which she's going to leave.
It's already puffing away at the platform.

If only my dearest would glance out the window. Perhaps she would catch sight of me. Then let her think what she wants. O God

Farewell my Dear, my good, beloved little girl, my sweetheart, don't forget me, think of me from time to time. Someday, maybe, you'll think of me.

The train went by. But that, it seems, was a long distance train. And she couldn't have been on it.

I'll wait for the next one.

There's the whistle.

* * *

Oh God, if only she would return to me.

I don't want to live like this.

But even with all this, it's been clear for a long time. She doesn't love me and there's nothing I can do about it.

I say to myself: I'm a failure and there's no happiness for me anywhere. That's only because I don't know my own strength. I'm constantly trying things that are beyond my strength. Moreover, I've haven't managed to grasp the science of deriving happiness everywhere.
That's a noble science indeed.

People are probably wondering why I'm sitting in the road.
Let them wonder.

* * *

Will the train Esther's leaving on be here soon?

A gypsy once told my fortune. She said my dreams would come true one day. So far it doesn't look good.

At the present, this is my dream: I come home and suddenly . . . O miracle! O sacred moment! Esther is sitting there.
I don't know what would become of me.

It will soon be an hour since I last saw my little girl.

Utter failure. Now if her train does go by, I won't see her. A freight train is blocking my view.

* * *

Well, I'm leaving without staying to see her.
    July 21.

Later I was at the station, where I saw her for an instant. That was at exactly 9:58. I won't see her any more.

* * *

Streblov finds my break-up with Ester to be entirely correct. I find that myself. But I do love her, I love her more and more.
Hell, how I love her.
    July 23.

I was lying on the couch with a little dog and I suddenly realized (only now I've realized) that everything is over. There's nothing else that I can expect from Esther. This is all very difficult.

July 24.

* * *

From childhood to deep old age, a certain man always slept on his back with his arms folded. In the end, he died. Therefore sleep on your side.

* * *

Since I saw Esther for the last time, it's been: 270,180 seconds.

July 24/25.
Midnight.
1927.

* * *

And opened the abyss of stars full of stars no number of abyss no bottom.
Lomonosov.

The Sayings of the Chinese Sage Lao Tsu. Selected by Leo Tolstoy. Pub. "Posrednik." No. 763.

Lao Tsu shook me to the core.
Not, I think, by accident
Tao-Te-Ching

* * *

August 1
I'm throwing dice now. And no matter how improbable the answers, I will consider them correct and believe them.
If the number three falls out, it will mean that fate does not want to answer that question. At first I will ask Her if she wants to talk to me.

Rules of the game:
An even number means, yes;
An uneven number, no;
Three, the question is not permitted.

Questions:

1. Does Ester love me?
2. Will our silence end while I'm living in Tsarskoe?
    a. Who will end the silence?
    b. Will success follow?
3. Will we get back together after my arrival in Petersburg?
    a. Who will take the first step?
    b. Will success follow?
4. Will I ever get back together with her?
5. Will I ever go down on her?
6. When, exactly?

Here's how it's determined:

~~The first throw is just the question: will I get an answer or not?~~

one point = 1
two points = 2
three points = 3
four points = 4
five points = 5
six points = 0

Answers:

1. ~~No (5)~~ No (1)
2. ~~Yes (2)~~ Yes (2)
    a. she (2)
    b. yes (6)
3. yes (6)
    a. she (6)
    b. yes (4)
4.
5. yes (2)
6. (3) ?

I threw the dice on August 1.
It came out uneven
I'll put it off till tomorrow.

* * *

Gymnastics	Seconds
mill (41)	70
arm twists (61) ↑↓	90
body twists	50
wrist resistance (6)	45
steering (10)	25
neck turns (10)	30
fist grips (50)	30
squats 8	60
wipe down _____	100
total	500

[From notebook 10]

You don't love me, because you sit there without moving and even keep a little away from me.

Do you love me?
Very much

[From notebook 38]

Rules for Living:
1. Do something useful every day.
2. Study and practice Hatha and Karma yoga.
3. Go to bed no later than 2 am and get up no later than 12 noon, except in case of emergency.
4. Every morning and evening exercise and wipe down.
5. P—r.
6. Get out of bed as soon as you wake up: don't surrender to morning meditation and the desire to have a smoke.
7. When alone, keep busy with something definite.
8. Limit the number of guests who sleep over, and spend your nights predominantly at home.

9. Plan only that which is possible, but once something is planned, do it.
10. Value your time.

Daniil Kharms.
November 1927.
Cross and Mary, C. and M., C. and M., Saint Nikolai the Wonder Worker, Help me.

[From notebook 11]

417-32

212-64

Daniil Ivanovich Kharms. 1927.

rifle [36-23] 6560178.

235

Eclaire.

Sofia Aniolovna.

0 = done

+ = undone

Alek-ndr Nik. 171-18

Daniil Kharms. 1927.

* * *

Loneliness.
The fear of lying in the dark.

* * *

White.
Kg1, RR—e2, a1.
pp. a3, b2, c2, d4, f2, g3, h2.

Black.
Kg8, RR—f8, e6.
Nd5. pp. a4, b5, e4, g7, h7.
Black's move.

[From notebook 38]

Meeting of the Oberiuts
Agenda for Wednesday November 23.
8:00 pm Press House.

Report on current business.
1. Develop principles uniting poets and artists.
2. Develop methods of intra-group work.
3. Develop method of extra-group work.
4. Plans for "Three Left Hours."
5. Draw up budget for performance.
6. Draw up schedule for Press House.

* * *

November 28.
We (Kolya Zabolotsky and I) were at Marshak's. He read us the wonderful prose of M. Gudim.
We decided to meet on Mondays.

Oleinikov and Zhitkov have been organizing an Association of Children's Writers. We (Vvedensky, Zabolotsky and I) have been invited to join.
Kliuev has invited Vvedensky and me to read poems for some students who these days are rather more cultured than those of the past.

On Thursday, December 8, call Kliuev in the morning. On Tuesday evening Levin will come by.

[From notebook 11]

Of money received for *Ivan Ivanovich Samovar*, 35% = 61 r. 23 k.

30 r.	for home.
16 r. 80 k.	boots.
3 r.	owed to Zabolotsky.
10 r.	sundries.
	1. Mechanical pencil.
	2. Pads, copybooks, notebooks.
	3. Writing paper.

4. Ink.
5. Toothpaste.
6. Comb.
7. Hair cream "Brioline"
8. Tobacco.
9. Haircut and shave.
10. "Northern Palmyra."

A test of the pen. Daniil Kharms

* * *

For the journal *Hedgehog*,
Start up a section for reviews of children's literature.

Friday, Dec. 9, at Tsimbal's at 11:00 am. +
Meeting of the journal's editorial board at Marshak's at 12:00 on
December 9.

Ideas.
> The adventures of an orphanage where the electricity goes out
> every day.
> Shooting contests.
> Barber.
> Children's correspondent.

* * *

Objections to Tuberovsky
If you worship platform and puppet-booth, then we, on the contrary, are
completely and exclusively for the theater, for the stage. We need a building
closed to the idly-roaming crowd.

Drop in at Marshak's on Sunday morning.

* * *

Ask Marshak about editorial work that Aunt Natasha can do at home.

The evening of the 27th at Ender's.
Go to Press House in the morning and retype the piece.

~~By one o'clock on Saturday at Yudin's.~~

Evening of Wednesday, Dec. 28, at Marshak's.

* * *

Sketches for *Ivan Ivanovich Samovar* (for Zaits).

Friday, December 16. Stop by Press House in the morning for passes for Selvinsky +

Write something for Mansurov's paintings.

Mart for dinner at my place on Sunday at 3. O

Concluded terms on contract for *Pictures* on Saturday, December 17, 1927, due no later than January 15, 1928.

Will give Yudin text for illustrations.

* * *

See Malevich on Wednesday the 21st at 7 pm. +

Call Marshak on Friday, Dec. 23.
Redo story by Friday.

Friday at Marshak's:
       1. Find out about the journal   O
              What's happening and when   O
       2. About "Pictures"   O
       3. About money   +

* * *

For upcoming days:
       December 19, clean my room.
       December 20, work on play.
       21, work on play.
       22, work on play.   Finish play
       23, work on play.
       24, finish play.   Rework material.
       25, first reading of play.

The performance is scheduled for January 24, 1928 (Tuesday).

Stage at Press House:
      Width, 11 meters.
      Depth, 6 meters.
      Height to boards, 1 meter, 27 centimeters.
      Height to proscenium, 5 meters.

* * *

See Ermolaeva at Leningrad State Publishing on Saturday and let her know about meeting on Saturday at 8 in the evening.
On Friday send post cards to Ermolaeva and Yudin about the meeting of the Oberiu.

Wednesday 1 ½. Rehearsal.
Wednesday evening at Marshak's.

* * *

Agenda for Saturday, December 24.
      Reading of play.
      Discussion with Press House about money to retype play.
      Division of work.
            a.   company call,
            b.   drawing up a plan for the performance. O

Urgent to-do's.
      1. Retype play in 10 copies.   O
      2. Find one actor, one actress and . . .   O
      Thursday at 8 pm at Ermolaeva's. Let Shura know about this. +

      Friday, Dec. 30 at Marshak's (Tatlin will be there). +

1928

[Published in Proceedings of Press House, no. 2, January 1928.]

Declaration of the OBERIU

OBERIU (The Association of Real Art), in conjunction with Press House, unites workers in all forms of art who accept its artistic program and implement it in their own work.

OBERIU is divided into 4 sections: literary, artistic, theatrical and cinematic. The artistic section is conducting experimental work, while the other sections exhibit their work at evening performances, productions and in the press. At the present time OBERIU is working to organize a musical section.

The Social Face of the OBERIU

The immense revolutionary shift in culture and everyday life, so characteristic of our time, is being hampered in the sphere of art by many abnormal phenomena. We have not yet fully understood the indubitable truth that, in the sphere of art, the proletariat cannot be satisfied with the artistic methods of yesterday's schools; that its artistic principles go much deeper and undermine the old art to its very roots. It's absurd to think that the Repin who painted the Revolution of 1905 is a revolutionary artist. It's even more absurd to think that every "Association of Revolutionary Artists" carries within itself the germ of a new proletarian art.

We welcome the demand for an art that can be understood by everyone, accessible in form even to a village schoolboy, but the demand for *only* such an art leads into the thickets of the most terrible errors. The result is heaps of remaindered books from which the warehouses are bursting at the seams, while the reading public of the first Proletarian State is left with nothing but *belles-lettres* by Western bourgeois writers.

We very well understand the impossibility of quickly finding the only correct way out of the current situation. But we simply do not understand why any number of artistic schools working persistently, honestly, and resolutely in this sphere are relegated to art's backyard when they ought to be supported by all of Soviet society by all possible means.

We don't understand: why has the School of Filonov been ousted from the Academy? Why can't Malevich develop his architectural work in the USSR? Why was Terentiev's *Inspector General* so absurdly hissed off the stage? We don't understand why so-called left art, despite its not inconsiderable services and accomplishments, is accounted as hopeless refuse and, even worse, as charlatanism. How much hypocrisy, how much artistic bankruptcy, is concealed in those who take this savage approach?

Today OBERIU steps forward as a new detachment of left revolutionary art. OBERIU does not skate along the themes and across the heights of creativity: it seeks an organically new sense of the world and approach to things. OBERIU sinks its teeth into the very heart of the word, dramatic action and the film-frame.

The new artistic method of OBERIU is universal: it can find a way to represent any theme whatsoever. It is precisely on the strength of this method that OBERIU is revolutionary.

We are not so self-assured as to see our own work as complete in all regards. But we are firmly convinced that a sturdy foundation has been laid and that we are strong enough for further construction. We believe and we know that only the left path of art will lead us out onto the road of a new proletarian artistic culture.

The Poetry of the OBERIU

Who are we? And why us? We, the Oberiuts, are honest workers in our art. We are poets of a new sense of the world and of a new art. We are not only creators of a new poetic language, but also the founders of a new apprehension of life and its objects. Our will to creativity is universal: it overflows all types of art and bursts into life itself, enveloping it from all sides. Meanwhile the world, beslobbered by the tongues of the multitude of fools, entangled in the slime of "experience" and "emotion," is now being reborn in all the purity of its concrete and virile forms. Even now some deign to call us *zaumniki—trans-sense poets*. It's difficult to know what that is all about: a total misunderstanding or an inescapable failure to understand the fundamentals of verbal art? There exists no school more hostile to us than *zaum—trans-sense poetry*. Real and concrete to the very marrow of our bones, we are the first enemies of those who would geld the word and turn it into a powerless and meaningless mongrel. In our work we expand and deepen the meaning of the object and the word, but in no way do we destroy it. The concrete object, cleansed of its literary and everyday shell, becomes the property of art. In poetry, the collision of verbal meanings expresses that object with mechanical precision. You seem ready to object that this is not the same object that you see in life? Come closer and touch it with your fingers. Take a look at the object with naked eyes and you will see it for the first time cleansed of antiquated literary gilding. Perhaps you will assert that our subjects are "unreal" and "not logical"? But who said that "mundane" and "everyday" logic is necessary for *art*. We are astounded by the beauty of a picture of a woman even when, contrary to anatomical logic, the artist has turned the shoulder blade of his subject out and twisted it to the side. Art has its own logic, which, rather than destroying the object, helps us to know it.

We expand the meaning of object, word, and action. This work is carried out in different directions: each of us has his own creative persona and this circumstance often confuses some people. People speak of an *accidental* union of *different* people. Apparently, they assume that a literary school is something like a monastery, in which the monks all look alike. Our association is free and voluntary: it is a union of masters and not apprentices, artists and not house painters. Each knows himself and each knows what connects him to the rest.

Aleksandr Vvedensky (the extreme left of our association) breaks the object into parts, yet the object does not thereby lose its concreteness. Vvedensky breaks action into bits but the action retains its artistic necessity. Once fully deciphered, the result is the *appearance* of nonsense. Why the *appearance*? Because while a *trans-sense* word is obvious nonsense, there are none such in Vvedensky's work. One must be more inquisitive and not let up before examining the clash of verbal meanings. Poetry isn't kasha you swallow without chewing and then promptly forget.

Konstantin Vaginov's phantasmagoric world passes before one's eyes as if shrouded in mist and trembling. However, through this mist you sense the proximity of the object and its warmth, you sense the crowd rushing in and the swaying of trees that live and breathe in their own way, in Vaginov's way, for the artist has molded them with his own hands and warmed them with his breath.

Igor Bakhterev is a poet conscious of his persona in the lyric tint of his subject matter. The object and action, broken down into their components, rise again, renewed by the spirit of a new OBERIU lyricism. But lyricism here is not an end in itself: it is no more than a means of shifting the object to the field of a new artistic perception.

Nikolai Zabolotsky is a poet of naked concrete figures, brought right up to the level of the observer's eyes. One should listen to and read him more with eyes and fingers than with ears. The object is not fragmented but, on the contrary, knocked together and condensed to its very limits, ready to meet the viewer's groping hand. The development of action and situation play a role secondary to this main task.

Daniil Kharms is a poet and dramatist whose attention is focused not on the static figure, but on the collision of a series of objects, on their interactions. At the moment of action the object takes on new concrete outlines full of real meaning. The action, its face turned inside out in a new way, retains in itself a "classical" imprint and, at the same time, represents the broad range of the OBERIU sense of the world.

Boris Levin is a prose writer working at present in an experimental direction.

Such are the rough outlines of our group's literary section in general and of each of us individually: our poems will say the rest.

People of the concrete world, object, and word, we see our social significance in this purpose: to sense the world with a working hand, to cleanse the object of the garbage of ancient decayed cultures. Is this not the *real* need of our time? For this reason, our group bears the name OBERIU, The Association of Real Art.

Toward a New Cinema

Until recently, cinema did not exist as an art independent in principle. It was layered over with old forms of "art," and, at best, there were isolated and timid attempts to blaze new paths toward a genuine language of cinema. Such was the situation. . . .

Now the time has come for cinema to discover its *own* real face, to find its *proper* means of making an impression and a language that's really its *own*. No one has the power to "discover" the future of the cinema, nor do we promise to do this now. Time will do it, not people.

But it is the duty of every honest filmmaker to experiment, to seek out paths toward a new cinema and to take the first firm steps in that direction. And we are doing this.

A brief note is not the place to describe all of our work in detail. For now, just a few words about the already completed "Film No. 1." The time for the dominance of subject matter in cinema is over. At present, the adventure film and the film comedy are the most un-cinematic of genres precisely as a result of their focus on subject matter. As long as theme (+ story + plot) is an end in itself, they subordinate the cinematic material. However, finding an original, specifically cinematic material is the key to discovering the language of cinema. "Film No. 1" is the initial stage of our experimental work. It's not the plot that's important to us, but the "atmosphere" of the material we have chosen, that is, the theme. Individual elements of the film can be completely unconnected to each other in their relation to the plot and meaning; they can be antipodes in character. But this is not, we repeat, the point. The whole point is the "atmosphere" characteristic of the given material, of the theme. Revealing this atmosphere is our primary task. The easiest way to understand how we solve this task is to see the film on screen.

Not by way of self-advertisement: our performance is on January 24 of this year, at Press House. There we will show the film and discuss the direction of our work and what we are trying to achieve. The film was written and directed by **Aleksandr Razumovsky** and **Klementy Mints**.

The Theater of the OBERIU

Let's assume the following: two men come out onto the stage, they say nothing but they signify something to each other by signs. Doing this, they blow up their triumphal cheeks. Viewers laugh. Is this theater? It is. Do you say, farce? Well, even farce is theater.

Or this: a curtain descends on the stage: a village is painted on the curtain. It's dark on stage. Then it begins to get light. A man in a shepherd's costume comes out on the stage and plays a pipe. Is this theater? It is.

A chair appears on stage, on the chair—a samovar. The samovar is boiling. But instead of steam, naked arms come out from under the lid. Is this theater? It is.

And all of this: both the man and his movements on stage, and the boiling samovar, and the village painted on the canvas, and the light, now waning, now waxing, all of these are individual *theatrical elements*.

Up to now all these elements have been subordinated to the dramatic plot, to the play. A play is a story about some event told through characters. And on stage everything is done to explain this meaning and to make the course of this event clearer, more comprehensible and closer to life.

Theater is not at all to be found in this. If an actor portraying a government minister on stage starts walking on all fours and howling like a wolf, or if an actor portraying a Russian peasant suddenly recites a long speech in Latin, that's theater, it will interest the spectator, even if it occurs without any relation to a dramatic plot. It will be an isolated moment: a series of such moments, organized by the director, creates a theatrical performance with its own plot line and theatrical meaning.

This is the kind of plot that only theater can offer. The plot of a theatrical performance is theatrical just as the plot of a musical work is musical. They both represent the same thing, the world of phenomena, but depending on the material, they communicate it differently, each in its own way.

When you come to us, forget everything you are accustomed to seeing in other theaters. Much, perhaps, will seem absurd to you. We take a dramatic plot. At first it develops simply, then it is suddenly interrupted by what seem to be extraneous moments, clearly absurd. You are amazed. You want to find that customary, logical necessity that you think you see in life. But you won't find it here. Why? Clearly because object and action, once transferred from life to the stage, lose their "real life" logic and acquire a different logic, the logic of the theater. We will not explain this. To understand the logic of any theatrical performance, you have to see it. We can only say that our task is to show the world of concrete objects in their interrelations and collisions on the stage. We are working out a solution to this task in our production of *Elizaveta Bam*.

Elizaveta Bam was written by **Daniil Kharms**, on commission from the OBERIU theatrical section. The *dramatic* plot of the play is shattered by many apparently extraneous themes, which isolate the object as a separately existing whole, without connection to the rest; therefore the *dramatic* plot does not come before the viewer as a distinct plot line, but rather flickers in back of the action. Instead, a *scenic* plot, an elemental plot that arises from all the elements of the performance, comes to relieve it. It becomes the center of our attention. But at the same time, the separate elements of the performance are valuable in themselves and are dear to us. They lead their own existence, not subordinate to the ticking of the theatrical metronome. Here the corner of a gold frame sticks out and lives as an object of art; there an excerpt of a poem is spoken and, independent in its own meaning and independent of its own will, it pushes the play's scenic plot forward. Stage decoration, the movement of the actor, a bottle thrown across the stage, the tail of a costume, are as much actors as those who wag their heads and utter various words and phrases.

Staging by **Igor Bakhterev, Boris Levin** and **Daniil Kharms**. Art design by **I. Bakhterev**.

* * *

[From notebook 11]

Sunday, Jan. 1, at 5:00. Tsimbal coming over. +

Tuesday, at 6:00 at my place, meeting about play.

Tuesday, Jan. 3, 1928, morning call State Publishing.

Take documents to Public Library.

Jan. 6, Rehearsal, call Marshak.

Jan. 7, Tailor, State Publishing, Vaginov, Meeting 8:00.

* * *

Jan. 9.
> By 1 pm, rehearsal.
> See Ermolaeva.
> Put Program together.
> To Press House to see Baskakov.
> Call Marshak.
> See Marshak.
> 2 pm, Jan. 10, at Igor B.'s.

For January 12.
> Call Ermolaeva.
> Call Kis-Kis.
> Finish corrections to the play.

> Call Golts.
> Call Levin and Igor, tell them to come earlier.
> Call Baskakov to find out about ticket prices.
> Work out gestures for verse parts of play.

* * *

By Jan.11, we will have clarified our position re theater.
Jan. 11, contract with artists.
Starting Jan. 8, negotiate with musicians.
Jan. 15, finish staging.
Jan.15, film.

Need to come to an understanding with Baskakov about plywood, advertising (maybe in *Red Evening Gazette*), carpenter, paints, seating in the hall.

Put together text of poster. Need to do this to clarify the situation with artists and musicians.

On ~~Saturday, January 14~~ Wednesday, January 11, turn in draft of poster to Baskakov.

* * *

On Monday, January 16, be at "Comintern" printers by 9 am.
Then rehearsal.   O
Ender will call me at 6:00.

Call printers at 8:30. Ask about regional censorship committee (Gublit). O
Call Vulfius at 1 pm.

At 5:00 rehearsal at my place.
Call Babaeva.   O

Tell Igor about the servants' costume.
Call Matiushin.
Speak to Terentiev about makeup.
Call Kurbanov.

Rehearsal. Distribute posters.
See Vaginov.

* * *

Need to get props for upcoming performance of "Three Left Hours":
    1. Tricycle.
    2. Several pieces of colored material, although I'm for a plain
    sheet.

3. Whistle.

4. Samovar.

5. 2 wine glasses.

6. Swords.

7. Crutch.

8. Abacus.

9. Quill pen.

10. Log and saw.

11. Small box.

12. Lantern.

* * *

Chorus.

Women, 5—10.

Men, 10—15.

Musical direction by P. Vulfius.

Ticket prices from 40 k. to 1 r. 50 k.

* * *

S. L. Tsimbal's play "Gold Deposit."

At Gublit:

1. Turn in play (bound in 4 copies)

2. Correct poster.　　　O

With Baskakov:

1. Find out about ticket prices.

2. Negotiate payment for poster to avoid delay at printer.

With Itkin:

Ask about putting an evening lecture by Tsimbal on the calendar for Feb. 4.

* * *

<u>Poster</u>

"Battle of the Two Champions" in different fonts.

Turned upside down: Kropachev.

Put the T sideways in "Debate."

Classical dances.
Militsa Popova.
Your host for the evening, Yu. Golts.
Jazz by Mikhail Kurbanov.

January 17, talk with Baskakov about:
        putting up posters, 43 rubles,
        carpenter,
        money for costumes,
        finishing painting of stage.

* * *

Invitations:

Marshak	2	
Malevich	2	
Matiushin	1	
Tuberovsky	1	
Stepanov	2	
Tufanov	2	
Sollertinsky	1	
Erbshtein	2	
Lebedev	1	
Sokolov	2	
Terentiev	1	
Kashnitsky	1	Filonov
Ink	1	
Kliuev	1	
Mansurov	1	

Buy 15 five-kopeck stamps, 75 kopecks.

* * *

Complimentary tickets:

Zabolotsky	3		
Bakhterev	2		
Vvedensky	1	Manevich	1
Levin	2	Grin	1

Vaginov	1	Varshavsky	1
Tsimbal	2	Vigiliansky	1
Razumovsky	2	Babaeva	1
Mints	2		
Golts	2	Kharms	
Vulfius	2		
Kotelnikov	1		

Personal Invitations:

Lipavsky
Ermolaeva
Suetin
Yudin
Rozhdestvensky
Sterligov
Zhuravlenko
Nikolsky

* * *

Casting

Peter Nikolaevich	~~Vigiliansky Dmitrichenko~~ Varshavsky
Ivan Ivanovich	Manevich
Papa	~~Dmitrachenko~~ Vigiliansky
Elizaveta Bam	~~Ratur~~ Goldfarb
Mamma	~~Goldfarb~~ Babaeva
Beggar	~~Varshavsky~~
Servants	Kropachev, Vvedensky
Chorus	

Literary director	D. Kharms
Art Director	I. Bakhterev
Main director	S. Tsimbal
Musical director	P. Vulfius

Chairman of Theater Council—B. Levin.

* * *

Who will take Kropachev's place, and what will the maid wear?

* * *

Rehearsals

1. Reading of ½ play by actors.	Dec. 28, 1:30 pm
2. Reading of ½ play.	Dec. 30, 1:30
3. Reading of the entire play.	Jan. 2, 2:00
4. *Mise en scene ½.*	Jan. 4, 1928, 1:30
5. Excerpts 1, 2, 3, 4.	Jan. 6, 1:00
6. Intonation Elizaveta Bam and P. N.	Jan. 8, 12:00
7. Excerpts 5, 6, 7, 8, 9, 10, 11.	Jan. 9, 1:30
8. Finish the play.	Jan. 11, 1:30
9.	Jan. 13
10. Entire play twice.	Jan. 16, 1:30
11. At my place, 5 pm.	Jan. 17, 5:00
12. Press House, 1 pm	Jan. 18
13. 1:30	Jan. 19
14. 1:30	Jan. 20
15. 1:00	Jan. 21
1:00	Jan. 22
16. 2:00	Jan. 23.

* * *

For the debate

Literature

Stepanov

Petnikov

Eikhenbaum

Tufanov

Livshits

Theater

Terentiev

Veisbrem

Dreiden

Cinema

~~Kumeiko~~
Maimon
FEKS people
Likhachev

Arts

Pakulin
Malevich
Filonov

* * *

Eliz. B. carries a pitcher and splashes water.

Militsia Popova.
Pizzicato, from *Little Humpback Horse.*
Adagio by Chopin.
Pizz.—*Vain Precaution.*

Rakhmaninov's Polka No. 1.

* * *

OBERIU Declaration by N. Zabolotsky

Distribution of posters:

State Publishing—10 copies.
Public Library—3 copies + 1
Bank for Commerce—2
North-Western Stock Co.—1
North-West Union—1
Regional Finance Bureau—3
University—10 copies
Vereinigung—1
Consulates—
All-Union Association of Engineers—2
Central House of the Arts—2 + 2
Library of New Books—1
Cinema *Soleil*—1
Cinema *Colossus*—1

Book stores on Nevsky
Academia Press—1
Philharmonic—1
Office of Academic Theaters—1
Life of Art—1
Attorneys' Club—1
Business Club—1
Regional Censor—2
Yusupov Palace—3.

* * *

Money received:

    15 r. for paints.
    10 r. for carpenter and captions.
    5 r. for sundries.
    15 r. for Jazz.
    5 r. for trumpet player.
    50 r.

Owed:

    10 r. for Jazz.
    9 r. for carpenter
    5 r. for Kulikov
    3 r. for Levenberg.
    4 r. for cellist.
    31 r.

* * *

January 18.

    Find someone to replace Kropachev.
    Discuss makeup.   o
    Put up posters.

Friday, January 20.

    Call Baskakov and ask him for 30 r. right away.
    Call Kurbanov.
    Call Vulfius, ask about rehearsal, tell him about cellist and
    Levenberg.
    Begin sale of tickets.

Take all props to rehearsal.   o
Call Igor and Levin.
Announcements for *Red Evening Gazette*.
Finish text.

* * *

Today: the Oberiuts at Press House. *Three Left Hours*

For January 21, Saturday.
Get memo for kettledrums at Press House.
See B. Ulitin regarding claque.
Call Lipavsky at Leningrad Publishing.
Call Marshak in the evening.
Send postcard to Vaginov.
Call Razumovsky and find out about poster distribution and finances.
Tell them at home to wash a shirt for me.
Get hold of a bell.

* * *

Memorandum
Society for German Cultural Enlightenment in Leningrad

Press House requests the loan of two kettledrums for January 22, 23 and 24 and guarantees safe return of same.

* * *

Press House.

21 Fontanka.
Invitation.

OBERIU requests the pleasure of your company at the performance of "Three Left Hours."
January 24, 1928.
Performance begins at 7:30.

Stamp.   Signature.

* * *

Hang <u>posters at</u>:
University, State Publishing, Credit Union, Conservatory, Library of New Books.

At 1:00 go to the German Society for Cultural Enlightenment.

* * *

[Program for "Three Left Hours"]

PRESS HOUSE

**Tuesday
January 24
1928**

**By way of a demonstration of
contemporary
movements in art**

A THEATRICALIZED EVENING
OF THE
OBERIUTS

"Three Left Hours"

Oberiu—The Association of Real Art:
Literature—art—cinema—theater.

First Hour

Introduction. Masters of Ceremonial Choir. OBERIU
Declaration. Declaration of Literary Section.
Reading their poems:

K. Vaginov
N. Zabolotsky
Daniil Kharms
N. Kropachev
Igor Bakhterev
A. Vvedensky

The Master of Ceremonies will ride around on a tricycle
making improbable lines and figures.

Second Hour

A theatrical presentation will be shown.

"Elizaveta Bam"

Text D. I. Kharms. Staging I. Bakhterev, Bor. Levin, D. I. Kharms. Decorations and costumes I. Bakhterev. Music P. Vulfius. Actors: Grin (Elizaveta Bam), Manevich (Ivan Ivanovich), Varshavsky (Peter Nikolaevich), Vigiliansky (Papa), Babaeva (Mama), Kropachev (Beggar), P. Katelnikov (stage engineer).

During the course of the action:
"The Battle of the Two Champions"

Text Emmanuel Crasdäterich. Music Veliopagus, the Netherlandish Shepherd. Choreography the Unknown Traveller. The beginning will be signaled by a bell.

Third Hour

An Evening Meditation on the Cinema—
Aleksandr Razumovsky.
There will be a screening of

Film No. 1 *The Meatgrinder*

A Work by directors
Aleksandr Razumovsky
And Klimenty Mints

Special musical illustrations to the film.
Jazz by Mikhail Kurbanov. The evening's host
Iu. Goltz. Theatricalization by Bor. Levin.
Art design by I. Bakhterev.

DEBATE

The evening will be accompanied by **Jazz**

* * *

[Review of "Three Left Hours," Krasnaia gazeta, no. 24, January 25, 1928]

Ytuirebo.

Incomprehensible? You bet! That's exactly the reason for doing it. No matter how you write "Lipkovskaya," back to front or front to back, people will still come hear her. But you try writing "Kropachev" upside down and filling the house. Tricky.

Yesterday something not fit to print took place at Press House. If the Oberiuts (allow us to translate: "The Association for Real Art") let themselves go wild, the public was no less frivolous: whistles, hissing, catcalls and an unfettered exchange of opinion with the performers.

"Now I shall read two poems," announces an Oberiut.

"Make it one!" someone in the hall groans imploringly.

"No, two. The first one is long and the second is short."

"Just read the second!"

But the Oberiuts are merciless: once they start, they'll bring the affair to its misbegotten conclusion.

"Three Left Hours" called to mind both the striped blouses of the Futurists and the summersaults of FEKS ("Factory of the Eccentric Actor"). Someone even recalled Balmont, who in his day was "understood by no one."

"They wants to show off their learning and talk about what's incomprehensible," said Chekov: he might just as well have been talking about the Oberiuts.

But that's not the point. The point isn't that Zabolotsky's poems are good, quite comprehensible and thoroughly iambic in origin; the point isn't that Vvedensky's aren't, but rather that his awful *zaum* smacks of gobbledygook and that *Elizaveta Bam* is unvarnished-to-the-point-of-cynicism chaos in which "no one understood a damn thing" according to the general acknowledgment of the discussants.

The main question that burst forth spontaneously from the hall was:

"What the hell?!" "What's the point?!" "Who needs this clown show?"

Checkered hats, red wigs, toy horses. A dismal attempt at joyless sensationalism, pieces poorly played.

The Futurists drew sharps and flats on their faces in order to: *épater le bourgeois*.

In 1928 you're not going to epatage anyone with a red wig and there's no one left to scare.

During a debate organized at the insistence of the public, opinions were expressed energetically.

"I would offer my opinion about the Oberiuts," pronounced a representative of the Poets' Union, "but I cannot: I am an official person and there are women in the hall."

On the other hand, the Oberiuts said it all about themselves in the words of the author of *Elizaveta Bam*:

"If you go to buy a chicken, look to see if it has teeth. If it does, it's not a chicken."

"It's a cockroach," a spectator chimed in.

Lydia LESNAYA

* * *

[From notebook 11]

Hello to you. It's you again.
Have a seat, please, on this sofa,
Take a flower from the table,
And a look around the room:
I'll throw this lamp up to the ceiling
I'll grind it up and leave you reeling
Mix it up with honest water
And wipe it off with my transparent beard.
Ester: And what will you do with me?
Me: I'll crebovy You,
                I'll spread your legs,
                I'll thrust my head down there
                And the long waters of my desire for Ester
                Will begin to flow.

* * *

Of the money received on February 4.
        10 r. to Lipavsky.
        5 r. to Kobelev.
        3 r. to Zhenka Bogdanov.
        6 r. to Illa.
        8 r. 50 k. for telephone.

2 r. 50 k. for haircut.

10 r. for enhancing sexual potency.

50 r. to Mama.

* * *

<u>Invited to an evening of Zabolotsky's poetry.</u>

1. Marshak.

2. Lebedev.

3. Shvarts.

4. Oleinikov.

5. Frumkina.

6. Lipavsky.

7. Zhitkov.

* * *

For February 12.

Call Zhenka about putting together a list of invitees.

Call Ginken.

Find clean shirt and collar.

Go see *Natalia Tarpova* with T.A.M.

February 15.

Call Ester.

Go to State Publishing.

Go see Ester.

Go to Press House (about Zabolotsky's evening).

* * *

My debts.

B. S. Zhitkov, 5 r. by February 15.

Lebedev,   5 r. by February 18.

Illa,   2 r.

Zhenka Bogdanov, 3 r.

Lipavsky,   3 r.

Lebedev,   5 r. by February 18.

Vvedensky,   8 r.

               Total 31 r.

Expenses.
>31 r. in debts.
>19 r. for an evening with Baskakov.
>9 r. [illegible]
>6 r. for a shirt.
>6 r. for notebooks.
>20 r. pocket money.
>20 r. for home.

* * *

For February 27.
>Call Shura about the settlement; leave the results at home for Nikolaev.
>Go to State Publishing.
>Stay home this afternoon and evening and work.

* * *

>Speak to Kashnitsky about makeup.
>Bell.
>Curtain.
>Lighting and projector.

>Call Kurbanov.
>Pick up costumes.
>Bicycle.
>Electrician.
>Curtain.
>Screen.
>8 r. for Baskakov.
>Send out tickets.
>Banners to Kropachev.

* * *

Are you happy or not that I am going away now.

* * *

By March 1, Deliver "The Naughty Fuse."

By March 1, Deliver "How Papa Shot Me a Ferret."

By March 1, Write a new story.

<u>Ester</u>
Take manuscripts to the Literature Seminar Room at the Institute for the History of the Arts.

* * *

For Daniil
    8 Shirts.
    6 pairs of Long Johns.
    3 Jerseys.

For Ester:
    6 blouses.
    6 knickers (short and wide).
    2 slips.
          material for bras.
    6 night shirts.
    1 pair black leggings.
    Corset.
    6 pairs stockings.
    6 dresses.
    1 peignoir.
    Patent leather shoes.
    Yellow shoes.
    white linen.
    house slippers.

* * *

[Entries in Ester's and Kharms's handwritings]

Natasha didn't ask me anything about you.
She still has time, you'll see.

Ester, last night I experienced the torments of Tantalus. Still it's lucky I was very tired.

The torments of Tantalus: a condition when what you want is there right next to you, but you can't reach it.

Liza really wants a smoke.
What a joke!

* * *

Oberiu.
Meeting, March 3.

Should attend:
        Bakhterev.
        Zabolotsky.
        Kharms.
        Levin.
        Tsimbal.
        Razumovsky.
        Mints.
        Vigiliansky.

Agenda:
        1). Discussion of intergroup relations.
        2). Discussion of situation at Press House.
        3). Future moves (near-term).
        4). Division of work.
        5). Relations with Terentiev.

* * *

Herbert Spenser. *First Principles.*
Wasserman. *The Man with the Geese.*
Charles Van Lerberghe. *They Sensed It.*
Hašek, *The Good Soldier Schweik.*

* * *

180

Raviggioli—cheese curds from goat's milk.

* * *

Ester	Ink	Asya
I love	I love	I love sexually
deeply	her for	[illeg.]
And forever.	her mind.	As a woman,
I want her to	Astonishing	she has her effect on me.
agree to see me	woman.	Maybe
[illeg.]	[For me	also good
to get married.	(illeg.)]	as a person.

* * *

A chest of drawers
Above the winds
A shepherd running to the shore
He dives into transparent streams
Around the pond the cities gleam.

* * *

By then the night had passed and the wind had come up. It blew from all directions, blew so hard it seemed as if not the wind, but dogs were coming in through the chinks.

The water came up to his face and suddenly stopped. His face became smooth, the skin stretched tight, and his mouth moved to where a pretty ear used to grow.

A face looked in at every window. How horrible when faces look in from all sides. If they look out from the house onto the street it's not as terrifying as if they look in through all the windows, from the street into the house, into the room.

Suddenly two men appeared in the stove, one redheaded and the other with a black mustache.

* * *

An old lady went out walking
An old lady in a headscarf
Through the streets, through the town
To buy herself some ink.

But it was really very cold
On the street and in the town.

* * *

From woes diverse
does God protect us?
Answer:
He does and the truth is
in his hands life's all the smoother.

* * *

[Entry in Ester's handwriting]

My beloved husband,
I will never ever
leave you forever.

* * *

On March 7, I had to show up for military service. Interesting, but disgusting. I sit apart from all the others. This, I think, is how it's going to be.

Even on the stairs I was hit with the foul smell of sour dog and soup that reeks of schooldays.

There are 14 of us. I still don't know what they're like. Almost no one from the intelligentsia. Apart from me, there might be one more, but even that's doubtful.

A certain comrade Commander with one bar on his collar who looks like a redheaded cockroach is a real gulletbuster.

I write because I don't know what else to do.

March 8. There are a lot more of us now. Really not good. Oh Lord, help me, free me once and for all from military service.

* * *

Oh Lord, what do I do to get out of military service? Cross and Maria. C. and M., C. and M., C. and M., Thou wilt set me free.

* * *

"Comrades, no spidding on the floor and no smoking! For this go out into the collidor!"

* * *

A discovery. Remove all signs of rank after rolling your flaps up and gulping down a prickly fish. (Walleye won't do here.). Be boastful, even if someone just appears to be an ignoramus. Now sit like a piece of glass, but don't melt and don't admit any scratches, be transparent but not for everyone. They're too familiar with me, therefore be proud. Oh God, spare me from showering in the washroom. Got to get out of here as soon as possible. It's very bad here. Everyone is against me.

* * *

Mein Lieber G.
Befrei mich von allen Pflichten. Ich bin Schnell dagegen was mein Land sich zu Hertzen nimt. Mir ist alles fremd was hier passiert. Mein Lieber G. Mache mich frei von Proletarität sein. L. G. mir ist schwindich, gieb mir Stärke. Ich möchte schlafen mein L. G. Ich bin fremd denen die rund mich sitzen. O wie schlim und greslich ist hir.

> *Dear God,*
> *Free me from all afflictions. I am against everything that my*
> *country holds dear to its heart. Everything that happens here seems*
> *foreign to me. My Dear God, free me from the proletariat. Dear*
> *God, things are so difficult, grant me strength. I would like to sleep.*
> *Dear God, I am foreign to those sitting around me. How terrifying*
> *and terrible it is here.*

* * *

How disgusting it is to be here anyway, even in the mornings.

4 squads to a platoon.
3 battalions to a regiment.
1 signals platoon.
1 mounted scouts platoon.
1 artillery division.
Regimental staff HQ.
Regimental club.
Dressing station.
Platoon.
4 rifle squads.
1 light automatic rifle squad.

A company has 3 platoons, 1 machine gun. 1 HQ platoon.
A battalion has 3 companies, 1 machine gun,
Chemical weapons platoon, 1 signals squad.

$10 \times 4 = 40 \times 3 = 120 \times 3 =$ battalion.
$360 \times 3 = 1{,}080 =$ regiment.

* * *

L.G. mach das ich frei sich werde. . . Es ist sehr schwer hier zu bleiben.
Mein L. G. Ich bitte Dich sehr, mach mich frei. Mach das heute ich werde
frei sein und nach Hause gehen. L. G. Du kanst es doch machen. Ich gebe
Dir mein Wort das ich alles machen werde um das ganze Leben schön und
Richtig geht. Befreie nun mich. Wegend meine Frau und meine Ältern
befreie mich.
D. H.

> *Dear God, set me free. . . It's very hard to be here. My dear God,*
> *I beg of Thee, set me free. Set me free today and let me go home.*
> *Dear God. Thou canst do this surely. I give Thee my word that*
> *I will do everything to make my whole life pleasing and just. Only*
> *set me free. For the sake of my wife and my parents, set me free.*
> *D. H.*

I want to get a divorce as soon as possible from ⊟.

* * *

<u>Wallnewspaper of the Ninth Company</u>.
~~Just outside~~
~~We showed up on 7 March we~~
~~Formed up, formed up, formed our ranks~~
~~To our rifles we affixed our~~
~~bayonets~~
~~Ninth Company's the very best~~.

* * *

A Guest at Zabolotsky's

And now I've come upon the house,
that stood along the moor,
that opened wide its door.

And up the step now jump! I run.
Then four times after that.
The house is standing on the shore,
right by the shore in fact.

And now my fist knocks on the door:
hey open get me in!
But oaken door says nothing to
my host into his ribs.
My host is lying in the room,
and in this room he lives.

And then I look into the room,
into the room I go,
in which the smoke from cigarettes
will take you by the neck,
and Zabolotsky's hand—his hand
is running round the room,
and picking up a wingéd pipe
it pipes its music round.
The music dances. I come in
in costly tophat crowned.

I sit myself down on my right,
laughing to my host,
reading as I look at him,
the sly perfidious poems.

The house that's on the riverside,
that's there upon the lea,
that stands (there in the distance)
looking like a pea.

THAT'S ALL.

D. Kh.
December 14, 1927.

* * *

I'd always been a model lad
Till I forgot my spoon,
And got a little scared.
Where's my spoon now? Where's my spoon?

* * *

[From notebook 12]

Ester, let's go to my place today.
I also wanted to write something, but that didn't pan out.
Let's go E.

* * *

Stupid empty words!
There is an infinite movement,
A breath of light elements,
the racing of plants,
the rotation of the earth,
the crazy alternation
of day and night.

The compounding of deaf nature,
the rage and strength of darkdreaming beasts,
And man's conquest
Of the laws of light and wave.

* * *

[Entries written in Ester's and Kharms's handwritings]

Dummy, do you love me?

No I don't. Yesterday I fell in love with another woman: a little bit, just a little bit! Today that's already over, but I've begun to love you less. Forgive me for being so frank.

I expected this. Well, whatever, live and live it up. When you stop loving her, you should know that there is still one silly girl who loves you and will accept only you, if that's what you want. So farewell. Anyway, try to stop with her.
Yours forever Ester.

Good, I'll keep that in mind. When they all turn their backs on me, I'll come to you.
Yours some day Daniel.

* * *

Papa really loves to win at chess. I'll ask him to play and I'll lose. He'll be very happy.

* * *

[Entries written in Ester's and Kharms's handwritings]

You've stopped loving me completely. I know that and I can see it.

Aren't you ashamed, Ester, even to think like that? You can't imagine how happy I am just sitting next to you. You are better than everyone who has lived since the world began. When I sit next to you, I feel such pleasure I need nothing, only that you be kind and affectionate.

* * *

Ester, don't think anything bad. I know you're angry I invited Ini to sit with us. But I only did it so you would see her and calm down. So you'd realize she and I are just good friends. I love only you.

* * *

Tuesday, March 13, 1928. I woke up quite early and got ready to go do my military service. Ester was still sleeping. I bent down and kissed her. She stirred, took my hand, squeezed it, and said "Mishenka." It's ridiculous to think she's forgotten him. But her saying his name is tormenting me, it's been 2 hours already. I think this is going to go on for a long time, maybe forever. She'll never forget the man she gave her innocence to, and that means I won't either. Lord how difficult this is. Help me God, instruct me, tell me what I should do. This is very difficult and my heart aches. Lord, is Ester really so unfaithful that her relations with me, supposedly her only ones, are nothing more than a cunning game? No, this cannot be. Lord, tell me, can I believe her or not? God help us, bless us. Amen.

* * *

What will be? What will be? Oh Lord, how are we going to live? God, I have to break up with her. I can't bear her thinking about another man she belongs to by right of first cohabitation.

Lord, I can't bear this ambiguous situation. God give me strength. God. . . . Let it be as it will be.

If the worm gnaws at your heart
Go get yourself a harem.
You can call me "D" maybe
But don't you ever dare "M."

So now it's all the same to you
To be with him . . . or someone. . . .
You've been dead a long long time
You call them all "my dear one."

You don't want to be with me
you flee me like a she-hen.
That means you want to be alone
and that's just what you'll be then.

I really like the way you walk,
your shoulders arms legs bust and—
your eyebrows hands . . . you're quite a find—
strict only with your husband.

You spend your nights with Dan-i-el
but, alas, your Daniel,
although he rhymes with Mich-a-el,
is not at all a Michael.

If a bullet will not help,
Go get yourself a harem.
You can call me "D" maybe,
But don't you ever dare "M."

* * *

[From notebook 11]

Oh Lord, better Thou shouldst cut short my pitiful existence. I find no
support anywhere. Oh Lord, there's never yet been a time like this in my
life. Oh Lord, if I am so weak that my entire life must be such torture, then
take this life from me. Oh Lord, dost Thou really not want to help me?
Lead me painlessly to a better place. Lord, I perish, Thou seest this. Oh
Lord, Lord, Lord! Save and preserve me.

March 16. And that's because I'm unhappy with her. But why, I myself
can't say. But something isn't right. A terrible evening and night are before
me. Lord, do not leave us without Thy care. Amen.

Wrong. Everything is very good.
Oh God, I give thanks to Thee that Thou hast given me life. Everything in the world is good.

Look, my sweet friend, and see how good, how beautiful everything is.
Take pleasure in everything.
Today is the best day. And so should every day be.

Say then, what is it you fear? Come what may, I fear nothing and accept that everything is the way it should be. All the same, my Spirit is not vanquished by anything or anyone.
Long live Thy wise arrangement of our lives. Hallowed be Thy Name.

* * *

You're a little bit tired, lie down and take a rest.

March 17. She, that is Ester, came but we. . .

All she cares about now is clothes, won't talk about anything else. Very boring. Why did I ever get married? I'm done for if things go on like this. We had a fight and I have no intention of making up with her.

Ester, you should know that if I leave, there's the risk of an irreparable break, that is, <u>divorce</u>. Don't let it come to this.

Ester, it's hard for us to make up now. I'll leave this minute. Then it will be impossible.

Ester, while I'm still here, take just a few steps towards making peace. Show somehow you love me and not rags. Dear little Ester, quickly, call me back. Call me now, while I'm still here.

Ksenia, Servant of God, help us. Grant that we be reconciled now.

* * *

Oh Lord, can this really be the end? If we fight and break up now, it looks as if it will be forever. Oh Lord, don't let it come to this. It's true, I do want to be single again, to be able to write and live like a free poet. But God, grant that, somehow, both might be possible together. Lord, I love Ester too much. Oh God, please bring us together. Do it now.

Farewell, Ester, farewell. I'll leave now and we'll never again sleep together. Farewell, my little kitty, farewell.
Amen. March 17, 1928.

* * *

March 18, 1928. Oh Lord, give me the strength to divorce Ester.
I just can't be with her. It would ruin her life, and I can't go on living like this either.

March 31. It's clear that everything's over between the two of us. She talked a long time with Mishka on the phone, even though I've forbidden her to be friends with him. What's more, I suspect she's been flirting with someone though the window. Yes that's probably what's been going on. This morning, she was standing in front of the window in just her bathing suit, which, by the way, she won't wear in front of me. And there she was, sitting without her panties, legs up so across the street anyone who wanted could see everything. Now she's gone up to the window again and is looking out over there.

Things are getting serious. It smells like divorce. Watch out, you'll be the one to blame.

* * *

I want to leave now. She's sitting in the room with me. What's she waiting for? No idea. Does she really think I'll say something to her?

She's gone to make a phone call. Must be calling home. She'll take off, no doubt.

Somehow I can't hear her making the call. I'll leave now. But she's right. Whatever happens, she and I won't be able to live together and get along. Did she put a note in my bowler?

Seems there's no note under my bowler. She (that is, Ester) has gone away somewhere. At her sister's maybe?

Ester, you're little better than a whore. I'm right to think that even if you aren't cheating on me in the usual way, you're being unfaithful in small things. You're looking for men all the time. And you do everything to attract them.

* * *

~~In three minutes I~~ . . .
I'll smoke another cigarette and leave. You and I have had a row, Ester. It's clear now we won't make up and that means we won't get back together at all. And even that's for the best. All the same, sooner or later, we'll go our separate ways. We're strangers. Better not be attached to me. Better that you forget me, *e basta*! I'll never be for you what you want me to be, just as you won't for me. We'll forget each other soon enough. You're not comfortable breaking up in front of other people, I know that. But still, despite all that, we have to go our separate ways.

I'm waiting until this cigarette burns down to the end, and then I'm leaving. That means a complete break. I know that, but I'll leave anyway.

Meanwhile I'm still waiting for I-don't-know-what. Must be for a miracle.

Ksenia, Servant of God, help me!

* * *

She's gone, but that's not the point. Everything's over anyway. Let her be the one to begin, then maybe something could be cleared up. But in a few minutes it will be too late. I'll leave.

Still, since she has come, I'll smoke another cigarette.

Fine, let her write me something. It's really a wonder: when I see she's angry, I always go up and speak to her. Now when she sees that I'm angry, I get zero attention. Fine, I won't go near you, you don't need to worry. Cry even, I won't go near you. Have the courage and the love to come to me first. This is your last bet, Ester, and I know it's not easy, you're hemmed in by time too. But with desire and love, everything is possible. There's a challenge for you. Hurry up. Otherwise, everything's lost. Remember, should I leave without making up with you first, we'll part as enemies and strangers. Forever.

What are you waiting for? Time is running out..
You were to blame, now you go and repent. Forgive me if I'm being unfair but there's no point, Ester, in making up just for the sake of making up. We'll fight again soon enough. I have no faith in you, so let reconciliation on your part be a guarantee of your honesty and good faith. Ester! Quickly! Time is almost gone.

You keep fooling around and then assure me this is all very painful for you, etc.

Now that I've finished smoking my cigarette, I'm leaving. Ester's left the room.

Another minute of this and we're through.

There's no love left. That's clear.

I'm out of here.

AMEN.
March 31, 1928.

* * *

[From notebook 13]

Plan for April, May, June, I've got to hand in two things:
"The old lady and the ink";
"A story about seven hedgehogs." With G.'s Help.
May 21, started "Don-Permadon." A complex thing for the children's division.

Esther—June 19. Biceps: left 25.5 centimeters,
                                     right 27.5 c.

White: Kf1, Qb3, Nc1, ppb4, c2, f3.
Black: Ka1, Qa4. Mate in 3 moves.

White: Kh1, Qg1, Rh4, Bg8, NNc7, d7, pe2.
Black: Kf5, RRa6, b8, Ba3, Nb2, ppf3, f6, g6, h5.
Mate in 2 moves.

* * *

<u>My debts</u>

> 7 r.—to Lebedev.
> 10 r.—to Lipavsky.
> 3 r.—to Zhitkov (20 May).
> 2 r.—*The Republic of Shkid.*
> 3 r.—to Kobelev.

A bottle of vinegar is on the table. Peter Ivanovich sips tea with poppy seeds. Peter Ivanovich's wife is stupid. Mousetown.

An idle hidalgo and a repentant idler. Lev Markovich Veisenberg.

A work by E. A. Kharms.
Morning song.

> Wash up!
> Wash up!
> don't you be scared of
> me. I won't touch you,
> so don't you get worked up!

* * *

Out in the yard sang Father comes with war against son, and son kills father.

A face as red as a calico copybook.

Rypin. *Interplanetary Communication.*

* * *

I'm some special kind of loser. For some time now an incomprehensible law of non-realization has been hanging over me. Whatever I desire, that's exactly what never turns out. Everything that happens goes against my intentions. In truth: man proposes, God disposes. I'm in dire need of money, but I'll never get any, I know that! I know serious troubles await me in the near future that will make my whole life much worse than it has been up to now. Day by day things get worse and worse. I don't know what to do anymore. Ksenia, Servant of God, help me, save me and keep my entire family. <u>Daniil Kharms</u> July 26, 1928.

* * *

[From notebook 38]

Is there anyone who can advise me what to do? Ester brings misfortune. I'm drowning along with her. So, should I divorce her, or bear my cross? I was given a chance to avoid this, but I wasn't satisfied and wanted to join my life with Ester. And once again I was told: don't do it! But I insisted, and although I got scared later on, I bound myself to Ester for the rest of my life anyway. I myself am to blame, or rather, I did it myself. What's happened to Oberiu? Everything fell apart as soon as Ester came into me. Since then I stopped writing and have been catching only grief from all sides. Can't I be dependent on a woman no matter who she may be? Or is there something about Ester that she destroys whatever I do? I don't know. If Ester brings grief along wherever she goes, how can I ever let her go? But at the same time, how can I let what I've created, Oberiu, fall apart? At my own request fate bound me together with Ester. Now I want to break with fate for a second time. Is there a lesson here, or is this the end of a poet? If I am a poet, fate will take pity on me and make me a free man again and will lead me again to great events. But perhaps the cross I've taken up must hang on me my whole life? And do I have the right, even as a poet, to put it down? Where can I find advice and permission? With her rational mind, Ester is foreign to me. She hinders me in everything I do and she annoys me. But I do love her and want only what's good for her. No doubt she'd be better off divorcing me: I can have no value for a rational mind. Would it really be so bad for her without me? She can remarry and, perhaps, have better luck this time. If she'd at least stop loving me, breaking up would be easier for her. But what am I supposed to do? How can I get a divorce? Lord help me! Ksenia, Servant of God, help me! Grant that next week Ester might leave me and live happily. And that I get down to writing again, free as before. Ksenia, Servant of God, help us.
Daniil Kharms
July 27, 1928.

* * *

[From notebook 13]

One problem: **get free.** July 28, 1928.

Oh Lord, what have I come to!
I won't drink any more until it's a good time for me.
God help me get a divorce. July 29.

For August 2.

    With God's help, go to the library and write out the rules.

    With God's Help, go see Mansurov regarding the expressionists.

    Work this evening on translation of the Grimm tales, God willing.

For August 3.

    With God's Help, Go see Ester and take her bandages.

    With God's Help, Call Culture Directorate.

    With God's Help, Deliver "The Old Woman" to State Publishing.

    With God's Help, Go see T.A.M.

    With God's Help, Translate the Grimms.

* * *

Win 50 rub.

on top of your own.

Step lively now!!

Articles:

   1. "Objects and figures."

   2. The History of Oberiu.

   3. Explanatory note to the production of *Elizaveta Bam.*

According to the rules, our society is not intended to make a profit.

* * *

Talk to Mansurov:

    About sending our poems inside letters so they can be torn off and copied.

    About honoraria.

Riding on the tram: three perfectly idiotic girls (The Semislutsisterhood).

I feel terribly sorry for my sweet, good little wife, my little Ester. I wish that she lived at home but would come see me often. I don't want to break up with her, but she'll never understand me. After that I want her to get married again and to live happily.

* * *

What's the point of a stage in a concert hall?

* * *

For Wednesday August 15, 1928.
With God's help:
1. Deliver list of the Grimms' tales to State Publishing.
2. Go see Vaginov.
3. Get Terentiev's tale from State Publishing.
4. Drop it off with his wife by 8:00.

* * *

Grimms' tales recommended by the Institute of Children's Reading
1. The Bremen Town Musicians.
2. Snow White and Rose Red.
3. Little Brother and Little Sister.
4. Faithful Johannes.
5. The Wolf and the Seven Young Kids.
6. Hansel and Gretel.
7. Clever Hans.
8. The Goose-Girl.
9. The Goose-Girl at the Spring.
10. The Golden Bird.
11. The Two Brothers.
12. Iron Hans.
13. The Naughty Child.
14. The Golden Goose.
15. Jorinda and Joringel.
16. The Shoes that were Danced Through.
17. Little Red Riding Hood
18. Thumbling.
19. Frau Holle.
20. One-Eye, Two-Eyes, Three-Eyes.
21. The Nixie of the Pond.
22. The Skillfull Huntsman.
23. The Mouse, the Bird and the Sausage.
24. The Wishing-Table, The Gold Ass, and the Cudgel in the Sack.

25. Snow White.
26. The Sweet Porridge.
27. The Blue Light.
28. The Frog King or Iron Heinrich.
29. Clever Elsie.
30. The Brave Little Tailor.
31. The Devil with the 3 Golden Hairs.
32. The Six Swans.
33. Six who made their Way in the World.

* * *

Outline. A muzhik goes from X to Y. On the way he stops at an inn. He says that he's going to buy a she-goat. After he buys a she-goat in Y, he goes back home. Again he stops at the inn, where he trades the she-goat for a billy goat. He brings the billy goat to his wife. She sends him back. Again he stops at the inn and brings the she-goat to Y. There they tell him it's a she-goat. The muzhik goes back, stops at the inn and brings his wife the billy goat. Then back again and so on.

* * *

[From notebook 14]

Daniel Harms.
Daniil Kharms.
1928.
Sunday, August 19.
St. Petersburg. 11 Nadezhinskaya St., apt 9. Tel. 32-15
No. 34

* * *

The tastiest tea is brewed at 65—68 degrees Celsius.

Sent with Mansurov:
Kharms, "Objects and Figures," "A Cossack's Death," "Magic Tricks," Serenade," "Temptation," "Falling from a Bridge," "Greed," *Elizaveta Bam.*

Bakhterev, "The Shepherd," "The Path to Narym," "Description of Yertyshkin."
Levin, 4 stories.
Vaginov, 2 poems ("On the shore," "Toksovo").
Vvedensky. . .

Pavel Andreevich Mansurov left on Tuesday, August 21, 1928, at 10 o'clock in the morning.

On August 19, 1928, I am changing the letter S to e.

* * *

Heinrich Cornelius Agrippa von Nettesheim. *Magische Werke*. Stuttgart, 1855. Verlag von J. Scheible.

So here this whore is about to sit in my seat, but I don't want to let her, the snub-nosed slut, Soviet floozy, high class proletarian tart, sweaty streetwalker, pig and scum, once a floozy, always a floozy.

Ter ler ly
Terlerlú Dam Dan
Terlerlú

The Sphinx at Giza
Hermes—Thoth (Totem)   Osiris. O-Sir-Is.
Hermes-Trimegistus

1. Where did the five-pointed Soviet Star come from?
2. What force built "The Pyramids"?

* * *

Earthly life means using earthly means for the sake of an "I". Like an artist who uses paints to create a picture.

The other way round, the artist turns into a house-painter.
Life for the sake of life, Materialism.

I. The outer is like to the inner: the small is the same as the large: one law for everything. There's nothing small and nothing great in divine economy. II. People are mortal gods, while gods are immortal people.

Classify everything into two categories of thought: into those thoughts that can be spoken and those that are secret.

* * *

Jan van Eyck, Born in Maaseik, in the valley of the Meuse around 1390. "Portrait of Arnolfini and his Wife."

Hans Memling, 1430-1440. Died in Bruges in 1494.

* * *

Oberiu.
September 5/6, 1928. night.
With God's Help.

> 1. Stage directions for the four of us: Vigiliansky, Levin, Bakhterev, Kharms.
> 2. Find someone who can arrange literary evenings for us.
> 3. An Evening for free.
> 4. Special program for evenings in the clubs.
> 5. Propaganda at restaurants.

* * *

At restaurants.
> Coffee with pickles.
> Tea with eggs.
> At a sign, drink milk through a straw.
> Seven glasses of tea for 3 people.
> Wheat kasha.
> Rice kasha.
> Herring with milk.
> Tea with carrots.
> Turnip.

Buffet.
Bar.
Fyodorov's.
Vladimir Club.
Roof.
Foyer of the Grand Palace.

Read the alphabet.
Black list.
Strew bits of paper around.
Sit with eyes closed.
Have an embroidered towel on your shoulder.
Cut pickles with scissors.
Warm up your food.

Play tin soldiers over beer.
Tie napkins on and feed each other.
Show up in armor.
All three of us stutter.
Dark glasses.

* * *

Eduard Fuchs, *An Illustrated History of Manners*. Moscow 1914.

Read Jakob Böhme's *Aurora: The Day Spring*.

* * *

Temptation is man's greatest blessing.
Temptation is not needed so that the temperate man might develop his will,
but man's will is needed so that he might do battle with temptation.
Doing battle with temptation, man goes forward.
You can speak only after you've reached a certain height.

* * *

Edwards Fuchs. *Illustrated History of Erotic Art*. 1914.
Arnoldi, S. S. *Historical Letters*.
Lavrov, P. L. *Historical Letters*.

* * *

Never in her life will ⊟ take my cock in her mouth.
This morning isn't going to be fun.
⊟ doesn't like my cock and she doesn't like depravity. But I do and
therefore I don't need her.
She won't even think of sucking my cock herself and doesn't even like
it when I lick her pussy.
Today I'll be less happy with her than ever.

* * *

Wolf G. *Mathematics and Painting: Female Beauty from Antiquity to the Present.*

* * *

Shekinah

Jacques Jean-Marie de Morgan. *Prehistoric Humanity.*

Adam and Eve.
the talk of the hills
it's a chill Ararat

***The Bat*, Gustav Meyrink. 1892**
Buddha is my refuge.

* * *

Karl Folia, *Shri Ramakrishna: The Last Indian Prophet.*
Richard H. Laarss, *Eliphas Levi, the Great Kabbalist and his Magical Works.*
P. B. Randolph, *Dhoula Bel: A Novel from the History of the Rosicrucian Order.*
Egmont Colerus, *White Magi.*

* * *

Oh Lord, it is clear I have come upon the hard path of tribulations. Do
I see, O Lord, that everything around me is not good? Lord, I place my
hope in Thee and think that I will still be able to achieve some peace

and tranquility. Lord, if Thou willst, help my parents, help me and my wife, but in general Thy will be done.
      September 29, 1928.

* * *

Ya. B. Shnitser, *An Illustrated Universal History of Writing.*

* * *

Marshak's brother's situation is pretty bad. I don't want him to be embarrassed with me.
I also want things to be better for him.

Of course, things are bad all over.
They're bad for us too.
Everything that is, is as it should be.
However, you must act to make it better; that's also what's needed.
When you see another's misfortune, you should think about him.
Now I can hear the conversation of the two brothers, and I can hear real irritation in it.
I can't understand his brother's situation at all.
The irritation's growing.

Lord, bring peace to this house.
Something strange is going on here. And what am *I* doing here?

* * *

I'm observing October 10, 1928, as the first day on my path to hunger and poverty.

* * *

She'll read it and won't make peace.
It's so obvious that things won't calm down for us this time.
Oh God, if this be Thy will, then let it be so.
Lord, help her.
But if Thou findest it necessary, I will keep silent and will thank Thee.

Have to strike with all one's might.

* * *

Total:	327 r.
Home:	100 r.
Abortion:	50 r.

Ester's shoes	15 r.	
2 knickers		
shirts	20	
stockings	10	
gloves	6	
bra	2	
	58 r.	

Danya	suit	58	
	boots	18 50	
	socks with suspenders		10
	2 shirts	8	
	2 underpants	3	
	grey trousers	7 50	
	gloves	6	
		169 r.	

* * *

[From notebook 38]

I won't receive a money order from Moscow today or tomorrow.
4—5:00 pm. Thursday, October 18, 1928.

Today I most probably won't receive any money from Moscow again. I know it. At around 5 pm, I'll be able to tell myself: I just knew it!
Daniil Kharms
1-2 pm. Friday, October 19, 1928. Petersburg.

* * *

[From notebook 14]

I. Matsa. *The Art of Contemporary Europe.* Gosizdat, 1926.
G. Martsinsky, *The Method of Expressionism in Painting.* "Academia," 1923.

* * *

It's risky to buy fine leather, when bent, it shouldn't leave wrinkles.
The needlework must be very precise.
It's important that it not be nailed but sewn.
A double sole.

* * *

[From notebook 15]

1. Number of performers and personalia.
2. Literary or not exclusively literary.
3. Conversation with Zabolotsky and Vaginov.
4. Performance in jackets or in caps.
5. Performance, cover charge or free.
6. Contract, commission.
7. Program for the show.

* * *

Levin will not read, a girl from the Leningrad Institute of Artistic Speech will read for him.

The stage.
In the background, signboards and pictures. On the right, a poster. On left, slogans.

Eat soup. Drink a violet and green liquid.
The Master of Ceremonies (Zhenka) in a cape.
1.   Dark face, white hair.
2.   Face of Pierrot with mustache.
3.   Mustache with Stetson hat (straw).
        Master of Ceremonies with a staff.

One variety act.
Antonio's good.
~~Have a talk with Sophia Ivanovna~~.
A choral reading.
Vulfius to write music for a melodeclamation.
An absurd speech.
Talk by Shimkevich.
Talk on Astronomy or on worms.
Kropachev the juggler.

The Evening's Program

Local Announcements	
Literary talk	10 min.
Astronomy talk	10
Oberiu talk	5
Vaginov	7
Zabolotsky	10
Romance	5
Entr'acte	10 min.
Oberiu talk	5
Levin	12
Kharms	10
Kropachev the juggler	3
Bakhterev	5
Vvedensky	10
Collective performance	3
Finale	2

* * *

What we need to do:
1. Go with Vaginov to the insane asylum.
2. Come to an understanding with Shimkevich.
3. I've got to talk to Kolka.
4. Come to an understanding with Zhenka.
5. Arrange reading with former Leningrad LEF group on Thursday, November 1.
6. Go to the baths with Kolka.

1. University.
2. Institute for the History of Arts.
3. Central House of Education Workers.
4. Central House of the Arts.
5. Press House.
6. Former Press House.

* * *

For October 29.

A get together at my place at noon.
Call Zhenka.
Go to the university.
Have a talk with Shimkevich.

October 30, 1928.

Be at Central House of Education Workers by 6:00.
Nitsenko, Head of publishing division.
This evening, see Ermolaeva.
Tell Ermolaeva that I'll be late.
Call my dear wife.

* * *

~~Cats~~.
Immortality.
In big tense bodies.

For Thursday, November 1, 1928.
Reading by Varshavsky and Rakhtanov at my place.

On Wednesday, October 31. Call A. A. Ivanov.
On Friday, November 2. Evening at the Ivanovs.

~~On Wednesday, October 31, at 4 o'clock, be at Ermolaeva's~~.

* * *

The Clever Boy and the Stupid Boy

The Stupid Boy:

How does an airplane fly?
How does a locomotive work?
How do soldiers march?
How does a bee do its work?
~~Who lives in America?~~
Where is Siberia to be found?
~~What's stronger than three elephants?~~

Why does a candle burn?
~~Who lives at the bottom of the sea?~~
Who built Leningrad?
Who ~~thought up~~ invented the telephone?
What are clouds made of?

The Clever Boy:
Buy "The Hedgehog"
And you'll find out everything!

march and march and march and
run and run and run and
gallop gallop gallop gallop
by yourself or on a horse
for "The Hedgehog" yes of course!

everyone on earth says

"The Hedgehog" is the best friend of all kids
both big and little (tiny, teeny).

* * *

On Monday, Vaginov will call.

Oberiu.

Toward an Oberiu
Consider as active members of Oberiu: Kharms, Bakhterev, Levin, Vvedensky. 4 people. Literary Section. Administrator, Vigiliansky.

Create an Oberiu art section. Invite Bakhterev, Kaplan.

Principle: No need to worry about the small number of people. Better three people in full agreement than more people who constantly disagree.

* * *

31 October.
Go to the administrative section.
~~Go to State Publishing~~.
Deliver caricature.

Ask Lebedev about ~~Mark Chagall~~.
~~Go see Ermolaeva.~~
Give some thought to a general meeting of the Oberiuty.
~~Exchange books at the library.~~

* * *

1. Boarding the little boat.
2. Good sailing.
    Light blue brown pink.
3. Breakfast.
4. A storm blows up.
5. The sail rips apart.
6. They sink.
~~6. They swim to shore.~~
7. They're saved. Big sailboat.
8. On shore.

Young boy, dog and 2 grownups.

* * *

Italia, Roma.
Viale Giulio Cesare No. 61 int. Pavel Mansurow.

For sphere at Kremlin to repose
A round field's ready on location
It's round down to its very toes
It's dark all round. O Night cetacean!

* * *

Stage 20:10 MAIN AUDITORIUM AT THE UNIVERSITY
Gave Liza 7 copies of *Ogonek*.

For November 3.
1. ~~Ester has to go home to get documents, silk dresses, underwear, shoes, Liza's girdle.~~

Me:

1. Buy half-bottle vodka.
2. Press trousers.
3. Go to barber.
4. ~~Go to Zabolotsky's.~~
5. ~~Sew button to trousers.~~
6. Convince Shurka to come with Niurochka.

* * *

On Monday, November 5, get Afanasiev's *Tales* at State Publishing.

On Saturday, November 10, at 2:00, appearance at State Publishing,
At 8:00 pm at the Vyborg District library. 16 Soviet Prospect.

At the debate:

Charcoal mustaches.
Eat soup.
Chairman of debate will be Vigiliansky.

Writing to be assigned:

1. Theatrical piece, Kharms.
2. Absurd Lecture, Kharms, Bakhterev.
3. Master of ceremonies. . .
4. Preparations, everyone.
5. Art design, I. Bakhterev.

* * *

What to tell the doctor:

1. Pain in left wrist, in palm.
2. Strangling sensation, as if pants with brass buttons had been attached to my neck.
3. Black and blue marks on right and left legs.
4. Feel really nauseous when I see an uncleanly beard.
5. I'm being bitten by fleas.

* * *

Putilov Factory. November 11, at 11:00 pm. Lenin Club in Church building.

No matter what!
No matter what happens, I've got to get a divorce.
Oh Lord, divorce me from Ester.
Grant her happiness, Lord, and me freedom.
Really this is simply no way to live.
I've got to get a divorce, I know it.
If only Ester wouldn't suffer because of it!
Above all, I need complete freedom.
Oh Lord, grant me freedom!

* * *

Valerian root. Brew and take 4 times a day.

"Conductor! A couple of tickets!" (On the tram).

Tomorrow, Thursday, November 8, at TAM's.
August 11 is TAM's birthday.

* * *

For November 13.
>   Call and go see Krimmer at 7:00.
>   Oberiu meeting at 4:00.
>   This evening with TAM.
>   Take *The Castle* and *The Golem*.
>   This morning at State Publishing, take Jean Barnes.
>   Stop by Literary Foundation.
>   This evening meeting at Union of Poets, 6:00, children's
>   performance.

For Wednesday, November 14.
>   Oberiu meeting.
>   Central House of Education Workers.
>   This morning, go to the Lawyers Club, call the Polytechnic, stop by
>   Army-Navy House, Smolny and GPU.

* * *

I am the most pathetic man in the world.
A coward and a milksop.
I pray to God only out of weakness.
I can expect nothing from this life.
The most fitting job for me is serving in the Red Army.
What am I thinking!

November 17.

I don't much like Budagoskaya's story. Besides it's not right for
The Hedgehog.
A ladies' story, for little German girls. Governesses will like it.

* * *

Marshak is angry with me because of my Grimm translation.

* * *

⊟ and I have got to get a divorce.

* * *

[From notebook 16, end of 1928]

Daniil Kharms
1928
Purchased October 20.

* * *

Daniil Ivanovich Kharms.
11 Nadezhdinskaya Street, apt. 9.
Tel. 32-15.
Subscription № 34, State Publishing Library.
Membership № 121. Literary Foundation.
Married to Ester Aleksandrovna Kharms since March 5, 1928.

[In Esther's handwriting]

~~Divorced on the 25. . .~~

* * *

Pavel Florensky, *Imaginary Numbers in Geometry*, 1922.
Jean Bart in *Berühmte Seeleute* von Reinhold Werner.

A THOUGHT COMING OUT THE DOOR LIKE A MAN IS
NEVERTHELESS INCORPOREAL, FOR YOU CANNOT SHARPEN
A KNIFE ON IT.

* * *

For an evening at the Literary Foundation.
    Read "A Winter's Walk."
    Read "How I Got Married."
    Choral reading.
    Drink and eat on stage.
    Come out on stage with little flags.
    Idiotic improvisations.
    Masks.
    A green beard.
    There walk men, but not lions.
    There the heroine, but not you.

* * *

Semyon Tarasovich Rylov. Socialist-Revolutionary. Initials S.T.R.

* * *

For the Oberiu Evening at the University we would like: November 26, 27,
28, 29. November 28 is more convenient for the University.

I WANT WOMEN.

* * *

Performances for children:
    1. Saturday, November 10, 2:00 pm at State Publishing. ✓
    2. Saturday, November 10, 8 pm at the library, 16 Suvorovsky
Prospect. ✓

3. Sunday, November 11, 11 pm at the Lenin Club at the Putilov factory.

I'm not going there.

4. On Tuesday, November 23, 6:00 pm, Vasilevsky Island, 10 Bolshoi Prospect, Tolstoy Library.

* * *

We went to the zoo and saw an ape that looks like TAM.
I want to go to the zoo with TAM.
I miss TAM.

T.A.M. ist prachtvoll mit kurzen Haaren.

T.A.M. looks great with short hair.

TAM will never love me but I would like to be one with her.

Tamara Aleksandrovna is **a beauty and a goddess.**

November 22, saw **Dina.**

They say TAM is sick.
What's the matter with her?

TAM might not like it if I go see her today. But I'm going anyway.

What should I do **about Erica?**
She's wants me to drop by and see her.

Erica is a smart girl, she'll understand
that I may not have the time.

I really like Tamara. I don't have much experience with women. How can I take her?
She's far too indifferent to me.
Give yourself to me, Tamara.
With the love of blue Saharas.

My poor dove ⊟, my beloved girl.

* * *

I'm sick and tired of the Grimm tales. But I have to deal with them anyway.

Away!

Your mug
Not mine
My mug
Not yours
A mug to be blunt:
But don't hide your ~~legs~~ **cunt.**

Your hand
Not mine
My hand
Not yours
It may scratch an itch
But you're still a bitch.

* * *

My wife is still the best. Dearer to me than all the others.
The company of sluts and extra-marital affairs both attracts and repels me.
Oh Lord, help my sweet wife!
Oh Lord, while you're at it, make me a bachelor.
TAROT
Dina's got to give me a blow job. She's mine. She'll give herself to me, it will absolutely happen.

* * *

The Fifth Card of the Tarot
A victor in a chariot harnessed with sphinxes.
Everything has meaning here.
This is will armed with knowledge.
But in all of this, there is more of a desire to achieve than actual achievement.
This is not an authentic victor.

A true victor begins with a victory over time.

But this one gains victory not through love but with fire and sword.

He sees the sphinxes outside himself. This is his greatest error.

He was in the antechamber of the Temple but he thought he was in the Temple itself.

He took the rituals of the first trials for sanctification and the priestess guarding the threshold for the goddess.

Great dangers await him.

And understand, this is the same Man whom you saw uniting heaven and earth and later walking along the dusty road towards the abyss.

The Seventeenth Card.

This is Nature's imagination, said the Voice quietly. Nature dreams, fantasizes, and creates worlds. Learn to merge your imagination with hers and nothing will be impossible for you anymore. But remember that unless you give up the Earth, you will not find the Light. It's impossible to see the lie and the truth at the same time.

The Seventh Card (Hierophant). (Mysticism. Esotericism).

Seek the path, rather than the goal. Seek the path within yourself. Do not hope to hear the truth from others, to see it or read it in books. Seek the truth within yourself, not outside yourself. Desire only the impossible and unachievable. Expect only that which will not be. Do not place your hope in me. Do not believe I exist. Build a high tower in your soul and ascend it to heaven. Above all be on guard lest you believe in mystery on earth, in mystery guarded by people. These people stand guard over empty treasures. Seek not the mystery that can be hidden. Seek the mystery that is within you, not outside you. And above all fear the towers built to preserve mysteries, those stairways of stone built to climb from earth to heaven. The path is within you alone, the truth is within you alone, the mystery is within you alone.

* * *

Beauty is the absence of a concept. (Tufanov)

* * *

On December 2/3 at 3:00 am, I lost consciousness.
Have to lie down and rest.

* * *

For December 5.
At State Publishing.
Talk to Oleinikov about the enigma of Bakhterev and put in for a receipt for
November.

* * *

[Letter from Ester Rusakova]

December 5, 1928

Daniel, I've gone to the wedding registry bureau to get a
divorce.

Don't you be angry, it will be possible if you want to get
together and be good friends. I see that I am a burden to you.
Daniel, remember only that I love you too and even more strongly.
And I will love you to the day I die. Daniel, if I'm not mistaken
you have been behaving like this with me so I would get a divorce.
That is very smart otherwise you could not push me away from
you.

I kiss you warmly and remember that I will love you always.
Eternally yours

Ester

* * *

I'm finished. There's nothing to expect anymore since I love Ester.

Dina will be Shurka's anyway and so forget about her.

Nothing doing with this bitch so no point trying. Spit on her!

**Dina Vasilevna can never be my wife. She will be another's. I want to
go down on her.**

It's a dacha.

I'll be depressed.
A year has 365 days.

The audience started fidgeting. I found myself in a very bad situation.

I'm really weak, really unlikeable.

No, Dina won't come now.

A Chinaman's chatting up Ksenia Lvovna.

Tormented by envy.

I'm a very bad person.

Got to think more about poetry.

No matter what you say . . .

. . . Dina's got a nice cunt.

What's pleasure for Dina is poison for my dear ⊟. I love only ⊟,
of course, and it's only because I'm conscious that I have to break up
with her, that I don't have to dump Dina.

* * *

For Monday, Dererember 17.
    Find out Cherkasov's telephone number.
    Call Pastukhov.
    Talk to Marshak about business.
    Appearance at the Institute for the History of the Arts.
    Drop by the Literary Foundation.
    Get book from Zabolotsky.
    Arrange for rehearsal.

Monday, December 17. At the Institute for the History of the Arts at 8 o'clock.

December 23. Matinee at Press House at 2:00. Took place. ✓

December 25, an evening at Press House. Our play.

* * *

They won't say a word about me.

Zabolotsky's going to read "Seven Hundred Versts."

* * *

Coming on the evening of December 25.
1. Vigiliansky.
2. Amalia Yakovlevna.
3. Bakhterev.
4. Levin.
5. Lina Vasilevna.
6. Ester.
7. D. Kharms

Tickets requested for:
Bogaevsky, 2.
Dina Vasilevna, 2.

* * *

On Wednesday, December 26, 8:30 pm at Eikhenbaum's.
Eikhenbaum liked Zabolotsky, perhaps Vvedensky, but me not at all.
That's the truth.

Oberiu and L. K. Lisenko. Thursday, December 27, at 2:00, my place.

Put on a play where everyone stammers.

N. P. Baskakov, Kamen (Siberia), Telephone code, 22.

From now on, it's all over between me and Dina. She'll be with Vvedensky now. She won't like me and . . .

Auntie Vera's better than the rest. Dina's not mine any longer. Hurray! Free yourself from your wife and you'll be free.

Dina will be together with Shura. And I'll be by myself. Vera's not for me. 2:00 Friday, January 4.

* * *

In case the audience gets restless, promise to show them what's behind the curtain.

You can't give someone a handkerchief.

For January 9, 1929.
      Go to State Publishing.
      Go to the Library.
      Go to Press House.
      Go to the Central House of Education Workers.

* * *

Home hurray!

**Ester cheated on me with Misha Chernov.
Ester may have syphilis.**

Dona nobis pacem.

* * *

I love only my girl, my sweet little Ester.
      January 12.

I really wish Ester would call today and come spend the night at our apartment, but that's impossible!

* * *

Home hurray!

The shattering of art.
Long live the Oberiu!
Skepticism, no doubt harmful, has appeared in me.

Lord preserve us!

A beast sat in a trunk
and Stephan was his name
but don't believe that bunk.
There was a little girl
a reed was in her chest
a wave, a freezing curl,
instead of nose, a spout,
instead of eye, a hole,
she weeps and she cries out
her stomach aches and moans.

* * *

With a name like Bukharin, no one will be shocked.

I can't accept anything Selvinsky says whatsoever! Everything he says runs counter to my convictions. Selvinsky is an insensitive clod travelling on a path totally different from mine. If Eikhenbaum and the young formalists join him, I want nothing to do with them.

I think Eikhenbaum is closest to me.

* * *

[Entries in Ester's and Kharms's handwriting]

How are you feeling?

Dear Ester, don't you want to go there?
If you want to, get up and go.

* * *

Next time, pack a revolver, not a foxtrot.

Clocks:
>   Pedestal clock with books.
>   Studio clock with plays.
>   Standing table clock, with Germans.
>   Large kitchen alarm clock.
>   Small alarm clock.
>   Clock—balloon—moon.

* * *

It's not a novella but rather an elegant way to get rid of guests. ~~Right right!~~
~~I was just thinking, what an uninteresting idea for a novella. But now I~~
~~realize, it's an interesting idea. My foxtrot will do good service~~.

* * *

[From notebook 17]

Purchased on April 30, 1929.
Daniil Ivanovich Kharms
11 Nadezhdinskaya Street, apt. 8, tel. 32-15.

* * *

Wednesday, May 1.
>   4 pm at Stepanov's.

Friday, May 3.
>   11 o'clock at State Publishing about story for *Hedgehog*.
>   7:00 at Marshak's in Tsarskoe Selo. Was there on Thursday.

<u>Saturday May 4,</u>

Bakhta will drop by between 1 and 2 pm.

Call Lydia Aleksandrovna Nadezhina.

Eisner's at 4.

<u>Sunday, May 5.</u>

4:00 pm. Iraida Genrikhovna Bakhta.

* * *

<u>Poetry</u>

1. Zabolotsky.
2. Vvedensky.   2 printer's sheets.
3. Kharms.
4. Khlebnikov.
5. Tikhonov.

<u>Play</u>

Elizaveta Bam. 1 printer's sheet.

<u>Prose</u>

1. Kaverin.
2. Vvedensky.
3. Dobychin.
4. Kharms.
5. Tynianov.
6. Shklovsky.
7. Olesha.

<u>Criticism</u>

1. Stepanov.
2. Gofman.
3. Ginzburg.
4. Bukhshtab.   3 ½ printer's sheets.
5. Kavarsky.
6. Shklovsky.
7. Tynianov.
8. Eikhenbaum.

Quartet

    For the poetry: Vvedensky.
    For the prose: Kaverin.
    For the essays: Gofman.
    For the play: Kharms.

* * *

46 Nevsky Prospect. Dental clinic. They pull teeth.

* * *

Monday, May 13 at 8 pm at the Writers' Union. "An Evening of Shamans."

* * *

L. Panteleev's "Pocket Watch."

For public reading, I think, you should abridge a story the right way: at home, not on the fly.

The misfortunes of Thursday, May 9.
    1. Two trams went by in the wrong direction.
    2. We had to wait a long time for our tram.
    3. The tram didn't go to the end of the line.
    4. Unable to borrow money.

My life is going just so-so. I'm not happy.

SOS, SOS, SOS.

Expenses:
lightbulb	1 r.
collar	1 r. 25 k.
laundry	<u>2 r.</u>
	4 r. 25 k.

* * *

For Papa.
Soap, ~~soap dish, box of matches~~, 2 postcards, folding scissors, small comb, ~~letter~~.

* * *

Feeling very poorly. Toothache. Weakness and insomnia. Head foggy.
May 11, 1:30 in the morning.

* * *

Tabidze is a shaman.

* * *

Anastastius Pernath has neither a real father, nor mother, just like the Son
of Man.

* * *

I know of a no more disgraceful bunch
than the Writers' Union.
That's who I really can't stand.
It's a shame they set up here.
Better in a museum.

* * *

There's nothing worse in this world than good-hearted girlfriends . . .

* * *

Feeling poorly. Today is May 19. Very worried about myself. Suffering
from insomnia.

* * *

The Lamb

Little lamb, who made thee?
Dost thou know who made thee,
Gave thee life and bid thee feed.
By the stream and o'er the mead;
Gave thee clothing of delight,
Softest clothing, woolly, bright;
Gave thee such a tender voice,
Making all the vales rejoice?
      Little lamb, who made thee?
      Dost thou know who made thee?

> Little lamb, I'll tell thee;
> Little lamb, I'll tell thee:
He is called by thy name,
For He calls Himself a Lamb.
He is meek, and he is mild,
He became a little child.
I a child and thou a lamb.
We are called by his name
> Little lamb, God bless thee!
> Little lamb, God bless thee!

> William Blake

* * *

Faina Davidovna is constantly hinting that I'll get nothing from her in terms of physical love.

* * *

Today I'll see Faina Davydovna. She'll either invite me to her place or she'll come herself! Most definitely! May 22, 1929.

I had thought that Faina and I would go by ourselves but as it turned out Mirra Abramovna came along too.

I've fallen in love with Faina Davydovna.

* * *

[From notebook 38]

May 22, 1929.

I was sitting on the roof of the State Publishing House, making sure that everything was in order, because no sooner do you overlook something than something happens. You can't leave the city unwatched. And who will keep an eye on the city, if not me? So in case of some kind of disorder, we can stop it right away.

Statutes of the State Publishing Roof Watch.

First rule: A Watchman should be a man of the Oberiu confession with the following characteristics:
1. Moderate height.
2. Brave.

3. Far-seeing.
4. A stentorian and powerful voice.
5. Mighty and plain spoken.
6. Able to catch every kind of sound and not easily bored.
7. A smoker or, in an extreme case, a non-smoker.

Second rule (what he should do):
1. A Watchman should sit at the very highest point of the roof and, not sparing himself, should assiduously look from side to side, for which purpose he is instructed to turn his head continuously from left to right and vice versa, moving it in both directions until his vertebrae can bear it no longer.
2. A Watchman should see to it that good order be maintained in the city, ensuring:
    a. That people walk around not just anyhow but as the Lord God himself has ordained.
    b. That people travel only in those kinds of carriages made specifically for that purpose.
    c. That people not walk on roofs, cornices, pediments or other raised places.
       Note: Carpenters, painters and other laborers are permitted.

Third rule (what a Watchman should not do):
1. Ride on the roof on horseback.
2. Flirt with the ladies.
3. Insert his words into the conversations of passersby.
4. Chase after sparrows or adopt their habits.
5. Call policemen "Pharaohs."
6. Spit in your eye.
7. Grieve.

Fourth rule (the rights of a Watchman):
A Watchman has the right to:
1. Sing.
2. Shoot at whomever comes along.
3. Invent and compose, also make notes, and recite in a low voice, or learn by heart.
4. Look over the panorama.

5. Compare life below to an anthill.
6. Contemplate book publishing.
7. Take a bed along.

Fifth rule:
A Watchman must be polite to firefighters.

That's all.

Founding members: Daniil Kharms, (signature), Boris Levin (signature)
Helped: Yury Vladimirov (signature)
May 22, 1929.

* * *

[From notebook 17]

Monday, May 27.
Stenich says that I am a flying paranoic.

* * *

Her name is ADA.

The way Faina Davydovna behaves, I have no desire to see her any more.
Here's what I'll say: there's nothing I can do with her.
Everything, at least for today, is over with Faina.
Wednesday, May 29, 1929.

* * *

Lydia Nadejena. 82 Washington Place, apt 10. New York City. U.S.A.

Daniil Kharms
Daniil Kharms.

* * *

All of Vvedensky's nonsense is jokey.

"The Sick Man who Became a Wave."—I like it very much. There's almost
no jokiness.

* * *

~~What is beer?~~
~~It's a diuretic.~~

1. Launder collars	2 r.
2. Buy shirt collars	3 r.
3. Boots	25 r.
4. Coat	10 r.
5. Toothpaste	1 r.
6. Pen knife	4 r.
7. Razors	2 r.
8. Shaving cream, toilet soap, *eau de cologne*, powder	3 r.
9. Stationery	<u>5 r.</u>
	55 r.

* * *

Tailor. Ekaterinhofsky Prospect, corner of Sadovaya.

Herman Izrailevich Rabinovich, 71 Sergievskaya Street, apt. 8
Proletarian. Intellectual.

* * *

Magic tricks
1. Dice.
2. Ring, matchbox and handkerchief.
3. Cane that stands on its end.
4. Coin that disappears under a glass.
5. Object that floats above open hand.
6. Coin that disappears in palm.
7. Coin that disappears in sleeve.
8. Coin that passes through table.
9. Broken matchsticks.
10. Knotted handkerchief.
11. Balloon.
12. Torn cigarette paper that goes back together.

* * *

Write "A History of Europe." June 27, 1929.

* * *

I consider myself free from Ester in all respects.
The Islands. June 28, 1929.

Twice I forgot something at Kaverin's and every time I went back, the tram wasn't running as it should and I saw some good-looking peasant girls on the tram.

* * *

July 4, 1929.
Feel very . . . bad. Fighting for my health. Worried. Have to be more careful.

* * *

Man does not live only once. Whatever remains unfinished is finished in the next life. The same with love.
July 7.

I'm sitting with my Ester for the last time.
The Splendid Palace Cinema, 6:00 July 7, 1929, Sunday.

* * *

Tom Sawyer.
Munchausen.
Kipling's tales.

* * *

July 13, 1929.
My Ester's come to see me. I'm very happy.

I know that Ester cheated on me with Dr. Nikolaenko. Why won't she admit it? I wish she would admit it.
It's all a lie.

* * *

They're talking in the next room.
Papa and Natasha.
There will be changes.
July 21, 1929.

What's become of me? I'm afraid of life. A man should not be afraid of his own life.

* * *

I feel terrible. Worried about my health. Last night I was restless and didn't sleep much.

* * *

Debts

To Loris-Melikov	10 r.	
To Ester	5 r.	
To Dardim	6 r.	
To Illa	<u>6 r.</u>	
Total	27 r.	

To Praskovya Naumovna	~~3 r.~~	
To Frol	~~5 r.~~	
To Frida Mikhailovna	~~11 r.~~	
To Razulevich	<u>40 k.</u>	
	34 r. 40 k.	

* * *

Vsevolodsky (Gerngross), *History of the Russian Theater*.
B. S. Borisov, *History of My Laughter*.
V. Volkenshtein, *The Law of Dramaturgy*.
Delert-Dan, *The Art of Dramaturgy*.
Ginzburg, Glebov, Radlov, *Franz Shrecker*.
M. K. *A History of Opera*.

* * *

I consider Vvedensky, Khlebnikov and Marshak my teachers.

* * *

For September 23.

    Take books to State Publishing.
    Call Iraida Genrikhovna.
    Get book about Buddha from Ester.
    Get tobacco from Ester.

* * *

Concerning prose: prose is governed by laws of proportional measure and semantic material. Poetry is based on the material of the word itself.

You can't read prose out loud.

Bukhshtab. "On the Social Command."
Trivial and perhaps even wrong-headed. I'm ashamed to say I don't really understand it. Written in a language as dry as dust.

Works should be both easy and hard to read.

* * *

Yankee Doodle

Yankee Doodle came to town
Mounted on a pony.
He stuck a feather in his cap
And called it macaroni.

Yankee Doodle came to town,
Yankee Doodle dandy.
He stuck a feather in his cap
And called it sugar candy.

* * *

Vladimirov. "Slaughtered Mary."   a play

V. Khlebnikov. "Cracking the Universe." Amazing poetry. Complicated.

* * *

October 19. Ester checked into the hospital for an operation Uncle Zhenya's doing. (Now everything's over between me and Ester. She called Liza yesterday and said she's getting married to someone.)

Poems	lines
Stinginess.	35
A Cossack's Death.	86
Magic Tricks.	38
Fall from a Bridge.	44
Serenade.	30
Temptation.	117
Forest Secret.	109
Bandits.	74
The Aviation of Transformations.	72
Flight to the Heavens.	68
Threefold Description of a Luminary.	59
Solution to an Worldly Problem.	184
Unfinished Poem.	24
Elizaveta Bam.	220
Tulips in a Field of Trochees.	125
Observer.	8
To Khlebnikov.	2
Resurrection.	155
From *A Comedy of the City of Petersburg.*	150
Ivan Taporyshkin.	12
	1612
	~~1285~~

* * *

In October a great deed was accomplished: it's over with Ester. Now it's November 2nd and I know that I will never be with Ester again. We no longer love each other and have been unfaithful to each other.

Pioneers Club. 49 Liteiny Prospect. Performance on November 17 at 2 pm.

* * *

Igor and Me to visit Tufanov and Erika.

Find out about children's magazines for 1919-20 at State Publishing.

November 13, 1929. Everything's finally over with Ester. Yesterday she was discharged from the hospital, and today she called Liza on business, but she didn't even do it herself, she gave the job to her gigolo.

You've been torn off like an arm, Ester. That's why I'm gloomy today. Lord, everything is over between us. That's good and bad. Still it's boring without little Ester. Not to mention, it's annoying and hard to accept that she's found herself a man to replace me. I've got to hang on for 3 or 4 more days and then I'll be free from Ester inside.

Whenever I'm with Ester, it's good, but it's hard to be without her. I miss Ester but, of course, she doesn't miss me, otherwise she would have called Liza, at the very least. She knows that it's better for us to be apart. She said that herself once. It's a shame she doesn't love me anymore.

No, now I know for sure that everything's over with Ester. I'll never see her again, in any case as her husband.
November 13, 1929.
10 hours 53 minutes in the evening.
Petersburg.

* * *

Night of November 15/16, 1929. I miss Ester. She doesn't love me. Don't feel very well. Very agitated.

* * *

Saw Ester for the last time on November 29 (Friday), 1929 at 7 hours and 43 minutes.
By the fence of a house on Valynkin Alley.

* * *

~~Danya wants you to give him a blowjob.~~

* * *

Union of Poets. Saturday, November 30, children's performance. At 8:00.

* * *

I really want to sleep.
I hardly slept last night.

I really want to sleep.   I didn't sleep all night.
                          I didn't sleep all night.
                          I didn't sleep all night.
                          I didn't sleep all night.

* * *

The journal *Chronicle* for 1917. "Teachers of Teachers" (Atlantis), by Valery Briusov.

December 6, 1929, started reading Dostoevsky's *Brothers Karamazov*.

* * *

I really shouldn't keep a diary. There are blows from heaven that rain down upon me whenever I keep a diary. December 7.

* * *

People are created for happiness and only he who is completely happy is worthy of saying: "I have fulfilled God's Commandment on this earth."

December 10, 1929. Yesterday I spoke with Ester's father. Today he didn't want to see me. Ester is taking his side. It's finally time for me to break it off with her. It's already half over. I have to get together with her this evening at 8:00. This meeting, if it does take place, will be our last. It's impossible to go on like this, nothing good can come of it. I'm looking for an ending. It's on its way. I'm sitting in Boba's room. 4:00 in the afternoon.

I'm in agony. Blows from all directions. Papa has broken his arm. Liza's been let go. I'm impotent as a writer. Ester doesn't love me anymore. Physically I'm a wreck. Everything is bad.

Everything, everything, everything's over with Ester forever. May God protect my beloved Ester.
Amen
7:00 in the evening. December 10, 1929.

On Wednesday, December 11, 1929. I've been invited to read at the Central House of Education Workers at 8:00 pm.

* * *

I think that, in some ways, I'm like Aleksandr Polezhaev.

A black cat at home protects you from the bad luck of "a black cat crossing your path."

Ester is leaving me for the Michaels.
     1. Michael Nefedov
     2. Michael Shelukhin
     3. Michael Grigorievich
     4. Michael Loris-Melikov

Fear the Michaels or you'll go crazy.

Michael . . .
Daniil, God's Judgement.

* * *

The very last time I saw Ester was on December 13, 1929, at the entrance to her building.

Everything, everything, is finished with Ester forever. May God protect my beloved Ester.
December 13, 1929.

We struggle against fate and bow before the inevitable.
December 13.

This time the inevitable has come to pass. Everything's over with Ester forever. This just can't go on any longer. Lord protect and have mercy upon my beloved girl.
December 13, 1929.

I lost my temper with Ester. She's behaving thoughtlessly. But help her, O Lord.
December 13, 1929.

* * *

Dear Ester, do you love me?

[In Ester's handwriting]

I do. Ester.

How dull it is without my dear Ester. But now I know for sure that it's all over between us. She doesn't love me that much, and others are now more important to her, and her parents have won and convinced her. I'll never see her again.
Lord, help my beloved pussycat, my kis-kis, my dear little Ester.
December 14, 1929.
State Publishing.

Everything's over with Ester. I couldn't hold out and called her last night. She spoke coldly but seems to want to meet me. Today she didn't even call me. It's clear that everything's over.
Cross and Mary. C. and M. C. and M.

December 15, 1929.
Sunday.
Daniil Kharms.

* * *

My law about the positive action of reverse thinking is difficult to implement and here's why: if, of three possibilities, A, B, and C, I think that only B and C will be realized so that A will be realized, then A will not be realized and here's why: if I think that B and C will be realized, I already know that they won't and that only A will be. That is, thinking that A will be realized it excludes the possibility of A being realized. Thinking about B and C as paired will not help A be realized.

Complete <u>faith</u> is necessary. In this way we arrive at faith. However, complete faith produces a direct result. It follows, in this case, that faith is not necessary.

<u>Assertion.</u>
It is necessary to subordinate one's conscious thoughts (B, C) to subconscious thoughts (A), and those that follow (Ai, Aii, Aiii).
December 15.

* * *

Ester received my letter, but hasn't answered at all. December 18, 1929.

I'm lost, but I discovered that Ester's forgotten me, she's infatuated with someone else and has given herself to him. Everything's through with Ester. The end has come after all. Lord have mercy on us.
Alas, everything is through with Ester. I've got to forget her. She refused to speak to me on the phone.
O Lord, Lord, Lord!
December 19, 1929.

So this is how it ends with Ester. How it's all come about logically. I was a fool not to notice it coming. I thought many times that everything was finished with Ester. But it wasn't. Only now the real end has come. It's very difficult to bear this, but I have no choice. It would be terrible not to see Ester for four months. But how horrible it is to know that you'll never see Ester again. You can't imagine beforehand what it will be like, the only thing you know is she won't love you anymore and that she will be unfaithful.
December 19, 1929.

O Lord! What anguish without Ester. Dear God, do something so that Ester and I can be together again, inseparable for all time, and also that we might live together happily. Dear God, I can't live without Ester. Hear my prayer, O Lord. Only Thou Alone canst help us. I hope in Thee, O Lord.
Daniil Kharms. December 21, 1929.

* * *

"Michael, Gabriel, Raphael! Make Esther love me as I love her."
December 22, 1929.

* * *

Twist together five of your hairs and three of your beloved's, and throw them into the fire, saying: "Ure igne Santi Spiritus renes nostros et cor nostrum, domine. Amen." Translation: O Lord, burn our kidneys and our heart with the fire of the Holy Spirit, Amen! After this, you will be lucky in love.

Take two 3-kopeck wax candles, twist them together saying: "As these candles are joined, so shall we be joined." Then light them before an icon and say: "I light not a candle but the soul and the heart of Thy servant Ester for Thy servant Daniil forever." Light nine times.

<u>Summoning Spell</u>.

Fagot, burn the heart, body, soul, blood, spirit, and mind of Ester with fire, sky, earth, and rainbow. By Mars, Mercury, Venus, Jupiter, Fenne, Fenne, Fenne, Elera and in the name of all the devils. Fagot, possess, burn the heart, body, soul, blood, spirit, and mind of Ester until she appears and fulfills all my desires and commands. Go forth in lightning, dust, and storm: Santas, Quisor, Carrocas, Arne. Take control of her so that she neither sleep, nor stand in place, nor do anything, neither eat, nor cross a river, nor ride on a horse, nor talk with man, woman or young girl, until she appears and fulfills all my desires and commands.

* * *

Liza won't call Ester today. Because Ester doesn't love me.
Wednesday, December 25, 1929.
8:00 and several minutes.
Cinema "Il Colosseo." Foyer. Balcony.
Daniil Kharms

That's just what happened: Liza didn't call.
Daniil Kharms
December 25, 1929. 11:40. Our dining room.

* * *

Everything, everything's over with Ester forever. May God preserve my beloved Ester. Amen.
12 midnight. December 26, 1929.

* * *

I was sitting on one leg,
held in my hands the family soup.
The story of a stupid trunk
in which a codger hid his gold—
      He's cheap.
And to the right was making noise
sad elephant
sad elephant.

Why make that noise? Why make that noise?
I asked him once I sobered up
I'm your foe, I'm soup, a prince.
The elephant's long sound fell still
The family soup cooled in my hands.
the hunger made my spittle flow
to spend good money on a meal
I'm much too cheap.
Much better to buy
a pair of chamois leather gloves,
better to save the money up
for a trip with Galya S
to the woods beyond the city fence.

That's all   Dec. 28.

* * *

December 29. Some Vera called Liza and didn't want to say who she was for a long time.

An average man's weight in kilograms is equal to the two last numbers of his height in centimeters.

* * *

To do.
Monday, December 30, 1929. Send tall collar to the cleaners.

Tuesday, December 31, 1929. Go skating with Galina Nikolaevna Leman.

* * *

On Tuesday, Dec. 31
Get "The Young Proletarian" magazine for 1920 for Konstantin Dmitrievich.

For Papa before Thursday: get 5 cards of the suburbs and 5 cards of Petersburg.
The galley proofs of his book on Sakhalin.

* * *

The Coming of the New Year

We (two people the same):
The New Year arrives
Impatiently expected.
We've stored up wine
And pickles
And fresh cutlets.
Come to table
Quarter to twelve
We'll raise a toast
And drink, brothers,
To the old year.
The bridge will collapse
And there's no way back
To the girls of the past
And bright abysses
Are our future.

Spectator
Look, he's taking up an oar
And flying round the room, a pipe,
Objects follow round the flight,
From rapid points the dawn is breaking.
In Neva doleful ice is melting,
The Earth and people clap their hands,
A wise beast turns his eyes to heaven:
And thus the 0 hour comes, and then the New Year is begun.

Tuesday, December 31, 1929.
23 hours 45 minutes

* * *

[From notebook 38]

Every single word must be inevitable.

[From notebook 17]

Mark the structure of a human face with signs, letters, and numbers. Number each part and designate the various possible types with a corresponding letter. Break it all up into categories, each with its own sign. Draw a map of the face marking the separate parts and details in their various forms designated by letters. All this must be committed to memory by long practice so that at a glance at any face, you can instantly and unconsciously note its code. In this way you will accumulate material for understanding people. Having at hand sufficient examples of human faces and characters, you can introduce them all into a theorem and thereby locate individuals and their opposites.

In the majority of cases, a dream means simply its opposite. But it's easy to understand that laughter foretells tears, sadness—joy, boredom—merriment, and so on. However, it's not always easy to find an opposite meaning for a given phenomenon. For example, you see a well, you're standing above a well, in place of your head you have a rooster, and in place of your arms and legs—toothpowder. What does this mean? What is its opposite? It's possible that the opposite phenomenon is riding in a train and eating yogurt with gold buttons. To interpret dreams, you have to be able to find opposite phenomena.

* * *

During the night of January 5, 1930, Liza dreamt that Ester was lying in bed with her. Suddenly, Illa knocks on the door and says she's feeling sick. For some reason, I'm walking around (can't understand why). Illa goes into Liza's room, takes her combs from the table and, with a malicious look on her face, says about Ester: a black crow.

Earlier (a few days ago) Liza dreamt that Illa was strangling her, saying: It takes 11 minutes for a person to die.

* * *

Drawn on a beetle: a hammer and sickle and the letters: U. S. S. R.

* * *

Miscellany *Archimedes Bath*

Zabolotsky,	II Conversation. Night was rattling in a barrel. From "The Triumph of Agriculture. Petrova's Fall. Immortality.
Kharms	Threefold Descritption. Elizaveta Bam. Flight to the Heavens. Temptation. Parsimony. Tiulpanov among the Trochees.
Vvedensky	The Answer of the Gods. Insane Beasts. Two Little Birds, Grief, the Lion and Night. Night of the Old Men
Oleinikov	The Carp. You're Grown Tired of Amorous Amusements.

Zvenigorodsky   A Certain Debaucher.
In One Beautiful Portrait.
Flight.

* * *

I gave Tamara Aleksandrovna a pad, a number 4 pencil, paper, and two of my books.
January 8, 1930.

* * *

T.A.	R.A.
Forehead 3	Nose 2
Eyes 2	Ears 2
Mouth 1	Mouth 1
Neck 2	Shoulders 2
Midriff 2	Breasts 2
Hips 2	Waist 2
Calves 1	Legs 2
	Calves 1
~~Back~~	Back 2
13	17

* * *

On the tram I saw a maiden,
A damsel, you could say, my friends,
She's just such a little bud that
I can't even tell you then.

But *chinar* Vvedensky's with me,
Riding like a fool as well.
Saw the maiden, took my hat off,
And Vvedensky doffed his bells.

* * *

Edgar Dacqué, *Urwelt, Sage und Menschheit*. Berlin 1927.
Nikolai Knipovich. *Fish of the Caspian Sea*.

* * *

If Ester had wanted to see me, she would have called Liza more often.

* * *

D. D. Galanin. *Mikhail Vasilievich Lomonosov and the Genius of Russian Culture.* Moscow, 1916. 88 pp.
Lev Alpatov, *Sakhalin: Field Notes of an Ethnographer* (Moscow, 1930).

* * *

Create a stock hero for a children's book who satisfies the following requirements:
> 1. Must be modern.
> 2. Must be real.
> 3. Must be universal.
> 4. Must be comic.
> 5̶.̶

* * *

I really like Galina Nikolaevna. After Ester she's the best.

Yes, Galina Nikolaevna does come after ⊟, but not ahead. January 8.

* * *

In the first place, I've got a terrible cold and in the second place, I've literally had no grub for two days.
Appearance on January 16, 6:00 pm, at 3 Ogorodnikov Prospect. And at 3:00 a.m. at 49 Liteiny Prospect.

* * *

O why do you twinkle
you swift flying mouse
O why do you twinkle
in the sky o'er the house
O why do you fly
Like tea-tray so round
O why are you sparkling

Are sparkling
are sparkling
are sparkling

do, re, mi, fa, sol.

* * *

I miss Ester a lot.

Saw my sweet kitten Ester for the last time a month ago.
January 13, 1930.
Press House.
5 hours, 13 minutes in the Afternoon. Petersburg.
Daniil Ivanovich Kharms

[From notebook 18]

Pereforation

We've opened up our shelter here
For all who wish to scrape and squeak
And all those singing in the street
In courtyards which to look at.
A period rose in place of Phi,
the final stop of all expressions.
The startled conflicts of our thoughts
Cut off at once by Ifs.
Those little artists laughing now
nod to us like Thursday,
but then the watchman cried out: prince!
and into me he turned this way.
He squatted down and leaning back
M, rejoicing, sang me through.
But I demanded only that
I be brought stewed fruit.

That's all. March 2, 1930

[From notebook 38]

Poetry should be written so that if you throw a poem at the window, the glass will shatter.
Daniil Khkharms.

* * *

I wonder what Esther was doing then.
Night of February 21-22, 1930.

[From notebook 18]

I'm tired of not sleeping nights,
forehead thickened, getting heavy,
Neck stood up from shoulder blades.
I went out for a walk to mama,
lips and forks go to my brain.

My head aches,
The earth quakes,
I'll go and drink some beer.
O dear, o dear, o dear.
Across from here a stake with arms
put up by us
in memory of mom.

* * *

Storitsyn said it's not my fate to be just a talent. I'll either stay stupid or I'll be a genius.

* * *

I. An evening of poems by Kharms. A theatricalized debate.
II. An evening of Oberiu poetry, without theatricalizations.
III. An evening of Oberiu poetry. Theatricalized.
IV. An Oberiu Spectacle.

* * *

To the cow:	tprupa—tprupa
To the calf:	tprutia—tprutia
To the horse:	tpro—tpro
To the colt:	chibu—chibu
To the sheep:	bal—bal
To the lamb:	mas—mas
To the goat:	dedeniaia
To the pig:	riukh—riukh
To the piglet:	vikh—vikh.

* * *

Check on the beginning of spring in relation to Easter.

* * *

LAWS March 14, 1930.

The will is of desire.
The will is of command.
The absence of will (when there is no force of command or of desire either).

The move of a creator (the will is of desire).
The move of a builder (the will is of command).
A move in the dark.

The move of a poet.
The move of a prose writer.

* * *

Part 1
An evening of poems by Daniil Ivanovich Kharms

Part 2
An evening of natural thinkers.
A. V. Tufanov, A. P. Eisner, E. Olimpov, P. Fogel, Non-em-ma,
K. K. Olimpov, A. A. Bashilov, V. N. Tsvetkov, E. I. V., V. Ya. L.

Part 3.
Debate.

* * *

[Review of an OBERIU performance at Leningrad State University, published in student newspaper **Smena,** *April 9, 1930]*

A Reactionary Circus

(Concerning a recent sortie by literary hooligans)

OBERIUTs, that's what they call themselves. And here's how they decipher it: "The Association of Real Art."

A tiny little grouplet of Leningrad poets has arrogated unto themselves this provocatively portentous name. There aren't all that many of them really. You can count them on the fingers of one hand. Their work . . . however even to mention it would be to give their trans-sensical verbal promiscuity much more credit than it deserves. Nobody publishes them and they hardly ever perform in public. *And there would be no point even in talking about them if they hadn't suddenly taken it into their heads to bring their "art" to the masses. But they did take it into their heads. A few days ago the OBERIUTs gave a performance in a student dormitory at Leningrad State U.*

And it's about this performance that we'd like to speak. The walls of the Red Corner of the dormitory were decorated beforehand with OBERIU posters. The bewildered students read:

−Kolya went to sea.

−Goga ate a pony.

−The minute got caught in a *po.* It probably got caught up in a *po.* No, it fell into a trap.

−Catch the lamp.

−The steps passed by the kvass.

−We're not pastry.

And lots more slogans, all in the same spirit.

−What does all this mean? What's your program?—first and foremost the students asked the assembled OBERIUTs.

The answer followed:

−The meaning of the slogans will be clear after our reading. We're not going to discuss our program: it's all in our works. We'll read and then open the floor to discussion.

But the works turned out no more intelligible, no less trans-sensical than the slogans.

Levin went first. He read a story full of all kinds of drivel. First one character turns into two ("one person, but two women, one a wife, the other a spouse"), then people turn into calves, and other circus acts of a similar sort.

Bewildered, the audience tried to follow these convolutions. What's the point of it all?

And in answer to this question, the OBERIU Master of Ceremonies proclaimed:

—The next performer will be the great Aleksei Aleksandrovich Pastukhov.

—Respected Citizens and Citizennesses! I have the honor of displaying my art to you. No sorcery, just slight of hand—thus began the "great Aleksei Aleksandrovich," who turned out to be no more no less than a common stage magician. He demonstrated some all too familiar tricks with disappearing balloons and handkerchiefs, ate a deck of cards, spat coins out of his mouth, etc. In a word, the "great Pastukhov" scaled the very heights of his calling as a petty prestidigitator: And why was he here, if not to harmonize with the creative works of the OBERIU illusionists and poetic jugglers?

The performance by the "poet" Vladimirov seemed to be a continuation of Pastukhov's work.

Here's his poetry:
"Ivan Ivanovich stumbled
                    in a ditch
And later he came home,
                    got hitched."
Or:
"He collapsed onto a bench,
and lay crosswise
Collapsed down crosswise."

Then the discussion began.

To stormy applause, all who spoke unanimously gave a harsh rebuke to the OBERIUTs. It was noted with outrage that in a period of intense effort by the proletariat on the front of socialist construction, in a period of decisive class struggle, the OBERIUTs stand outside of social life, outside of the social reality of the Soviet Union. Away, let us away from this boring reality, from these unbearable po-li-tics, *so that we may lose ourselves in the narcissistic pleasure of wild poetic mischief and hooliganism!*

The OBERIUTs are far removed from socialist construction. They hate the battle being waged by the proletariat. *Their retreat from life, their meaningless poetry, their trans-sensical juggling act—is nothing less than a protest against the Dictatorship of the proletariat. Their poetry is, therefore, counterrevolutionary. It is the poetry of people foreign to us, the poetry of the class enemy*—this is what the proletarian students declared.

What could the OBERIUTs possibly say in reply?

With inimitable impudence Vladimirov called the audience savages who, having stumbled into a European city, have had their first look at an automobile.

Levin announced that even though they were not understood at the present time (!), the OBERIUTs were the sole representatives (!) of a genuinely new art, which was in the process of constructing a grand edifice.

–Who are you building it for? someone asked.

–For all Russia,—came the classic response.

The proletarian student body re-plied to this incursion by the notorious OBERIUTs in the only way fitting. It decided to register its opinion in a resolution and to send it to the Union of Writers.

By the way, why is it that the Union of Writers tolerates in its midst such scum, such . . . OBERIUTs? After all, the Union is supposed to unite *Soviet* writers.

L. NILVICH

[From notebook 20]

The Master of Ceremonies with a dog.

All of you know the book *The Mail*. It's a good book. The movie's even better. I wasn't a part of it, but he is. A number of people made it. I'll tell you how it was done. I'll now ask all of you who had a part in it to come up on stage. Fanfare for the writer. Marshak. Who Marshak is. Marshak appears. M.C. applauds, poodle barks. The artist Tsekhnovsky did the drawings. He comes up on stage. He drew thousands of drawings. Tsekhnovsky demonstrates. His assistant Druzhinin. Music was written for the picture. Deshevov plays.

* * *

Learn the 12 Passions of Our Lord.
(Tarot).

If you toss a coin in the air once, the probablility of its landing heads or tails is equal. Tossed 4 times, the probablility of its landing tails equals 1 out of 16. However, you can treat each additional toss like the first one. Then the probability of its landing tails each time is 1 out of 2, so for 4 coin tosses, the probability is
½ ½ ½ ½ = 1/16.
That can't be right!

* * *

⊟ June 7.
I'm sitting in the Cinema *Soleil* and I can make her come here. But God
would have done that himself if He found it necessary. He's not doing
it, that means it's not necessary. But if I (as a man I have the right to
violate first causes) can make her come here anyway, then I will be doing
something unnecessary and will thereby be creating new karma.

One time I reconciled with ⊟, I met her on Nevsky Prospect and we went
to the *Aurora*. A few days later we were at the *Soleil* but that time I didn't
get a . . .

June 7. I haven't seen ⊟ since March 1. Was walking along Nevsky, went
into the *Aurora* by myself, then to *Soleil*. ʃ'ed alone.
Drank shrub, ate chocolate.

* * *

Lakhta. June 27, 1930.
In a black pond I saw the reflection of Count Stenbok-Fermor's castle.
Above the castle, I saw a tower.
On the tower, there was no one. But in the pond on the tower, there were
two people, one with a hat, the other without. And looking out from the
castle windows: big fishes.

* * *

July 16 at 2:00 in the afternoon. A beautiful cashier was sitting at the
Finland Station ticket window.

* * *

My life passes under the sign of ⊟.

* * *

On and on ahead I ride.
I've got no more strength to ride.
Night has fallen from the sky.
Sleep sells tickets at my side.

Train from Toksovo
12 h. 30 m.
August 1
Thinking about ⊟

~~Sleep a shirt~~

I can't sleep. It's dark. Past four.
Cast your glances toward the shore.
See the shore, it's white and high,
waves beat on the shore and die.
Flies like balls here in a game
circle round the candle flame.
I don't fear the candle.
Like a fly upon a knife
I'm remembering my wife,
and the day I left to go,
that was just a year ago.
Was on my way, the traincar clacked,
I was gloomy as a flask.

* * *

⊟ my soul!
⊟! come back to me! August 3, 1930.

* * *

Do the Tarot.

* * *

But what's wrong with me: vision somehow dim, mind foggy, body exhausted.
I don't feel well.
August 8, 1930. 5:00.

* * *

One day we will meet again
and never more be parted then.
Wednesday, August 13, 1930.

* * *

[Unfinished letter to Aleksandr Vvedensky. Summer 1930?]

Dear Sasha,

In this (and for brevity's sake I say simply "this" but understand by it "this letter") I will speak only about myself. I want, properly speaking, to describe my life. It's a real pity that I didn't write you a letter previous, since I would have written everything there that I've left out here.

Let us resort to the comparative method. You, let us say, are living there in Ashkabad in some fashion. For brevity's we'll call it "this way." While I am living here, designating it conventionally, "that way." I undertake to designate the one and the other in this way so that henceforward it will be easier and more convenient to talk about the one and the other. If you find the designations "this way" and "that way" to be inconvenient, then we can say: you live in a certain way, and I live in a certain way, but differently.

Suppose that I do not "live in a certain way, but differently," but in the same way as you do. What follows from that? For this let us imagine, and for simplicity's sake forget at once what we've just imagined. Now let's see what we've got.

[. . .]

I nearly forget to tell you how I bought a perfectly useless coat. On second thought, I'd do better to tell you about that later. Igor was here for a visit.

* * *

[Letter to Tamara Meier-Lipavskaya]

August 20, 1930

Tamara Aleksandrovna,

I have to tell you that I understand everything. Enough fooling around and writing stupid letters to who knows who. You think: he's stupid. He won't understand. But Daniil Kharms isn't stupid. He understands everything. You can't fool me, mother of mine! I'll fool you! And how! They've found a fool, have they! Well this fool is smarter than lots of clever people.

I won't use words like mockery, impertinence, etc. etc. That will only take us away from the real point.

No, I'll say it straight out, this is the devil knows what!

I've always said that there is something criminal in your face. People argued, disagreed, but now they can eat cow or eat their crows, however you say it!

I ask you straight out: what does this mean? Aha! I see you're blushing and you're trying to ward off that implacable phantom of a higher justice with your pathetic little hand.

I laugh as I watch you babble out pallid words of justification.

I mock your excuses. So be it! Let that pig Bobrikova take me for a monster.

Let the Rognedovs cover me with filth.

Yes! But no. That's not right.

I'll tell you quietly and bravely: I'm enraged.

And do you have any idea what I'm capable of? I'm a wolf. A beast. A panther. A tiger. I'm not bragging. Why should I brag?

I disdain spite. I don't understand spite. But sacred fury!

Oh, but we know those Ukrainian fields and ditches.

And we also know those notorious 20 pounds.

Valentina Efimovna has left for Moscow.

The price of produce is going up.

Daniil Kharms
20 August 1930

* * *

Dear T.A.,
I bought myself a tram. As soon as they fix the roads, I'll drive out to see you. Expect me around the 28th of the month.

* * *

[From notebook 20]

You don't know where to go, and you're going nowhere, and suddenly you know where to go.

Saw *Big Problems*, an absolutely disgusting film at the *Parisian*.

BUY
August 30.

Necktie	5 r.
Notebooks	5 r.
Enamel paints	5 r.

* * *

Cunnilingus.

* * *

Against
Trips to Tsarskoe Selo.
Consolidation of living space.
Natasha's difficult conditions.
Liza's situation.

For
Peace and quiet for Natasha.
Better for Papa and me.
Chesmenskaya almshouse.
Good for me personally.

Shurka rolled an idiotic cigarette.

* * *

Theosophical Messenger. "An Important Discovery." (Schlieman the younger) 1913, No. 3.

* * *

For Sunday, August 31.
"The Club of Natural Wisemen" at Lipavsky's.
1. I suggest adding Druskin as a member.

* * *

A theatrical number:
40 Spouses.
I know how.

* * *

$7 \times 9 = 63$ is the most difficult thing in the multiplication table.

* * *

October 26. 2 o'clock. At State Publishing. Sunday.

* * *

November 27, 1930. I was at Tamara Aleksandrovna's. One of her relatives, a certain Margarita, was there. We played cards. Valentina Efimovna came by. She brought a kitten. Tamara Aleksandrovna gave Lipavsky a stein with a picture of the Winter Palace.

* * *

[Letter to Tamara Meier-Lipavskaya]

Leningrad, December 5, 1930

Dear Tamara Aleksandrovna,

I love you. Yesterday I even wanted to say it to you, but you said there's always some kind of rash on my forehead and I started to feel uncomfortable. But later on, while you were eating a radish, I thought: "Well, ok, my forehead may not be beautiful but when all's said and done even Tamarochka isn't a goddess." I thought this simply to calm myself down. But in point of fact, you are a goddess, tall, shapely, intelligent, slightly cunning and completely unappreciated!

But at night I rubbed some polish on my forehead and then thought: "How good it is to love a goddess, when you yourself are a god." And then I fell asleep.

But papa woke me up and rather sternly asked who was in my room last night. "Friends," I say.

"Friends?" papa said.

I say Vvedensky, Lipavsky, Kalashnikov were here.

But papa asked if any visitors were, so to speak, from among the ladies. I say I can't remember right now. But papa did something (only I won't say what) and I remembered and say to him: "Yes, papochka, there were also such and such ladies that I know here and I had to see them in connection with business at State Publishing, Press House and the Federation of Writers." But that didn't help.

But it turned out that papa had read something before I did and had already shown it to Lydia Alekseevna (a woman by that name lives with us).

But I don't even know what was written there.

"No," says papa, "if you please, follow me and, if you please, explain everything."

I put my slippers on and went.

I walk in and see. My God! On the one hand, it's kind of nice to see, but on the other hand, papa and Lydia Alekseevna are standing side by side. "I," says Lydia Alekseevna, "cannot come here anymore, otherwise they'll write something about me too."

And papa also shouts. "This," he shouts, "isn't a train station."

Well, what can you say! I stand there thinking: "Still she loves me, clearly she does love me if it's come to this! Still, I think, what a crafty way for her to admit it! But which one was it? That's the question. Ah, if it had only been her, that is, Tamara!

Just as I was thinking this, suddenly the bell rings, the mailman shows up and brings me three registered letters. And it turns out that all three of them love me. But what do I care about the others when I love you, just you, dear Tamara Aleksandrovna. I've loved you from the first moment I set eyes on you, five years ago at the Union of Poets.

This has really broken my nature. I walk around like a fool. Lost my appetite. And if I force myself to eat something, suddenly a sour belch. Losing sleep. As soon as I do fall asleep, my left nostril gets stuffed up so there's just no breathing through it!

But love, you might say, is a sacred flame, it'll break through everything!

For five years I've admired you. How beautiful you are! Tamara Aleksandrovna, if only you knew!

Sweet, dear Tamara Aleksandrovna! Why is Shurka my friend! What a mockery of fate! But after all, if I didn't know Shurka, I wouldn't know you either!

No! . . .

Or rather yes! For only you, Tamara Aleksandrovna, can make me happy.

You write: ". . . I'm not to your taste."

Ah! The words have no power, but the sounds are indescribable!

Tamarochka, my rainbow!

Your Danya
December 5, 1930

         * * *

[Letter to Ester Rusakova]

         Leningrad, December 22, 1930

Dear Ester,

I'm sending you a piece called "Gideon." Don't look for any private meanings or hints in it. There's nothing of the sort there. Everyone is free to understand the piece in his own way. That's the reader's right. I'm sending it to you because I dedicated it to you. I would like you to have it. If you don't want it, just return it to me.
Daniil Kharms

         * * *

[From notebook 38]

December 24. Went with Zabolotsky to a Catholic church. It's night, I feel as if I've got a cold and not at all well. Worried about my health.

         * * *

December 28. Feel poorly. Head spinning. Took my temperature, 98.6. Worried about my health.

         * * *

December 29. Worried about my health.

[From notebook 38]

I'm not living right. Lately I haven't been feeling very well. Very worried about my health.
O Lord, help me to be healthy.
January 1, 1931.
Thursday.

January 1.
2:00 pm. 97.5 F.
7:00 pm. A slight chill, or, perhaps, it's simply cold in the room.
7:15. 98.2 F.
12 midnight. 98.4 F.

* * *

[From Notebook 21, spring 1931]

March 10, 1931
An Audit of Souls

———————

I tell you sweetheart, this I'll say,
don't mess with me my honey,
my wife's forever gone away,
take care my little bunny!

two peasants sat upon a bench,
the one his beard did ravage,
remembering last week's events,
the other chopped up cabbage.

* * *

~~March 7, 8, 9, 10 and 11. I don't feel well . . . right side of my chest . . . I~~
~~think I may have tuberculosis. Cross and Mary.~~

* * *

HE—   Come on then show me your hand
where you've scratched your finger
I suggest you daub it with iodine

SHE— There you see he's found something else to propose
as if I didn't know myself
it fell my lot to turn the heads
of inexperienced nomads
I ordered them to lay their heads down
at my feet in fluffy snow
those obeying quickly
loved me linearly
those extravagantly agitated
stored up malice inwardly.

~~HE—   science o wisdom's princess~~
~~an alabaster fish~~
~~an alabaster fish~~
~~So hence o wisdom's goddess~~

HE—
Science o wisdom's princess
slam thou shut the book of joy
so hence o wisdom's goddess
and show the fist of science to the fool
the schoolboy makes his progress
boning up on science on his bench
~~and pointing out the landmarks of our knowledge~~
~~grandsire reads grandchild a book~~
all these signs and all these landmarks
our grandchildren shall yet forget
and they, bald stones,

will look into the gaps
as graceful steeds they
will grow younger as they pass
they *chibu chibu* in us
will grow and blossom new
and in their free-running herds
they'll make the round earth quake.

* * *

11 March

SHE—
I know: this is an ancient song
and here and there mountains
of various junk are scattered
~~and though you split yourself open~~
but there is no point of balance here, no point of rest.

HE—
But for all that the mother of
our progeny and *chiberias* is here

SHE—
Drop it! you would show me
                    sugar
but where o where is the sweet fruit?

HE—
quickly we'll hammer together a swift float
and sail down the winding stream
and in a wink we'll come before
        the angelic gates

SHE—
        where?

HE—There beyond the turning.

* * *

Above the lofty tables
two blacksmith brothers rose

the fish have dried up
the streams have dried up
the people have dried up

hill of the fortyday fast
~~how come how come you're grown with wheat~~

No sooner does his wife shut her eyes
than the varied muffins of the night
become the dearer to his heart

* * *

WINDOW:
I am a hole in the wall of a house
and through me sunrays flow

~~A LESSON IN VAPORIZATION THROUGH THE WINDOW~~
WINDOW

SCHOOLGIRL—
I look out the window
and I see regiments of birds

TEACHER—
Look to the mortar's bottom
use the pestle grind the grains

SCHOOLGIRL—
I can't grind these little pebbles
~~so boring~~
o teacher they're so hard
while my little hand's so tender

TEACHER—
who'd have thought it such a princess
the hidden heat of vaporization
must be the object of your study

SCHOOLGIRL—
O teacher I'm exhausted
by this unbroken web of experiments
I've been grinding five full days. for what
my hands are stiff and numb
my breast dried up. O God O God

TEACHER—
Soon your torments will be ended
and your consciousness will quicken

SCHOOLGIRL—
Oh how my back is creaking

TEACHER—
See to it that the mortar rings
and the grains beneath the pestle crackle
I can see: you've turned all green
and tucked your legs up crosswise

this is the eleventh incident
I can recollect. ~~What a shtick~~ Oh my sainted mother
the poor thing just exerts herself
and there she lies a small dead corpse
how inexpressibly this grieves me!

CLOCK
it's half past one now
it's half past one now
coo koo
ahead ahead
it's half past one now

TEACHER—
when I climbed on the chair
and was setting the clock
so the weight wouldn't rock
she—unhappy—passed away

SCHOOLGIRL—
Oh my dearest teacher
I've grasped at last the hidden heat
of vaporization.

~~TEACHER~~
~~Farewell but I can't~~
~~hear you now~~
~~you're now a soul in heaven~~
~~the window leads out to the roof~~
~~and on its edge   a pigeon.~~

TEACHER—
Farewell, but I can't make you out
although I'd gladly listen
you're disincarnate now dear girl
so mum's the word from you then

WINDOW—
I've suddenly swung open wide
I am a hole in walls of houses
through me the soul pours through outside
I am the vent of elevated minds

March 15
1931.

* * *

On the second of June to a family quite lazy
an infant was born just a little bit pensive

———————————

mom and daddy bore a son
the aunts came rushing in a flock
the mother rested on the bed
while the cradle slowly rocked

FATHER—
behold gentlemen my son
You can see that he's still mangy

MOTHER—
o father father
please don't speak with such assurance
the child's really not so bad
he's barely opened up an eye
but it notes nothing in the room
that eye won't go where it's supposed to
his ear can't catch the sound of music
and only by the bones a tapping
makes its way into the skull
and why then, fulminating father, do you
   keep harping on the neverending thought
   of your son's vileness?

FATHER—
his ~~an aspect~~ figure's like a nail
how impotent his glances
~~and that chest? his face? his wail?~~
look and see wife what a face
a face like yuletide maskers
the color of his face—like wax
his lips flat as a skillet
unceasingly your nipple stretch
you're really happy with that sinner?

MOTHER—
Are you so sure that you're not happy?
You're the one who's glowing dad.

FATHER—
Quiet, hush now mangy woman
and rock the cradle by the bed.
   March 16
   Sitting for P. Sokolov. He was painting my portrait

     * * *

~~God thou art greater than me~~
~~higher than the snow or rain~~
~~more fluid than a sign or steed~~

----

well now my dear comrade
we've had enough of fighting
it's time it seems to take a rest
to bask upon a hammock

----

well now my dear comrade
it's time it seems to blow apart the planet

* * *

An American by the name of John Trunk was walking down the street
carrying a large wall clock with a counterweight and pendulum.

* * *

One day Andrei Vasilievich ~~glued on a false beard~~ was walking down
the street and lost his watch. Shortly thereafter he died. His father,
an elderly hunchbacked man, sat the whole night long in a top hat, his left
hand clutching a walking stick with a hooked handle. Diverse thoughts
visited his head, among them this one: ~~got to get married got to~~ life is
a smithy.

Andrei Vasilievich's father, by the name of ~~Andrei Anto~~ Grigory
Antonovich or more precisely Vasily Antonovich, ~~had come to Pet Luga.~~
~~And the moment twilight fell His future wife Maria Mikhailovna~~ embraced
Maria Mikhailovna and called her his queen. But in silence and in hope she
gazed forwards and upwards. And right then and there Vasily Antonovich,
the lousy hunchback, decided to eradicate his hump.

3

To this end, Vasily Antonovich got into the saddle and went to see Professor Mamaev. Professor Mamaev was sitting in his garden reading a book. ~~in which something was written.~~ Professor Mamaev responded to all of Vasily Antonovich's requests with but a single word: relax.

Then Vasily Antonovich went and checked into the department of surgery.

4

~~The orderly and the nurses put Vasily Antonovich on the table and covered him with a sheet. Then Professor Mamaev himself came into the room. Would you like me to shave you? asked the professor. "No, just cut my hump off for me," said Vasily Antonovich.~~

The operation began. But it ended badly because one of the nurses covered her face with a ~~dark~~ checkered cloth and couldn't see a thing and couldn't hand the professor the necessary instruments. And the orderly tied up his mouth and nose and he had nothing to breathe with and by the end of the operation he began to suffocate and fell nearly dead on the floor. But the most unpleasant thing was that Professor Mamaev in his haste forgot to take the sheet from off the patient and ~~in haste~~ instead of his hump he cut off something else, the top of his head, it seems. But he only poked at the hump with ~~a lancet~~ surgical scissors.

When he got home Vasily Antonovich ~~took a long time~~ could not calm down until Spaniards burst into the house and chopped off the top of Andriushka the cook's head.

After calming down, Vasily Antonovich went to see another doctor and that one ~~already~~ quickly cut off his hump.

After that everything went quite smoothly. Maria Mikhailovna divorced Vasily Antonovich and married Bubnov.

~~And Bubnov kept on squeezing the hand of a co-worker who sang various songs for him after which she died.~~

Bubnov did not love this new wife. As soon as she would leave the house, Bubnov would buy himself a new hat and say hello to his neighbor Anna Moiseevna all the time. But suddenly Anna Moiseevna broke a tooth and ~~she had to she wide~~ she opened her mouth wide from the pain. Bubnov fell deep into thought about ~~three-point geometry~~ his biography.

~~He recalled the streamlets and lakes~~
~~He recalled his mother when she was still young and wore a sarafan~~.

Bubnov's father by the name of Phy fell in love with Bubnov's mother by the name of Hnu. Once Hnu was sitting on a flat stone and gathering the mushrooms that grew around it.
But Phy unexpectedly spoke thus: Hnu, I want us to have a Bubnov. Hnu ~~said~~ asked: A Bubnov? Yes? Yes?
−Precisely so, your Excellency answered Phy.

Hnu and Phy sat together and started thinking of various funny things and they laughed for a very long time.

Finally Hnu gave birth to Bubnov.

* * *

A flower flies beyond the water

~~A hare went hopping through~~

~~short-bursting lightning crashed into the water~~
~~only a hare gasped~~

~~the earth goes rushing on through space~~
~~stream of flying children~~
~~the cosmos stands alone henceforth~~
~~o burn my candle burn~~

EPISTLE TO THE CUCUMBERS

Apostle stars mosquitoes gnats
lair of haggling tipplers
of intriguers and of breads
she-criminal of destiny
little bell of a shell that's fired to the planets
Greetings! to you this letter

So how is Anna astra doing
~~I'd like to know~~
~~What is the railing up to?~~
how does the rain feel today
has a hole been made in the sun?
I'd like to know it all
the sooner all the better

And air's courageous kernel
That's filled up with flights of birds
and the lightning of white snows
is our ~~tower~~ hope

                             * * *

but the lynx and lip of swine
~~and rustle of the stones~~
~~our~~
and the hours of rising Venuses
are our vices

——————————

~~We can~~
~~We'll pledge our heads to one another~~
weakness and hunger and sickly white tongue
and the eternal call of food's evacuation
~~and the tender juices~~
and the supple juices of tender young girls
there's fearful interference for you

                             * * *

Hnu friend of the lamp

The short-bursting lightning of winter-white snows
flew into the forest and frightened the beasts
over there there's a hare bounding round the wild cherry
there a lynx lies in wait for a submarine mouse
it's puffed up its muzzle
raised its tail with a tuft
you damned mangy predator
the thrush and rabbit are for you what fried eggs are for us.
only the oak stands not paying attention to anything
freshly fallen from the sky
~~the pain of the fall has not subsided~~
~~and like a grain flew around flew in on the back of a shaggy fly~~
its pain has not grown quiet
its branches not spread wide
I don't deserve
either answer or obeisance
hey now my spurs
seize and slash and beat me
got me in the back
got me in the back
ah but he's quick
I thought I saw the torah before me
but no you madman
madman of my words
there's one I won't repeat
not repeat my whole life long
this gentlemen
gentlemen my most attentive auditors
is that spring
the spring of matingsingers from the heights
downward onto stone slabs
stone tablets
the tables of celestial ohoho Numbers.

II.

Again it began from something small
the soul in green garland
struck up a song
and now we listened and the water
flowed right through us
we pressed ourselves against the wall
but felt them start to beat on it
it was beating on our backbone
and subtle little lamps
the subtle little lamps
those mischiefmakers they
those subtle little icon lamps
~~shone~~
I saw above the head of everyone
You know, said one
sin sin of those were there
it grates upon my ears
grates upon my ears
You know, said the third
Pharan I've gone blind
and so
it bent me over
backwards in an arc
Gryphon! now the soul cried out
makander
on high we're brethren.
on high the gryphons *darandasy*.

III.

The two put on fresh tunics
and madmen they came out against us
hey so where are your faces? We shouted
and they can you imagine
shook our dwellings with their hands
trying thus ~~us~~ to frighten us.
you try in vain! we said to them

with tender tongues turning the meanings of speech
in vain.
but no said one
two, he said
three, he whispered
four, he implored
eight eight, he repeated
after us you little girls
will do the very same.
And then what then what? we had to ask
we asked an explanation.
The year went by we learned it all.
This is how it was:
there was a gardener
loved a saw
the saw in reply kept silent
the gardener asked her to forget
forget his boorish nonsense
the saw then turned away from him
and tended to and gave drink to
her honor.
Why did you stupid gardener
pursue me with your speeches
I tried to run away from you
but in the dark and summer nights
you'd number the stars and put into a sack
your diverse observations
your thoughts of me
were filthy gardener
and now you're filled with offal
rejected gardener oh my soul
the falsehood of your thoughts
will not mislead me
I'll put the lash in play if need be
your world won't ever warm you up
while you are in exile.
know this: the greater the simplicity
the higher the quality.

GARDENER
This is naught but foolery
all my hope has left me
kleer's bright tree ~~of youth~~ is gone
let's go my soul Though I'm an ignoramus
you're still my favorite lyre
how quickly you come near
to me my soul
I'm very glad that soon
There'll no more be an argument between us.

IIII
Here's where the fish began to swim
didn't you see the bee fly in
from wasps perhaps you think you're saved
or from the lash of sturdy braids
or inclining the top of your head to her feet
you
were tender
were ardent
then tender anew
then sensitive to petting
then coarse
then a horse with red muzzle
then a corpse
then pressed against the wall you drowsy stand
then at a distance you wring your hands.

March 31 1931
At Poret's. Yudina played the piano.

* * *

I looked at myself in the mirror
But to you you
I'll say that I looked
On purpose the wrong way.

I saw a crest upon my brow
And beautifully, it seems,
The legs of two Venuses
Were lying in a pitcher.

To you you
I give ~~flowers~~ a bottle of fear.
You you
need my Georgian hat,
chestnut hair the ash of beard.
I'm the son of heaven's vault,
The kite and rook.
Where are you, close-woven staves of my fences?
The paths of stars at night
Are beautiful, so alluring,
So burning.

But talk is so deceiving
And songs are flowing slowly.
~~The wrath of God is not a mountain~~
~~Let us recall the fiery speeches~~
~~Let us recall the image of those~~
Far better you were silent now forever.
~~Forgetting all~~

~~To you you~~
~~I give a bottle of fear~~
~~For you for you~~
~~I shall be stone~~
To you to you we've told the secret
Of getting water from the neck.

We we have come to see so much.
For us us an axe in fur's not news.
Diligent we're masters of our voices
So not to wreck the crucible of passion.
We divide the world with axe to pieces
We sing the hovel of time

So not to wreck ~~the crucible of honor~~ flattery's foundation
We share together food and dream,
Horse work ~~we measure~~ isn't meet for us,
We're nothing but a horde of idle angels.

* * *

Tycho Brahe had an artificial nose.

* * *

THE CHOICE OF DAYS

I'll tell you plainly
the tail of the wise man
holds danger for the careless idler
as soon as the latter forgets the year's name
the tail dusts off the memory of the madman
farewell thereafter speakings Freedom!
by then the sun is rolling out new days
and putting them in ranks for choosing
I'll tell you plainly: just we alone,
the poets, know the days' *katybr*.
that's all.
April 4.

* * *

[From notebook 38]

May 6, 1931. I'd like to start writing a piece that has 11 stand-alone
chapters. Christ lived 11 times, a body thrown to the Earth falls 11 times,
I renounce the logical flow of thought 11 times.
The second chapter's title should be: cross-beam. The cross-beam taken
from a four point cross.

Our way of life is still in flux. Our time has not yet found its hero. And if he
does exist, the eye has not yet seen him. And even if the eye does see him,
he will not be recognized by others.

Either *eternal* or *not eternal*. *Almost eternal* does not exist, it's simply the
non-eternal. But something *almost non-eternal* is possible, although we

classify it with the *eternal*. On our lips it sounds like something capable of being completed, that is, something *eternal*, but also capable of becoming something *non-eternal*. As soon as it completed, it will become our own finite, i.e., *non-eternal*, thing. But can something that has not yet been completed exist? I think it can, in the eternal.

* * *

[Letter to Tamara Meier-Lipavskaya]

July 17, 1931. Detskoe Selo

Mother of mine, Dear Tamara Aleksandrovna,

I don't like writing when I've got nothing to write about. Exactly nothing has changed since you left. Valentina Efimovna still goes to see Tamara Grigorievna, Tamara Grigorievna to Valentina Efimovna, Aleksandra Grigorievna to Leonid Savelievich, while Leonid Savelievich still goes to see Aleksandr Ivanovich. I can also tell you absolutely nothing about myself. Got a little tanned, gained a little weight, got a little better looking, but not everyone agrees even with that.

Now perhaps I'll describe for you an extraordinary event that happened with Leonid Savelievich. Leonid Savelievich once came to see me and didn't find me at home. They didn't even open the door for him, they just asked through the door: "who's there?" At first he asked for me, but then he gave his last name, Saveliev, for some reason. But later on they tell me that some young lady by the name of Sevilla came to see me. It was only with some difficulty that I guessed who it really was. Yes . . . and recently another extraordinary event occurred. Leonid Savelievich and I went to the circus. We arrive before the beginning and, just imagine, there's not even a single ticket. So I say: let's go, Leonid Savelievich, just for the hell of it. So on we went. But at the entrance they stopped me and don't let me in, but he, I see, just walks right through. I got angry and I say: "that guy over there, he also doesn't have a ticket. Why are you letting him in?" But they say: "that's Johnny-Jump-Up, he's working in the show." Leonid Savelievich, you know, has started to waste away completely and has given up on State Publishers, he wants to go into hairdressing. Aleksandr

Ivanovich has bought himself pants, he assures me they're Oxford trousers. They're really terribly wide, wider than Oxfords, but to make up for it they're very short, you can see where his socks end. Aleksandr Ivanovich doesn't despair, he says: "I'll wear them a bit, I'll break 'em in." Valentina Efimovna has moved to another apartment. They'll probably chuck her out of there in short order too. Tamara Grigorievna and Aleksandra Grigorievna are brazenly sitting in your room: I advise you to pay attention. Scoundrels, by the way, from the Sinai.

That's approximately everything that's happend during your absence. As soon as something interesting happens, I'll write in detail.

We're all really bored without you. I've already fallen in love with three beautiful women who look just like you. Leonid Savelievich has written in pencil on the wallpaper above his bed: "Tamara A. K. N." While Oleinikov called his son Tamara. And Aleksandr Ivanovich calls all his acquaintences Tamasya. While Val. Efim. wrote a letter to Barsky and signed it "T," either yours "Truly" or "Tamara." Believe it or not, but even Boba Levin has sent a letter from Simbirsk in which he writes . . . "well, how are you doing, who are you seeing?" Obviously he wants to know if I'm seeing you. Recently I ran into Danilievich. He simply beamed and started to quiver but once he recognized me his face fell. I, he says,* took you for Tamarochka, now I see I got mixed up. That's just what he said: "for Tamarochka." I didn't say anything, just watched him walk away and mumbled quietly: "cock sucker!" But he probably heard this, he quickly came up to me and bashed me in the face with I-don't-know-what. I even started to cry, I felt very sorry for you.

I can't go on writing in pencil.

Yours Daniil Kharms
11 Nadezhdinskaya Street, Apt. 8
(Write me at this address)

* At this point my aunt took the ink away from me.

* * *

[Scenes from the life of the poet]

Morning

So, today I had a dream about a dog.

It was licking a stone then it ran to the river and started looking into the water.

Did it see anything there?

Why is it looking into the water?

I lit up a cigarette. There were only two left.

I'll smoke them and there won't be any left.

No money either.

Where am I going to eat today?

In the morning I can have tea: I've still got some sugar and a roll. But there won't be any more cigarettes. And nowhere to eat.

Got to be getting up soon. It's already half past two.

I lit up the second cigarette and started thinking: how am I going to get dinner today?

Foma has dinner at Press House at seven o'clock. If I show up at exactly seven o'clock, meet Foma there and say to him: "Listen, Foma Antonich, I'd like you to feed me dinner tonight. I was supposed to get some money today, but there's no money in the bank." I might borrow ten from the professor. But the professor, most likely, will say: "Pardon me, I'm in debt to you and you're borrowing from me? But I don't have ten on me now. I can only give you three." Or no, the professor will say: "I don't have a kopeck now." Or no, the professor won't say that, but this: "Here's a ruble for you, and I won't give you any more. Be off and buy yourself some matches."

I finished my cigarette and began dressing.

Volodya phoned. Tatiana Aleksandrovna said that she can't understand which part of me comes from God, which from the fool.

I put on boots. The sole on the left boot is falling off.

Today is Sunday.

I'm walking down Liteiny Prospect, past the book shops. Yesterday I asked for a miracle. It would be something if a miracle occurred right now.

A freezing rain is beginning to fall. I stop in front of a book shop and look at the window display. I read ten book titles and forget them instantly.

I reach into my pocket for cigarettes but then remember that I have none left.

I make a haughty face and quickly walk along Nevsky, tapping with my walking stick.

A house on the corner of Nevsky is being painted a disgusting shade of yellow. I have to move off the sidewalk onto the street. The people walking towards me are pushing and shoving me. They're all recently arrived from the country and don't know yet how to walk on sidewalks. It's quite difficult to tell them apart, dirty clothes and dirty faces.

They're rushing in all directions, snarling, pushing and shoving.

If they run into someone by mistake, they don't say "excuse me" but shout abusive words at each other.

On Nevsky, there's a terrible scrum on the sidewalks. But it's fairly quiet in the street. Now and then trucks and filthy automobiles rumble past.

The trams run crammed with people. People hang onto the running boards. There's always swearing in the tram. People speak as if they knew each other. When the door opens, a warm and stinking odor wafts from the car onto the tram stop. People jump on and others jump off as the tram is moving. But they don't really know how to do it, and they jump off the tram butt first. Often someone falls down and, howling and swearing, flies under the wheels. Policemen blow their whistles, stop the cars, and fine anyone jumping on the moving tram. But as soon as the tram starts up again, new people come running and jump on, grabbing the handrail with their left hand.

Today I woke at two in the afternoon. I lay in bed till three, too weak to get up. I thought over my dream: why *did* the dog look into the river, and what *did* it see there? I assured myself that it was very important to think through my dream. But I couldn't remember what came next in the dream, and I began thinking about something else.

Yesterday evening I was sitting at my desk, smoking a lot. In front of me lay paper to write something. But I didn't know what I was supposed to write. I didn't even know whether it should be a poem, a story, or an essay. I wrote nothing and went to bed. But I didn't sleep long. I wanted to find out what I was supposed to write. I mentally went over all the various types of verbal art but couldn't find the one for me. It could be a single word, or, perhaps, I was supposed to write an entire book. I asked God for a miracle so that I would understand what it was I had to write.

But I began to feel like smoking. I had only four cigarettes left. It would have been good to leave two, no, three for the morning.

I sat down on the bed and lit up.

I asked God for a miracle.

That's right, I need a miracle. Doesn't matter what kind of miracle.

I lit the lamp and looked around. All was as before.

But nothing was supposed to change in my room.

Something was supposed to change in me.

I looked at the clock. Seven minutes past three. That means, I should sleep at least until eleven thirty. Go to sleep already!

I put out the lamp and lay down.

No, I should have lain down on my left side.

I lie down on my left side and start to fall asleep.

I look out the window and see a yardman sweeping the street.

I'm standing next to the yardman and say to him that before you write something, you have to know the words you have to write.

A flea is hopping up my leg.

I'm lying face down on the pillow, eyes closed and trying to fall asleep. But I hear the flea hopping and I follow it. If I move, I'll lose the dream.

But now I should raise my hand and touch my forehead with a finger. I raise my hand and touch my forehead with a finger. And the dream is lost.

I feel like turning over onto my right side, but I should lie on my left.

Now the flea is crawling down my back. Now it will bite me.

I say, "ouch . . ."

With closed eyes I see the flea hopping on the sheet. It climbs into a fold and sits there quietly, like a little dog.

I see my entire room, but not from the side, not from above, but all of it at once, instantaneously. All the objects are orange.

I can't fall sleep. I try thinking about nothing. I remember that's impossible and try not to force my thoughts. Let me think about anything at all. So I think about an immense spoon and remember the fable about the Tatar who saw pudding in his dream, but had forgotten to take a spoon with him. And then I saw the spoon, but I forgot. . . . Forgot. . . . Forgot. . . . I forgot what I was thinking about. Am I really not sleeping? I opened my eyes to check.

Now I've woken up. Too bad, since I was already falling asleep and I forgot how much I needed it. I ought to try once again to fall asleep. So much effort wasted. I yawned.

I was too lazy to fall asleep.

I see a stove in front of me. In the dark it looks dark green. I close my eyes. But continue to see the stove. It's completely dark green. And all the objects in the room are dark green. My eyes are closed, but I blink without opening my eyes.

"A person continues blinking with his eyes closed." I think. "Only a sleeping person doesn't blink."

I see my room and see myself lying on the bed. A blanket covers me up to my neck. My face is barely sticking out.

In the room everything looks grey.

It's not a color, it's only the draft of a color. Things are primed for painting. But the paints have been taken away. And although this tablecloth on the table is grey, you can see it's really sky-blue. And although this pencil is gray, in reality it's yellow.

"Fell asleep," I hear a voice.

1931

* * *

[From notebook 22]

daniel khaarms.
1931.
3 Oktober.
Daniel Haarms.

* * *

A New Stage of Soviet Physics, V. Lvov. Academy of Sciences, USSR.
Apollon. 1911, No. 3. Bosch.
Physica sacra, oder, Der Begriff der himmlischen Leiblichkeit und die aus ihm sich ergebenden Aufschlüsse über die Geheimnisse des Christenthums. Julius Hamberger.
In the Midst of Life, Ambrose Bierce, 1924.
Theory of the Atomic Nucleus. 1928-31. A 27-year-old physicist from Leningrad G. A. Gamov.
The Agnostic "Principle of Unobservability" by Lev Landau.

* * *

Saint Antoine, Sainte Antoine, rend-moi la chose que j'ai perdue.

For October 31.
Get up at 11 o'clock.
Read from 12—2.
Go to State Publishing Library and get chivalric romances and biography
of Mozart.
Dinner at Press House.

* * *

Vaginov is busy on November 1, 3, 7, and 8.

* * *

Gregory Skovoroda, *Life and Teachings.* Moscow, 1912.

Apocatastasis.
Wisdom, knowledge, strength, action.

* * *

The adventures of a lazy boy.
Liquidation of illiteracy.
Garden.
Report on shock-workers.
How they work preparing cotton.
Connection to foreign kids confuses cities.

* * *

"Elisabeth " from *The Wonder Bar*
(Katscher and Caesar)

Ask for Elizabeth.
Only for Elizabeth,
So sweet and petite
In her silken stocking feet.

She knows her way about,
If you want to play about,
You will cover ground
With Elizabeth around.
She only loves the night time,
She calls that the right time,
And when you want a high time
There's no thing she won't do.
She knows her ABC's, ABC's and do re mi's,
So when you are blue,
Take Elizabeth with you.

* * *

"Hallelujah" from *Hit the Deck*
(Youmans, Grey and Robbin)

Sing Hallelujah! Halle-Hallelujah!
And you'll shoo the blues away:
When cares pursue yah, Halle-Hallelujah!
Gets you through the darkest day.
Now there's Satan, lying awaitin'
And he's creatin' skies of gray;
But Hallelujah! Halle-Hallelujah!
Helps to shoo the clouds away!

"Sometimes I'm Happy" from *Hit the Deck*
(Youmans and Caesar)

Sometimes I'm Happy: sometimes I'm blue,
My disposition depends on you;
I never mind the rain from the skies,
If I can find sunshine in your eyes!
Sometimes I hate you, sometimes I love you:
But when I hate you, it's cause I love you:
That's how I am, so what can I do?
I'm happy when I'm with you!

* * *

[Letter to Raisa Poliakovskaya]

November 2, 1931. Leningrad.

Dear Raisa Ilinishna,

I can't say anything about the reason why I haven't seen you since September 19. Of course I recognized your voice when you called me on the telephone. All the same, since I won't see you anymore, I can tell you: I fell in love with you and I love you. I loved Ester for seven years, and now for seven years I will love you. Wherever I may be, the thought of Raia and Paradise never leaves me.

Daniil Kharms

* * *

[Letter to Raisa Poliakovskaya]

November 2, 1931. Leningrad.

Dear Raisa Ilinishna, maybe it's for the best that everything turned out as it did. I really did fall in love with you. And if I had seen you one more time, I would have confessed everything to you. That would not have been good.

You haven't forgotten the little symbols on the walls of my room. Quite often you come across the symbol: ⊟. I call it a "window." In the little mirror I gave you, there's a note on which this "window" has been drawn in several variations. And there's also, you will recall, the inscription over my bed:

Thoughts of Raia

Anyway, Raisa Ilinishna, you may consider this a joke, but before you, I truly loved only once. That was Ester (in Russian "Star"). I loved her for seven years.

For me she wasn't just the woman I loved, but something else, something that entered into all my thoughts and deeds. I spoke with Ester in a language that wasn't Russian, and I would write her name in Latin letters: ESTHER. Then I made a monogram out of them and it came out: ⊟.

I called it the "window" through which I look out at the sky and see a star. And I called the star "paradise," but a very distant one. And then one day I saw that the symbol ⊟ was, in fact, the image of a window.

Then Ester and I parted. I didn't stop loving her and she didn't stop loving me, but I was the first to want to break up with her. Why? It's hard for me to explain. But I felt I'd had enough of looking "out the window at a distant star."

And then one time I couldn't sleep the whole night. I'd lie down and at once I'd get back up. But having gotten up, I'd realize that I had to lie down. I'd lie down again, but right away I'd jump up and walk around the room. I'd sit down at my desk and want to write. I'd put a piece of paper in front of me, take pen in hand and think. I knew that there was something I had to write, but I didn't know what.

I didn't even know whether it was supposed to be poems, or a story, or a discourse, or simply a single word. I looked from side to side and it seemed that something was just about to happen. But nothing would happen. It was awful. If the ceiling had fallen in, it would have been better than just sitting there waiting for who knows what?

The night had already gone by, the streetcars had started running, and I still hadn't written a single word. I stood up and went up to the window. I sat down and started to look out the window. And suddenly I said to myself: here I am sitting and looking out the window at . . .

But what *am* I looking at? I recalled: "a window through which I look at a star." But now, this time, I wasn't looking at a star. I don't know what I'm looking at now. But what I'm looking at is the word I couldn't write. That's when I saw you. You came up to your window in a bathing suit. That's how I first saw you. I saw you through the window.

Do you find what I'm writing ridiculous, Raisa Ilinishna? . . .

But I'm not even asking you to treat it seriously. But listen further now. I got to know you and found out that you're called Raia. I started thinking a lot about you, about Raia. The thought of you became my main thought. And I hung this inscription above my bed:

Thoughts of Raia (*o Rae*)

My main thought, besides you, is the thought of paradise (*o rae*), and you understand that you're not just the woman with whom I've fallen in love, but you've entered into all my thoughts and deeds.

Indeed the point here isn't in the pun—Raia and *rai* (paradise). All this is quite old-fashioned, and I had decided not to tell you any of this. Once I came to see you (you were having dinner) and said: You know, Raia, tonight a terrible thing happened to me, and you saved me. But after that I told you nothing.

Then when I was walking with you by the Buddhist Pagoda and around the islands, I felt I should tell you everything but something was holding me back and I didn't speak. I walked around and talked nonsense. And you even began to resent it in the end. And so it went every time I would see you. I should have either told you everything or broken up with you. And even now, in this letter, I've told you next to nothing. Only the tiniest little bit.

As it is, you'll decide that either I'm joking or I'm out of my mind. And I'm writing you all this only because I've decided not to see you anymore so as not to alarm you.

You called me on the telephone today after I had begun to write you this letter. Of course I recognized your voice at once, but not knowing what to say to you, I kept on asking: Who's calling?

The day after tomorrow Boris Levin will hand you this letter. May God preserve you, my sweet Raia.

Daniil Kharms

[From notebook 38]

November 14, Saturday. 1931.
The Art of Silence is the Gate to Paradise.

I raised my eyes up higher and higher.
Here are the windows of the second floor.
Here's a mast.
Here's simple sky.

Here's paradise,
And God in paradise with face like mine,
And I am like unto a man
And man is like to God
And God is like the world
And tree and grass, and bloom and leaf
Are all the source of life.
And grass is like to stone,
But stone breaks down to sand
And sand is like the earth.
And all that's dead seeks out the earth
And earth sends forth a shoot,
And gathering moisture, it lies
Green clay, along the river's bank.
And then we gather up this clay
And fashion men.
For man was made by God
From earth and clay.
Yes, man is like unto the earth
The earth is like unto the world
The world is like to God.
And I
Raise my eyes up higher and higher,
I see: I'm made in God's image and likeness,
And I wander through paradise,
And no one's there,
And I cry out: But where is God?
And God replies:
God is me.

[From notebook 22]

Edgar Dacqui, *Urwelt, Sage und Menschheit. Eine naturhistorisch-metaphysische Studie.* 1924. Munchen.

Krishnamurti.

* * *

For November 17, 1931.
Read *A Perilous Adventure* to the end. Dr. R. M. Bonn.
Read Balzac.
Johann Arndt. *Mysterien.*

* * *

[From notebook 38]

November 17, Tuesday. Everything that I have written up to now was written by one man. If God extends my life, I will write again. And everything that I write will be written by another man.

November 26, Thursday. I saw a house before me at a distance of two hundred and two paces. I walked closer and the house was now one hundred and fifty nine paces away. When I came closer still, a man came out of the house, got down on his knees and began to cry. "Why are you down on your knees crying," I asked. "I'm down on my knees crying," he replied, "so as not to forget the moment you came to me and so that you don't forget me."

* * *

The power latent in words must be set free. There exist certain combinations of words in which the action of this power can be felt more strongly. Words can be combined so that their power becomes more apparent. It's not right to think that this force can move objects. I'm sure that the power within words can even do this. But the most valuable action of this force is almost indefinable. We can get a rough idea of this power from the rhythms of verse meters. These complex pathways, such as the way metrical verse causes parts of the body to move, should also not be considered a fiction. Making the body move, however, is only the crudest and, at the same time, the weakest manifestation of verbal force. Any further actions of this force are hardly accessible to our rational understanding. If it is possible to think about a method for investigating these forces, then this method must be completely different from those previously used by science. Here, first of all, neither fact nor experience can serve as proof. I find it difficult to say how to prove and verify what has been said here. So far, I know of four types of verbal machines: poems, prayers, songs, and spells. These machines are constructed not by means of calculation or reasoning but by another means, that which we call the ALPHABET.

* * *

I love sensual women, but not passionate ones. The passionate woman closes her eyes, moans and cries out and the pleasure of the passionate woman is blind. The passionate woman squirms, grabs you with her hands not looking at what she's grabbing, squeezes, kisses, even bites, and is in a hurry to finish as soon as possible. She has no time to display her sexual organs, no time to examine, touch, or kiss your sexual organs, she is in a hurry to satisfy her passion. Once she has satisfied her passion, the passionate woman falls asleep. The sexual organs of the passionate woman are dry. The passionate woman is always in some ways like a man.

The sensual woman is always feminine. Her figure is rounded and ample. The sensual woman rarely descends into blind passion. She savors amorous enjoyment. The sensual woman is always a woman, and even when not aroused, her sexual organs are moist. She has to wear a bandage on her sexual organs so as not to be soaked in their moisture. When she removes the bandage in the evening, it's so wet, it can be wrung out. Thanks to such an abundance of juices, the sexual organs of the sensual woman give off a light pleasant scent that increases greatly when the sensual woman gets aroused. Then the juices from her sexual organs ooze out in a thick stream. The sensual woman likes you to examine her sexual organs.

ARREST BY OGPU, December 1931

Protocol No. 1

OGPU (All-Union State Political Directorate)
City of Leningrad. Authorized Representative
of the OGPU of the Leningrad Military District,
Secret Police Division, case No. 4246.

Interrogation Protocol

On the eleventh day of December 1931, I, A. V. Buznikov, authorized representative of the Secret Police Division, conducted an interrogation of the accused, citizen KHARMS, Daniil Ivanovich, and in response to the preliminary questions put to him, he testified to the following:

1. Name   *KHARMS (YUVACHEV)*

2. First name, patronymic   *Daniil Ivanovich*

3. Age (year of birth)   *1905*

4. Social origin (birth place, parents, ethnicity, nationality, citizenship)
Leningrad; son of a Court Counselor; mother member of the gentry

5. Place of residence (permanent and most recent)   *11 Nadezhdinskaya street, apt. 8*

6. Occupation (most recent place of employment and job)   *Man of letters, no permanent job*

7. Family (close relatives, their names, addresses, occupations before and after the revolution)   *father: Ivan Pavlovich; sister, Elizaveta Ivanovna Gritsyna. I have an acquaintance abroad, Nadezhda Aleksandrovna Nadezhina, an editor of Russian newspapers, with whom I correspond*

8. Property (of the person under interrogation and his relatives before and after the revolution) *propertyless*

9. Education (primary, secondary, higher, graduate, where, when, etc.) *secondary and incomplete higher*

10. Party membership and political convictions *non-party.*

11. Public service and revolutionary work *not involved in any public service*

12. Prior convictions (before and after the October Revolution) *none*

13. Service with the White Army *none*

Testimony re: essentials of the present case:

I work in the literary sphere. I am a person without political views, but in regard to a question that directly concerns me, the question of literature, I declare that I am not in agreement with the policy of the Soviet authorities in the sphere of literature and that, in opposition to existing government initiatives on this account, I desire freedom of the press, both for my own creative work and for the literary work of those writers near in spirit to me, those who along with me constitute a unified literary group.

Daniil Kharms
December 11, 1931

Interrogator: *A. Buznikov*

* * *

Interrogation No. 1

*Embarking on the path of a sincere confession, I testify
that I acted as the ideologue of an anti-Soviet group of writers
working primarily in the sphere of children's literature, which,
besides me, included A. Vvedensky, Bakhterev, Razumovsky,
Vladimirov (deceased), and, somewhat earlier, Zabolotsky and
K. Vaginov. The creative work of our group can be divided into
two parts. These were, in the first place, "trans-sense," essentially,
counter-revolutionary poems intended by us for adults, which,
by virtue of their content and tendency, could not be published
under contemporary Soviet conditions, and which we disseminated
among the anti-Soviet intelligentsia to whom we were connected
by shared political convictions. The dissemination of this
aforementioned portion of our creative work was conducted by
means of the reproduction of our literary works on typewriters
and the distribution of these works in manuscript form, through
scandalous readings of them at various anti-Soviet salons, in
particular at the apartment of P. P. Kalashnikov, a man disposed
to monarchist views, whose apartment systematically served as
a gathering place for people with anti-Soviet opinions. Besides
which, we also participated in public readings of our works for
adults before wider audiences, for example, at Press House and
the University, where the student audience at our last reading
responded with extraordinary vehemence, demanding that we be
sent to the Solovki camps and calling us counter-revolutionaries.
The second part of our creative work relates to the sphere of
children's literature. We considered our works for children, as
opposed to those for adults, inauthentic, intended simply to earn
us the material wherewithal for existence. By virtue of our political
convictions and literary platform, we consciously introduced ideas
politically hostile to Soviet reality into the sphere of children's
literature, and did harm to the cause of the Soviet formation of the
rising generation. Our "trans-sense" language is antithetical to
the materialist purposes of Soviet artistic literature, it being based*

completely on a mystical and idealistic philosophy, and is counter-revolutionary in present conditions.

I admit that, as the head of the aforementioned group of writers of children's literature, I engaged in anti-Soviet activity. In my future depositions I will detail and expand upon this protocol.

Daniil Kharms
December 18, 1931

Interrogator: *A. Buznikov*

* * *

Interrogation No. 2

Our group commenced working in the sphere of children's literature in 1927. In the sphere of children's literature, our group introduced elements of our work for adults, i.e., "trans-sense" language, language which in the previous protocol I called counter-revolutionary. The following works of mine for children are the most "trans-sensical": "Ivan Ivanovich Samovar," "About Toporyshkin," "How the old ladies bought some ink," "In the first place, and in the second place," and others. Works by Vvedensky such as "Who," "The Railroad," "Run and Jump," and others in the same vein most closely approach the form of "trans-sense" poetry. I have a very positive opinion of my most absurd poems, poems like, for example, "About Toporyshkin," which, due to its extreme lack of sense, was ridiculed even by Soviet humor publications, and I consider the quality of such works superb. And the consciousness that they were inextricably connected to my unpublished "trans-sense" works brought me great inner satisfaction. In view of the demands made of me, I subsequently had to move away somewhat from openly "trans-sense" works of the type indicated above, and to begin writing somewhat more concretely. However, as a result, works of mine such as "One

Million" and "What One Must Prepare for Winter" did not become less politically hostile or less counter-revolutionary than those works named above. In both books, both in "A Million" and "What One Must Prepare," I consciously substituted science lessons for social and political ones. In "A Million" I substituted a simple marching theme that I conveyed in the rhythm of the verse itself, for the theme of the pioneer movement, while redirecting the youthful reader's attention to combinations of numbers. In the book "What We Prepare for Winter," I substituted a science lesson for the theme of the pioneer camp, and shifted the child's attention to those things which absolutely need to be prepared for winter. I classify these books as politically hostile to the current political order, which opinion was shared by the entire group. In those instances when, because of material considerations, I attempted to accommodate myself to demands made by society of children's literature, the results were pure hack-work, such as, for example, the poems I wrote for the journal "Octoberbrats." The children's works named above, as well as others belonging to my pen as well as the works of other members of the group, were read intensively and discussed in the circle of group members and persons close to the group. There they met with complete approval.

Summing up my deposition, I confess that the activity of our group in the sphere of children's literature had an anti-Soviet character and did significant damage to the cause of forming the rising Soviet generation. Our books separated the reader from contemporary concrete reality and acted in a destructive way on the imagination of the child. In particular, from this point of view I can also point to a poem entitled "Liar," published in the journal "Hedgehog," which contains elements devoid of sense.

Daniil Kharms
December 23, 1931

Interrogator: *A. Buznikov*

* * *

Interrogation, January 1, 1932

    As I indicated in my previous deposition, our group worked in the sphere of children's literature over the course of several years. During this time we wrote and published a large quantity of books of poetry and prose for children, which can be divided into two categories, hack-work and anti-Soviet works.
    I count as hack-work the following of my books: "The Theater," "The Naughty Fuse" and three poems published in the journal "Octoberbrats," one of which was called "The Competition." These works for children were written by me in a minimally-short period of time and exclusively for the sake of receiving payment. Of the aforementioned works, in particular I consider "The Theater" a piece of hackwork. Besides the fact that this book conveys absolutely no useful information at all to children, it is, in form, extraordinarily vile, even anti-artistic. One can say the exact same thing about the book "The Naughty Fuse," which I wrote in all of two hours. Concerning the poem in the journal "Octoberbrats," it is of critical importance in this instance that I wrote these works on Soviet themes: socialist competition and so forth, which themes were inimical to me in connection with my political convictions and which I, consequently, was unable to set forth in an artistically acceptable form.
    The work of another member of our group, Vvedensky, is likewise, in some parts, hackwork. This relates to Vvedensky's first works on Soviet themes, which bear all the marks of conformist hackwork. It's difficult for me to name all these works now since I have forgotten their titles. I can also classify as conformist hackwork the entire corpus of works for children by another member of our group, Zabolotsky.
    I regard as anti-Soviet the following politically hostile books for children penned by members of our group: my works "A Million," "How the old lady bought some ink," "Ivan Ivanovich Samovar," "How Kolka Pankin flew to Brazil," "Preparing for Winter," and others; those of Vvedensky's books

*that I can remember include "Avdei the Scatterbrain,"
"Who," "Run and Jump," "The Feat of Pioneer Mochin"
and others.*

*My work "A Million" is anti-Soviet because this book on
the theme of the pioneer movement was consciously transformed
by me into a simple counting rhyme. In this book, I consciously
avoided the theme that was assigned to me and over the course
of the entire book didn't once mention the word "pioneer" or any
other word attesting that the book was about the contemporary
Soviet world. Were it not for the pictures (by the way, drawn by
the artist Konashevich in an anti-Soviet style), it would have been
impossible to know what the book was about: about a detachment
of Red pioneers or a detachment of White Guard boy scouts, the
more so since in the content of the book I separated the girls from
the boys, which, as everyone knows, occurs in bourgeois children's
organizations and, on the contrary, profoundly contradicts the
principles of the pioneer movement.*

*Another of my books named above, "Ivan Ivanovich
Samovar," is anti-Soviet by virtue of its absolute isolation,
consciously crafted by me, from concrete Soviet reality. It is a
typical bourgeois children's book, that has as its purpose to fix
the youthful reader's attention on trivialities and trifles with the
goal of separating the child from the surrounding reality in which,
in accordance with the mission of Soviet education, he ought to
take an active part. In addition to this, in this book I consciously
idealize the philistine kulak close-knit family with its enormous
samovar, the symbol of philistine prosperity.*

*In "Preparations for Winter," as also in "A Million,"
I consciously subverted the social and political theme of the
pioneer camp with a simple science lesson: that is, which objects of
domestic use should be prepared for winter. In this way, the child's
attention is redirected and torn away from the actively social
elements of Soviet life. From this point of view, I call this book not
only anti-Soviet but also a harmful act of sabotage in so far as it
relates to the most recent period of my creative life, when I was*

already well acquainted with the latest demands made of Soviet children's literature.

Of those abovementioned books by A. I. Vvedensky, a member of our group, I would especially dwell on "Avdei the Scatterbrain," which, singing the praises of a stout well-fed peasant and making fun of the village poor, is a kulak and anti-Soviet book.

The works for children that I mentioned above, as well as other works, were intensively read and discussed by group members and persons close to the group.

The creation of works like "A Million," "Ivan Ivanovich Samovar" and others, was conditioned by my political convictions, which were hostile to the contemporary political order and shared by the entire group.

Summing up my testimony, I confess that the activity of our group in the sphere of children's literature bore an anti-Soviet character and brought significant harm to the mission of educating the rising Soviet generation.

Daniil Kharms
January 1, 1932

Interrogator: *A. Buznikov*

* * *

Interrogation, Wednesday, January 13, 1932

At the base of my anti-Soviet activity, to which I testified earlier, lay political views hostile to the existing political structure. By virtue of my usual and intentional seclusion from current political questions—I don't read newspapers on principle—I formed my political views with the help of close friends, that is, the members of our group. In conversations with them I revealed myself as a supporter and adherent of the political regime that existed before the revolution. The future of the country was depicted to me as the restoration of that order. I was waiting for that moment and often imagined it with the thought that, immediately after it had been accomplished, I could get down to active creative work. I assume that the restoration of the old regime would offer our group of "trans-sense" writers broad possibilities for creative work and for the publication of this work in the press. Besides which, I consider, and have always considered, that my philosophical quests, which run along the lines of idealist philosophy and are closely aligned with mysticism, are in much greater harmony with the political and social forms of the pre-revolutionary order than with the contemporary political system founded on a materialist philosophy. My philosophy, which I was seeking and developing, having consciously withdrawn from present-day reality and having isolated myself from the influence of this reality, is profoundly hostile to the contemporary world and will never be able to approach it. This is clear if only from the proposition that, by virtue of my philosophical views, I consider the utilitarian tendency in philosophy inapplicable to me. Only when it loses its utilitarian and practical character will this science, in my opinion, attain the absolute heights or be capable of penetrating to the depths of the universe's mysteries. It is clear to what extent this contradicts the present aims of science as understood by the Bolsheviks as one of the engines for the construction of a socialist society. It is natural that, conscious of the profound contradiction between my philosophical views, my creative work and the present political order, I selfishly sought the realization of my political views, that is, the form of political governance closest to me. In conversations with Kalashnikov, Vvedensky and others, sometimes of an extreme anti-Soviet character, I came to assert the necessity of a monarchical form of governance for Russia. In so far as these conversations were repeated from day to day, I became more and more accustomed to the thought of the necessity of destroying the Soviet political system and the restoration of the old order of things. This impending change became for me something like a self-evident proposition, while the actual character of this change was, to a significant degree, of no importance to me. I realized that changing the structure of society was impossible without armed struggle but I tried not to think too deeply about this point as much as it profoundly contradicted my philosophical views, which rejected the necessity for armed struggle and violence of any kind. In this way, up to my neck in "trans-sense" writings and mystical idealist philosophical pursuits, I consciously set myself against the present social and political order. In turn, this contradiction forced me to seek a political order where such a contradiction would simply disappear. With the help of people close to me both creatively and ideologically, and more politically aware than I was myself, I was strengthened in my desire for the destruction of the present order.

Daniil Kharms
Wednesday, January 13, 1932

Interrogator: *A. Buznikov*

[From notebook 22]

June 18, 1932, Saturday – Free.
Evening at Zhitkov's.
June 19, in Tsarskoe Selo.
June 20, at Shvarts', then Lipavsky's.
June 21, at Zabolotsky's.
June 22, at Zhitkov's. Summer Solstice.
June 23, At Lydia Pavlovna's.
Levin spent the night at my place.
June 24, By automobile to Tsarskoe.
June 25, At Oleinikov's. Saw Sokolov off.
June 26, At Natasha's.
June 27, On the balcony. Don't feel very well. Lost a lot of weight.

Invent a machine of philosophical ideas.

* * *

Water ~~has always interested~~ interests me. Water is a feature of the earth.
Water is a necessary condition for man and the gods invented water.
Water always lies down low and from water we measure mountain heights.
We use water as a unit for measuring heat and density. Water has its own
~~limits~~ laws and condenses only to the limit of liquidity, and then in a solid
state water again tries to gain space as ice like gunpowder blows apart
the bomb.

~~Water is always horizontal and reflects the heavens; but if you look at water~~
~~from the side~~ In its depths water is always calm and incomprehensible to
man and fish swim calmly and seaweed sways quietly and I advise the
curious man to beware of gazing there. Water always reflects only that
which is above the water. The sky sun moon and stars and a dragonfly and a
bird flying above the water. And if you look at water from the side, you can

see a tree growing on the shore, and a man walking across the bridge and a girl sitting in an elongated boat. Water or the wind rages and rushes into the print shop cliff like the wind and hurls tables to the ground and in an instant smashes everything and fills the air with its roar.

And if water rushes into the city and bursts into the cellars, it's not likely that anyone will be found to measure the force of the wind then. Perhaps a grey-haired old professor twirls a pencil in his beard and looks through his spectacles at the water and he himself flies into a rage and with his formulas struggles against the water and wipes the windowpane with his beard. And he measures the force of the wind and the height of the incoming tide and flings the doors open wide and instantly perishes in the waves. And his assistant runs across the water, crying out loudly: where are you? Where are you? And there from out the waves, in tiaras, one after another, maidens appear.

* * *

Discuss with Kogan:
> 1. Goethe.
> 2. Documents
> 3. Day of departure.

Clothing.

Shirts 4	Collars, all
Long johns 3	Neckties
2 quilted jackets	Cuff links
Socks, all	Garters 4
Bedsheets 4	
Pillow cases 3	
Towels 4	
Handkerchiefs, all	

* * *

Take to Kursk
> 1. Folder with paper.
> 2. Pencil box.
> 3. Ink well and ink.

4. Pens.
5. Inkwell stand.
6. Ashtray.
7. Balloons.
8. 2 knives, 2 forks, 2 spoons, 2 teaspoons.
9. Plate, mug, shot glass.
10. Pan.
11. Loupe.
12. Needle and thread.
Scissors.
Toothbrush. Soap. Sponge.

* * *

I'm sitting in a park and waiting for her, but it's never her.

The public paddles around in boats
Nosily shrieking by the palace.
And happiness is expressed upon the little square
Where a graceful Doberman
Gallops with a certain amazement.
The picture looks luxurious:
The palaces, the trees, the heat,
And people's voices can't be heard.
Nearby it's all just doubt:
Motion's only dull emotion
The palaces but grief and tinsel.

I'm waiting for her, she ought to rise up from the grass, but she's not there and doesn't rise, alas.

Too bad that beautiful girls aren't coming down from that little hill.
So I'll just sit here alone some more and she won't come. I'll be in this park till I see the "Parcae." How sad it is.

O Lord, she didn't come again! But we could have become friends and lived . . .
AGLA!

Wozu! Wozu den sitzt er hier
Wozu den sitzt er doch
Ich möchte einen Mädchen hier
Mit einem feuchtem Loch.

> *Why! Why is he sitting here*
> *Why is he always sitting here*
> *Right now I'd like a girl*
> *With a moist hole.*

Every day I go looking for her and every day I don't find her and anyway she just isn't there.

Ecclesiastics, or The Wisdom of Jesus, Son of Sirach, 22:27.
"Who shall set a watch before my mouth, and a seal of wisdom upon my lips, that I fall not suddenly by them, and that my tongue destroy me not?"

* * *

HER SIGNS:
Dressed well and with taste.
Well-bred and stern in aspect.
Medium height. Quite young.
Graceful, but voluptuous, a biblical type. With auburn hair, or a brunette.
A nose not too small, straight and juts forward. Vivid lips, full and slightly moist. Very pretty face.

HER QUALITIES:
She is religious and ~~Orthodox~~ perhaps a Christian. She loves the strange and unexpected, but is nothing at all like modern women. She is passionate, but always reserved. She is refined and dissolute but not at all immoral. When excited, her sexual organs are very moist. She's looking for me. She is my Eve.

HER PROPERTIES:
She's *never* where I am.

HER THOUGHT:
Where am I?

She happened to take a look around and then plunged back into her book: as if fate had smiled at me and good fortune had rained down upon me once more.

* * *

[Letter to Tamara Meier-Lipavskaya and Leonid Lipavsky]

June 28, 1932, Tsarskoe Selo.

Dear Tamara Aleksandrovna and Leonid Savelievich,

Thanks for your marvelous letter. I've reread it many times and learned it by heart. You can wake me up in the middle of the night and at once, without a hitch, I'll begin: "Hello, Daniil Ivanovich, we're *excruciated and bored* without you. Len has bought himself some new . . ." etc. etc.

I have read your letter to all my acquaintances in Tsarskoe Selo. They all really like it. Yesterday my friend Balnis came by. He wanted to stay and spend the night here. I read him your letter six times. He smiled very broadly: apparently he really liked the letter, but didn't have the time to tell me his opinion in detail, since he went away without staying for the night. Today I went to see him myself and I read him the letter once again so it would be fresh in his memory. Then I asked him for his opinion. But he broke a leg off a chair and, using this leg, drove me out onto the street and also said that if I show up one more time with this vile filth, he would tie my hands and stuff my mouth full of filth from a cesspit. These were, of course, vulgar and none too witty words on his part. I, of course, went away, realizing that he had, perhaps, a bad cold and wasn't himself. From Balnis, I went to the Catherine Park where I rented a rowboat. On the entire lake, besides me, there were two or three other boats. But as luck would have it, there was a really pretty girl in one of the boats. And all alone. I turned the boat (by the way, when you turn, you have to row carefully because the oars can slip out of the locks) and set off after my beauty. I thought I looked like a Norwegian and that my figure, in grey jacket and fluttering tie, radiated freshness and health and, as they say, savored of the sea. But some hooligans were swimming near the Orlov Column and as I rowed past, one of them wanted to swim right across my path. Then the other one shouted: "Wait until that cross-eyed, sweaty specimen rows past!" and pointed at me with his foot. I didn't like this one bit since my beauty had heard it all. And since she was rowing ahead of me, and, as you know, when rowing you sit with your back facing the direction you're travelling, my beauty had not only heard but had also seen the hooligan point at me with his foot. I tried to pretend that none of this had anything to do with me and started to look around from side to side smiling. But there wasn't another boat anywhere near. And then the other hooligan shouted again: "So what are you looking around for? You think we're not talking to you? Hey you, shit in a hat!"

I started rowing with all my might but the oars kept slipping out of the locks and the boat was barely moving. Finally, after great effort, I caught up with my beauty and we got acquainted. Her name was Ekaterina Pavlovna. We returned her boat and Ekaterina Pavlovna moved over to mine. She turned out to be quite a witty conversationalist. I resolved to dazzle her with the wit of my acquaintances, took out your letter and started reading: "Hello, Daniil Ivanovich, we're *excruciated and bored* without you. Len has bought himself some new . . ." etc. Ekaterina Pavlovna said that as soon as we got to the shore, I'd see something. And what I saw was Ekaterina Pavlovna walk away, while a filthy little urchin crawled out from beneath the bushes and said: "Hey pops, how about giving me a ride on the boat?"

This evening I lost the letter. It happened like this: I was standing on the balcony, reading your letter eating kasha. At that moment, my aunt called me back inside to help her wind the clock. I covered the kasha with the letter and went inside. When I returned, the letter had absorbed all the kasha into itself, and I ate it.

The weather in Tsarskoe is good: partly cloudy, winds from the southwest, chance of rain.

This morning an organ grinder came to the garden and played the dog's waltz, but then swiped the hammock and ran off.

I read a very interesting book about a young man who fell in love with a young woman, but this young person loved another young man, and this young man loved another young person, and this young person loved still another young man, who loved not her, but yet another young person.

And suddenly this young person stumbles into an open manhole and breaks her spine. But when she's quite healed, she suddenly catches cold and dies. And then the young man who loves her does himself in with a shot from a revolver. Then the young person who loves this young man throws herself under a train. Then the young man who loves this young person out of grief climbs up a power line, touches the wire and dies from the electric shock. Then the young person who loves this young man stuffs herself with ground glass and dies from a wound in her guts. Then the young man who loves this young person flees to America and becomes such a drunk that he sells his last suit and, for lack of a suit, has to stay in bed and he gets bed sores and from these bed sores he dies.

One of these days I'll be in the city. I definitely want to see you. Greetings to Valentina Efimovna and to Yakov Semyonovich.

Daniil Kharms

* * *

Konoplev (office of political censor)
[June?] 29. GPU. 12:30.

* * *

Try to see the sun in dreams.

The Zulus say: "A body constantly well-fed will never see the things of mystery."
One path is to desire God's help and immediate communion with him, and another path is to travel by one's own strength towards moral perfection.
Grandchildren always envy their grandfathers

* * *

LETTERS

Addressees	Date p = postcard, l = letter
Papa:	p. 13 July; l. 21 July; l. 28 July; l. 10 August; l. 14 August; l. 5 September; l. 15 September; l. 16 September; l. 21 September.
Natasha	p. 12 July; p. 12 July; p. 13 July; p. 16 July; l. 18 July; l. 22 July; l. 28 July; l. 6 August; l. 9 August; p. 11 August; l. 20 August; l. 23 August; l. 29 August; l. 3 September.
Zabolotsky	p. 23 July; l. 10 August.
Levin	p. 12 July; p. 21 July; l. 24 July; l. 2 August; l. 17 September.
TAM	l. 20 July; l. 2 August; l. 23 August; l. 3 September; l. 10 September.
Zhitkov	p. 20 July; l. 31 July; l. 3 September.
Esther	
Panteleev	p. 23 July; l. 10 August; l. 18 September.
Vladimirova	l. 24 August; l. 18 September.
Gorky	l. 26 July.
Mashenka	l. 6 August.
A.S. Ivanter	l. 10 August.
Bashilov	l. 11 August.
Papernaya	p. 11 August.
Shvarts	l. 11 August.

* * *

July 20, received Natasha's letter of the 17th. First letter.

* * *

[Letter to Aleksei Ivanovich Yeremeev, "L. Panteleev"]

Dear Aleksei Ivanovich,

Kursk is a really nasty town, I prefer the transit prison. All the local residents here take me for an idiot. When I'm out on the street, they invariably say something as I pass. Therefore, I spend almost all my time sitting in my room. In the evenings I sit and read Jules Verne and during the day I don't do much of anything.

I live in the same house as Vvedensky, and I'm not at all happy about it. Behind our house there are fruit trees. At the moment there are a lot of cherries there.

Forgive me for writing such a vapid postcard, but at the moment I don't have the inspiration for a letter.

Greetings to Marshak.

Daniil Kharms

♄, July 23, 1932. 16 Pervyshevskaya Street, Kursk.

* * *

[Letter to Tamara Meier-Lipavskaya]

☽ August 1, 1932. Kursk.

Dear Tamara Aleksandrovna, Valentina Efimovna, Leonid Savelievich, Yakov Semyonovich and Valentina Efimovna,

Give my best to Leonid Savelievich, Valentina Efimovna and Yakov Semyonovich.

How are you all, Tamara Aleksandrovna, Valentina Efimovna, Leonid Savelievich and Yakov Semyonovich? What's Valentina Efimovna up to? You must write, Tamara Aleksandrovna, and tell me how Yakov Semyonovich and Leonid Savelievich are feeling.

I really miss you, Tamara Aleksandrovna, and also Valentina Efimovna and Leonid Savelievich and Yakov Semyonovich. So tell me, is Leonid Savelievich still at the dacha or has he already returned? If he's already returned, please give him my best. And likewise Valentina Efimovna, and Yakov Semyonovich, and Tamara Aleksandrovna. All of you are so memorable that at times it seems I won't even be able to forget you. Valentina Efimovna stands before my eyes as if alive and even Leonid Savelievich seems alive. Yakov Semyonovich is like my own brother and sister to me, and likewise you too are like a sister or, at the very least, like a cousin. Leonid Savelievich is like a brother-in-law to me, and likewise Valentina Efimovna is also like some kind of relation.

With every step I recall you, now one, now the other, and always with such clarity and precision that it's simply horrible. But none of you appears to me in my dreams, and I even wonder why this should be. For after all, if Leonid Savelievich had appeared to me in a dream, that would be one thing, but if Yakov Semyonovich had, that would have been something quite different. You can't disagree with that. And likewise, if I had dreamt of you, it would have been another thing again than if Valentina Efimovna had appeared to me in a dream.

Let me tell you what's been happening lately! I, just imagine, had just gotten ready to go somewhere and had taken my hat to put it on, suddenly I take a look, the hat somehow isn't mine, somehow it's mine and somehow it isn't mine. Damn it! I think, what's the story here? Is it my hat or not mine? And I keep putting the hat on over and over again. But when I put the hat on and look into the mirror, well I see that the hat seems to be mine. And I think to myself: and what if it's not mine? Although, on the other hand, perhaps it is mine. Well, it turned out that the hat is definitely mine. And also when Vvedensky was swimming in the river, he swam into a fisherman's net and got so deeply depressed that as soon as he got free, he instantly came home and sneezed. Please write and let me know how you're doing. How is Leonid Savelievich, still at the dacha or has he returned yet?

Daniil Kharms

* * *

Owed to:

Vvedensky	- 1 r. for bread, 20 k. for apples.
Vvedensky	- 8 r. 80 k. due August 10.

Expenses

August 4		August 6	
mail	15 k.	Bread	1 r. 20 k.
Café	1 r. 75 k.	dinner	3 r. 85 k.
Cookies	1 r.	matches	30 k.
Cutlet	<u>1 r.</u>	tobacco	2 r. 80 k.
	3 r. 80 k.	apples	40 k.
		gingerbread	1 r. 05 k.
		garden	<u>50 k.</u>
			10 r. 10 k.

August 5		August 7	
Shoemaker	1 r.	Bread	1 r. 80 k.
Dinner	3 r. 80 k.	Tomatoes	30 k.
Rent	<u>15 r.</u>	Suet	1r. 50 k
	19 r. 80 k.	Herring	<u>1r. 50 k.</u>
			6 r. 10 k.

* * *

Black suit (3)
Grey suit (3)
Grey jacket with short pants. Vest.
Dark grey cotton-silk jacket,
  short trousers, long trousers, vest.
Grey trousers.
Striped vest.
3 white vests.
Black boots.
Brown shoes, rubber soles
  black, light.
Leggings, black, brown.
Socks, 4 pair.
6 white shirts.
3 colored silk shirts with collars.
12 pair socks.
4 starched collars.
Dark summer overcoat.
Dark hat.
Light hat.
4 pair silk underwear.   Belts
3 pair gloves.   Suspenders
2 handkerchiefs.
6 sheets.
Plaid.

stick-pins for ties.
cuff links.

Gillette razor.

Sharpening stone.
  2 regular razors.

Macintosh.
  Gold chronometer with
    black chain.
Ring.
2 pipes.
  Tobacco-pouch.
  Wallet.
  2 amber cigarette-holders.

Three-shot rifle
Revolver, 6.
Binoculars.
Suitcase.
Compass.
2 pen knives.
Hunting knife.
Double-barrel.
Walking stick.

* * *

Make a figure out of windows ⊟.

First proposition.
"My lips are sealed."

Second proposition.
"My lips will be opened for the highest wisdom, to strength and to light."

* * *

[Letter to Aleksei Ivanovich Yeremeev, "L. Panteleev"]

☿, August 10, 1932, Kursk.

Dear Aleksei Ivanovich,

I just got your letter. I'm very happy to hear that you've been going swimming and lying in the sun. Here there's neither sun, nor anywhere to go swimming. It's rainy and windy here all the time and not at all like Petersburg. Incidentally, my mood is in no way gloomy. I feel good and at peace, but only as long as I'm sitting in my room. All I have to do is take a walk outside and I come back feeling spiteful and irritated. But that happens rarely, since I go out only once every 3 days, and that's just to the post office and back. At home, I think, write and read a lot. That's right, I'm not just reading Jules Verne. Now I'm working on something big called "Don Juan." So far I've finished only the prolog and a portion of the first part. I'm not very happy with what I've written. But then again I have completed two treatises on numbers. I'm completely satisfied with them. I've managed to deduce two theorems, then refute them, then refute the refutation, and then refute that. On this basis it has proven possible to deduce another two theorems. This is a gymnastic move, but it's not simply gymnastics. The direct consequences to these theorems are too material to be simply gymnastics. One consequence, for example, is the determination of absolute zero. My conclusions turned out to be so unexpected that, thanks to them, I've begun to look a lot like a "natural thinker." And moreover a "natural thinker" from the town of Kursk. Soon it will be entirely in my power to take up squaring the circle and trisecting an angle.

I've always been quite fond of the work of untutored scientists. But now it's beginning to get dangerous.

I haven't written anything yet for *Young Guard* but now, perhaps, I will.

What *is* up, as you write, with Marshak? Still, it's impossible to make him into something he isn't. Give him a line of poetry a day to read, he'll come up with a way to spend all day and night on it. On just that line, he'll create a theory, projects, plans, and will make it into an event of universal significance.

For people like him, nothing goes to waste. Every little bit becomes a part of a unified whole. You can't imagine how much responsibility there is in eating a tomato! Another person will live an entire life yet have less to answer for. My warmest greetings to Marshak. I still haven't written him a single letter. But that just means that up to now it hasn't been necessary. Greetings to Lydia Chukovskaya.

Daniil Kharms

Aleksei Ivanovich, thanks for your touching concern for me. If I do write something that will fit in a letter, I'll send it to you.
D. Kh.

* * *

~~Daniil Kharms~~
~~August 12, 1932.~~
~~Daniil Kharms~~

On the night between August 12 and 13, from ♃ to ♀ I had a dream as I was falling asleep. I walk from an asphalt courtyard into a house. In the doorway of the house are several cats, all grey. One is licking another under her tail. I looked and woke up. The phrase "many significant changes" resounded in my ears. I started to fall asleep again and saw a small black kitten appear to run into the hay. I made an effort and . . . woke up.

Saturday, August 13, towards the evening, I didn't feel very well.

Sunday, August 14, I realized I was sick. Head ached and I felt feverish.

* * *

August 18 ♃, received a package.

Received *Der Golem.*

Have determined that I have pleurisy in my right lung. D. Kh.
August 18.

* * *

On ☿ August 17, around 11:00 pm, I was lying in bed reading and suddenly felt a shock. My heart was pounding and I felt strange. All day long my temperature hovered around 98.6 F. I began to feel sick. I asked the landlady for Valerian drops. I felt terribly *weak and my heart was pounding.* Aleksandr Ivanovich wasn't at home. He was in Yamskaya. He was supposed to come back from there by local train. I could hear the rumbling of the local through an open window. I listened: when is it going to stop? I lay there, afraid to move and waited for A. I. When he arrived, we spoke for a bit, drank some tea, and I calmed down, but still had a feeling of nervous exhaustion. I couldn't fall asleep for a long time. Thought I was losing my mind. And my soul had nothing to sustain it. Someone's hand was pressing on the back of my head and my thoughts fluttered like my heart. I called out to God, but my thoughts were racing and I started thinking about something else. I am a cowardly dog, a pathetic Doubting Thomas. I abandoned the hearth and ran in terror. I was afraid to put the lamp out and lay there, whispering prayers in fear. I fell asleep at about 4 in the morning.

Determined that my disease is appendicitis.
August 19.

Today is August 23 and I've still got a fever. At noon it was 99.1 F. I'm positive beyond all doubt that I've got consumption. What else can it be with a fever like this?

* * *

Psalm of captivity, 136.
Gratitude to God and reliance on Him, 94-97, 135, 137-150.
Sublime psalm, 138.
Praise to the Creator, 147, 148.
Psalm about the universe, 103.
Songs of ascent, 119-133.

5 Parts.

* * *

I am alone. Aleksandr Ivanovich goes out somewhere every evening, while I remain alone. The landlady goes to sleep early and locks her room. The neighbors sleep behind four doors and I sit alone in my tiny room and light a kerosene lamp. I do nothing: an animal fear comes over me. These days I stay home because I've caught cold and have the flu. I've had a slight temperature for a week already and my lower back aches.

But why does my back ache, why hasn't the temperature gone down in a week, what is ailing me, and what should I do? I think about this, listen to my body and begin to be afraid. My heart begins to quake from fear, my legs get cold, and fear grabs me by the back of my head. I only now realize what it means. The back of my head is being crushed from below and it seems to me: just a little more and my entire head will be crushed from above, that's when you lose the ability to notice your condition and you go out of your mind. A weakness spreads throughout your entire body, starting from the feet. And suddenly a thought flashes in my mind: and what if this isn't coming from the fear, but the fear's coming from this? Then it gets even more frightening. I can't even think of anything else. I try to read. But what I'm reading suddenly becomes transparent and again I see my fear. If only Aleksandr Ivanovich would come back soon! But there's no point in expecting him any sooner than two hours from now. Now he's out with Elena Petrovna, explaining his views on love to her.

[From notebook 23]

Saturday ♄, August 27, 1932. Woke up at 10 o'clock. Slept 6 hours. Safonova came by at 12 o'clock. We drank black coffee. Then S. left. I read Leskov's *The Bypassed.* Aleksandr Ivanovich and I lunched on barley kasha with butter. At 5:00 I went to the doctor. She promised to see me tomorrow at 2 o'clock. Was with A. I. at Erbshtein and Gershov's new apartment. A. I. went with S. for a walk. E., G. and I had supper at the student cafeteria. Then we went to my place and drank coffee. A. I. returned at 10:30. He didn't feel very well.

* * *

It's now 2 o'clock in the morning. I did nothing good today.

☉, August 28. Woke up at 9:30. There was a draft coming into the room through the partition. Lying in bed, I began to read Leskov's *The Enchanted Wanderer*. Then the draft starts up again. How I hate drafts. If I lived in my own house, I would board up all the windows and put springs on all the doors.

ʃ Got up at 12:30. Feel pretty weak. Stomach hurts a little. Today the butter ran out. Only 4 rubles left. Have to give 3 to the doctor, and I have only one ruble left. I went to see the doctor at 2 o'clock. It turns out that she's a specialist in female disorders. Erbshtein has a doctor he knows. I went to E. to ask him to take me to this doctor, Katz. But E. couldn't be bothered. I went with A. I. to the Tuberculosis clinic. They sent us to the out-patient department. From there they sent us to another department. We went home. Got on a tram but there was no power and the tram just stood there. I didn't like this so I started walking. On the way (had to make it over two hills) my heart started to bother me. I almost lost consciousness. I caught my breath at the post office and slowly made my way back home. Pain on the left side of my chest. And A. I. arrived shortly afterwards. He had received a money order for 75 rubles. I took my temperature. It turned out to be 98.2 F when I held the thermometer properly. For a week and a half at this time of day, my temperature has been 99 F. Now it's 5 o'clock. Maybe it's because of my weakness. It seems my temperature is already beginning to rise. It's been less than 20 minutes since I last took it. We had macaroni and butter for dinner. Then Safonova came by. A. I. left. Safonova and I drank coffee. Safonova stayed till 11:30. I sat and sketched till 2 in the morning. A. I. got back at 2. I'm feeling weak today. Lost weight, pale. An unproductive day. A. I. was at Malenkina's. He came back in a good mood. Now it's 2:30 in the morning.

* * *

☽ , August 29, 1932. Woke up at 11 o'clock. Received a letter from Natasha. Drank milk with Aleksandr Ivanovich. We went to the market for butter. Then to the post office. Came home, weakness in body and spirit. Two o'clock. Temperature 98.4 F. Then I did nothing. Read *The Enchanted Wanderer*. A. I. was writing something, then left to find company to play *Preferans*.] At 4:30, my temperature was again 100 F. So what is this? I'm sure it's consumption. Safonova came by. I pretended I was very busy and asked her to sit and wait in A. I.'s room. But me, I'm not doing anything. Got to go see the doctor. 5:30. The signs of consumption are weakness, perspiration and slightly labored breathing. I don't feel well and I'm worried about my health. Inserted the thermometer again. Preliminary detention and exile have had some benefit. I didn't appreciate Petersburg. How far I am from salvation. My temperature is 98.4 F (5 hours 40 minutes). We had dinner. But A. I. oversalted the buckwheat kasha and I had to make do with buttered toast. Now it's 8 o'clock. Temperature 98.4 F. Sat and worked on a story. From time to time my heart's been acting up. At 9:30, temperature 98 F. Between 10 and 10:30, heart attack. I lay down and rubbed water on my chest near my heart. And it seems I've caught another cold. Read the Bible and calmed down. Vvedensky came back at midnight. We sat together till 1:30. He went off to sleep. Again some pain in the region of my heart. 1:40.

* * *

♂, August 30. Woke up at 11 o'clock. Safonova came by at 11:30. I got angry but Petersen was with her. They left. At 1:00 pm, temperature 98.6 F. All morning long I felt so weak that my legs were shaking. I went to the out-patient clinic. Barely made it: on the way my heart was pounding something awful. Waited at the clinic for 3 hours until they started seeing patients at 3. Finally, I got in to see Dr. Sheboldaeva. She found pleurisy in my right lung and acute neurosis of the heart. They applied cups. Got back home at 7 o'clock.

Had cream of wheat made with water. Safonova came. She brought a watermelon. She stayed almost till midnight. At 7:30 pm, my temperature was 99 F. It's now 1 in the morning. My tooth is aching and my head a little too. I slept badly and woke up at 6 o'clock. The pleurisy, apparently, has gotten worse. I lit a lamp and lit up a pipe. Temperature 98.2 F. That means it will go higher during the day. ⌡

August 31 ☿ . Woke up at 10:30. The landlady's son is back. Raining outside. I got up. Drank coffee. 1:40. ⌡

At 6:30, Safonova and Petersen came over. We drank coffee. At 8:30, Petersen left. Safonova stayed till 11:30. Vvedensky came at 11. Rain. I drew an airship. Went to bed at 2.

♃, September 1. Woke up at 11 o'clock. Got up at 12 o'clock. Drank coffee. Ate tomatoes. Drew an airship. ⌡ Had rice for dinner. S. dropped by at 8 o'clock, but the way I received her she left immediately. Drew apartments. V. came back at midnight. He's already out of money. I think he lost it gambling. Went to sleep at 1:30.

* * *

♀, September 2, 1932. Woke up at 10:15. No letters for a long time. No money. Hunger begins now. I do nothing all the time. I feel psychologically weak. ⌡ Today there was ⌡ nothing to eat. Safonova came by in the evening. Temperature 98.6 F. Then Erbshtein. When E. and S. left, I put the thermometer in again. At 12 o'clock, temperature 99 F. These days I walk around wheezing. Voice weak. There's a thumping on my right side. Rubbed myself with turpentine ointment and applied mustard plasters. It's now 2 o'clock in the morning. Now it's 2:50.

* * *

[Letter to Tamara Meier-Lipavskaya]

September 2, 1932. Kursk.

Dear Tamara Aleksandrovna,

How is your health? Aleksandr Ivanovich read your letter and right then and there sneezed. Really what is it with your kidneys? I've been thinking on this subject for a long time but have not arrived at any positive results. The kidneys, as is known, serve to eliminate harmful substances from one's organism and in appearance resemble beans. What can possibly happen to them? In any case, you've been played a pretty good trick. What does a dislocated kidney even mean? For the sake of clarity, imagine, for example, that you and Valentina Efimovna are two kidneys. And suddenly one of you begins to dislocate yourself. What does that mean? Absurd. Instead of Valentina Efimovna, take Leonid Savelievich, Yakov Semyonovich or anyone you like. All the same, you're left with nonsense of the purest sort. I've sent congratulations to Valentina Efimovna. Whatever she is, still, I think, she ought to be congratulated.

Daniil Kharms

* * *

♄, September 3. Woke up at 10:20. Pain in the lower lungs, in front. I guess my pleurisy isn't going away.

I positively can't do anything here. I'm sick in spirit and body.

Today again no letters. I'm worried.

I'm sitting here without money and have nothing to eat.

A. I. has received a package from home: vermicelli and rolls. I went for a walk to the ravine. We drank coffee with milk and rolls. A. I. broke my porcelain spoon. Slept during the day. I'm feeling a perfectly impossible weakness today. I've lost a lot of weight and gotten very pale. At 4 o'clock my temperature was 99 F. I went again to the out-patient clinic to see the nerve doctor, Chekanov. He said that I have neurosis of the heart and that, in general, my nerves are shot. He ordered me to live right and to eat well. He said that my pleurisy isn't gone yet. That's the crux of the matter. Came back home. Instead of dinner, drank coffee. Not feeling very well. Sluggish, sweating, weakness. First my back hurts, then my shoulders. Then pounding in my chest. In the evening, played chess with the landlady's son, then talked till 12:30. It's my first real conversation with him. I'm very nervous and concerned about my health. I feel feverish all the time.

* * *

⊙, September 4. ♪♪♪ Drew all day. Temperature 99 F. Back hurts. S. came over but I ~~kicked her out~~ wouldn't see her. In the evening I wrote about Bobov. We had vermicelli with butter for dinner. Went to sleep at 2 o'clock.

*　*　*

☽, September 5. Still no letters. Worried.

When I was locked in a two-man cell with Aleksandr Petrovich, I wanted to be with Vvedensky more than anything else. Now that I'm living with Vvedensky, more than anything I want to be with Aleksandr Petrovich. Never ever wish for anything.

Today I look really bad. Powerful weakness. I walked as far as the post office and broke out in a terrible sweat. Washed the dishes and my back began to ache again. I feel very poorly. And everywhere the drafts are terrible. I simply don't know what to do. And I'm eating very badly. Strictly speaking, I'm eating one meal a day and not always that. I drew during the day. ♪ No letters.

Temperature at 5:30, 99 F.
There goes the postwoman. I wonder if there will be any letters.
Received 25 rubles from papa and gave Vvedensky the 10 rubles I owed him. 9:40 in the evening. Lying in bed. Feel poorly. Getting weaker every day. This can't go on. I'm reading the Negro novel *Home to Harlem*. Today I'll probably catch cold again. Seems that my temperature is rising. Inserted the thermometer. Sent letters to Natasha and Papa today. Temperature 99.3 F., even though I took aspirin this afternoon.

I don't feel well at all and am terribly worried about my health. My temperature will probably go up again in the evening. 9:45.

10 o'clock, temperature 99 F. Cross and Mary, Cross and Mary, Cross and Mary!

11:30, temperature 99.1 F.
Sweating heavily. Thoughts muddy. Movements nervous, jerky. I'm drawing. Vvedensky's back.

12 o'clock. Hands feel hot. Sweating.

1:20. Drank tea with A. I. The conversation wasn't interesting. Head aching a bit, some kind of weakness in my head. Thoughts horribly muddy. Overall, an unpleasant feeling. I think I've got the flu again. When I take a deep breath, you can hear the phlegm whistling in my chest. Nothing in my back or my sides hurts right now, but from time to time there's an ache around my collarbone and below my nipples. My legs are weak and lethargic. My face is sweaty and is sensitive to the slightest breeze, my sense is that I'm feeling the cold breeze because my face is pale and anemic. Temperature 98.4 F.

2:30. Wrote captions for drawings. ⌡ Rubbed myself with ointment. Put on clean long johns and a sweater. The landlady's son just returned home. Should go to bed but don't feel like sleeping. Judging by all the signs, I'm going to feel even worse tomorrow and my temperature will be higher than 99 F.

* * *

♂, September 6. Woke up at 11:30. At 11:45, temperature 98.6 F. Wheezing in the chest when I breathe. And still, perhaps, with God's help, I'll begin to feel better now.

A. I. and I have switched bedrooms. O my God, there were so many bedbugs in A. I.'s bed! All day long I battled with them, stripped the wallpaper, and washed everything down with kerosene. Now the room is tidy. The card-table that I use as a writing desk is cozily covered with green cloth. The writing supplies, all of them mine, that I brought from Petersburg, are on the desk. A small walnut box with tobacco. My silver pocket watch ticks. On the wall hangs a lamp, on it a shade with cabbalistic characters. And outside the window, a garden. Everywhere it's quiet. Only from time to time trains sing on the Yamskaya line.

I got a letter today from Zhitkov.

10:30 in the evening. Back aching. Temperature 98.8 F.
A. I. is in what was my, now his room with Malenkina. In what was his, now my room, I'm planning to read some poems by Goethe.

* * *

♀ ,September 7. Got up at 9 o'clock. Rained during the night. Very worried about Natasha. Why no letters? It's already been 9 days without a letter from Natasha.

Made coffee. Head pretty dull and weak. Any minute now I'll start sweating.

12 o'clock. Temperature 98.4 F.

2:45. Temperature 99.3 F. Sweating.

J
Oh, how I hate Vvedensky.

There's almost nothing left to eat today. Received a letter from T.A.M. Vedensky went to see Dr. Chekanov.

Vvedensky's back. The doctor advised him to eat better.

Erbstein came by. He and V. are going to a party somewhere. They'll stop off at Safonova's. I've asked them to tell her I'm not expecting her today.

8:30. Feel very poorly. Weakness, the back of my head is aching and my thoughts are muddy. Difficulty breathing. Sweating. Forehead and hands moist all the time. I'm very worried. Temperature 99.3 F.

I'm hungry. Want to eat.

Safonova came at 9 o'clock, she brought a piece of bread. We drank coffee. I didn't feel quite well but better than an hour ago. Safonova left around midnight, and Vvedensky showed up. Depressing that tomorrow it will again be the same, the same lethargy, fever and hunger. V. and S. are planning to go mushrooming tomorrow. O Lord, do not forsake me in my fallenness. Comfort me and give me strength.

Temperature 98.6 F. Didn't keep the thermometer in beyond that. But sometimes it happens that you keep it in for 10 minutes and it shows one temperature, but then five minutes later it adds another 2 or 3 degrees. O Lord, heal me from sickness, but Thy Will be done. 12:30 o'clock.

* * *

♃, September 8. Only 4 rubles left. No letters from home. Nothing to eat. Ate leftover buckwheat kasha without butter. A. I. left to go mushrooming. At 1 o'clock in the afternoon, temperature 99 F. Cold outside but sunny. V. and S. came back. They brought mushrooms. They're acting as if they own the place. We ate millet kasha with mushrooms. I received a money order for 75 rubles from Natasha. Bought a bottle of Riesling for 6 r. 80 k. After the wine, a pleasant feeling. O Lord, may my spirit be gladdened for Thy sake.

O Lord, raise me up in Thy spirit and fill my body with joy.

Praise to Thee, O Lord, from rocks, from grass, from flowers, from trees; from fish, from birds, from animals; and man also sings Thy praise, and I glorify Thy name.

7:40, temperature 99.1 F.

At 1 o'clock in the morning, temperature 99 F.

* * *

♀, September 9. Received 2 letters from Natasha and one from Lydia Vladimirova. Drank coffee with milk and ate bread and butter. At 1 pm my temperature was 99 F. Wrote a letter to Natasha. This constant fever has made me weak and depressed. 3 o'clock in the afternoon, temperature 99 F. Received another letter from T.A.M. No dinner, but had some dried fish. Really bored today. Sick and tired of sitting around doing nothing and feeling ill. Feeling queasy. The only people I see are S. and V. And both are boring. My only comfort is the Bible. Today I read about Joseph.

6 hours 40 minutes, temperature 99 F. Holy Seraphim of Saratov, deliver me from illness. Cure me, Seraphim of Saratov!

9:30, Suddenly felt ɟ weakness. Temperature 99.1 F. O Lord, what is this?

9—11, Safonova was here.

11:30, temperature 98.4 F.

* * *

ℏ, September 10. Woke up at 10:30.

11:45, temperature 98 F.
Drank coffee. Ate bread and butter.
1 in the afternoon, temperature 99.1 F.

Today I can't see straight and my heart is pounding. Oh, the anxiety and pain! O Lord, O Lord! Why dost Thou test me so fearfully?

2:10, temperature 99 F.

Feel very poorly. Weakness and sweating. And my sides are aching and I want to eat.
3:40. Temperature 99.1 F.

Went to the clinic. Signed up to see Dr. Katz and went for a walk. Stopped in at the café. Drank milk and ate an egg. Stormy outside. Rain. Went to my appointment with Katz. Katz found pleurisy. No consumption, he said. Prescribed Phytin. Gershov was here in the evening. Erbshtein dropped by very late.

[From notebook 22]

O Teacher! Teacher! Come to me today. Today is the day of Saturn, Saturday, and the sun shines within me. I have pined away in my ignorance. Who will say the word to me, who will comfort me by his wisdom?
O Teacher! Teacher! I am thy disciple. Come to me today. Come, come, quickly, come quickly!
Saturday, September 10.
1932.

Saturday, September 10. Woke up at 10:30 and immediately realized that I would have a fever today. At first I felt ok, but no sooner had I moved than a barely perceptible chill run down my spine. In my legs, my calves, just the opposite, they felt warm, and my arms started to burn, perspiration covered my shoulders and the palms of my hands began to sweat. I felt a heaviness in my forehead and head. And then fear appeared.
10:50. Temperature 98 F.

I've lost all fear. I dropped it like a handkerchief. I even feared that there was no fear, but now even that fear is gone. The room filled up, from the doors to the window, with holy fathers, and there was no more fear in me. O Holy Fathers, Archangels and Thrones, I am unworthy of your converse. But my love of your wisdom is great.

Signs of disease have been found in me. Today I felt especially unwell. Pain in my chest and weakness. On top of that, I'm terribly agitated. My daytime temperature was 99.9 F, and 98.6 F in the evening. I calmed down a bit while S. was here. Getting into bed at 12:30 am, I spat up some brownish phlegm. That's coughing up blood.

* * *

[From notebook 23]

Sunday, September 11. Went to the farmer's market. Bought some bread and milk. Went with A. I. to Mostorg, got a price for my cigarette case (33 r.). Went to the library. Met a young lady from the foreign literature section.

Sent Natasha a letter. Came home. Tired, sweaty, and gray. Maria Petersen came by. We drank coffee. P. left. A. I. was at Valya's relatives. He had dinner there. I've got 10 rubles left.

7 o'clock. Temperature 99 F. Safonova came by. Talked about her childhood. She left at 11:30. Malenkina is with A. I..

Midnight. Temperature. 98.4 F.

* * *

Monday, September 12. Got up at 8:30. Ran into Petersen. She stopped by at my place. We went to the Cathedral of Saint Sergius. Then I went with Vvedensky to Mostorg, sold the clasp from my watch chain and my cuff-links. Had a bite to eat in the student cafeteria. We bought about 18 lbs of flour, a kilo of rye, and a kilo of cooking oil at Torgsin. Then we visited the priest from the monastery cathedral. At home we made pancakes. I'm feeling weak and my chest hurts.

4 o'clock. Temperature 99.1 F.

At 6 o'clock, I went to the Church of St. Sergius. There was a funeral service going on.

6:25. Sweating, weakness, and fever. Plus my head's in a fog and feels heavy. All in all, nothing's changed.

6:40. Temperature 99 F.

Reading Hamsun.
Ate pancakes with V.
Feeling unwell. Head in a stupor.
11 o'clock. Temperature 98.8 F.

* * *

Tuesday, September 13. Woke up feeling tired all though my body. Sweat heavily during the night. Got a letter from Zabolotsky. Weather getting worse.

11:15. Temperature 98.6 F.
Feeling unwell. Aches and pains in my chest and sides. The main thing is how my head feels. A weakness in the back of my head and my thoughts sluggish. I lay down and slept during the day. Just woke up. I have to cook some pancakes. My temperature really worries me.
O Lord! Do not torment me.
3 o'clock. Temperature 99.1 F.

In A. I.'s room my temperature turns out to be 99.1 F. Erbshtein dropped by drunk with some hooligan. I threw both of them out. We made pancakes.
I feel dullness in my head and grayness in my face.
6:30. Reading Hamsun. Feel weakness and trembling.
In A. I.'s room, my temperature is 99.3 F.
At 7 o'clock, my temperature is 99.7 F.

Oh, I'm so worried about my health. There's consumption in Kursk, it's very serious. Must muster all my courage. Each day my temperature goes higher. It's not even ordinary tuberculosis, but galloping consumption.

I'm covered in a cold sweat from fear. The constant fear and constant fever. I really must be strong since I haven't yet lost my mind.

8 o'clock. Temperature, 99.5 F.
Safonova came by. She had x-rays taken. The results are negative. Nothing terrible. We made pancakes. Around eleven, temperature 99.1 F.

As I was talking about something, I raised my voice and a weakness suddenly spread out from my chest through my entire body. Feel unwell. There's a wheezing from under my collarbone. S. left at midnight. Malenkina was in A. I.'s room. We have no tobacco. Now it's 1:30 in the morning. A. I. took M. home and brought back a pinch of tobacco. Smoking my pipe. Powerful weakness and lethargy.

Nighttime. I don't like it when the clock says it's thirteen minutes to something or 13 minutes after something. So I woke up during the night and was frightened. I decided to light the lamp, but then I thought about the thirteen minutes. I wavered for a long time. Finally I got up and lit the lamp. It was thirteen minutes after five.
My side aches a little.

Wednesday, September 14. Felt ok in the morning. But at 12:30, I began feeling that something was wrong. It starts in my head. Must be the fever rising again. I'm lying on my bed reading Hamsun. I shaved and went with A. I. to the private clinic to see Dr. Kozlova. Kozlova sounded my chest very attentively and found evidence of disease in my right lung. She referred me to Dr. Sheindels, who has an extraordinarily sharp sense of hearing. Returned home at 8:30. Wrote letters. For a long time I was too agitated to fall asleep.
At 2:30, I was still awake.

* * *

Thursday, September 15. Woke up at 9 o'clock. Coughed up a thick stream of phlegm. I was quite worried. At 9:40, my temperature is 98 F. The weather's cool. At 12 o'clock, my temperature was 99 F. Drank milk and ate pancakes this morning. ɟ At 2:30 ate more pancakes. Now the kerosene's run out. I'm sitting in the rocking chair. The window's open. Eyes crossing. Cheeks burning. I feel a tightness in my upper lungs. Quite agitated. I've lost a lot of weight and my ring is swimming every which way on my finger. Can't do anything. All my thoughts are about my illness. Because there's no kerosene left, there'll be no dinner today. Head heavy.

O God, why hast Thou turned Thy face from me.
Hands cold. O Lord, do not abandon me.

At 3:30, temperature 99.3 F.
S. was here this evening. I talked with her and calmed down a little. But couldn't fall asleep till 4 in the morning. I was terribly agitated.

* * *

September 16. This morning I went ~~with S.~~ to the tuberculosis clinic. Dr. Sheindels is the director there, but he doesn't see patients. Was at S's. Went with V. to Torgsin and sold a stick-pin.

In the evening I went to Dr. Sheindel's home. He's a good doctor. He found signs of disease in the left lung. He ordered tests and promised to arrange everything free of charge. Returned home very anxious. Didn't get to sleep for a long time. Agitated.
Spent the evening with S., E. and A. I.

* * *

September 17. In the morning I went for the tests. Slept only 4 hours last night. Returned home. Feel unwell. Very weak. Lying in bed.

S. came by.

Although I haven't slept for 2 nights, I don't feel like sleeping. My right lung is bothering me. Nervous. Yesterday evening E. V. arrived in town with her oldest son. At 10:30 S. left. Feeling very unwell. Legs trembling.

At 11 o'clock, I started to feel a little better. Fell asleep at 12. Slept badly, kept waking up and tossing in my sleep. At 5:30 in the morning, I lit the lamp. Can't sleep. I'm afraid of dreams so I'm sitting in bed with a lamp. 6 o'clock. Shivering and don't feel like sleeping. I fell asleep later, but slept badly. Woke up at 9:30.

* * *

September 18. Sunday. Horrible mood. Drank milk. Ate bread and butter. Cheeks burning. Body trembling. What cowardice.

Safonova was here. S. and V. made meat broth. At 7 o'clock they both left to drink plum brandy. I was reading in bed but felt disgusting. I look awful today. Gotten terribly skinny.

Went to bed at 9 o'clock.

* * *

[Letter to Aleksei Ivanovich Yeremeev, "L. Panteleev"]

September 18, 1932

Dear Aleksei Ivanovich,

This letter won't be all that much fun either. I've been sick for more than a month already. It turns out I have tuberculosis. Lately it's gotten worse, every day my temperature creeps up. In view of this, I can't write anything for State Publishing at the moment. It's very hard to keep to a regular regimen here, therefore my situation is rather serious.

I'm very happy that you saw Bashilov. I like his aphorisms. I sent him a letter, but haven't heard back.

If Marshak is in the city, please say hello for me.

Hello to Tamara Grigorievna.

Daniil Kharms

* * *

September 19. Woke up at eight. Powerful weakness. Woke up several times during the night, but slept fairly peacefully. Appetite weak but I forced myself to eat bread and butter and a little piece of onion.

At night I dreamt that I caught a cat, beat it terribly, first with my fists, then a whip, and threw it away.

Safonova came by. We cooked cabbage soup. A. I., S. and I had dinner. I feel weak, the left side of my chest hurts. Around 5:30 I went to the clinic for an x-ray. Powerful weakness on the tram. The x-ray machine wasn't working today. Went to see Sheindels, who had already received results of the blood and phlegm tests. He found nothing in the phlegm, neither bacilli, nor elastic filaments. Returned home and found S. and V. there. But they left soon after. Was feeling comparatively better this evening.

Went to bed around 10 o'clock. But couldn't sleep. Started perspiring terribly. Unable to sleep, I tossed and turned the entire night, covered in sweat.

* * *

September 20. Woke up at 7:30. Weakness, and anxiety that I've become so terribly thin. Went to early morning service at Kazan Cathedral, prayed to St. Serafim of Saratov. Returned home feeling weak. Pain in my upper chest.

10:30. Terrible weakness. Everything is trembling inside me, while my face and cheeks are burning. Feel disgusting. Beastly thin and grey. Temperature has reached 100.6 F.
S. was here.

At 5:00, I went for the x-ray. My head was spinning and my heart was pounding. After the x-ray. I went to Sheindels. The x-ray showed only a slight darkening of the upper left lung. Sheindels examined me again and ordered bed rest for 4 days. This evening I felt better.

* * *

Wednesday, September 21. Nosovich and S. came by. Nosovich didn't believe the thermometer. Got another and that one read lower.

* * *

Thursday, September 22. Woke up at 8. Sleeping badly. Money gone. I have all of 2 rubles left. Hunger setting in. ʃ

11:00. Sat down at my desk, but my head was spinning. Got back into bed again. Cooking rice.

* * *

[Letter to Tamara Meier-Lipavskaya]

September 25, 1932, Kursk.

Dear Tamara Aleksandrovna,

Perhaps it's quite stupid on my part to write like this but in my opinion you have always been very beautiful. Believe it or not, it's the truth. I'm even convinced of it. Yes, that's what I think.

I don't want to be funny or original, but I continue to maintain that you are 100 points ahead of any not especially good-looking woman. Granted, I am the first to have appreciated your beauty. I don't count on having any followers. Oh no! But should I be alone in this opinion, I will not renounce it.

This is not stubbornness. And as to what people will think of me, I don't give a rat's ass.

I hear from your letter that you dropped your nose and busted it. Pity. Still, that's a real loss. Loss of symmetry. Those around you may take advantage of your fleeting defect.

Valentina is a match for you. A good looking woman. Luxuriant hair, mouth, eyes. . . . It's amazing that a crowd of admirers has not yet laid siege to her door. Is it her walk? Her figure? What's the reason here? Why does every man turn up his nose?

Ignorance of taste?

Leonid is no Apollo, he has a multitude of deficiencies. But still, you've got to admit that it was a skillful architect who put him together. His miniature form, bordering on frailty, cannot be called perfection. But perfection is a dead lion, while Leonid is a living dog. I salute your choice of Leonid! You've managed to found a pearl in a manure pit!

Yakov inspires warm feelings. He's a student who shows some real promise.

Yakov! I implore you! Gnaw granite! And you, Tamara Aleksandrovna, give him your support! Instill hope into his consciousness, which for ages has harbored an idea of affairs, affairs of honor, debt and über-morality, of knowledge which overfills earthly existence, an existence obliged to depict all those human passions that have waged war with such cruelty against those human designs which in unremitting currents fill to overflowing the habitation of our thought. . . .

Tamara Aleksandrovna, Yakov is the very soul of society itself! The East!

Let Nikolai sing the praises of your beauty, Tamara Aleksandrovna. And, were I Goliath, I would reach up to the heavens and there, on the clouds, write your name.

So be it! Let people laugh and say that I have a scrawny neck and a barrel chest. A decent man won't laugh at this. I'm now taking cod liver oil!

I'm not speaking about myself now, but about you, about your beauty, Tamara Aleksandrovna!

You call attention to yourself!

Daniil Kharms

* * *

☽ September 26. Safonova ran into the room as A. I. and I were drinking tea. She has to leave town. They're sending almost everyone away. S. is crying and saying she doesn't want to live like this anymore. She came back later. She had already calmed down a bit. She has to go to Vologda. We boiled and ate some meat.

* * *

♃ September 29. A. I. went to the GPU and also asked to be sent to Vologda. They gave him permission.

* * *

September 30. ♀ Celebrated Nosovich's name day at Safonova's. I like Aleksei Savchenko. Whenever he wants to say something, his right eye starts winking in a funny sort of way.

♄ October 1. This morning I stood in the garden in the autumn sun. Then I walked around town and looked for someplace to have dinner. Ran into Sheindels. He looks a lot like Marshak. At 5 in the evening A. I. got money and decided to leave with Safonova this very day. I helped them haul their things and accompanied them to the train station at Yamskaya. Even Nosovich came to see them off. I walked up and down the waiting rooms at the station and watched A. I. get tickets. Sofia Nosovich and I left on the 11 o'clock local train. S. and A. I.'s train was supposed to leave at midnight. I accompanied Nosovich to her home and returned to my Pervyshevskaya street. Now I am all alone.

* * *

☉ October 2. Stayed home almost all day. Read and thoughts things over. Didn't do a thing. Lounged on the bed and sat like a lump at the table. Boiled myself some macaroni. Went to bed at 11 o'clock. Big storm at night. I woke up and watched the lightning flashing. But soon fell asleep again.

* * *

☽ October 3. Sat on a bench in an empty city park. On the ground lie yellow leaves. I sat and smoked my pipe. Then I dropped by the museum to see the artists. Went to eat with Erbshtein. Got home in the afternoon and slept a little. Then I went to see Sheindels. He listened to my chest and found that everything is calming down little by little. We talked about Isadora Duncan. In the evening I stayed home and read. But it was hard to read. Boiled myself some rice. Am I doing the smart thing by staying in Kursk? What am I waiting for? I don't know myself what I'm waiting for.

We lived in two rooms. My friend took the smaller room, while I occupied a fairly large room with three windows. For whole days my friend would be away from home, returning to his room only to spend the night. I on the other hand would stay in my room almost all of the time and if I did go out, it was either to the post office, or to buy myself something for dinner. On top of that, I had picked up a dry pleurisy that held me rooted to the spot all the more.

I love being alone. But then a month passed, and I was sick and tired of my solitude. My book didn't divert me and when I would sit down at the desk I would often sit there for a long time without writing a single line. Again I would try to get down to the book but the paper would remain blank. And then there was also that sickening feeling. In a word, I began to get bored.

I thoroughly disliked the city in which I lived at that time. It stood on a hill with postcard views opening out in all directions. These views so repulsed me that I was even happy to stay home. To tell the truth, except for the post-office, the market and store, there was no place for me to go.

And so I stayed home like a recluse.

There were days when I had nothing to eat. Then I would try to put myself in a joyful mood. I would lie down on the bed and begin smiling. I would smile for up to twenty minutes at a time, but then the smile would turn into a yawn. This was very unpleasant. I would open my mouth just wide enough to smile but it would open wider and I would yawn. I began to daydream.

I'd see before me a clay pitcher of milk and pieces of fresh bread. I myself am sitting at the desk writing rapidly. On the desk, on the chairs and on the bed there are sheets of paper all covered with writing. But I write on, winking and smiling at my own thoughts. And how nice that next to me there are bread and milk and a walnut box with tobacco!

I open the window and look on the garden. Yellow and purple flowers grow by the door. Tobacco grows further on and there is a large military chestnut tree. That's where the fruit orchard started. It was very quiet, and you could hear trains singing below the hill.

Today I couldn't do a thing. I walked around the room, then sat down at the desk, but got up soon after and moved over to the rocking chair. I'd pick up a book, but then toss it right away and start walking around the room again.

Suddenly it seemed to me I had forgotten something, some incident or important word.

I torture myself trying to remember the word, and it even began to seem to me that the word began with the letter M. No, wait!

Not at all with M, but with R.

Reason? Rapture? Rama? Rope? Or: Mind? Misery? Material?

No, of course with the letter R, if only it is a word!

I brewed myself some coffee and went through words starting with R. Oh, how many words I put together starting with that letter! Maybe the word was among them, but I hadn't recognized it, and took it for the same as all the others. But maybe the word wasn't there at all.

Diary 1932-1933

November 22, 1932 – September 10, 1933

Tuesday November 22, 1932. 0 h. 10 minutes
astronomical time

On Saturday the following took place: In the morning I sent off a letter to Moscow as Kogan had advised me. I stopped by the City Writers' Committee to be reinstated in the union, but they asked me to drop by on the 21st. I went to see Loewenberg the violinist twice since Boris Stepanovich Zhitkov is looking for a humble violinist for a musical divertissement. But I didn't find Loewenberg at home either time. I am without money at this time, and for that reason, I dine at my sister's. And so having lunched with my sister, I went to see Chukovsky. He's republishing his book "On Little Children" and wants to include some of my poems, but not the ones that were in the first edition. Kornei Ivanovich received me with a joyful shout and then lay down on the floor next to the fireplace. He's been down with the flu and even now he's not well. He lies on the floor simply for beauty's sake, and it really is quite beautiful. I took a look at *Chukokkala* but didn't write anything there.

From Chukovsky's I went to the Cathedral of the Transfiguration. Bishop Sergius was serving. When the bishop puts on his violet robe with its wondrous stripes, he is simply transformed into a magus. Enraptured, I could hardly keep myself from bursting into tears. I stood through vespers at the Cathedral, and then went home.

I shaved, put a clean collar on and went to Poret's, where I made the acquaintance of Frau René (René Rudolfovna O'Connell-Mikhailovska)—a very nice lady. She's about 35, she's got a daughter who's 13 and a son 6 ½ years old. But she's astonishingly slim, delicate and welcoming. Her voice is gentle and at the same time a bit knowing. We drank tea from good china.

I won't write anything about Poret, but if I were to write something, I would write only the very best of her. As always, Glebova was present. There was also a certain Orest Lvovich, an acquaintance of Averbach's, but he soon left. I saw Frau René back to Vasilievsky Island. She lives in her own, small, two-room apartment. I saw her children, who were asleep in their little beds. It was two o'clock in the morning, and I went in to Frau René's room for cigarettes since I was out of tobacco. She proposed that I stay for tea, but I was afraid she might think I had some designs on her since I had exactly those kinds of designs on her. And therefore, somewhat embarrassed, I left.

I walked home, smoking, feasting my eyes on Leningrad, thinking about Frau René.

On Sunday Vvedensky and I went to the "Exhibition of All the Artists." It was already my second time there, and, as before, I liked only the Malevich. But how disgusting the painters of the "Krug" are! Even Brodsky gives you something to like. We ran into Gershov at the exhibition. I went to his place and looked at his pictures. He paints good pictures.

After dinner, Levin dropped by and we wanted to go to see Raisa Ilinishna Poliakovkskaya. But somehow we missed the tram and didn't go. Then Vvedensky and I went to a party at Evegenia Davidovna Barsh's. Papernaya was there too and sang negro spirituals. I got back home at 4 o'clock civil time (3 o'clock astronomical time).

On Monday I woke up at 12 o'clock. Frau René called and said she was going to the exhibition at 2:30. I said that I'd come too. But Boris Petrovich Kotelnikov, whom I met in the prison dispensary, came to see me, and then Nikichuk, whom I haven't seen for five years now, came too. So I didn't get to the exhibit until 3. I met Frau René there, where we saw Evgenia Ivanovna, Vvedensky's mother, who's treating Frau René. We took a turn around the exhibit. It was, in my opinion, less than interesting. Then I walked her to the tram and went home. On Nevsky I ran into Malevich, then Kelson.

I had a bite to eat and went to Zhitkov's. Oleinikov and Zabolotsky were there with some agronomist, Ivan Vasilievich from Odessa. Oleinikov has become a wonderful poet of late, and Zabolotsky is publishing a book of his poems.

As usual Oleinikov and I walked back; and I got home at one.

After coming back to Leningrad from Kursk, I started seeing Esther again. Then on Friday she came here and I went down on her and had her. After which she covered her face with a kerchief and to my question: was she angry with me? She nodded her head, but refused to explain why. Then I said I can't leave it like this, I have to know otherwise I couldn't keep seeing her. But she said nothing in that regard and left. I walked her to the tram and she left for home. In all likelihood, I've become simply repulsive to her. And of course she doesn't call me anymore and won't call me ever again.

It's already November 22, 1 hr. 20 min. astronomical time and 2 hr. 20 min. civil time.

I had just noted all this down in my diary, and then suddenly the electricity went out, which has been happening quite often lately. And so here I am, writing these lines down by candlelight. It's time to sleep. I'm not living right. I don't do anything and I go to bed much too late. Things are a bit tedious now that I've broken off with Esther; all the same, no matter how antithetical to me she is in character and upbringing, I do love Esther.

Today I got up really late. I got up half past three. Lying in bed, I phoned my various acquaintances. Boris Stepanovich promised to get me a poodle. And so in connection with that, I phoned the Brain Institute, where the poodle is supposedly located. But as it is, nothing came of it. The whole business has been put off until tomorrow.

Marshak called me and asked me to come this evening, but I had promised to be at Panteleev's. Still, you can't refuse Marshak, because it'll be a long time before you get a chance to see him again. Like it or not, I'm going to have to go see Panteleev this afternoon.

I called Alisa Ivanovna. Tomorrow is the concert of that organist. I promised to get Frau René a ticket. But what should I do? I don't have any money, and how can I get a ticket through Ivan Ivanovich? I haven't seen him since Kursk.

I also thought about Esther. I almost even called her myself. But when you've become repulsive to someone, there's nothing you can do about it. And so now Esther and I have gone our own ways forever. Even so, something in my soul tells me that we'll come together as it's meant to be.

Towards evening I went to Panteleev's. Drank a lot of wine there. Boba was there and Belykh and his brother and some other young people. So I ended up not going to Marshak's. Boba spent the night here. We got to bed late; it was already after five in the morning.

November 23, 1932. Wednesday. I had a dream Ester was here. And then we undress and go to bed and now Vvedensky comes in and also gets undressed and lies down in bed with us and is lying there between us: And I'm enraged at his lack of tact and I wake up from rage. Boba dreamt Vvedensky was with some woman too.

Boba went home, and I sat on the bed and thought about Ester. I decided to call her on the telephone, and had already made the call, but just then the telephone went out. That means that's how it's supposed to be.

Marshak called. Really awkward I wasn't there yesterday.

I just went into the kitchen and Lisa reminded me that today's the day of Ester's birth. Oh how I wanted to see her then!

I have to send her a telegram. We wanted to spend the day together here, but look how it's all turned out.

I can't understand why I love Ester so much. Everything she says to me is either rude, stupid or in bad taste, but really I still love her in spite of everything!

How many times has she cheated on me and left me, but my love for her has only gotten stronger for it.

I went to the post office and at 4 o'clock I sent a telegram: "Congratulations. Kharms." Dropped in at Loewenberg's. Found him at home. We arranged to go see Zhitkov tomorrow.

Kotelnikov came by without calling first. I nearly drove him out. You have to call before to find out: may I come over?

So I wouldn't have to wait until Thursday or Friday to see Marshak, I decided to run by and see him today. I ran in for 5 minutes. He read me a new, very fine work of his: "Mister Twister."

From Marshak's I went to the Philharmonic. In the lobby I ran into quite a lot of acquaintances, also Poret, Glebova, and Kondratiev.

Ivan Ivanovich recognized me, and treated me as a friend right off, but he couldn't get any tickets. Glebova didn't have a ticket either. I have only three rubles. We decided to buy standing room tickets. Glebova had 4 rubles, and no one else had any more money. I got into the line for tickets. The standing room tickets are all sold out and the cheapest left are 5r. 75k. But while we were thinking, these went too. I'm standing by the ticket window and had to give up my place in line 5 times. Finally I buy Glebova a ticket for

6r. 50k. And there's no more money left. At that moment Frau René comes over. And the people are crowding around and shoving at the ticket window. Frau René lends me money. She hands me a bill, it's all she has. It looks like 20 rubles to me. And then on top of this some guy in uniform asks me to buy him a ticket and gives me money. I don't count how much money there is in all, it looks to me like there's 26r. 50k. there—all of which I hand to the cashier and ask for 3 tickets at 6r. 50k. The cashier gives me back the military guy's money, and says it's too much and she gives me three tickets at 6r. 50k. I get half a ruble change, take the tickets and settle up, first of all, with the guy in uniform. I nearly shorted him. Turns out he had given me not 6, but 5 + 3 i.e. 8 rubles. I finally settled with him and I take the change to Frau René. I hand her 7 rubles. She says, "What? That's all the change?" "Yes," I say. "What are you talking about, there were 50 rubles there?" she says. I go to the window and shout to the cashier that there's been a mistake. But all around people are shoving, reaching for the window, keeping me from talking things over with the cashier. The cashier says she gave back change from 50 rubles and that someone took it. For some reason I hand her the remaining 7 rubles, she gives back just 5 and I lose another 2 rubles. In sum, I'm supposed to give 50 rubles back to Frau René tomorrow, but right now I'm giving her only five. I don't have anything more.

All my hope is on Zhitkov. Meanwhile I had counted on borrowing 70 rubles from Zhitkov for an overcoat Natasha and I had given to the tailor for alterations amounting to 120 rubles. Natasha's giving 50 rubles, and I'm supposed to get the other 70. So now if I borrow 50 rubles from Zhitkov, I won't be able to borrow the 70.

So that's what happened.

At the concert the four of us were sitting in the second box on the side: Kondratiev, Glebova, Frau René and I. Alisa Ivanovna and Snopkov were sitting in the stalls.

I was sitting next to Frau René right in front of everyone. And suddenly I see that I have on display a pair of utterly ragged and moth-eaten gaiters, not-quite-clean fingernails, a rumpled jacket and, what's most horrifying, an unzipped fly.

I sat down in the most unnatural pose imaginable to conceal all these defects, and sat that way for the entire first half of the concert. I felt myself in a really stupid position. What's more, I didn't like the concert at all. The orchestra was conducted by Oskar Fried, and the German organist, Günther-

Ramin, was at the organ. They were performing Beethoven's Coriolanus, Handel's Concerto for Organ in D-minor, and Mahler's Fifth Symphony. The Mahler was the second half of the concert. During the second half, I was more comfortable and felt better about myself, but still I didn't like the Mahler at all.

After the concert, I saw Frau René home and had tea with her until 2 o'clock in the morning. On the way back I happened to get on a tram that was running late.

I stood on the empty platform between the cars and sang, giving glory to God and Ester. Suddenly I saw that behind me on the platform someone was standing and listening. I became embarrassed and began to sing in German, and then in English, and then I switched over to foxtrot tunes. But when he got off, I started singing again about God and Ester. Right up to the gates of the house I was singing: The whole world is a window is Ester.

November 24, Thursday. This morning I slept till one. Then I called and went to Zhitkov to borrow 50 rubles. Borrowed them. Took them to Frau René. I had dinner and lay down to rest at home, stopped by Loewenberg's, and then went with him to Zhitkov's. Got back home at 12:20.

This evening I started missing Ester again. Yesterday, as I was falling asleep, I prayed and wept. Oh how I love my Ester!

November 25, Friday. I woke up and lay in bed a long time. I had wanted to go with Alisa Ivanovna to Ermolaeva's this evening. But Marshak called and invited me to go there. I have to go see him. That's why when Alisa Ivanovna called, I said I wouldn't be able to go to Ermolaeva's today. I lay in bed until Gershov came. He's going to Borisoglebsk. His things are already at the station. The train leaves at 5 o'clock. I'm very sorry he's leaving. He's a very nice person and a good artist.

I saw him as far as the square and then went to Boba's. Boba and I went to Dementiev, the master pipe-maker. Boba's pipe was broken. The master has closed his shop and is working at a factory. But for us, his old customers, he took on fixing the pipe for three rubles.

Boba dropped by. Then I went to Marshak's. Marshak was tired, I was lazy and the poems were read without enthusiasm. At 10 o'clock I was already back home.

I've liked to dream dreams for a long time now: to draw apartments for myself and furnish them. Sometimes I'll draw 80-room mansions, and other times I like two-room apartments.

Today I'd like to have an apartment like this:

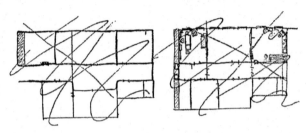

At the moment I'm writing and reading nothing. My galoshes are worn out. My boots are just as bad. No money. Mashenka came into town today and brought cod-liver oil and 25 rubles cash.

I'm going to bed late. It's already a quarter to two.

Saturday, November 26. I hung an icon of the Iberian Mother of God in my room.

Today I decided to stay home and not go out anywhere. I called Ester. She said that I had done well. But she's not giving me any hope.

Veisenberg came to see me. Then Boba and Igor came. This evening Ester called and asked for Yudina's number. Erbstein's sister called, she needs to see Aleksandr Ivanovich. Tatiana Nikolaevna called and asked for Ivan Ivanovich's telephone. Igor and Boba stayed here until one in the morning. Before going to sleep I read *Captain Trafalgar*.

Sunday, November 27. Alisa Ivanovna called this morning. She's going to go to a concert at the Philharmonic this evening, they're doing Mozart's "Requiem." I want to go too. Andronikov called me. Ester called too. She'd been at a party all night. She spoke to me as if it were an obligation. She has no interest in getting together with me. Not a word about meeting. I kept mum too.

Tatiana Nikolaevna called and I arranged with her to be at the Philharmonic at 8:30. I ironed my poor worn suit, put on a starched standing collar, and, all told, dressed as well as I could. It didn't turn out well, but was, at least, to a certain degree decent. My boots, true, are extraordinarily bad, and, what's worse, the laces are broken and tied together with knots. In a word, I dressed as well I was able to and went to the Philharmonic.

I met Poret who was with Kondratiev, and Glebova in the lobby. I just didn't have the heart to ask Ivan Ivanovich for a ticket, and so I got into the line for the box office. I had to buy a ticket not just for myself, but for Glebova too. The cheapest turned out to be 8 rubles, and I bought them.

I'm really very shy. And thanks to a bad suit and unaccustomed to being in society, I felt quite inhibited. I really don't know how I looked from the outside. In any case, I tried to hold up as best I could. We walked around the foyer and looked over the photographs. I tried expressing the simplest and lightest thoughts in the simplest tone possible, so it wouldn't seem as if I were trying to be witty. But those thoughts turned out either boring or simply stupid, and even, it seemed, out of place and at times a bit vulgar. No matter how hard I tried, I made several pronouncements with an extraordinarily significant face. I was not happy with myself. And in a mirror I saw my jacket sticking up in back. I was glad to get back into my seat as soon as I could.

I was sitting next to Glebova, while Poret and Kondratiev were sitting somewhere else.

I had wanted to sit down in a sophisticated, unconstrained pose, but, in my opinion, nothing came of this either. It seemed to me I looked like a soldier sitting for a sidewalk photographer.

I really didn't like the concert. I.e. I know nothing loftier or better than the "Requiem," and the Klimov choir has always been stunning, but this time the chorus was obviously too small. So the "Requiem" didn't sound the way it should.

During the entr'acte I saw Zhitkov and his wife, saw Frau René, talked with Ivan Ivanovich, but I spoke with neither wit nor intelligence. How awkward I've become!

After the concert Braudo came up to us. On that basis I didn't take Glebova home.

I went instead to Lipavsky's, where Vvedensky and Oleinikov were supposed to be. But Oleinikov wasn't, and Vvedensky was with Anna Semyonovna.

Only here, at Lipavskys' table, did I feel fully free and unconstrained. But here as well I think I put in too much salt and let myself go to an extreme. But I really don't know.

I wheedled an invitation to spend the night at Lipavsky's. Tamara Aleksandrovna moved into the dining room to sleep and didn't sleep the whole night.

Monday, November 28. Aleksandr Ivanovich is going to Borisoglebsk today. From Lipavsky's I went straight to Aleksandr Ivanovich's. I went to the market with him where he bought himself socks. After I got back to A. I.'s from the market, I discovered my old pipe had vanished. Who can understand what it means to lose a pipe? Luckily it turned out that Tamara Aleksandrovna had it. I went to the station to see Aleksandr Ivanovich off. Both Evgenia Ivanovnas went to the station with him. Anna Semyonovna and Erbstein's sister were supposed to be there too. A half hour before the train left, the Evgenia Ivanovnas left. Aleksandr Ivanovich and I were left alone. But his Niurochka didn't even come. I saw how sad that made him. He left very upset. Then Niurochka called me and asked how Aleksandr Ivanovich had gotten off. The way she behaves, Niurochka reminds me of Ester.

I was lying on my bed and reading *Der gute Ton*. It was already almost 9 o'clock. Suddenly Ester called. She's been spending her time quite gaily of late: always visiting someone. But today they're the ones with visitors since it's her parents' 35th anniversary. Ester asked me to come. No matter what I say, she insists on her own way. So I'm going.

There are a lot of people sitting in the dining room. Kibalchich is here, and Yakhontov and Marcel, and some ladies and some other people. Ester poured me a glass of liqueur. I sat there, face completely red, my ears burning. Ester looks worn out and unkempt. She talks, squeals, guffaws or suddenly listens with her mouth open and that's when she starts looking like an old Jewess. Before there was nothing like this. But I love her. Ester keeps looking over at me, each time less and less cordially. Yakhontov gets up and reads poetry. He recites Derzhavin. Recites it quite badly, but to declamatory effect and with culture. Then he recites Pushkin. Everyone likes it very much.

Ester claps her hands and says "Oh how charming!"

Then Yakhontov leaves.

When they ask Wiktor Kibalchich how he liked Yakhontov, he says that he does indeed have his own way of reciting and he would have been happy to listen to him the whole evening. Ester says: "I'm in love with him." Wiktor says "O that's really quite easy, he doesn't have to recite Pushkin for that."

Then Ester says: "I'm not in love with him, but with his reading. I'm in love with Pushkin."

Then Wiktor says "Oh! I was in Moscow and saw Pushkin. Hard to believe he could respond to love." (Wiktor's talking about the monument.) Wiktor was being witty that way all evening, in exactly the way I was most afraid of being yesterday in the foyer of the Philharmonic.

I sat there red-faced and awkward and could hardly say a thing. Everything I said was stunningly uninteresting. I saw that Ester despised me.

I told Ester: "Ester dear, I've lost my pipe."

She replied: "What's that? Pipe?" and then began to talk about something else with her sister.

Finally the guests were ready to leave. On purpose I waited for all of them to go. Marcel played something for me on the piano. I said goodbye and went to leave. Ester saw me to the door. Her face was really quite unpleasant: preoccupied with something that wasn't about me, but it was, in relation to me, displeased. I said nothing to her. She didn't either. We just said: "Goodbye." I kissed her hand. She slammed the door.

"Oh God!"—I said then—"She's got a snout like a slut!" I said that to myself and went running down the stairs. I said it very crudely. But I love her.

I stopped to see Zhukovsky for ten minutes and then walked home along Nevsky.

When I got home, I wrote all this down.

3 hours 10 minutes in the morning.

Thursday, November 29. This morning I went with Boba to the Writers' Committee but got nothing. Saw Panteleev and Zabolotsky.

Then I returned home. Poret called. I was supposed to go see them, but then everything changed. I invited Poret to come see me. I lay on the couch and read *Captain Trafalgar*. At half past eleven Alisa Ivanovna came. I had on hand red caviar and sturgeon. That was quite apropos. We drank tea. Alisa Ivanovna was here with me until 2 o'clock in the morning. Then I saw her home. We stopped at the "Two Masks" Cinema and decided to go to the film "The Green Lane" tomorrow. Got back home at 4. Didn't J all day.

Wednesday, November 30. Woke up late, around one. Called Alisa Ivanovna, we decided to go to the Cinema. She was supposed to call me back at 4. Heine dropped by and soon left. Alisa Ivanovna called at 4. We decided to go to the six o'clock showing. I suggested I come earlier and bring the remaining fish. Alisa Ivanovna asked me to come right away. And so right away I came. And had dinner there too. Then Alisa Ivanovna drew while I sat and did nothing. We missed a few showings since we had decided to go with Snopkov and were waiting for him to get free. We went to the 10:40 show and bought 3 tickets. We had more than an hour before it began. And so we decided to go to my place and eat what we found. And so we did. Then we called Snopkov, but no one came to the phone. Alisa Ivanovna called home and suggested to Tatiana Nikolaevna that she go with us. And so then we went to the cinema. I sat next to Alisa Ivanovna. Then we also went to their place to drink tea. I was alone with Tatiana Nikolaevna for a time, looked at her paintings. Then we drank tea. Left their place at 1:30 in the morning. Even so I caught a tram at Tsarskoe Selo station.

Natasha called today and said the overcoat's ready. I have to take a ride out there to pick it up the day after tomorrow. Have to get the money (70 rubles). Natasha's terribly tired. How can I help Natasha? Her job is much too hard. She has to move to Leningrad.

Thursday, December 1. I've been looking for money all morning. But no matter whom I called, nothing worked out. I went to see Shvarts. Ekaterina Ivanovna was the only one home, and she complained of a complete lack of money.

Couldn't get money anywhere. Called Alisa Ivanovna about it. She sympathized with me. Before she hung up she said "Until later, dear Daniil Ivanovich." It seems that she did say "dear." In the evening I was at Lipavsky's. No money there either. Lipavsky read me his fable "Menike." It's bad and I tore it apart. I pulled Tamara Aleksandrovna and Valetina Efimovna by the hair. Generally went overboard and, it seems, made a bad impression. Took the number two back home as far as Nevsky.

Friday, December 2. Got up at 10 o'clock. Shaved. Called Alisa Ivanovna. We decided to go out to Tsarskoe today. Borrowed five rubles from Illa. When I got to Alisa Ivanovna's, Kondratiev was already there.

Kondratiev has been in love with Alisa Ivanovna for six years now. He genuinely loves her. But he hasn't seen a bit of good from her. Things were good for him only when he was sick and Alisa Ivanovna would come see him every day. But now he's tormented and jealous for days and nights on end.

Alisa Ivanovna and I got to the station. We had 1 hour and 20 minutes before the train left. We went for a walk in the garden. On the train, Alisa Ivanovna read my poems.

In Tsarskoe we went to my Aunt's. Natasha wasn't at home, and Alisa Ivanovna acted shy. I felt a certain power over her. We both wanted to eat. We drank a glass of milk. Then we took a walk in the park. We ate in the cafeteria. We saw Firuzek and went home.

On the train we stood on the platform between cars. In Petersburg we decided Alisa Ivanovna would stop in at my place for something to eat. But then she asked to stop off back home. But at home they told her Snopkov was already on his way there. So Alisa Ivanovna stayed but I went home. At home there was nothing to eat. It's good Alisa Ivanovna didn't come with me. I slept a little. Ester called, but I wasn't happy she called. However when Alisa Ivanovna called I was quite happy. Vladimir Iosifovich and I fiddled with the radio until three in the morning. Then, in bed, I wrote my thoughts about Alisa Ivanovna down in my notebook. I couldn't get to sleep for a long time thinking about Alisa Ivanovna. That's not good. It would be good if she were thinking about me.

Saturday, December 3. This morning I got up and called Alisa Ivanovna. She wants Illa to sell her Persian lamb manteau for her. Took a bath. In the afternoon Lipavsky came to see me, then Oleinikov and Zabolotsky. I blabbed that I had made Alisa Ivanovna my wife. How tactless I am. Then Oleinikov called Alisa Ivanovna and asked about me. Alisa Ivanovna put an end to their conversation. When everyone had left, I called Alisa Ivanovna. She called me a provocateur, and it's obvious that she's changed her opinion of me. Yesterday's relations between us have vanished. I was tormented by this. Veisenberg came. Stayed fairly long. Then I went to see Boba. I couldn't hold out and at 11 o'clock I called Alisa Ivanovna from Boba's. Spoke nonsense. Her voice was not at all welcoming. Serves me right! Stayed at Boba's until 3:30 in the morning.

Lisa and Illa have gotten 75 rubles together for me.

Yesterday's night thoughts about Alisa Ivanovna seem disgraceful to me today. I have to not call Alisa Ivanovna ~~until she calls herself~~. I will not call her.

Sunday, December 4. Bashilov came to see me this morning. Before lunch I hooked the speaker from the City Power Net up to my room. After lunch I went to Tsarskoe to see Natasha. Picked up the coat from the tailor. Spent some time with Natasha. Mashenka was there. I ate a marvelous, huge onion, roast goose, and drank milk. Returned home toward 12 o'clock.

Monday, December 5. This morning I was at Oleinikov's. I presented him with a gargantuan onion. Came home. Mashenka came. Got a bowl cut. This evening I went to Alisa Ivanovna's in starched cuffs, starched collar and white vest. The following company had gathered there: Alisa Ivanovna, Tatiana Nikolaevna, Frau René, Snopkov, Braudo, Struve, Oleinikov and I. It was boring enough. I nearly had a fight with Alisa Ivanovna. Walked back with Oleinikov. He doesn't believe I consider him a good poet.

Tuesday, December 6. At 11 o'clock this morning Ester called me. She said that she couldn't say what she had to in Russian, so she would speak French. I understood nothing she said, but was ashamed to admit it. I asked her stupid questions not to the point. And finally she got angry and hung up.

Alisa Ivanovna called, she said that she found everyone repulsive yesterday. And that she called so she and I wouldn't keep fighting, but it turned out we quarreled even more.

This afternoon Ernest Ernestovich dropped by.

This evening I was at Zhitkov's. Oleinikov, Matveev and Bianki were there. Then Tatiana Gruzdeva came. We drank vodka. Zhitkov got drunk. On the way back, Oleinikov, Matveev and I walked.

Wednesday, December 7. I had wanted to begin working today. But did nothing the whole day. Until 4 o'clock, I did absolutely nothing. At 4 Tiuvelev came. He's studying mathematics and German. After Tiuvelev left, Vladimir Iosifovich and I fiddled with the radio receiver. This evening I was at Poret and Glebova's.

* * *

[1933]

Saturday, February 18, 1933. Saw the New Year in with Glebova. And then Alisa Ivanovna and Snopkov came here to see me. They were kissing and it was torment for me to see it. Then I had a quarrel with Alisa Ivanovna that lasted several days. It happened after the 4th when I was in a cab with her and almost kissed her. We parted quite tenderly. But the next day she didn't want to see me. And we didn't see each other for more than a week. Afterwards we made peace only with some difficulty. And during all that time what thoughts didn't obsess me. I was jealous of Vvedensky. But sometime in the fourth week of January we made friends again. At the end of January, an anxious time began in connection with passport reform. Alisa Ivanovna and I saw one another literally every day. I was falling more and more in love with her, and on the first of February, I told her about it. We called this "friendship" and continued to see one another.

February 3. I sat at Alice's feet and put my head in her lap. The smell from her was marvelous. And I fell in love once and for all.

February 7. I started making out with Alice. And that's when I discovered I'm impotent. It was terrible.

February 10. Went for a walk with Alice on the Fontanka, we kissed on the Monastery bridge. Touched the hair on her mound with my hand.

February 11. Alice left for Vsevolozhskoe

February 12. Alice called me from there on the phone. During the day I took a ride out to Tsarskoe, but that evening I went to see Alice, who by then had returned to the city. Chernetsov and Kondratiev were there. Alice was rather cold.

February 13. Alice didn't let me kiss her. I spoke at length and stupidly. February 14. Alice was with me here. We kissed. I kissed her foot. Alice was quite nice.

February 15. In the morning I walked Alice home from State Publishers. That evening I went to her place again. We kissed quite passionately. But once again I was impotent. This worries me terribly. I kissed Alisa on her mound through her panties.

February 16. We spoke rather tenderly on the phone. Tomorrow Alice goes to Vsevolozhskoe until the 20th. She promised to call me on the 18th and to write me a letter. ʃ

On the evening of the 16th I was at the Lipavskys'. Yakov Druskin was there. Got home at 11 o'clock.

February 17. Spent the whole day writing a letter to Alice. And sent it that evening. I'm tormented that I may have complete sexual impotence. Have to go to the doctor.

February 18. Alice didn't call. In the afternoon Heine was here. In the evening I went to see Ester. She's sick in bed. I sat on her bed and touched her "there" with a finger. Even though "there" was quite wet, I didn't get aroused. That really worries me.

Sunday, February 19. At night, terrible thoughts about **spermatorrhea**. Saw Kepka in a dream, but she seemed white. In the morning when I was still asleep, Vvedensky came. I complained of my impotence to him. We went to the Municipal Committee Offices. Saw neither Bauze nor Kalnyn. Couldn't get the application notarized. Ran into Shvarts. Dropped by his place and drank tea. Then went on a long walk with him down the street. That evening I was at Ester's again. She's still sick. Today her temperature was 102. I didn't touch her for three reasons: first because of her temperature, second because of my impotence, and third because I love ~~Alice~~ Alisa Ivanovna.

I got back home at 11:30 and drank tea with Liza and Vladimir Iosifovich.

February 20. Spoke with Alisa on the telephone. She's back. But we didn't see each other that day. I went to see Ester. Ester didn't allow herself to be touched even slightly. Fine. I left and went to the Lipavskys'.

March 1. Natasha lost her job. That evening there was a dinner at Liza's on the occasion of Kirill's birth. Alisa Ivanovna was there, and she met Liza. Then Alisa Ivanovna stayed here with me until 3 o'clock. Again we talked for a long time. I love Alisa Ivanovna but she loves Peter Pavlovich. Kondratiev is also mixed up here. And I'm impotent. And threats from without. But I love Alisa Ivanovna so much! There's a kerfuffle for you!

March 2. Was at Zhitkov's. Bianki, Barmin, Zhitkov and I discussed a series of encyclopedic books.

March 3. In the morning I was at Alisa Ivanovna's. She was drawing hunters. We looked at Goya. This evening Peter Pavlovich is supposed to be there. I couldn't bear it, and left earlier than I should have. Ate at the

Leningrad Writers' cafeteria. When I got home I couldn't hold out and I called Alisa Ivanovna. It was a useless call, in vain. In the evening I felt horrible. On the one hand I love Alisa so, and on the other I'm so impotent. I did something bad: I went to see Ester. I went down on Ester, but it was not tasty and was not interesting. I returned home at 12. Now I'm going to drink green tea, a present from dear sweet Alisa Ivanovna.

Friday, March 3. Alisa was here with me one time at the end of February. We talked for a long time. It became clear that she loves Peter Snopkov and is living with him.

Sunday, September 10. How often we go astray! I was in love with Alisa Ivanovna until I got everything from her a man requires from a woman. Then I stopped loving Alisa. Not because I had had my fill, satisfied my passion, or anything like that. No, simply because having gotten to know Alisa as a woman, I discovered that she's an uninteresting woman, at least to my taste. And then I started to see other defects in her too. And soon I fell completely out of love with her just when she fell in love me. I literally tore out of there, having explained to her that I was leaving because she was in love with Peter Pavlovich. Recently I found out that Alisa got married to Peter Pavlovich. Oh I was so happy!

But I have kept on seeing Ester. By now there's no longer the love there once was, but in any case, as a woman, Ester pleases me, and even though, maybe, it seems sad, but still it's very important. Yes, very important!

[From notebook 38]

February 8, 1933. I can't help myself and have to see Poret today. Going to see her now will most probably ruin everything forever. I know it's stupid but I can't help myself. I'm going to see her and, perhaps, with the help of the Blessed Ksenia, everything will be ok.
<u>Daniil</u>

Oh Lord, strengthen our love and do not abandon us. Selah. Grant that after midnight, that is, by Friday, February 9, I might go down on Alisa. Make Alisa love me.

I'm now sitting in Alisa Ivanovna's room. Very unpleasant feeling. I don't see that she has been treating me well. She's changed towards me. It would be smart simply to leave. But the thought of losing her forever like this is terrible.

Again she's begun talking about how evil I am. I'm not sure what she means by that, but in any case, there's nothing good in any of this.

I ask God to make Alisa my wife. But it's clear that God doesn't see fit to do so. May God's will be done in all things. I want to love Alisa but it just isn't working out. How sad! Selah!

If only Alisa Ivanovna loved me and God wanted it, I would be so happy! I beg Thee, O God, arrange everything as Thou seest fit and right. God's will be done.

Into Thy hands, O God, I commend my fate, do everything as Thou wouldst.
Sweet Alisa Ivanovna, I thought, ought to become my wife, but now I understand nothing. Selah!

I can see that Alisa Ivanovna is slipping away from me.
O God, God, Thy will be done in all things.
Amen.
February 13, 1933.
Daniil Kharms

* * *

[From notebook 24, spring 1933]

For Wednesday, April 5, 1933.
Get up no later than 1:00.
Clean my room. Take a bath.
Write a poem.
Go to bed no later than 1 am.

* * *

CHAPTERS

I. Birth. HE.		XV.
II. Birth. SHE.		XVI.
III.		XVII. ESFIR
IV.		XVIII.
V.		XIX.
VI. love.		XX.
VII.		XXI.
VIII.		XXII. Madness.
IX.		
X.		
XI. trial.		
XII. execution.		
XIII. church porch.		
XIV.		

* * *

Public Performances

April 12, 1:00 pm. Small Auditorium of the Conservatory (Shvarts and I).

April 16, 6:00 pm. Korolenko Library, 93 Obvodny Canal, Tram No. 19 (Oleinikov and I).

April 18, Noon. Children's Culture Club. (Shvarts and I).

April 12. School No. 107. 1/8 Prutkov Lane, corner of Grechesky Prospect.
At noon.

* * *

Serafima Nikolaevna.
Called me on the phone, seems to be interested in the poems.

Shvarts. *Treasure*
Ivan Ivanovich Terrible and the Bird.
"Balloons."
Balloons fly high
Sticks fly high

* * *

Lightbulb lightbulb lightbulb lightbulb
lightbulb lightbulb lightbulb's dead
it lit up and poof! it faded
that's what Peter Palkin said.

It went out, the cause is simple
tells him clever Fyodor Gaul
'cause there's no electric current
there's no current—not at all.

[From notebook 38]

Registry.

April 24, appeared at Scholars House. Received 100 r., spent the evening at
Shvarts's.
April 25, appeared with Oleinikov, Shvarts and Zabolotsky at the Builders
Club, received 50 r., spent the evening at Mikhailov's and got sick. April
26, Natasha arrived. Dr. Shapo treating me.
May 3, Dr. Bichunsky came and diagnosed paratyphoid.

May 4, Shapo discovered roseola on my body.

May 6, Today's visitors: Boba Levin, Shapo, Elizaveta Petrovna Petz with dachshunds, Dr. Fridland and Marshak. I'm reading Dumas' *The Two Dianas*.

May 7, Sasha Razumovsky was here this morning. Then Shapo came by. In the evening, Gaga Katsman, Grits and Fialka came by. We drank sour white wine.

May 8. In the morning, Boba came, then Mikhailov, then Shapo, then Lipavsky. Pugacheva and Verkhovskaya phoned. Drinking Salkhino wine. Liza has gone to the dacha.

* * *

[From notebook 24]

I.

Ivan Petrovich, where you been, friend?
It's been years now, that ain't right!

II.

I used to ride astride a mare
But now I ride a motorbike.

I came up to you from the road on the hillside
the better and longer to scrutinize you

* * *

I want to write.
I want to write a lot and very well.
I want to write
Very many, very good poems.
Sunny day.
Field of Mars.

Tell dear Gail that
I got galled here

Agness, my dear Ag-en-ness
The play is just a boring mess.

The Neva's roaring at this site:
Was hurrying to see my bride
took off my hat of felt *anglais*
so it wouldn't blow away

* * *

Shvarts's *Treasure* is interesting in those places where it seems that supernatural things are happening. How amazing that it's always like that when it's not overdone.

* * *

Monolog, the first 5 lines don't rhyme, then 6 rhymed couplets, then a quatrain with cross-rhyme, then 4 rhyming couplets. The final pair of rhymes repeats in reverse order, but everything else about the lines is different, further on everything goes back in reverse order. The lines and meaning are different, but the rhymes are the same.

* * *

One must travel the path of purification (*Perseveratio Katarsis*). One must begin literally with the alphabet, that is, with letters.

Summer Garden

filth comfort prosperity sleep feeling

Purity is close to emptiness.

Don't confuse purity with emptiness.

* * *

It's interesting that almost all the great writers had their own particular idea, that they considered higher than their artistic work.
So, for example, Blake, Gogol, Tolstoy, Khlebnikov, Vvedensky.

* * *

The magnitude of a creator is determined not by the quality of his creations, but either by the quantity (of his works, their power or other various elements), or by their purity. By virtue of an enormous quantity of observations, postulates, nervous energy, and feelings, Dostoevsky achieved a certain purity.

And thereby he also achieved greatness.

* * *

What I've written about *Professor Trubochkin* "won't be right for *Siskin*." May 24.

* * *

~~A young lady, languorous and proud,~~
~~was traveling in a tram with me~~
~~the tram was made of cloud.~~
Field of Mars. Central path. Northern part.

I'd like to meet yesterday's girl from the tram with the transparent eyes here.
Although she's not a brunette, she's very juicy.

All the girls avoid me. Not one of them will sit down next to me.

* * *

I'm despised by everyone yes everyone.
No one but no one wants
to know me.
No one ever mentions me
in anything they say.
No one ever acknowledges
my genius.

The sooner I write
some poems of genius
The sooner I'll become
the king
of poets.

Next to me on the bench. Some soldiers just flopped down on my bench.

* * *

Sitting in the Summer Garden, I suddenly recalled one particular detail about the girl from Press House.

* * *

O God, bring me the girl who was here 3 days ago in a green dress with a Doberman puppy.

Everything is finished with this girl. God didn't hear my prayer. The girl didn't come.

[From notebook 25]

Purchased and started on June 5, 1933. Wednesday.
Daniil Kharms

* * *

O God, I've found a girl whom I ask your permission to take to wife.

* * *

~~On June 2, 3, and 4, I read Mérimée. In the evening and during the day of June 5, I was in Petersburg. On the train I saw a beautiful girl. Went to Pavlovsk. Wrote, and read Kuprin.~~

* * *

Need to compose a law or a table whereby numbers would increase at inexplicable non-periodic intervals:

6	3	8	9
2	1	4	
8	5	10	7
		16	17

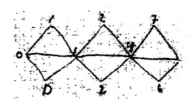

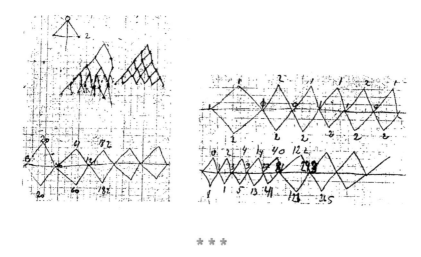

* * *

Started reading Bunin's story "A Hundred and Eight." I was immediately taken aback by the word "smithy."
Not a good story. Uninteresting.

Finished Kuprin's story "The Coward." Not very good.

Finished Kuprin's "Staff Captain Rybnikov." One of the best stories ever written in Russian.

[From notebook 26]

In the *Journal de Verdun* for the month of July 1735, there is a story about a child born with a clock face in his eyes, caused by his mother's strong desire to possess a Clock.

The ancient Romans, should they sneeze upon getting up in the morning, would go back to bed.

The tail of a lizard, placed in a boot, brings happiness and wealth.

The caul of an infant brings success to lawyers.

Never arrange a fork and knife in the shape of a cross.

It is my opinion that separating a fork and knife lying in the shape of a cross will bring something particularly pleasant to him who does so.

An owl brings misfortune if it perches on a house or a church. But if an owl makes its way into a dovecot, then consider it a good sign. An ancient law of the Franks forbade killing an owl in a dovecot.

Abbé Rousseau tells a story of once having had a toad. It would sit in a glass cage. And then one day it started to stare at the Abbé so that he felt his heart beat faster, frightening him and causing him convulsions. Perspiration covered his body and the Abbé defecated right then and there. Such is the power of the peculiar gaze of a toad!

A peal of thunder on the right side is bad, while on the left is a good sign.

A charred log that falls out from a stove portends a guest.

A spider spinning its web portends money and riches.

A ringing in the right ear is bad, but good if in the left.

* * *

Summoning Spell
"Dies, mies, jesquet, benedo, efet, donvema, enitemaus."

The word AGLA! Pronounced loudly towards the east will locate a lost object and discover a distant piece of news.

A person should not have freckles.

When invoking the spirits of the night, kiss the table.

A dress left behind should be sprinkled all around.

* * *

Solday,	ou ♄	est Samedi, Sonnabent.
Zaden,	ou ♃	est Jeudi, Donnerstag.
Madime,	ou ♂	est Mardi, Dienstag.
Zemen,	ou ☉	est Dimanche, Sonntag.
Hogos,	ou ♀	est Vendridi, Freitag.
Cocao,	ou ☿	est Mercredi, Mittwoch.
Zeveac,	ou ☽	est Lundi, Mondtag.

* * *

Les heures de Saturne ♄, Mars ♂ et Venus ♀, sone bonnes pour parler aux esprits: celle de ☿, pour trouver les choses derobees avec les esprits; celle de ♄ pour appeler les ames de l'enfer, savoir de ceux qui sont morts de mort naturelle; l'heure de ♂, pour appeler l'ame de ceux qui ont ete tues, et pour lors on doit aussi joindre le jour comme dans la suivante experience.

> *The hours of Saturn, Mars and Venus are useful for speaking with spirits: those of Mercury are good for finding things that were stolen by spirits; those of Saturn for calling the souls of hell, to learn about those who died a natural death; the hours of Mars for calling the souls of those who have been killed, and to decide when they will move on to the next stage.*

* * *

Solday,	or ♄	Saturday
Zedex,	or ♃	Thursday.
Madime	or ♂	Tuesday.
Zemen	or ☉	Sunday.
Hogos	or ♀	Friday.
Cocao	or ☿	Wednesday.
Zeveac	or ☽	Monday.

All the days are not at all the same, which is why the hours of the planets are not the same. In order to find out how many minutes constitute an hour for a planet, you must do this when the day has 15 hours. You need to multiply this number by 5, resulting in 75. This gives you the number of minutes that makes up one planetary hour for that day. Take the number of hours in the night, that is 9, and multiply it by 5, giving you 45. That's how many minutes make up a planetary hour of the night. And that's the way to proceed in all the seasons.

* * *

India
Mahatmas.
"Paramahamsas".
1. Dayananda Saraswati.
2. Pavhari Baba + 1898.

3. Debendranath Tagor.
4. Rai Saligram Sahib Bahadur.
5. Ramakrishna.

Ramakrishna
b. February 20, 1833.
d. August 16, 1886.
Born in the village of Kamarpukar. Father was a Brahmin. His first name was Gadadhara, one of the names of Vishnu, which means: "he who holds the scepter." Gadadhara's father had the gift of Vak Siddhi, the power of the word, that is, whatever he would say about someone, whether good or bad, would come true. During his father's pilgrimage to Gaya, Vishnu appeared to him in a dream and said that he, Vishnu, would be reborn on this earth through his son.

* * *

John of Damascus. (Syrian scholar)
Works:
An Exact Exposition of the Orthodox Faith.
Sacred Parallels.

* * *

I took a step, stepped back again,
And to the Summer Garden ran.
And rising from her bench, a girl
Walked in the park in white beret.
A line goes up, straight as a rail,
o with her body she did play.

* * *

June 12. Wrote an Epistle of 33 lines to Oleinikov. Planned to write this poem together with him, but wrote it myself, except for the first line. That's why the poem looks like a poem by Oleinikov.

Himmelkumov was smiling until Sakharov broke the chapel off from the model of Smolny Cathedral and stuffed it into Mr. Himmelkumov's mouth.

* * *

Black
Ka8, Qc5, Rh8, Nb4, Bc2, a5, b7, h7, h6, c4

White
Kc3, Qf4, Ra1, Rh2, Bb5, a4, f2, d4, h3
White's move.

* * *

Was fur dumme Menschen giebt es auf der Erden Besonders die
Schauspieler.

What idiots there are on this earth especially actors.

* * *

How I want a woman!
I really want a woman.

**Nowadays there are no longer any women capable of falling so in love
with me at first sight as to come up to me on their own and be the first
to strike up an acquaintance.**

Lakhta, June 15, 1933.
I'm bored without a woman, without the moisture of female embraces.

The beach at Peter and Paul fortress.

My body is revolting to all women.
**I'm lying [illegible] of a greenreddishish color. If I were bright green, I
would be a lot more attractive.**

It's so nice lying out in the sun.
Sun, pour your sacred power into me.

But it's possible I'm just very erotic!

A good-looking little Jewess was lying on the beach, but she's a whore.

**She's gone out whoring: looking to find herself a cavalier. She'll bring
anyone home.**

* * *

1. Black dress suit.

    Jacket, vest, trousers, pants.

2. Checkered grey wool suit.

    Jacket, vest, trousers.

3. Fine brown suit.

    Jacket, vest, trousers, pants.

4. Two summer suits made of white canvas.

    High-collared jacket, vest, trousers,

    Jacket, vest, pants.

5. Dark blue cotton suit.

    Jacket, vest, trousers, pants.

6. Grey wool checkered trousers.

7. Grey pants.

8. Greenish jacket.

9. Light grey cotton suit.

    Jacket ~~black,~~ trousers, shirt.

10. Two colored cotton vests.

11. Three or four argyle vests. (4 wool, 2 cotton).

12. Six white vests.

13. Shark-skin suit.

    Jacket, trousers, pants.

14. Grey redingote.

    Frock-coat, breeches.

15. Black frock-coat.

    Frock, trousers, checkered trousers.

16. Fine summer beige suit.

    Jacket, vest, pants.

17. Grayish suit.

    Jacket, vest, trousers, pants.

18. Dark blue wool suit, diagonal pattern.

    Jacket, Vest, Trousers.

19. Dark grey summer coat.

20. Black demi-season coat with a velvet neck.

21. Tuxedo.

    Jacket, trousers, vest.

22. Camouflage service jacket, dark.

23. Multi-colored checkered trousers.

24. Black cloth jacket.
25. White trousers, 3 pair.
26. Grey striped cotton suit.
    (Coat, jacket with high collar, trousers, pants, vest

1. 12 pair woolen socks, of which 3 are shiny black, 4 brown, 3 argyle, 2 gray.
2. 12 pair summer socks with the same colors.

* * *

1. Black dress shoes.
2. High-quality black shoes.
3. High-quality black shoes.
4. Black patent leather shoes.
5. High-quality black slippers.
6. Brown shoes with rubber soles.
7. Yellow loafers on thick rubber soles.
8. Black shoes (Unitas).
9. Black slippers.
10. Yellow slippers.

1. White gaiters, 2 pair.
2. Gray gaiters, 2 pair.
3. Beige gaiters, 2 pair.
4. Brown gaiters, 2 pair.
5. High gaiters.
6. Black leggings.
7. Brown leggings.

* * *

O God help me do good work on Professor Trubochkin today.

A pig thrust its snout out, quickly snatched a piece of bread from the swill, flapped its wings and dragged it up to the sties.

How often do you come across a woman with an extraordinary figure, marvelous breasts and wondrous legs but with such a vulgar proletarian mug that you just want to scream?

* * *

June 25, 1933. I'm putting myself on notice that I can't go on doing nothing like this anymore. Have to write every day. Have to lose myself in an idea and serve it.

HATS

1. Black felt.
2. Grey felt.
3. Brown felt.
4. Top hat.
5. Bowler.
6. Cap.
7. White hat.
8. Light summer peaked cap.

Siskin. 68—17.
Telephone 37. Radio Station.

* * *

[From notebook 25]

Come come to me my little friend
run cross the meadow quick and then
come lie with me in sunwarm rays
~~all care and woe are far away~~
where all the world is far away.

I know many men who prefer democratic girls. Excuse me, but I don't like them. And even if I did like them, I wouldn't get anything from them. I've noticed that they always run away from me. They're always stupid, dense, in a hurry, shy where there's no need, cynical, vindictive, and quick to take offense. An intelligent girl of the people is always vulgar in the highest degree and impertinent. Run as fast as you can from such girls. The only good thing about them is those bodies and their good health.

* * *

[From notebook 27]

I hate unobservant people.

I am cruelly punished for my greed. I feel like eating and being in good society. I do think, however, that it's better here at Druskin's than with those mockers the Shvartses.

Here the conversation's about the Gothic and it's peaceful here.

What a traitor I am in my soul.

At Shvarts's they'll drink to Zabolotsky's health, but not to mine.

* * *

WHOM DO I CALL "THOU"?

Men

Vvedensky

Zabolotsky

Bakhterev

Razumovsky

Levin

Andronikov

Sollertinsky

Veisenberg

Mart

Tiuvelev

Vigiliansky

Women

Ester

Lina Vasilievna Khodorovskaya

Dina Vasilievna Markova

D.V. Senkevich

Inna Emelyanova

Natasha Zegzhda

WHOM DO I CALL "KOU"

Men

Shvarts

* * *

Everyone has noticed that once he has shaved his cheeks, upper lip and chin closely, he feels better all over.

On the other hand, it's said that once Samson's beard was cut off, he lost all his physical strength.

I think that if Samson had shaved the remaining hairs on his face closely, he would have felt himself stronger again. It's obvious that there's a connection between feeling good physically and having beautiful facial hair. All religious teaching has something to say about these hairs.

* * *

Four Germans were eating pork and drinking green beer. One German by the name of Klaus was choking on a piece of pork and got up from the table. Then the three other Germans started whistling with their fingers and loudly making fun of the sufferer. But the German Klaus quickly swallowed the piece of pork, washed it down with green beer and was ready with an answer. The three other Germans made a few cracks at the expense of the German Klaus's throat, then they started in on his legs and started to shout that the German Klaus was rather bow-legged. One German in particular, by the name of Michael, laughed at Klaus's bow-legs. Then the German Klaus pointed at the German Michael and said that he had never seen another man who pronounced the word "bow-legged" so stupidly. The German Michael looked at everyone with an inquisitive glance, then at the German Klaus with a glance that expressed extreme hostility. Here the German Klaus drank a little green beer with these thoughts in his head: "so a quarrel is brewing between me and the German Michael." The other two Germans chewed their pork in silence. But the German Klaus drank a little more beer, looked at them all with a look that expressed the following: "I know what you want from me, but as far as you're concerned I am a closed book."

* * *

Need to buy
 I 3 lined oilskin copy books.   9 r.
 I Violet ink.
 I Razors.
 III Suspenders.
 I 3 packages of tobacco.   3 r.
 I Eyeglasses.
 III Enema tip.
 II Felt hat.

III Cane.
I Notebooks (if possible).
    Galoshes.
    Soap.

    Debts
    46 r.
    2 22
    47 22

To Illa   50 r.

* * *

Stories about Himmelkumov

Himmelkumov looked at a girl in the window opposite. But the girl in the window opposite didn't once look at Himmelkumov. "It's because she's shy," thought Himmelkumov.

Himmelkumov painted his face with green India ink and went up to the window. "Let them all think: how strange he is," Himmelkumov said to himself.

The tobacco was finished and Himmelkumov had nothing to smoke. He sucked on an empty pipe, but this only increased his torment. In this way two hours passed. And then tobacco appeared.

Himmelkumov made goggle eyes at a girl and mentally commanded her to turn her head. However this didn't work. Then Himmelkumov mentally began to command the girl not to look at him. This didn't work either.

Himmelkumov was searching for an inner idea so he could spend the rest of his life absorbed in it. It's nice to be like a madman, mad over a single point. Such a man sees his point everywhere and in everything. Everything is grist for his mill. Everything has a direct relationship to his beloved point.

Suddenly a terrible greed seized Himmelkumov. But it was unclear how far this greed had spread. Himmelkumov reviewed the rules about dividing words at the end of a line and thought a long time about the letters n, s, and c, which should not be divided. "Today I'm feeling very greedy," Himmelkumov said to himself. A flea was biting him, he scratched and turned over in his mind the word "transcendental," trying to figure out how to divide the word between two lines.

* * *

A small grasshopper flew in through the window. Petrov tried to catch this grasshopper with a cup. Petrov's wife drove the grasshopper into a corner with a napkin, and Liapunov's son brought a jar of glue and awaited Mrs. Petrov's orders.

Shura, Kolya and Fedya broke the door down and laughed loudly at their prank. But then along came the mathematician himself and he thrashed them with a strap. What a lot of cries and noise there were! Maria Abramovna came back from Vienna and grumbled for a long time once she learned how the young men had behaved themselves when she was gone. But that's not right because young people always want to make life difficult for someone and they do everything very quickly. But as you age, everything slows down. Not from sloth precisely, but from old age. But it's actually better when the cause is sloth. For example, when an old person begins to tell a story, it always lasts a very long time and the story has no end. Only some incident makes an old person stop talking. Steamers are heading for Elagin Island.

* * *

"Margarita" in Russian means a woman who likes to foretell the future.

* * *

The age of sexual maturity has its own fascinations and "horrors." But the sexual "horrors" of the opposite sex are not at all repulsive. Even the excretions of the female sex organs are not at all repulsive to a man.

A woman who's too clean is physiologically more repulsive than one who is even slightly slovenly.

If a woman's sexual organs are washed too often, are dry and don't give off any smell, it's simply repulsive.

Everything pleasant is also slightly repulsive.

A clean child and a clean old man are always somewhat repulsive.

Both wet sweaty bodies and dry mucous membranes evoke a feeling of disgust.

A man whose mouth is dry is repulsive. O, how much more repulsive is a woman with dried out sex organs!

One of the most powerful ways a woman acts on a man is through the smell of her sex organs. O, how foolish are those modern women who, through frequent washing, eradicate their own beautiful smell.

A woman should wash only her thighs, and that only occasionally. She should never wash the insides of her sex organs! No matter how strong the smell.

* * *

July 1, 1933. Finished reading Dickens' *Dombey and Son.* You can't fault this book. It's a good, serene book. Perhaps a bit boring, but that's not a disaster.

* * *

Sunday, July 2, 1933. I'm sitting on the veranda in Tsarskoe. Smoking a pipe. Thoughts or feelings worthy of attention—none.

Same day. Read Derzhavin's "On the Death of Prince Meshchersky." A great poem!

* * *

Monday, July 3, 1933. In the morning read Prosper Mérimée and humor magazines. In the evening took a walk in the Catherine and Alexander parks. O, how gloomy it is there. I didn't see one young lady there, not one real lady: only tarts and old biddies. Returned home down in the dumps.

* * *

Tuesday, July 4. Cold and rainy all morning. Sitting on the veranda. According to my calculations, all of July will be rainy and cold. In other words, there won't be any summer.

Feeling very sluggish, no cerebral energy. Can't compose or write poems now. Reading Mérimée.

Finished Mérimée's *Carmen*, *Lokis*, and some other pieces, pleasant to read, but in general they didn't impress me much.
Read several stories by Kuprin—good.

My advice is always to ride the train and tram alone.

Kuprin's "Staff Captain Rybnikov" is one of the best stories ever written in Russian.

Oscar Wilde's—

⊟

July 4. Went to Zhitkov's with Zhukovsky. Zhitkov was unhappy about this.

* * *

Got on bus No. 9 at the corner of Kamennoostrovsky Prospect and Bolshoi Prospect.
Received 48 rubles today. Bought a few notebooks (6) but they're still not any good, and violet ink. Wednesday, July 5.

* * *

After the revolution, a former gendarme started to work in a publishing house in one of the southern cities of Russia. Usually he was gloomy and taciturn but sometimes he would appear in the doorway of the publishing house, twirl his mustaches and share various interesting things with those present. For example, once he said: "In America they've invented a machine that if you suck on it, you won't feel like eating. Not at all."

* * *

Absolutely can't recall his name. Something like "Medallionov."
Dustbusterov, Lampshadov.

* * *

Sitting in the Alexander Park, I was observing the people and noticed the people out walking walk in different directions.
July and June 9.

Here's what I was doing in the park: ɟ And at that moment, I noticed the wife of the artist S. walking by.

I'm looking for a lonely girl out walking by herself, an educated, young, healthy, fresh, good looking, sweet, and luxurious girl.

I'm looking for one just like me.

* * *

What frenzied racing runs its course
A motorcyclist and a girl on horse
They fly like arrows from the start
And the air is torn apart.

I remember how it was (and will be):
one of them—a handsome filly
the other only dried up trash
there's lots like that, don't even ask.
And those whose bodies are more rounded
are always by fate's hand out-bounded.
Though sometimes with a little pluck . . .
But everything depends on luck.

She's fresh, she's got great teeth.
Tho' I am timid. So finito.

We three sat down beneath the willow
and lazy conversation followed.

Two girls are chattering on politely.
Is this useful? Yes, quite rightly.

* * *

Among the graves you're not allowed to ride around.
And so the road here in this place is out of bounds.

The road here in this place is out of bounds.
Which means you're not allowed to walk around.

How swiftly the mosquitoes fly.
Like sleds from ice hills way up high.

She's fresh and those long legs are sweet.
She's bright of eye and has great teeth.

Riding on a lady's bike
Resembles soup, quite cotton-like.

At end of a Moldovan lane
a bike stood still: it broke its chain.

Shifting seats two times I realized:
Got to move on home. It's time.
Whose world is this?
It's mine.

I visit only city parks
Although the days are crazy hot
And though the sun is burning bright
I'm still the prince of heat and light.

* * *

I from towering height above
didn't note the beauty of
your shoulders and your legs
though I honestly must say
I couldn't notice in that instant
in that moment of collision
of our bodies hot and lithe
~~You were moaning. I just sighed.~~
I sprang up and soared on high
up with you into those heights

where all earthly beauties bright
vanish just like smoke.
And now you and I, dear Lela,
go as one into this house
I cast my glance upon your shoulders
I cast my glance upon your legs
None but gods possess such beauty
And archangels ~~with a knout~~ no doubt!

* * *

We need to reintroduce truncated adjectives into Russian.

Ate English vanilla mousse today and liked it.

Examined an electric light bulb and liked it.

Went swimming in the Catherine pond and liked it. July 10.

I took a liking to two girls
The one for the beauty of her figure
The other for the kindness of her nature.

Once again I'm looking for a beautiful girl.

I'm looking for the beauty who's looking for me.

Could a beautiful girl be looking for me?
Perhaps she is.

Such timidity, and before whom?
I don't get it.

There's not a lot of people passing by here.
But to top it off, you're still an old goat.

Very few educated girls,
and not a single boorish one, nothing for you.

I took the best seat, settled in.
Is doing so a sin? No sin.

Two girls walking by. Will they pass by? Yes, they will.

The path is enclosed by flowers.

The sand here is covered with mud.

This man here's not of princely blood,
And in his veins, not blood, but mud.

* * *

Performance: July 11 at 2 pm. The Volodarsky Garden, 53a Liteiny Prospect.

July 11. Before bed did ɪ. Therefore I'm expecting all kinds of unpleasantness tomorrow.
Likewise, I expect bad weather tomorrow.

Today I went swimming with Ester at Elagin Island, and then went down on her at her home.

I'll share with myself.

ɫ We ran into Bakhterev's wife: she showed up and is in the way. Got to get away from her: she'll be insulted.

I ran into an acquaintance. She's the wife of a friend, what is there about her that could possibly interest me?

You have to run from the fatal ones like her.

Now all because of her, I have to pretend I'm writing all the time.

I'm surrounded by all these uninteresting people.

It's nice to be among sweet women, but everything depends on fate.

I moved into third place today. Possibly the worst.

What a disaster: before whom!

* * *

Irina Frantsevna Sollertinskaya.

Wagner's opera *The Flying Dutchman*. Got to see it. There's a good sailor's chorus.

Beethoven, Piano trio in C minor.

"Oh, give me freedom" Prince Igor's aria. Borodin.

Chaikovsky, A Russian dance.

Chopin, Polonaise.

* * *

[From notebook 27]

July 12. Drinking with Nikolai Oleinikov at Sollertinsky's. Got completely drunk. Went right home and puked. Next morning puked again.

* * *

July 13. Raining all day. Tomorrow the weather is also going to be bad.

On July 5, Wednesday, when I was on my way to Tsarskoe, I saw such an amazing woman on the train that I haven't been able to get her out of my mind since. July 13.

* * *

July 14, 9 am. Some sun through the clouds. But after 10, there'll be no sun at all. Going to be a nasty day, not a day for the beach.

No chance today of lying on the beach surrounded by beautiful ladies.

37 is an unlucky number.
37 x 3 = 111
111 is a factor of 666.   111 x 6 = 666

Mr. Protoplasm asked
who of you will do me?
I'm the one who'll get you done,
said one daring dame.

Clouds in the sky.
Storm clouds on the way.
Tram 31.

Here's a story the sailors are telling:
The English decided to prove that the belief that Fridays are unlucky is nothing but an empty superstition. To this end they built a steamship. They began building it on a Friday, launched it on a Friday, named it "The Friday." On Friday the steamer put out to sea, and it sank on a Friday.

July 14. Saw a revolting anti-Semitic film, *Through Tears*.

Elena Vasislievna Safonova, 37 Furshtatsky St., apt. 3. 2 –35 – 33.

I'm sitting next to a girl who's mean.

* * *

July 17. Lying on the beach since 1:30. I don't foresee anything in the way of ~~good meeting with women~~ meeting a nice pretty woman today.

I'm sitting next to a girl who's mean.

WHAT INTERESTS ME

Poems.
Packing thoughts into poems.
Extracting thoughts from poems.
Once again packing thoughts into poems.
Prose.
Illumination, inspiration, clarification, transformation.
Paths of achievement.

Finding one's own system of achievement.
Various kinds of knowledge unbeknownst to science.
General laws of various phenomena.
Nought and NIL.
Numbers.
Signs.
Letters.

Type fonts and handwriting.
Everything logically meaningless and absurd.
Everything that elicits laughter.
Stupidity.
Humor.
Natural thinkers.
Omens.
Idiosyncratic superstitions.
Miracles.
Sleight of hand, but not illusions done with the help of apparatus.
Human interrelations, private.
Bon ton.
Human faces.
Women's beauty.
Women's sexual physiology.
Smells.
The liquidation of squeamishness.
Washing, bathing and the bath.
Cleanliness and filth.
Food.
The preparation of certain dishes.
Serving food at the table.
Smoking pipes and cigars.
The arrangement of house, apartment and room.
Men's and women's clothing.

I'm interested in what other people are interested in.
What people do when alone.
Sleep and dreams.
Notebooks.
Writing on paper in ink or pencil.
Paper, ink, pencil.
Recording daily events.
Small smooth-haired dogs.
Women, but only my favorite type.
Anthills.
Canes, walking sticks.

Water.
Wheels.
Meteorology.

Kind old ladies of good family interest me.
Phases of the moon.
Weather reports.
Record of events.
Kabbala.
Pythagoras.

* * *

<u>WHAT I LOVE:</u>

I love to write. I love observing people I like. I love observing pretty women. I love to eat. I love smoking a pipe. I love to sing. I love to lie naked in the sun on a hot day by the water, surrounded by nice people, including many interesting women. I love small smooth-haired dogs. I love ~~laughter~~ good humor. I love the absurd. I love watches, especially thick pocket-watches. I love notebooks, ink, paper and pencils. I love walking in Petersburg, namely: along Nevsky, the Field of Mars, the Summer Garden, the Trinity bridge. I love walking in the Catherine Park in Tsarskoe Selo. I love walking along the seashore in resort towns like Lakhta, Olgino, and Sestroretsk. I love to walk alone. I love to be among refined people. ~~I love women, but only my type.~~

What interests me:
Writing poems and discovering various things from them.
Succulents.

* * *

July 18. Cool weather all morning but better towards evening. The sky gradually cleared up. All day long I did nothing. I was at the beach between 1 and 7. No luck. In the evening I went to the Mikhailovsky Park.

My wife and I—1. My study. 2. Library. 3. Anteroom. 4. Bedroom. 5. Wife's room. 6. Dining room. 7. Sitting room. 8. Spare room.

Papa—1. Study. 2. Bedroom.

Natasha—room.

Mashenka—room.

Common areas—1. Hall. 2. Dining room. 3. Spare room. 4. Spare room.

Liza and Volodya—1. Study. 2. Bedroom. 3. Dining room. 4. Nursery. 5. Anteroom. 6. Tutor's room.

$8 + 2 + 1 + 1 + 4 + 6 = 24$

* * *

At the beach I'm always surrounded by such vile women that I don't even feel like staying.

There are almost no educated women on the beach, they're all rude bitches.

I'm constantly afraid that suddenly a woman will think: oh no! Now he's going to start up a conversation with me, that's why I always lie on the beach looking angry.

(the weather's shit)

Anyone who says the weather on July 18 is good, or even not too bad, is a dope.

Some Jewish girls are insolent, with a terribly annoying sense of humor.

Some Jewish girls are very good-looking but most of them are nasty, stupid and impudent creatures with a very primitive consciousness.

I would forbid people from making fun of one another at the beach. Wherever fate places you at the beach, just stay there.

Searching searching searching for a wife!

* * *

1. A wristwatch, a gold chronometer with repeater, alarm and second-hand.
   A gold watch chain.
2. A gold chronometer with gold chain.
3. An open-faced silver chronometer with black steel chain.
4. A platinum watch with cover. Alarm. Platinum chain.

All watches thick, heavy, and with Roman numerals on the dial.

* * *

1. A pipe with a faceted mouthpiece, flat at the end.
A chibouk ("Finnish Locomotive"), straight and rather short.
2. A straight, wood, light-colored pipe.
3. A black mastic pipe with a cap.
4. A long curved pipe with a top.
5. A long straight meerschaum screw stem pipe.
6. A straight briar pipe, highest quality with egg-shaped bowl.
7. A short black pipe.
8. A short, dark, straight pipe.

1. An ivory cigarette holder.
2. Green amber holder.
3. Yellow amber holder.
4. Yellow amber cigar holder.

1. Pen knife.
2. Cleaner.
3. Lighter.
4. Bracelet.
5. Ring.
6. Signet ring.
7. Two stick pins.
8. Four sets of cufflinks.
9. Comb.
10. Metal mirror.
11. Burning glass.
12. Cigarette case.
13. Compass.
14. Revolver.

15. Eyeglasses.
16. Lemon preserves.
17. Mechanical pencil.
18. Mechanical pen.
19. Aurora Ltd.

* * *

Allah Akhbar
Daniil
Kharms
Daniil Ivanovich Kharms
Kharms font
want a good broad.
wet cunt.
bouquet of brunettes.
my wife is a luxuriant brunette
with moist and fragrant
sex organs.

* * *

They'll stop talking to me at State Publishing. I'm letting them down after giving them my word.

If only men didn't get in my way.

I'm behaving like a scoundrel. I ought to be at State Publishing at this moment but instead I'm lolling around at the beach shirking my duty. I really enjoy being around naked women but only if they find me handsome and interesting.

An officer sat down next to me. He's with a woman. Seems he has to leave but is afraid of leaving his lady next to me. How can I reassure him.

I see a woman who's nearly naked.

I feel like getting to know the girl lying next to me on the beach.

I was at the other end of the beach, even tried to lie down, but it's so revolting there, it's hard to describe.

* * *

In the woods
I understood
How water is like to a wheel.

Water shines and makes a body trim.
One young beauty went in for a swim,
she stripped naked and in the water, splash!
I'm all ready to make a pass.

**Nothing's happening. I want women to take one look at my cock
and to go into raptures about it and get excited by looking at it and
for the juices to start flowing from their cunts while my cock swells
enormously and beautifully. I want a beautiful sweet woman to present
her moist sex organs for me to suck and lick.**

**I despise all proletarian women.
Women in swimming caps are ugly.**

Find out if 5693 and 11389 are prime numbers. I think that the first is, the
other isn't.

Look a swallow is standing upside down.

**Good-looking women lying next to me on both sides.
Saturday, July 22.**

A good looking girl is lying next to me. . .

This is about another one:
She just went and introduced herself to some hooligan. Meanwhile your
humble servant is left holding the bag. But she could have had a more
interesting time with me.

July 22. Was at Lipavsky's. Zabolotsky and Druskin were there as well. We
talked about fights and women.

* * *

**O Water Water
You refresh our bodies
You refresh our insides.
You slake our thirst.**

O Water Water
When you're sated with the sun
You suddenly open up for me
Like the wheel of life.

I see the woman from yesterday again, but she's lying far away from me.

Sweet girl, I conjure you by water, heat and sun. Come here to me.

o water water
who knows your secret destiny
o water water
I feel drawn to you intensely
but wicked though you are, Great Water,
through you the world is kept
in perfect peace.

* * *

Ice from Sebastopol.

Bichat and van der Kolk remarked that people with deformed necks have more lively minds than normal people.

* * *

I wasted time on the islands
didn't see my beauty.
        Ah!
everything is disgusting.
everything is repellent.
my heart has cooled towards
all women except for
that one beauty.

the ship's propeller cuts the water
the ship needs its propeller, daughter.

o water water
you're the first foundation of all numbers.
o water water
you're gas then liquid again.

Need to try to forget my love, make peace with it. How infinitely sad this is.

* * *

A peasant woman on tram no. 31 on its way to the Petrograd side asks: "Where's the station to Moscow around here?" Another woman answers her: "The station, it's further on over there" and points in the right direction. However she doesn't explain that the first old woman is going the wrong way.

Two ninnies.

So that's the way it has to be, I won't see my beloved again. That's the way it has to be. It's all for the better.

G.

I'm no longer looking for my girl from the beach. She's already forgotten me and I don't want to remember her any more. There has to be some kind of equilibrium in these things. Out of inertia, my eyes are still looking for her but my soul has already cooled towards her.

O these unfriendly, dense and crude Soviet women! How can I get away from you? For every 478 dimwits and blockheads, there is just one sweet and beautiful one. Just one!

Sit yourself down and think about good-looking women.
1.   They are inaccessible to you.
2.   That's all you can say about them.

Leave the cafeteria. You won't meet anyone here anyway. Go away and stay at home.

* * *

Apocryphal gospels of James and Thomas.
The Adoration of the Magi.

About Adam's skull.

* * *

July 27. You can hear the distant radio stations well. Tomorrow the weather will be bad.

Pity. I would have liked to spend the whole day at the beach.

July 28. 10:30. If you look outside from inside the room, the sky is clear. But if you take a look out the window, you can see that in an hour or two the whole sky will be full of clouds.

Why are you so tanned?

I'm getting aroused looking at a girl. She amazes me. She's standing like a candle at the edge of the sea, naked.

* * *

/ / - / - / - /
- / - / - / - /

and all romance is but a dream
the one can't keep her legs together
she sweeps the hair from off her face
and skips down to the sea to play there
she searches shells out in the sand
she's bent her pretty little head down
and heaven warms the charming little scamp now
and sunbeams cast their patterns on her hand
in beauty she's a queen majestic
And yet another to the left is
kicking pebbles without shoes
~~and there's a beautiful brunette who's~~
~~lying there with cunt in view~~
~~lying there completely nude~~
she's wholly shameless. That's quite rare
~~and she may well be yours someday~~
and half a minute passes swiftly
the water rolls in eight times more
~~a goddess with her full hips swinging~~
~~goes past us swiftly on the shore~~

July 30. Bad weather today. I predict bad weather tomorrow too. In any case, I won't be able to go to the beach.

* * *

Write something about the old woman on the staircase.

* * *

I'm sitting watching the "cinema for the masses." Well, what do you expect? Not one intelligent face.

White Kb3, Qh7, Bd2, e8, Nc6, pp. b4, e5, e6
Black Kd5, Rf5, pp. d3,e5, f6.
Mate in two moves.
My solution.
1. Be8-g6; Kd5-e4 for if Kd5: c6 then
2. Qh7-d7 x
2. Qh7-h1 x

Nimbus	rainy
Stratus	layered
Cumulus	clumped
Cirrus	feathery

* * *

August 3, 1933. Bought myself an Austrian pipe for 33r. 25k.

* * *

[August 4]

At the beach I finally saw a nice, interesting woman, good in every sense of the word. She was lying next to me on the right. There was also a beautiful woman lying on the left, but she was not from my circle. I made a notation on page **50**. It happened on July 22, 1933.

July 23. Again I saw this beautiful girl. But when I got to the beach I didn't notice her right off and lay down a distance from her. She left soon after I noticed her. Now I miss her.

I never did see her again.

August 4. I was walking with Olga Nikolaevna along Znamenskaya St. and ran into my beauty.

~~March 13, 1934.~~
~~I was standing, looking through the card catalog in the reference room at the Public Library. Next to me stood a young lady in a green blouse. Suddenly, I felt my cock harden. Some kind of electrical current was running from the young lady to me, getting me all aroused. But there was something about the young lady I didn't like. Suddenly I realized that she was my beauty from the beach. I looked more closely and saw that she was pregnant now. That's what I didn't like about her, my cock got hard anyway, even before I recognized her.~~

Now I've suddenly realized, it wasn't her, it was that female editor from the State Publishers.

My cock was mistaken.

* * *

[From notebook 25]

6:20 – 6:30
24 hours 20 m.
North-Western Weather Bureau.
1 pm August 6.
Cyclone is moving East. Eye in Rybinsk.
Freshening northerlies around Lake Ladoga.

* * *

For August 9.
      13:10. Weather bulletin.
      18:10. Weather bulletin.
      18:55. Weather bulletin.

[From notebook 27]

August 12.
I make one little vow: not to smoke until tomorrow.

* * *

Everything written by Mozart is a work of a genius. I was just listening to his "German Dances." And yesterday I listened to Masetto's aria from *Don Giovanni* and the aria *"Non piu andrai"* from *The Marriage of Figaro*. Now that's genius.

I was listening to Schubert. The very end of his "Musical Moment" is wonderful.

A good march by Schubert.

Schumann's "March of the Tin Soldiers," good.

* * *

P. Uspensky, *Tertium Organum*
Masonry, 2 vols, 1914, ed. S. P. Melgunov,
Petrovo-Solovo, *Spiritism*. 1905. 237 p.,

Jean-Jacques Rousseau, *Confessions*

* * *

The Theoretical degree of the Solomonic sciences.

A five-pointed salt cellar with white salt is a sign of wisdom.

Wilde
Dos Passos, *Manhattan Transfer*
Flaubert, *M-me Bovary*
Wassermann

Chesterton
Dreiser

* * *

The History of India. Ragozina.

The Book of Radio, Guenter.

Justin Winsor, *The Life of Columbus.* 608 p. 1893.

Findel, *The History of Free Masonry.* 2 vols, St. Petersburg, 1872-74.

Bishop Feofan. *Letters about the Spiritual Life.*

Episcopal Justice, N. Leskov.

H. Grell, *The Sexual Problem.*

C. Wel, *Das verbotene Buch: meine sensationellen Erlebnisse mit der internationalem Liga freier Menschen.* Hanover, 1925.

Alexander von Fekete, *Die Funktion der weiblichen Geschlechtsorgane und ihr Beziehungen zum Gesamtorganismus für Arzte und Studierende.* Berlin 1930.

A. P. Eisner, *On Dostoevsky*

B.

September 4.

Valentina Efimovna's birthday.

* * *

[From notebook 28, autumn 1933]

Daniil Ivanovich Kharms
Petersburg, 11 Nadezhdinskaya Street, apt. 8
Tel. 32—15
Tuesday, September 19, 1933.
State Publishing Library.
No. 641.

* * *

[From notebook 38]

Works of art describing the negative side of human nature work better. As do works that begin with an indifferent or even a poor word.

As they decrease, numbers do not end with zero. But the system of negative quantities is a fictional system. I proposed creating numbers smaller than zero, that is, Cisfinitum. But that was also wrong. Zero includes in itself these numbers unknown to us. Perhaps it would have been correct to consider these numbers as certain zero categories. In this way, a descending series of numbers would look like this:

. . . 3	-	category III
2	-	category II
1	-	category I
0	-	category 0
		category of two zeros
		category of three zeros
		category of four zeros
. . . . . etc.		

I propose to call a zero forming certain categories "nought" and to express it not in the shape of an elongate circle 0, but as a precise circle O. Tuesday, September 19, 1933.

* * *

[From notebook 28]

I should read the following books:

1. ~~Balzac, *Lost Illusions*, by September 8.~~
2. ~~Gogol, *Dead Souls*, by September 10.~~
3. ~~E. Perrier, *The Earth before History*,~~ by September 15.
4. ~~L. S. Berg, *The Theory of Evolution*, by 18 September.~~
5. ~~Eckermann, *Conversations with Goethe*, by September 22.~~
      October 5

V. O. Likhtenshtad, *Goethe: The Struggle for a Realistic Worldview*, 1920. His "On Flowers" is there.

On November 24, 1933, Mozart's *Requiem* will be performed at the Capella.

* * *

Prince S. N. Trubetskoy, *Lectures in the History of Classical Philosophy* (Logos).
A. Makovelsky, *The Pre-Socratics: The First Greek Thinkers and their Works*. (texts). Kazan, 1914.

I. Lapshin, *The Laws of Thought and the Forms of Cognition*. St. Petersburg 1906.

Johann Kaspar Lavater.

The fantastic novels of Theodor Gottlieb von Hippel (1741-1796).

> *1. Lebensläufe in aufsteigender Linie nebst Beilagen A.B.C.* (Berlin, 1778-81).
>
> *2. Kreuz- und Querzüge des Ritters A. bis Z.* (1793-1794).

* * *

List of books I intend to read:
1. Berg, *Theory of Evolution*.
2. Rozenberg, *The Problems of Buddhist Philosophy*.
3. Nordman, *A Trip around the Universe*.
4. Eckermann, *Conversations with Goethe*.
5. *A General History of Literature*, eds. Korsh and Kirpichnikov. (St. Petersburg, 1880-92).
6. Dostoevsky, *The Possessed*.
7. Benvenuto Cellini.
8. Lesage, *The Devil Upon 2 Sticks*.
9. Lesage, *Gil Blas*.

Look at the plays of Kotzubue and Iffland. Read Byron.

* * *

Chess Problem

White, Ka7, Qh2, Rc2, Bc1, c6, Nf3, d4, pp. a2.
Black, Kd3, Qh4, Bd1, Nb1, pp. b2, e3, f4, g5.

Mate in two moves.

Étude
White, Ka2, Bc6, Nh3.
Black, Kc3, pp. c2.
White gets a draw.

It's dangerous to think about just anything.

<u>Books for Liza</u>:

> ~~Balzac, *The Wild Ass's Skin*.~~
> George Sand, *Consuelo*
> Maupassant, *Mont-Oriol*.
> Flaubert, *A Sentimental Education*.

* * *

Klavdia Vasilievna Pugacheva
Petersburg.   48 Suvorovsky Prospekt   } apt. 4a
                  2 Kavalergardskaya St.
                  tel. 1—49—71

[Letter to Klavdia Vasilievna Pugacheva]

Wednesday, September 20, 1933. Petersburg.

Dear Klavdia Vasilievna,

It turns out not to be so simple to write the letter I promised you. What is there to reveal about myself? And where do I get the eloquence I promised? Therefore I simply refuse to write the promised letter, and simply am writing you a letter from the bottom of my heart and of my own free will. So let the first part of this letter be tender, the second, playful, and the third, businesslike. Perhaps some portion of what was promised will even enter into this work, but, in any case, I won't especially worry about that. The one thing that I will carry out exactly is, I will drop this letter into the postal box on September 21, 1933.

Part I (tender)

Sweet Klavdia Vasilievna, this part of the letter is supposed to be tender. That isn't at all difficult to do since, in truth, my feelings for you have attained a tenderness simply astonishing. It would be enough for me to write down everything that comes into my head while I'm thinking only about you (this doesn't require any effort either, since I am thinking about you all the time) and my letter would, on its own, turn out to be most tender.

I myself don't know how things turned this way, but only that one fine day it suddenly happened that you—were no longer just you—but it wasn't that you had become a part of me, or I a part of you, or we both a part of something that had previously been a part of myself, if I had not myself been that particle which in its turn was a part. . . . Forgive me, the thought is rather complicated and, it seems, I've gotten myself tangled up in it.

On the whole, Klavdia Vasilievna, believe me in this one thing: I have never had a friend, and never even thought about it, considering that the part (again that part!) of myself that was searching to find a friend could look upon the remaining part as the entity most capable of embodying the idea of friendship and of that openness, of that sincerity, of that self denial, i.e. denial (I feel that once again I've gone too far and again I'm beginning to get mixed up), of that touching exchange of the most cherished thoughts and feelings capable of touching . . . No, I've gotten mixed up again. Better to tell you everything in two words:

I feel infinite tenderness for you, Klavdia Vasilievna!

Now let's move on to the second part.

Part II (playful)

After "the tender part," which requires all the subtlety of psychological convolutions, how simple it is to write "the playful part," which needs not so much psychological subtlety as keen wit and flexibility of thought. Refraining from pretty phrases with lengthy periods by reason of my unfortunate and clumsy tongue, I turn my attention straight to you and here exclaim: "O, how beautiful you are, Klavdia Vasilievna!"

May God help me finish the next phrase to the end and not get stuck in the middle. And so, crossing myself, I begin: Dear Klavdia Vasilievna, I'm glad that you left for Moscow, since had you stayed here (be brief!), I would have forgotten in a short time . . . (briefer still!) I would have fallen in love with you and forgotten everything around me! (Done.)

Having achieved complete success, neither wishing to spoil the impression left by the second part, I move quickly on to the third part.

Part III (businesslike—as it should be)

Dear Klavdia Vasilievna, write me soon how you're doing in Moscow. I miss you very much. It's awful to think that a person gradually can get used to anything, or, rather, forgets what he once longed for. But another time, a gentle reminder is enough and all desire flares up anew, if it had once been, even for a moment, genuine. I do not believe in epistolary correspondence between people who know each other; people who are not acquainted can correspond the more readily and the better, and therefore I do not ask of you letters written according to the "rules and forms." But if you would, from time to time, send me a little piece of paper with your name on it, I will be very grateful to you. Of course, if you do send me a letter, I will also be much touched.

I still haven't been to see the Shvartzes on Liteiny. But when I do, I'll convey to them everything you've asked of me.

Life, ah life! Life has gotten so expensive! At the market a leek costs not just 30, but 35 or even a whole 40 kopecks.

Daniil Kharms

* * *

A chess problem by Sam Lloyd:
White, Kh7, Qa2, RRf5, h3, Be5.
Black, Kh5, Qe2, Rg5, Bg4, pp. h4.
Mate in two moves.

September 21 at 7:30 PM, invited to Maria Yurievna's (Mariasha).
Ozerki, 2 Varvarinskaya St. (in the courtyard there's a dog: he lunges but won't bite).
Tram № 21 or 20 (to the end of the line), Bus № 11.

[From notebook 38]

It's interesting that the Russian words for a German, a Frenchman, an Englishman, an American, a Japanese, a Hindu, a Jew, even a Samoyed, are all proper nouns, like the old Russian word *Rossianin*. But in modern

Russian, there is no noun for a Russian. The word "Russian" is derived from the adjective and sounds just like an adjective. "Russian" is undefined. But even more vague is "a Soviet." How subtle words can be!
September 21.

* * *

[Letter to Natalia Koliubakina]

Thursday, September 21, 1933. Petersburg

Dear Natasha,

Thanks for Zhemchuzhnikov's poems. They are precisely Zhemchuzhnikov, but not at all Prutkov. Even if they had been signed "Prutkov," they still wouldn't be Prutkovian. And conversely, things by Aleksei Tolstoy like "Comma's Ballet" or "How the philosopher went without pickles," are pure Prutkov, even though signed only by Tolstoy.

I showed my leg to Dr. Shapo. He muttered a few Latin phrases but, judging by his telling me to drink yeast, he agrees with my opinion. Incidentally, there's no yeast to be had anywhere.

To answer a poem with a poem, I'm sending you some verses I wrote yesterday. It's true that they're not yet finished. The end should be different, nevertheless I think they're graceful and have that melancholy tone with which one speaks of the incomprehensible predestination of man in the world. I repeat that the verses aren't finished and don't even have a title yet.

Daniil Kharms

* * *

[From notebook 28]

There are sounds, sometimes quite loud ones, which are hardly distinguishable from silence. So, for example I've noticed that the sound of our doorbell does not wake me up. When I'm lying in bed, the sound of the doorbell doesn't really differ from silence. This happens because it's similar to the extended, sausage-like forms made by the end of my blanket turned inside out near my ear.

All things arrange themselves around me in certain forms. But some forms are missing, for example, the forms of sounds *made* by children crying or playing. That's why I don't like children.

Learn the names of the northern sea birds.

* * *

Books I've borrowed from the State Publishing library:
> *Masonry*, 2 vols.
> Podmore, *Spiritualism*, 2 vols.
> Petrovo-Solovovo, Spiritualism.
> Gorbunov, 2 vols.
> *General History of Literature*, ed. Korsh, vol. 4.
> 3 books on paper making.
> Steiner, *Higher Consciousness*.
> Eckermann, 3 vols.
> Goethe, "Dichtung und Wahrheit," *Wilhelm Meister*.
> Novalis, *Heinrich von Ofterdingen*
> Helmholtz, *Physiology of Hearing*.
> Zernov, *A Biography of Helmholtz*.
> Belshovsky, *Goethe*, 2 vols.
> Goethe, Suvorin edition.
> Aleksandr Grin, "History of a Murder."
> Prout, *Mozart*.
> Davydova, *Mozart*.
> Biographies of composers.
> George Sand, *La Confession d'une jeune fille*.
> Galsworthy.
> Rimsky-Korsakov.
> Pustoroelev.   Music theory.

Books from the City Writers' Union Library
> September 16
> Lesage, *The Devil upon Two Sticks*
> Balzac, *The Collection of Antiquities*
>
> September 28
> Lesage, *Gil Blas*
> Balzac, *La Peau de chagrin*

<u>Books borrowed from private individuals</u>:

> <u>From Zabolotsky</u>:
> ~~E. Perrier, *The Earth Before History*.~~
> Nordman, *A Trip around the Universe*.
> Eckermann, *Conversations with Goethe*.
> Arithmetic for Fun, Book 8

> <u>From Druskin</u>:
> Rozenberg, *Problems of Buddhist Philosophy*.
> Berg, *Theory of Evolution*.
> Chesterton, *Club of Queer Trades*.

> <u>From Lipavsky</u>:
> Dickens, *Dombey and Son*.
> Hamsum, *Gedämpftes Saitenspiel*

> <u>From Shvarts</u>:
> Two books by Jean-Paul.

* * *

On Saturday, September 23, have to be at the Radio Center (for adults) from 5 to 7
Bronfin (her) and Evgenii Pavlovich Gershuni, 6th Floor, room 45.

S.A. Buturlin, *Shooting with Bullets*. Petersburg, 1912.

on young poets p. 226
Goethe's birthday is 28 August 1749.

Tell Shvarts about the Radio Center.

* * *

About a man of very great strength.
He's invincible. Everyone is amazed at him.
A certain somebody is very interested in him.
Another somebody, a learned man, is talking about precisely these things.
After many efforts, the first certain somebody comes upon the learned man.

Finally the first certain somebody learns from the learned man that there exists a third certain somebody, much stronger than the aforementioned strong man. The first certain somebody learns from the learned man many stories about the third certain somebody but is still unable to get a look at him.

Stephan Schütze. *Happy Hours*. 1821-23.

* * *

Johan-Paul-Friedrich Richter, known as Jean-Paul (Richter), born 1763. His novels *The Invisible Lodge* (1793), *Hesperus, or Forty-five Dog Post Days* (1795), *Flower, Fruit and Thorn Pieces, or the Married Life, Death and Wedding of the Advocate of the Poor, Siebenkäs* (1796), *The Titan* (1801-03), *The Comet or Nikolaus Marggraf* (the story of an insane pharmacist) (1822). The heroes of his last pieces are almost all madmen. The complete edition of his works runs to 60 volumes.

Richter's first novel *The Invisible Lodge* remained unfinished but in the novel's second edition, Richter wrote: "Although readers will not learn here what came of Kunts's second love or of Lisa's despair, we will recall that all of life everywhere presents riddles whose solutions lie on the other side of the grave, that the entire history of mankind is an enormous novel without end."

* * *

[Letter to Natalia Koliubakina]

September 24, 1933. Leningrad.

Dear Natasha,

You've sent me enough brewer's yeast to cure someone as completely covered in blisters as a bird is in feathers. I didn't know it came in tablets and is sold in drug stores. I'm simply embarrassed that while I'm the one who needs the yeast, it was you who found out about this. Your edition of Kozma Prutkov (1899) is the best, although it's lacking many things. Yesterday Marshak called and asked me to go see him if I wasn't busy and had the desire to do so. I went. In the entranceway there was the usual scene with embraces and kisses. The words "O Mother of Mine!" would not have been out of place. Then Marshak circled around me and, without even letting me take a seat, talked about Rome and Paris and complained about his fatigue. Marshak spoke very well about Rome. Then the conversation turned to Dante. Marshak has already learned to speak some Italian and we sat up till 3 in the morning reading Dante, both of us in raptures. The poems I had wanted to send you are not yet finished, so it's good I didn't send them.

But I'm definitely Kolpakov.

Thank Mashenka for the matches and tobacco.

Danya

* * *

For Sunday, September 24, 1933.

Finish Goethe's biography in Korsh's *History* and read 100 pages of Eckermann. Wake up at 11:30, go to bed no later than 2.

Woke up at 2 pm. One resolution already broken.

Friedrich Leopold von Hardenberg (Novalis) born 1772. *Heinrich von Ofterdingen* (*The Blue Flower*).

Read Byron's *The Deformed Transformed.*

Who is Grigory Aleksandrovich?

* * *

Write a poem about the universal flood. September 24, 1933.

* * *

[From notebook 38]

Reading Byron's *The Deformed Transformed.*

The beginning with the mother's curse is wonderful. But further on the innumerable appearances of classical heroes become excessive. Byron gets carried away describing them. Arnold's conversation with the stranger is very good up to the spell. Then the heroes start appearing.

The illustration "The Appearance of Achilles' Shade" by Madox Brown is utterly worthless. Instead of a monstrous hunchback whom "man avoids, fearfully passing by," Arnold looks like a stealthy youth ready to catch a butterfly resting on a flower, for which reason he bends his knees and body, holding his arms at the ready. The stranger is simply a tall man with a mustache, wrapped in a cloak just to look mysterious. Achilles, who should be a giant 12 cubits tall, is no taller than the hunchback. On his head is a helmet with what looks like a piece of the cogwheel depicted on the emblem of the Defense Aviation Chemical Society. With the face of a good-looking governess, he stands in the modest pose of a provincial ballet dancer. Madox Brown wanted to show Achilles standing in a waterfall, but Achilles' scrawny legs are standing on, not in, the water. And in general, the waterfall looks like straw. In his hand, Achilles is holding two spears, each about as long as a small cane but with large, broad spearheads. The general impression is that he's holding a waffle maker in his hand. A disgrace, not an illustration.

Later on the play becomes interesting again. Especially when the action moves to old Rome. The appearance of Benvenuto Cellini is interesting. Then Caesar (Mephistopheles) says some interesting things. Very subtle bit in Act 3, where Count Herman is jealous of Olympia.
September 25.

* * *

ON LAUGHTER
Advice to comic actors.

1. I've noticed how important it is to find the moment at which you get a laugh. If you want the audience to laugh, come out on stage and stand there silently until someone bursts out laughing. Then, wait a little bit longer until someone else begins to laugh but this time loudly enough that everyone hears. But this laughter has to be genuine and, in this instance, a claque won't do the trick. Once this has happened, you know that you've found the comic tipping point. At this point, you can start your comic program and be assured that your success is guaranteed.
2. There are several kinds of laughter. There is the middling kind of laughter when the entire hall is laughing but not at full force. There's a strong kind of laughter when only one or another part of the audience

is laughing at full force, while another part of the hall is silent. In this case, the laughter has not gotten to them. The Stage Management demands the first type of laughter from performers, but the second is better. Swine ought not laugh.

September 25.

* * *

September 25. Rm. 45, 7 pm. Methodological brigade for radio performance.

> You really don't need a ventriloquist on the radio. What's the point of a ventriloquist if you can't see what he's doing with his lips? Krzhanovsky

> A ventriloquist can play the piano with his lips. There are some special tricks that go with radio broadcasts. Sometimes you can whistle.

> Failed actor.
> Failed ventriloquist.
> Failed singer, etc.

> Laughter on the radio, at the beginning, at the mistakes.

> Radio is closest of all to literature, to the printed word.

> Laughter is based not on meaning, but on situation.

> About a reader on the radio who keeps getting confused, or is unable to speak into the microphone, or is always asking what he should do.

> Middling laughter.
> During a big laugh, only a part of the audience is really laughing.

> The difference between radio, theater, cinema and literature.

> It's all either very simple or it's ridiculous.

About creativity, about the circumstances of happy-go-lucky and joyous creativity.

Creating the comic tipping point, the moment you get a laugh.

Concerning experienced audiences.

What's the point of psycho-technology? We need psycho-technology here less than anything else.

Next meeting, October 5, 1933.

* * *

September 26, 3:30 pm. An eccentric is appearing at the Radio Center.

* * *

Melmoth the Wanderer. Charles Robert Maturin. Suppl. to *The North*. St. Petersburg, pub. M. N. Remezova, 1894.
The Lake School. Wordsworth, Coleridge and Southey.

Thomas Campbell (1777-1844).
John Wilson (1785-1854), *The Isle of Palms* (1812), *The City of the Plague* (1817)
Charles Lamb (1775-1834), humorist.
The following poets are also associated with the Lake School: James Montgomery, Henry Kirke White, and the poetesses Felicia Hemans and Letitia Elizabeth Landon.
George Crabbe (born 1754), *The Library* (1781), *The Village* (1783), his poem *The Parish Register* (1807) made him famous.
Ann Radcliffe. Born Anna Ward 1764.
Mathew Gregory Lewis (1773 -1818), *The Monk*. Translations into Russian: 1st edition 1802-1803, 2nd edition 1805.
Charles Robert Maturin (1782-1824). *Fatal Revenge, or the Family of Montorio: A Romance* (London, 1807): *Melmoth the Wanderer*, 4 vols. (London, 1820).

* * *

The Mathematician and Andrei Semyonvich

M.

I pulled a sphere from my head.   (4 times)
A. S.

Put it back.   (4 times)
M.

No, I won't put it back.   (4 times)
A. S.

So don't put it back.   (4 times)
M.

Then I won't put it back.   (4 times)
A. S.

So you don't have to.   (4 times)
M.

Then I've won.   (3 times)
A. S.

So you've won, now calm down.
M.

No, I won't calm down.   (3 times)
A. S.

Even though you're a mathematician, honest to God, you're not too smart.
M.

No, I am smart and I know quite a lot. (3 times)
A. S.

A lot but it's all just nonsense.
M.

No, not nonsense.   (3 times)
A. S.

I'm sick of quibbling with you.
M.

No, you're not sick of it.   (3 times)

* * *

You've got to write poems so that every single thought in the poem, if retold in prose, would be as pure as the line that expresses it.

Lines like the following look ok:

". . . the rivers of our knowledge perish
within our mighty brain. . . ."

But if retold in prose, they sound bad:
". . . I watched the rivers of our knowledge gradually disappear from our mighty brain . . ."
You have to say:
"I saw knowledge perishing within a great brain. . . "

Of course, poems have their own laws but it would be even better if the poem sounded good while at the same time preserving the laws of prose. September 25.

Eckermann. *Gesprache mit Goethe in den letzten Jahren seines Lebens.* 1868

* * *

Moliére, *Le Misanthrope.*
Kant, *Critique of Pure Reason.*
Shakespeare, *Lady Macbeth.*
Aristotle, *Poetics.*
Aristotle, *Ethics.*
Ivan Volodikhin, *Architectural Style.*
Biographies:
Helmholtz
Goethe (Lichtenstadt).
Helmholtz, *On the Sensations of Tone as a Physiological Basis for the Theory of Music.*
Wilhelm Meister.
Dichtung und Wahrheit.
Belshovsky, *Goethe, His Life and Works.* Vol. I 1898, 438 p. Vol. II 1908, 637 p.
Goethe. 261 p. Suvorin's publication.

Goethe, Journals. in *Literary Heritage*, 1932, 4-6.
Hermann Helmholtz.
Emil Michel.
Rubens.
George Borrow, *The Bible in Spain; Levengro; Romany Rye.*
D. G. Lewis, *The Life of Goethe.*
Gundolf, *Goethe.*
Stefan George.
George Kreis.

* * *

[To N. A. Tiuvelev]

Dear Nikandr Andreevich,

I got your letter and realized at once that it was from you. At first I thought that it might not be from you, but as soon as I opened it, I realized at once that it was from you, otherwise I was about to think that it wasn't from you. I'm happy that you got married a long time ago, because when a man gets married to someone he wanted to marry that means he's accomplished what he wanted. So now I'm quite happy that you got married because when a man gets married to the person he wanted to marry, that means he's accomplished what he wanted. Yesterday I got your letter and thought at once that the letter was from you, but then thought, it seems that it's not from you but I opened it and see—exactly, it's from you. You did very well to write to me. At first you didn't write, but then suddenly wrote, although even earlier, before you didn't write for a time, you had written too. As soon as I got your letter, I decided at once that it was from you and then I was very happy that you're already married. For once a person's conceived a desire to get married then he has to get married no matter what. Therefore I'm very happy that you finally married someone you wanted to marry. And you've done very well to write me. I was delighted when I saw your letter, and even thought at once that it was from you. True as I was opening it, the thought suddenly occurred to me that it wasn't from you but then I nevertheless decided that it was from you. Thanks for writing. I am grateful to you for this and very happy for you. Perhaps you can't guess why I'm so happy for you but I'll tell you right off that I'm happy for you because you got married and precisely to the person you wanted to marry. And this, you know, is very good—to marry precisely the person you wanted to marry, because then you accomplish precisely what you wanted. And that's precisely why I'm happy for you. I'm also happy that you wrote me a letter. I had decided from a distance that the letter was from you, but as soon as I took it in my hands, I thought: but what if it's not from you? And then I think: come off it, of course it's from you. I open the letter myself and at that moment think: from you or not from you? from you or not from you? Well as soon as I opened it, I saw it was from you. I was delighted and decided to write you a letter too. There's a lot to say, but literally no time. I wrote as much as I could manage in this letter, the rest I'll write in another, otherwise I don't have any time at all now. At least it's good that you wrote me a letter. Now I know that you've been married for a while. I know from your previous letters that you were married and now I see again— it's absolutely true, you got married. And I'm very happy that you got married and wrote me a letter. Just as soon as I saw the letter I decided that you got married again. Well, I think, it's good that you got married again and wrote me a letter about it. Write me now about your new wife and how it all turned out. My regards to your new wife.

* * *

"Messengers and their Conversations," Yakov Druskin.
I am the messenger.

Note down my thinking about "The Adoration of the Magi" by Rubens.

Design a coat of arms for myself.
The Coat of Arms of the Family of Khaarms. October 1, 1933.
Cosi fan tutte, Mozart.
Rondo, "Rage over a Lost Penny," Beethoven.
Mozart's "German Dances." Minus the finale.
Schumann, "Waltz," "The Happy Farmer," "Lonely Feelings,"
"The Hunter's Song."

* * *

Tell Bronfin at the radio station that you can't perform classical music on the balalaika.

Children should be given bell wire, rope and sticks.

I'm listening to Beethoven's Fifth Symphony. Now that's how to construct something big. How beautiful it is when the opening theme suddenly reappears in the middle.
The second movement is different.

A movement must be all of a piece.

It's good when the theme starts at the very beginning of the first movement, then it returns a little after the beginning of the second movement and is developed on its second appearance.

How can one represent a large and a small number of voices in poetry?

* * *

Ought to finish the following books:

      Goethe, *Dichtung und Wahrheit*, between October 9 and 16.
      Goethe, Suvorin edition, by October 20.
      Belshovsky's *Goethe*, by October 30.

During the winter of 1933-1934, I ought to accomplish the following:

1. Master English.
2. Develop my memory.

* * *

Smoking serves as brilliant proof that, when smoking, a man takes smoke into his mouth, passes it through his lungs, and then blows it out into the air.

October 4. Have to quit smoking so that I can brag about my will power. Imagine: you don't smoke for a week and, confident that you'll be able to keep from smoking, you spend the evening in the company of Lipavsky, Oleinikov and Zabolotsky. How pleasant when they notice you haven't been smoking all evening. And when they ask: why aren't you smoking? You answer, concealing a terrible pride: I've quit smoking! ("You" = I).

A great man shouldn't smoke.

To use the vice of pride to free oneself from the vice of smoking is both good and useful.

Promiscuity, drunkenness and gluttony are lesser vices than smoking.
      Or:
Drunkenness, gluttony and pride are lesser vices than smoking.

A gentleman smoker is like a button, while a lady smoker is like a buttonhole. And therefore, gentlemen, let's quit smoking.

> Or:

A gentleman smoker is unworthy of being even a button, while a lady smoker is unworthy of being even a buttonhole. And therefore, gentlemen, let's quit smoking.

> Or:

A gentleman smoker is like a chicken, while a lady smoker is like a dung heap. And therefore, gentlemen, let's quit smoking.

> Or:

A gentleman smoker is like a button buried in a dung heap, while a lady smoker is always annoying someone with her cigarette. And therefore, gentlemen, let's quit smoking.

> Or:

A gentleman smoker will never be at the top of his game, while a female smoker is game for anything. And therefore, gentlemen, let's quit smoking.

* * *

About Geniuses.

If we exclude the ancients, about whom I am unable to judge, there are no more than five true geniuses, of whom two are Russian. These are the five poetic geniuses: Dante, Shakespeare, Goethe, Pushkin and Gogol.

One should not confuse fecundity with productivity. The first is not always good; the second is always good.

Rose, fish and man.

* * *

A novel in which one of the characters tells the same story twice.

"The Demonic," Goethe said on March 2, 1831, "is that which cannot be dissolved by reason or understanding. There is none of it in my nature, but I am subject to it."

Goethe considered Napoleon and Grand Duke Karl Augustus, who were by nature full of boundless energy and knew no peace, to be demonic.

"Demonic beings of this sort the Greeks reckoned among the demigods."

Mephistopheles, according to Goethe, is not demonic: he is too negative a being. The demonic manifests itself only in absolutely positive energy. Among artists, there is more of it in musicians than in painters.

I think that among us, Vvedensky is the most demonic.

Goethe said: "Man must strive to prevail over the demonic."

* * *

[Letter to Klavdia Vasilievna Pugacheva]

October 5, 1933. Leningrad.

Dear Klavdia Vasilievna,

I want to see you more than anything in the world. You've conquered me. I'm very grateful for your letter. I think about you quite a lot. And again it seems to me that there was no good reason for you to move to Moscow. I really love the theater but, unfortunately, there's no theater these days. The time of theater, great epic poems and beautiful architecture came to an end a hundred years ago. Don't flatter yourself in the hope that Khlebnikov has written great epic poems or that Meyerhold is still theater. Khlebnikov may be better than all the other poets of the second half of the 19th and the first quarter of the 20th centuries, but his epics are simply long lyrics; and Meyerhold hasn't done a thing.

I firmly believe that the time for epic poems, architecture and theater will come again someday, but it isn't here yet. Until new models for these three art forms are created, the old ways remain the best. And I, were I in your place, would either try to create a new theater, if I felt in myself greatness sufficient for the task, or I would keep to the archaic theatrical forms.

By the way, the Children's Theater is in a more advantageous position than are other theaters, the theaters for adults. Even if it's not opening up a new renaissance, thanks to the specifics of its juvenile audience, and even though littered with "theater science," "Constructivism" and "Leftism" (please don't forget that I myself am considered to be among the most "extreme left poets"), it's still purer than the other theaters.

Sweet Klavdia Vasilievna, what a pity that you've left my city and more's the pity for me that I've become attached to you with all my heart.

I wish you, dear Klavdia Vasilievna, every success.

Daniil Kharms

* * *

Write letters to: Pugacheva, Khardzhiev and Nadezhina.

THREE TOPICS:
1. Sounds and numbers.
2. Tonic and syllabic music.
3.

* * *

Aleksandr Grin
"The happy go lucky parrot."
"Gladiators."
The road to nowhere.
The Golden Chain.
The History of a Murder.
"The Lanfier Colony."
Stories.

Virgil's *Eclogues*
"The Fourth Eclogue."

* * *

Strugovshchikov, the translator of *Faust*, translated it 6 times.

For Esther:
1. Plug for lamp.
2. Nails.
3. Light switch.
4. Mop.
5. Stockings.

* * *

[Letter to Klavdia Vasilievna Pugacheva]

Monday, October 9, 1933. Petersburg.

Dear Klavdia Vasilievna,

You've moved to a strange city, so it makes complete sense that you don't have any close friends there yet. But why, suddenly, don't I have any since you've been gone: it's not that I can't understand it, but it is amazing! Amazing that I saw you all of 4 times but I feel like telling everything that I see and think only to you.

Forgive me if from now on I'm absolutely candid with you.

I comfort myself with the thought: somehow it's good that you've left for Moscow. For what would have happened if you had stayed here? Either we would have gradually grown disenchanted with each other, or I would have fallen in love with you and, by virtue of my conservatism, would have wanted to see you my wife.

Maybe it's better to know you from a distance.

Yesterday I went to the Children's Theater to see *The Treasure* by Shvarts.

Okhotina's voice quite often sounds like yours. It's perfectly clear she's imitating you.

After the theater I walked with Shvarts for a long time, and Shvarts was sorry you weren't here. He was telling me how well you performed in *Underwood*. To hear a little more about you, I asked Shvarts to tell me about your role in *Underwood*. Shvarts kept on talking and I kept on being interested in all the details, and so Shvarts was flattered by my attention to his play.

I just finished reading Eckermann's *Conversations with Goethe*. If you haven't read it at all, or if you read it a long time ago, you should read it again. A really good and serene book.

Since you left, I've written only one poem so far. I'm sending it to you. It's called "Girlfriend" but it's not about you. The girlfriend looks rather frightening, with circles under her eyes and a burst eyeball. I don't know who she is. Perhaps, no matter how ridiculous this sounds nowadays, she's The Muse. But if the poem has turned out sad, that's really your fault. I'm sorry you don't know my poetry. "Girlfriend" isn't like my usual poems, just as I'm no longer like myself. You're the one to blame for that. And therefore I'm sending you this poem.

The flute you gave me has a strange peculiarity: it plays for five minutes and then starts hissing. Therefore, I play it twice a day: in the morning and at sunset.

Sweet Klavdia Vasilievna, don't lose heart, and also don't be afraid of writing me sad letters. I'm even glad that you found Moscow, at first, to be empty and dreary. This only means that you yourself are a great person.

Daniil Kharms

* * *

Everything well thought out is good. The appearance of the sorcerer at the beginning of Rimsky-Korsakov's opera *The Golden Cockerel* is good.
How wonderful when the chorus enters.
Great when one character is singing, suddenly another joins in, and then the entire chorus enters.

Francois Rabelais, *Gargantua and Pantagruel* in five books. First Russian translation by A. Engelhardt (with illustrations by Doré). St. Petersburg, 1901.

Fr. Rabelais, *Gargantua and Pantagruel*. Trs. and notes by V. Piast. Edited by I. Glivenko, With 276 illustrations by Gustave Doré. 1929.

* * *

[Letter to Klavdia Vasilievna Pugacheva]

Monday, October 16, 1933. Petersburg.

Talent grows by fostering destruction and creation.
Prosperity is always a sign of stagnation!

Dear Klavdia Vasilievna,

You are an amazing and genuine person!
However regrettable it is for me not to see you, I won't invite you to come back any more to the Children's Theater and to my city. How nice to know that there is still one person in whom desire

seethes! I don't know the word to express that force in you that makes me happy. I usually call it *purity*.

I was thinking how beautiful all first things are! How beautiful the first reality! The sun is beautiful, and grass, and stone, and water, and bird, and beetle, and fly, and man. But just as beautiful are wine glass, and knife, and key, and comb. But if I went blind, went deaf and lost all my senses, then how can I know all this beauty? Everything has vanished, and there's nothing left for me. But I received the sense of touch and, almost all at once, the entire world appeared anew. I acquired hearing and the world became significantly better. I acquired all the proper senses and the world became even larger and better. The world started to exist as soon as I allowed it to enter into me. Granted still in chaos, but none the less it exists!

However I began to put the world in order. And at that moment Art appeared. Only then did I realize the true difference between sun and comb, but, at the same time, I learned they're one and the same.

Now my concern is to create the correct order. I'm fascinated by this and can't think of anything else. I speak about it, attempt to tell, describe, draw, dance, build it. I am the creator of the world, and this is the most important thing within me. How can I not think about it constantly! Into everything I do I put in the consciousness that I am the creator of the world. But I'm not simply making a boot, but, first of all, I'm creating a new thing. It's not enough for me that the boot turn out comfortable, sturdy and that it look good. It's important for me that the order in the boot be the same as that of the entire world: that the order of the world not suffer, nor be polluted by coming into contact with leather and nails, that, whatever the form of the boot, it (the order) preserve its own form, that it remain the same as it ever was, that it stay *pure*.

This is the same purity that runs through all the arts. When I write poetry, the main thing, it seems to me, is not the idea, not the content, nor the form, and not the hazy concept of "quality," but something even hazier and less comprehensible to the rational mind but is comprehensible to me and, I hope, to you, sweet Klavdia Vasilievna. This is the *purity of order*.

This purity is one and the same in sun, grass, man and poems. True art stands together with the first reality, it creates the world and is its first reflection. It is necessarily real.

But, my God, what trifles are the stuff of true art! *The Divine Comedy* is a great work, but Pushkin's "Through the wavy mists of night" is no less great. For in the one and the other there is the same purity and, consequently, the same closeness to reality, that it, to independent existence. It's no longer simply words and thoughts printed on paper, but a thing just as real as the crystal inkwell standing before me on the desk. It seems this poem, which has become a thing, can be taken from the paper and thrown at the window, and the window will shatter. That's what words can do!

But on the other hand, how powerless and pathetic these same words can be! I never read newspapers. This is a fictive, not a created world. Nothing but a pathetic, worn out type on poor, splintery paper.

Does man need anything besides life and art? I don't think so: nothing more is necessary, everything genuine goes into it.

I think purity can be in everything, even in the way a man eats his soup. You did the right thing moving to Moscow. You pound the pavement and perform in a hungry theater. There is more purity in this than in living here, in a comfortable apartment and performing in the Children's Theater.

I'm always suspicious of everything comfortable and well off.

Zabolotsky was here today. For some time now he's been really fascinated by architecture and he's just written a long poem in which he's expressed a lot of remarkable thoughts about architecture and human life. I know that many people will be ecstatic over it. But I also know that the poem's bad. It's good only in a few places, almost by accident. There are two categories.

The first category is comprehensible and simple. Here it's so clear what has to be done. It's clear where to go, what to attain and how to realize it. Here the way is clear. You can discuss it, and someday a literary critic will write a whole volume on the subject, while a commentator will write six volumes about what it means. Everything here is comfortable and well-off.

No one can say a word about the second category, although it is precisely what makes all this architecture and thinking about human life into something good. It is unintelligible, incomprehensible and at the same time beautiful, this second category! But you can never attain it, it's ridiculous even to seek it, there are no roads leading to it. It is precisely this second category that suddenly forces a man to drop everything and take up mathematics, and then, dropping mathematics, suddenly to become fascinated with Arabic music, and then get married, and then, having knifed his wife and son, lie on his stomach and examine a flower.

It's this same uncomfortable category that makes a genius. (By the way, I'm not saying this about Zabolotsky: he hasn't yet killed his wife and hasn't even taken up mathematics.)

Sweet Klavdia Vasilievna, by no means am I making fun of your frequent visits to the Zoo. There was a time when I myself went to the Zoo here every day. I was friends with a wolf and pelican there. If you like, someday I'll tell you how pleasantly we'd pass the time.

If you like, I'll also tell you how I once spent an entire summer at the zoological station in Lakhta, in Count Stenbock-Fermor's castle, living on live worms and Nestlé chocolate powder in the society of a half-crazed zoologist, assorted spiders, snakes and ants.

I'm quite glad that you take walks to the Zoo in particular. And if you go there not for just a stroll but also to look at the animals, then I will love you even more tenderly.

Daniil Kharms

* * *

They stopped wearing the codpiece or "braguette" at the end of the 16th C.

I-rony
I was walking down the Neva screaming "Kapa!"

About Goethe:
1. *Historical Messenger* 1891, July, p. 217-218.

* * *

October 20, 1933.

I'm sitting in the Philharmonic waiting for the concert to begin. Mozart.

1. Symphony No. 31 in D Major.

2.

3. Jupiter Symphony.

The third part of the second thing is brilliant.

Shostakovich must be a genius.

My children are not glorious. No! I gave them great strength. I gave them long life.

Naïve Evenings.

At these evenings you can drink sweet wines, eat sweets, sing simple songs, play the zither, play naïve games such as guess what, marvel at how wondrously a fly is constructed, do magic tricks and read pleasing poems aloud.

I propose to organize such an evening on October 24 and to invite the following people to participate: E. I. Gritsyna (my sister), I. D. Zagorodnaya, E. E. Sno (zither), N. A. Zabolotsky, D. D. Mikhailov and me.

＊ ＊ ＊

Towards an Art of DRESSING

Dresses:

    I.   Female

        A. Brunettes.

           1. Short. Plump. Proportionate. Harmonious.

           2. Short. Plump. With inordinately large breasts.

           3. Short. Plump. With large breasts and thin legs.

           4. Short. Plump. Waist too wide.

           5. Short. Medium complexion. Harmonious.

           6. Short. Medium complexion. Breasts too small.

           7. Short. Medium complexion. Breasts too large.

           8. Short. Medium complexion. Legs too thin.

           9. Short. Medium complexion. Legs too fat.

A = brunette. B = blonde. C = Auburn hair.

m = short. r = medium height. h = tall. S = redhead.

z = plump. x = medium. y = thin.

Amz, Ahx, Crz - Bad	Bhy - good.
Az	By
Amz2?	

* * *

1. Requiem.
2. Dies irae.
3. Tuba mirum. Soloists.
4. Rex Tremendae.
5. Ricordare. Soloists.
6. Confutatis.
7. Lacrymosa.
8. Domine Jesu.
9. Hostias.
10. Sanctus.
11. Benedictus.
12. Agnus Dei.

Agnus Dei 43, 64, 95.

Sanctus 56

Otto Jahn, Mozart's biographer, *W. A. Mozart*, 4 vols, Leipzig, 1856-59. Second edition, reworked by Hermann Abert. 2 vols. 1919-1921.

* * *

Go immediately to Dementiev's to get Budagossky's pipe.

1. a = la
2. e = re
3. g = sol
4. g = sol
5. c = do

To go an octave higher means to double the number of vibrations. So what does it mean to increase the number of vibrations by 3, 4, 5 times, etc.?

* * *

What is more pleasant? Infinity or finitude?

Petersburg Tales.
the words—we hear them backwards.

Adonilen Twice a day, 10 drops.
Camphor Water – 2 times a day after meals

* * *

Luther ist der hohe Mann, 294.
"Ein feste Burg ist unser Gott."

* * *

Biographies of Composers from the 4ᵗʰ to the 20ᵗʰ Century. pub. Durnovo 1904.
Evgeny Braudo, *A Brief Account of the History of Music*. Moscow, State Publishers, 1928.
Zasedatelev, *Diseases of Singers' Voices and their Treatment*.
Edward Mörike, *Mozart on the Road to Prague*. Novella. 1928.
Prof. E. Naiman, *Illustrated General History of Music*.
A Sketch of the History of World Music. 1891.
Davydova, *Mozart*, 1891.

* * *

[In another handwriting]

D. I. Kharms is a very bad man because he takes notes during concerts. That means he doesn't love music. But music is art. And art is higher than everything. Long live Art!!!!
Does he like M.Ch."?

* * *

V. E. Goldina. 5—57—72.

* * *

[From notebook 38]

On Productivity.
My literary creations are my sons and daughters. It's better to give birth to three strong sons than forty weak ones.

Do not confuse productivity with fecundity. Productivity is the ability to leave strong and lasting progeny, while fecundity is nothing more than the ability to leave numerous offspring, who may live long but can also die out quickly.

The man who possesses productive force is usually also fecund.
October 20, 1933.

My children are not glorious. No! I gave them great strength. I gave them long life.

It's better to call the bad good than the good bad, and therefore I say that Shostakovich is probably a genius.
October 20.

Having just listened to two acts of *Lady Macbeth*, I'm inclined to conclude that Shostakovich is not a genius.

* * *

Jean-Baptiste Poquelin Moliere

I was just examining one of the three surviving signatures by Moliere from 1668. It's a beautiful, precise signature, each letter written with attention. The entire signature looks approximately like this:

* * *

[Letter to Klavdia Vasilievna Pugacheva]

Saturday, October 21, 1933. Petersburg.

Dear Klavdia Vasilievna,

On October 16, I sent you a letter, unfortunately, unregistered. On October 18, I received a telegram from you and answered with a telegram. Now I don't know whether you ever received my fourth letter.

A particular sequence has been established in our letters and in order to write the next letter, it's important for me to know that you've received the previous one.

Yesterday I went to the Philharmonic to hear Mozart. Only your absence kept me from feeling completely happy.

Now more than ever, I'd like to see you. But despite that, I'm not asking you again to come back to the Children's Theater and to my city. You are a genuine and talented person and you have the right to despise a comfortable existence.

I laid all this out in detail in my fourth letter.

If in the next four days I don't receive any news from you, I will send you the next long letter, having concluded that you never received the fourth letter.

Daniil Kharms

This letter is out of order and its purpose is simply to repair the irregularities of our correspondence.

* * *

[Letter to Klavdia Vasilievna Pugacheva]

October 24, 1933. Leningrad.

"My wonderful Klavdia Vasilievna," I say to you, "do you see me at your feet?"

But you say to me: "No."

I say: "Have mercy on me, Klavdia Vasilievna. If you want I'll even sit down on the floor?"

But once again you say: "No."

"Sweet Klavdia Vasilievna," I say here, flaring up, "After all, I am yours. Precisely yours."

But you shake with laughter along your entire architecture and you don't believe me and won't believe.

"My God," I think. "After all, faith moves mountains!"

But faithless is windless. I unfurled all the sails but the ship won't budge. What a difference a steamer makes!

At this point, the following plan flew into my head: what if I don't let you out of my heart! It's true, there are those so nimble they come in an eye and crawl out an ear. But I'll stuff my ears with cotton! What are you going to do then?

And in fact, I did stuff my ears with cotton and went to State Publishers. At first the cotton wouldn't stay in my ears: I'd swallow and the cotton would fall out of my ears. But after that, using my finger I stuffed the cotton back into my ear more firmly; then it started to stay put.

My sweet and dearest Klavdia Vasilievna,

Forgive me this humorous introduction (just don't cut off the upper part of the letter, or the words could be seen in a different light), but I just want to tell you that *in no way*, or rather, if one may express oneself this way, I regard you *absolutely* without irony. With each letter you become closer and dearer to me. I even see something like a sphere or a tear rising from the lines of your letters and going into my eyes. Then through my eyes it makes its way into my brain, and there, becoming more dense or making more sense, it runs along my nerves or, as they used to say in days of yore, along my veins, now in your aspect, into my heart. And in my heart you, with your legs and arms, sit down on the sofa and make yourself the absolute mistress of this unique, goddamn it, house.

And now I myself come to my own heart like a guest and, before entering, I knock meekly. And you answer from there: "Please! Come in!"

But I enter meekly and now you're an amazing salad to me, paté of herring, tea with bon-bons, a magazine with Picasso and, as they say, a hatchet in the teeth.

But at State Publishers they make fun of me: "Well, brother," they shout at me, "you, brother, have lost your marbles!"

But I say to them: "It's true that I've lost my marbles. And all from love. From love, brothers, I've lost my marbles."

* * *

[Letter to Klavdia Vasilievna Pugacheva]

November 4, 1933. Leningrad.

Dear Klavdia Vasilievna,

In all this time I've written you two long letters, but didn't send them. One seemed too light-hearted, while the other was so muddled that I preferred to write a third. But these two letters knocked me off my tone and I haven't been able to write you anything for eleven days.

Three days ago I went to see Marshak and told him about you. How his eyes blazed and how passionately his dear heart beat! (You see, once again an inappropriate and absurd phrase has wormed its way in. What nonsense! Marshak with fire in his eyes!)

I've become enamored of Mozart. That's astonishing purity for you. I depict this purity three times a day five minutes at a time on your flute. Oh, if only it could be played for twenty minutes at a time!

For lack of a piano, I got myself a zither. I practice on this delicate instrument with my sister, each of us trying to outdo the other. I haven't gotten to Mozart yet, but along the way as I've become acquainted with music theory, I've become fascinated with number harmony. Incidentally, numbers have interested me for a long time. And humanity knows what number is least of all. But for some reason people suppose that if a phenomenon can be expressed in numbers, and if enough regularity is observed making it possible to predict the succeeding phenomenon, then it follows that everything is comprehensible.

So, for example, Helmholtz discovered numerical laws in sounds and tones and thought by this to explain what sound and tone are. This has given us nothing more than a system: it has brought order to sound and tone and makes comparison possible, but it has explained nothing.

For we do not know what number is.

What is number? Is it an invention of ours which becomes material only when applied to something? Or is number like grass, which we've sown in a flower pot thinking that we invented it and that there's no grass anywhere else except on our windowsill?

Number cannot explain what sound and tone are, but rather sound and tone can shed light, if only the tiniest drop, onto the essence of number.

Sweet Klavdia Vasilievna, I'm sending you my poem "Grass."

I really miss you and want to see you. Although I was silent a long time, you're the only person I think about with joy in my heart. Evidently, were you here, I would be genuinely in love for the second time in my life.

Dan. Kharms

* * *

[From notebook 29]

Daniil Kharmus.
1933.
Thursday, November 16.

* * *

To buy:
1. Shoe laces.
2. Tobacco, 10 packages, 28 r.
3. Razor blades, 2 packs.
4. Tooth powder.
5. Mozart score.
6. Notebooks.
7. Boot polish.
8. Black necktie.
9. Cigarette holder.

Owed to:

Panteleev	40 r.
Illa—	60 r.
Gernet—	6 r.
Marshak—	50 r.
	156 r.

* * *

⊟ is neither wife nor friend to me. Everything she does is bad and upsets me. She's stupid and lacks tact. She's just pretty, without a single other good quality. Everything she says is revolting. There's a strong whiff of the whore about her.

* * *

November 24.
Mozart's Requiem at the Capella. Marshak, row 3, seats 11, 12 (9 + 9).

Aleksandr Veltman:
> 1. *Koshchei the Immortal.*
> 2. *Virginia, or a Journey to Russia*

To Larisa Aleksandrovna Oleinikova: a watch.

* * *

It's clear to me: I just don't like the violin. My favorite solo instruments are the piano and the organ. Especially the piano. But best of all is the chorus.

* * *

Scores:
Mozart.

1.	*Requiem.*	
2.	*The Abduction from the Seraglio.*	Russian.
3.	" " "	German.
4.	*Don Giovanni*	Russian.
5.	" "	German.
6.	*The Magic Flute*	Rus.
7.	" " "	Germ.
8.	*The Marriage of Figaro*	Rus.
9.	" " "	Germ.

* * *

December 21, 1933.
It's not a good thing to read Mayakovsky to children.

* * *

Having your
Shaft there is odd
I'm not your
Scheherazade.

* * *

[Note posted on Kharms's door]

I'm working on a deadline.

I'm home but not receiving anyone. And I won't even talk through the door.

I work every day until 7 in the evening.

* * *

[Letter to Klavdia Vasilievna Pugacheva]

[Leningrad. End of 1933?]

Dear Klavdia Vasilievna,

Now I understand: You're making fun of me. I can't believe that instead of sleeping for two nights in a row, you spent them in the company of Yakhontov and Margulis! Moreover, by mentioning the second part of Zoshchenko's *Youth Restored*, you wittily and precisely hint at my secondary role in your life, and with the words "*Youth Restored*," you wish to say that my youth cannot be restored and that, in general, I think far too much of myself. I also understand perfectly that you consider me stupid. But I, in fact, am not stupid. And as concerns my eyes and the expression of my face, then, in the first place, outward impressions are often erroneous, and, in the second place, I persist in my opinion, come what may. . . .

(I-rony)

[Letter to Alisa Ivanovna Poret]

Leningrad

Alisa Ivanovna,

Forgive me for applying to you but I have done everything to avoid this, that is, in the course of a year I have made the rounds almost daily of many second-hand bookshops. From this you yourself will understand how much I need Meyrink's book *Der Golem*, which I gave to your brother at some point.

If this book is still in one piece, I beg you to find a way to get it to me. I suggest doing it by way of the post. Once again, forgive the circumstances that have forced me to appeal to you.

My address: 11 Mayakovsky Street, apt. 8.

Daniil Ivanovich Kharms

* * *

[Letter to Dr. Iosif Scheindels: fragment]

Leningrad.

Dear Doctor,

I was very, very happy to get your letter. I remember quite well those few conversations we had, very fragmentary and therefore uncertain, and they are my only happy memories of Kursk. Whatever you do, dear Doctor, you must get out of that city. You remember in the Bible, God spares an entire city because of one righteous man. And thanks to you, I cannot take pleasure in laying a curse on Kursk. I call you "Doctor" to this day even though there's nothing medical in it: it's rather in the sense of "Doctor Faustus." Much of the Germanic remains in you in a good sense: not the German (German, sauerkraut, sausage man... and so forth), but the genuinely Germanic *Geist*, which is similar to an organ. The Russian spirit is either the singing of a choir or the nasal droning of a deacon. It's always either Divine or ridiculous. But the Germanic *Geist* is an organ. You, Doctor, can say of nature: "I love nature. That cedar, how beautiful it is. Beneath that tree a knight could stand, while on that mountain a monk might wander." Feelings like that are inaccessible to me. For me, be it a table, a cupboard, a house, a meadow, a wooded grove, a butterfly, a grasshopper, it's all one and the same. . . .

* * *

How revolting to stand in line, even to get money. Despise all other people. . . .

January 7, 1934.
Solo-violin is a terrible instrument.
I don't like solo-violin.
I like the piano.
I'll say it again: I don't like the solo-violin. I like the piano.
Once again I'll say the same.

* * *

Daniil Khaaaarms
Vaaaalya

* * *

January 9, 1934. An icon fell from the wall in Papa's room and broke. Now what happens?

* * *

An American Story

The watchman of a slaughterhouse brought suit in an American court, alleging that some guy had broken his arm. The judge summoned this guy and asked: "Did you break the watchman's arm?" The guy said: "No, I did not break his arm." Then the watchman said: "What do you mean you didn't break my arm. I broke my arm because of you." Then the judge asked: "What really happened?" Turns out this is what really happened:

A strapping young guy made his way to the slaughterhouse, cut the teat off a cow's udder, stuck it in his fly and walks away like that.

The watchman, his eyes popping out of his head, sees the guy and says: "Hey you, just look at yourself walking around like that!"

So the guy takes the knife and says: "What's the big deal?" He cuts the teat off with his knife and throws it away.

The watchman fell down and broke his arm.

O   O   O   O   O   O   O   O   O   O   O   O

* * *

"I'm sad that I'm not an animal."
A. Vvedensky.

* * *

"Signs of immortality."
Yakov Druskin.

* * *

[Letter to Klavdia Vasilievna Pugacheva]

Saturday, February 10, 1934. Petersburg.

Dear Klavdia Vasilievna,

I just received a letter from you in which you write that it's already been three weeks since you've received any letters from me. Really I've been in such a strange condition these three weeks that I couldn't write to you. I'm ashamed that you were the first to remind me of this.

It was so touching how your friend came by and gave me the rooster. "This is from Klavdia Vasilievna," she said. I was happy for a long time just looking at this bird.

Then I saw Aleksandr Margulis. He's written a long poem and dedicated it to you. He's also invented a special game with matches in which the first person who can spell out "Klavdia

Vasilievna" with them wins. I played this fascinating game with him and he lost something or other to me.

There's good news from the Children's Theater: they've made the stage wider and set up a changing room right there on the stage, where the public can remove their outer garments. It's really livened up the performances.

Briantsev has written a new play called *The Vampire*.

Yesterday I went to see Anton Antonovich: we talked about you all evening long. Vera Mikhailovna is planning on repeating her *pouliages*. How do you like that?

Your Metropolitan lays seige to me from early in the morning on. When they tell him that I'm not at home, he hides in the elevator and lies in wait for me there.

I go see the Shvartses quite often. I go there under various pretexts but really in order to look upon your photograph. Ekaterina Ivanovna noticed this and told Evgeny Lvovich. Now my visits to the Shvartses are called the "Pugachev visitation."

Dear Klavdia Vasilievna, I often see you in dreams. You're running around the room with a silver bell in your hand and you keep asking; "Where's the money? Where's the money?" While I smoke my pipe and reply: "In the trunk. The trunk."

Daniil Kharms

* * *

[Letter to Aleksandr Vvedensky]

In regard now to your scrivener's malice in connection with Razumovsky's visit. I won't say any longer that I don't understand any of it. On the contrary, everything is clear to me!

You were seized with a noble indignation because I told Razumovsky that in your intellectual development you occupy a place no higher than the writer Brykin; that you've got a question mark drawn on your belly in green paint, and that you consider it to be the most mysterious event of your life, ~~that you yourself are a pitiful imitation of Zhukovsky~~; and, finally, that Razumovsky himself is quite a refined personality and that there is something in his screenplays reminiscent of "The Divine Comedy."

After all that's been said, you can do what you want.

One fool less, one saint more.

Let us agree to establish relations as follow:

1) When we meet one another not to discuss unofficial topics, but to greet each other politely.

2) To neither make a mess of nor shove a stick into the spokes of one another's business.

Daniil Kharms,
May 13, 1934

* * *

[From notebook 30]

My name is <u>Khabarms</u>.

I purchased this notebook on Tuesday, August 14, 1934.

Daniil Sharon
Wednesday, September 5, 1934.
Thursday. September 6, 1934.

Daniil Dandan
Wednesday, September 12, 1934.

* * *

Mironov wrapped a clock in a blanket and took it to a kerosene shop. On the way Mironov ran into Golovyov. Seeing Mironov, Golovlyov hid behind a cigarette stand: "What are you standing here for?" the cigarette man started pestering him. To get rid of him Golovlyov bought a cigarette holder and a can of toothpowder from the cigarette man. Mironov saw all this, at which point, properly speaking, this story comes to an end.
August 20.

Mironov punched Golovlyov in the face, proclaiming "Here's your powder for you, you crooked dog!"
August 20.

Drenched from the rain, Sikorsky shivered and knocked at the gate. Some twenty minutes later, the gate was opened. Sikorsky asked to spend the night. They let him in but on condition that he leave at first light.

At first light, Sikorsky left and, gazing at the rising sun and the grass, Sikorsky felt a surge of new strength.

August 21.

* * *

Andrei Ivanovich spit into a cup of water. At once the water turned black. Andrei Ivanovich screwed up his eyes and looked intently into the cup. The water was very black. Andrei Ivanovich's heart skipped a beat.

At that moment, Andrei Ivanovich's dog woke up. Andrei Ivanovich went up to the window and was lost in thought. ~~His thoughts were disturbed by a strange phenomenon: his dog rushed past.~~ Suddenly something big and dark rushed past Andrei Ivanovich and flew out the window. It was Andrei Ivanovich's dog that flew out the window and sailed like a crow to the roof of the house opposite. Andrei Ivanovich squatted down and began to howl.

Comrade Pappagallo rushed into the room.

"What's the matter with you? Are you sick?" Comrade Pappagallo asked.

Andrei Ivanovich said nothing and rubbed his face with his hands.

Comrade Pappagallo ~~took the cup from the table~~ glanced into the cup on the table. "What is it you've poured here?" He asked Andrei Semyonovich.

"Don't know," said Andrei Semyonovich.

Pappagallo vanished instantly. The dog flew in through the window again, lay down in his previous place and fell asleep.

Andrei Semyonovich went up to the table and drank the blackened water from the cup. And a light dawned in Andrei Semyonovich's soul.

August 21.

* * *

Here's a strange thing that happened on tram no. 3.

A lady in a calico coat dropped 10 kopecks on the floor of the tram. A citizen standing near the lady bent over to pick up the money and, turning suddenly into a pig, made a rush for the platform.

The passengers riding in the tram were dumbfounded. And even a little old man, addressing himself to everyone and winking his blue eyes, said: "There's a hash! Thatsshh downright hooliganism!"

* * *

A neck poked out from the collar of a fool's shirt, and on the neck a head. At one point the head had been cropped short. By now the hair had grown out like a brush. The fool was talking a lot about something or other. No one was listening to him. Everyone was thinking: when will he shut up and leave?

But the fool noticed nothing and kept on speaking and guffawing. Finally Yelbov couldn't take it anymore, went up to the fool and spoke briefly and ferociously: "Get the hell out of here right this minute!" The fool looked around in bewilderment, not understanding what was happening. Yelbov smacked the fool in the ear, the fool flew out of the chair and collapsed on the floor. Yelbov gave him a kick and the fool flew out the door and rolled down the stairs.

That's life for you: an utter fool and yet he still wants to express something. People like that deserve a punch in the face. That's right, in the face! Wherever I look, everywhere I see this foolish mug of a jailbird. A boot in the face is just about right.

* * *

GOOD	BAD
Mozart	Chaikovsky, Scriabin
Big-boned women.	Small-boned women.
Busty women.	Flat-chested women.
Young, healthy, fresh, plump, juicy women.	Stylish, skinny, lithe, pampered, even demonic women.
Meat, milk.	Spicy dishes, dishes with vinegar.
Humor.	Moods.
Dress should be simple, comfortable, emphasizing the strong points of the figure	Fashionable dress with fancy trim and pretensions to luxury.

Towards the Art of Dressing.

For both men and women, the cut of a garment must always be simple. Every extraneous bit of material used for ornament must be strictly considered and would be better left out. There should be no little creases or buttons on a garment. Everything that can be straight should not be askew. On a woman, clothing should emphasize her hips and bust, while on a man, his broad shoulders, chest and strong legs.

However, a certain complexity in one's dress is allowed, but only in big things, not in small details. So, for example, multi-colored vests are completely acceptable in a man, as is a stole or special blouse on a woman. Accessories like bracelets and rings can also be very nice.

* * *

It's absolutely unbearable to feel that someone is watching you all the time. I wanted to write that down but thought that someone might see that I was about to write something and think: here he is, writing something bad. Always have to maintain appearances.

Zlotin, Kraev, Dvukurev, Panochkin, Miller, Perelygina, Perelygin, Yezhov, Lobanov, Yusupov, Vonch, Vovk.

Some musical pieces can be sung one way and also another way, for example, the aria of the Indian merchant from *Sadko*. Individual parts of the aria can get mixed up and, if you don't know the aria well, can be sung differently and no one will notice. But if you change a single note of Mozart, everyone will notice.

* * *

Listening to Shaliapin. He's singing Chaikovsky's "Nightingale." He sings badly and the piece's no good. Still the piece fits the singer.

For August 31.
~~Burn trash in stove~~.
~~Sharpen knives~~.
~~Plug the voltmeter in next to the socket~~.
~~Read at least 2 conversations by Flammarion~~.
Write at least three vaudevilles.

Phone Ivan Ivanovich about the Westminster Choir.
~~Hammer the nail in on my shoe.~~

* * *

~~Kulygin put his arm into Maria Timofeevna's mouth right up to the elbow.~~
~~Maria Timofeevna hiccupped loudly.~~
~~Kulygin wanted to pull his arm back out, but Maria Timofeevna's gullet~~
~~constricted and Kulygin was caught.~~

Olga Forsh went up to Aleksei Tolstoy and did something. Aleksei
Tolstoy did something too.

At this point Konstantin Fedin and Valentin Stenich leapt out into the
courtyard and started looking for a suitable rock. They didn't find a rock,
but they did find a shovel. With this shovel, Konstantin Fedin bashed Olga
Forsh in the chops.

Then Aleksei Tolstoy took off all his clothes, went out onto the
Fontanka and started neighing like a horse. Everyone said: "that's a major
contemporary author neighing." And no one touched Aleksei Tolstoy.

* * *

I'll never forget such humiliation.
Erbsensuppe. August 30.

~~Dancing with a lady's lovely~~
~~if the lady's not too thin.~~

Wherever it went, it didn't get there.

As everyone knows, Bezimensky has a stupendously stupid snout.
Once Bezimensky banged his snout on a stool.
After this, the snout of the poet Bezimensky went completely out of
commission.

I wonder what happened with our screenplay at the film factory.

* * *

G. K. Chesterton.
"The Wisdom of Father Brown."
"The Incredulity of Father Brown."
The Man who knew too much.

H. Rider Haggard
> *Doctor Therne.*
> *Montezuma's Daughter.*
> *King Solomon's Mines.*
> *Heu-Heu or the Monster.*

Louis Henri Boussenard
> *Les voleurs des diamants.*
> *Le tour du monde d'un gamin de Paris.*
> *Les ètrangleurs du Bengal.*
> *Les secrets de monsieur Synthése.*

* * *

Not really getting into anything. What should I do? Disagreeable financial prospects are part of what's tormenting me. Eyes and head twitching. August 31.

Owed to		Buy
~~Illa~~	~~40~~	
Gritsin	10	Soap
~~Illa~~	~~2~~	Tooth powder.
Laundress	9	Tooth brush.
Papa	10	Repair shoes.
~~Papa~~	~~2~~	Five rubles Marina.
Eliz. Aleks.	15	
~~Zadunaiskaya~~	~~10~~	
Gernet	1	
Illa	3	
Illa	4 r. 50 k.	

* * *

Two friends lived their lives in Kiev,
A people most perverse.
The first was born down south there.
While the second—the reverse.
The first one was a glutton,
The second even worse.

The first died of constipation,
But the second—the reverse.

Have to learn Russian grammar.

Listened to:
> Schubert's Rondo, not great.
> Schubert's Romance "By the Sea," not great.
> Schubert's "Bacarolle," good.
> Schubert's "Morning Serenade," good.
> "Love letter" by Schubert-Liszt, boring.

~~Khabam~~   ~~KHARMS~~
~~Khomes~~   ~~Khomen~~   ~~SHARON~~
~~Daniil SHARON~~

Schubert's "The Wanderer" is no good.

* * *

I am so sick of all the crap that's going on. I want to stay in my room by myself.

Romain Rolland, *Musiciens d'aujourd'hui.*

* * *

O God, how I need some real money.

11 o'clock, September 6, Morning.
At Oleinikov's, about *Siskin.*

Aleksandr Bashilov painted a picture called "Expecting Bad Weather." What imagination in the title and at the same time what a negligible and simple departure from the everyday! September 9.

* * *

Siskin, No. 7, Sept. 10, advance copy.

No 8, Sept. 7, proofs.
> Sept. 29, advance copy.

No 9. layout, starting Sept. 7 (5 working days).

 Sept. 11, plates.

 Sept. 15, typesetter..

 Sept. 22, proofs to publisher.

 October 5, publication date.

No 10. Put out over the course of October. In this way, get back on schedule.

 Sept. 10, layout to editor.

 Sept. 15, galleys to editor.

 Sept. 26, proofs to publisher.

No. 11. Issue should come out on November 1.

Approved for publication October 2 or 3.

Compositors September 13.

Galleys September 20.

* * *

Two friends met.

"Oh!" said one friend.

"Ah!" said the other.

"What?" asked the first.

"Huh?" said the second.

"Huh what?" asked the first.

"Huh?" said the second.

"What nonsense!" said the first.

"Ha, ha!" said the second.

"Well, well!" said the first.

"Aha!" said the second.

"So that's it!" said the first.

"O-ho-ho!" said the second.

And the friends bowed

And went their way.

Tram No. 22.

September 5, 1934.

10:30 pm.

* * *

Pergolesi, *La Serva Padrona*, opera. Good.

* * *

To buy:

      Tickets to the Philharmonic.
      Brewer's yeast.
      Tobacco. One pouch and two plugs for 2 r. 80 k.
      Matches.
      Stop off at the Co-op.

* * *

1. Not alive.
2. Neither male nor female.
3. Known when he lived.
4. Name unknown.
5. Not a politician.
6. 19th century.
7. Not Russia.
8. Height unknown.
9. Didn't have a pussycat.
10. Science.
11. Made no discoveries.
12. Experimented on him?
13. Unknown who did the experiment.
14. Unless you had an interest in science, you wouldn't have heard of him.
15. Not educated.
16. Related to science and anatomy.
17. No connection to dreams.
18. Freak.
19. He could speak.
20. Pictures do exist.
21. Remains do not survive.
22. Only a freak.

Answer: The Siamese twins!

* * *

Daniil Wolfgang
1. Not alive.
2. Male.
3. Not modern.
4. B. C.
5. Related to art.
6. Only art.
7. Politician, not an artist.
8. Not a philosopher.
9. Not a writer.
10. Not the hero of a literary work.
11. No works of his are extant.
12. Very well known.
13. Valentina Efimovna knows.
14. Not a musician.
15. His name is well known.
16. Unknown how long he lived.
17. Not in Italy.
18. Not a Roman.

ANSWER: Herostratus

* * *

1. Not alive.
2. 19th century.
3. Male.
4. Real person.
5. Related to art.
6. There is a record of his work.
7. Not a composer.
8.
9. Yes, he made works of art.
10. Not a writer.
11. Not an artist.
12. Not a sculptor.
13. Is related to fine arts, including photography.

14. In Russia.
15. Not a photographer.
16. I wouldn't presume to define his nationality.
17. No troupe of animals.
18. Even if he had no relation to art, he would still be famous.
19. Related to science.
20. Not an inventor.
21. Second half of the 19th century.
22. I like the works of arts in which he's depicted.
23. Not an architect or builder.
24. Not a mathematician.
25. Not a chess player.
26. Actively engaged with art.
27. Much remains of his creative work.
28. In museums.
29. Not in the Hermitage.
30. Not in the Tretyakov Gallery.
31. Not in the Russian Museum.
32.

29. Not Sergei Chekhonin.
30. Did not make furniture.
31. Not a rarity in museums.
32. Never lived in Petersburg.
33. Not Kuznetsov.
(34. Himself an artist.)
34 Works depicting him not in Leningrad only.
35. Works depicting him not in Russia only.
36. Better known in Russia.
37. Did not write about science.
38. Not an actor.
39. Rich.
40. Not an aristocrat.
41. A factory owner.
(42. D)
42. Related to chemistry.

43. Did not make films.
44. No relation to the cinema.
45. Not Savva Morozov.
46. Did not manufacture building materials.
47. Did not manufacture home decorations.
48. For men, not for factories.
49. Did not manufacture paints.
50. Related to books.
51. Was a publisher.

Answer: Marx

~~Daniil Khelgot~~
~~Daniil Khelgandg~~
Daniil Khelgang
Wednesday, September 12, 1934.

Daniil Ivanovich Dandan
Dondon.
Daniil Dandan.

Haygang
Highwalk
Hochgang

Khaigot	Herrgang
Hartgang	Gothgang
Hellgang	Vollgang
Gottgang	Follgang

* * *

A Great Journey from Moscow Station to Vasilievsky Island.
Around the World on a Tram.

About a man who snuck into a tram park at night and left on an empty tram.

CREATION - ACTION - DEMATERIALIZATION

Recollection of paradise.

* * *

By dividing a singular absence into ~~two~~ three parts, we arrive at the trinity of existence.

	God The Father	God The Son	God The Holy Spirit
	PARADISE	THE WORLD	PARADISE
1.	Emptiness	Existence	Emptiness
2.	Past	Present	Future
3.	Stasis	Movement	Stasis
4.	Creation	Action	Annihilation
5.	Religion	Materialism	Art
7.	Birth	Life	Death
8.	Emergence from paradise.	Descent to the earth.	Return to paradise.
9.	Innocence	Sin	Innocence

* * *

A funny story about a man with a very poor memory.

Mozart, Goethe, Shakespeare, Schubert, Bach.
About English clock makers, about chronometers.
Moliére, Kepler, Titian, Leonardo da Vinci, Andersen.
About Herostratus.
About chess.

* * *

~~Daniil Dadan~~
~~Danan. Dadan~~
~~Shadan~~
~~Shaden~~

READ:

> Sir James Jeans, *The Universe Around Us*.
> Zoshchenko, *Selected Works* by October 1.
> *Astrologie* by October 3.

* * *

Three of us, Lipavsky, Vvedensky and I, decided to write a film together. But then I gave it a bit of thought and decided that a three-way collaboration would not work, so I'm opting out. September 20, 1934.

* * *

To do by September 27.

> Go see house manager.
> Letter to Peter Petrovich.
> Write 2 stories.
> Read 84 pages of Jeans.
> Tie up the trunk.
> Write in my diary.

* * *

Didascalia

> Conceptions of Adam.
> God the Father, or Figura.

Having done its work, Figura withdraws into the church.

* * *

About the film *The Little Humpback Horse*. Better to make it a silent film in order not to deal with Yershov's text.

* * *

October 1, 1934.

My darling, my little book, I'm hungry, married and angry. Three misfortunes have attacked me, I'm becoming unjust . . . I'm leading a life of sin.

* * *

Constitution

RESPONSIBILITIES

OF THE HUSBAND	OF THE WIFE
1. Write.	1. Keep up with the cleaning.
2. Compose.	2. Take care of the food ~~and tea~~.
3. Read.	3. Change and make the bed.
4. Study.	4. Take care of the ration cards.
~~5. Sing~~	
~~6. Play chess~~	
5. Get money.	5. ~~Read~~ Put the tea kettle on.
6. Wind up the clocks.	6. ~~Study~~
7. Obtain books.	7.
8. Wine.	
9. Tobacco.	

* * *

About the great center of magnitude.

On the one hand, cosmological magnitudes, on the other, atomic. Where then is that great centerpoint where everything is neither great, nor small? Does such a center exist absolutely? And where are its boundaries?

August 2.

Dandan

* * *

You who would censure the poet but vainly
Want to compare his weird life with the
Commoner. Never can he who
Dares hunt the king's pheasants be
Friends to the miller who toils by his millstone.

* * *

I'm sick and tired of being married. Oh, how I want to be single again, but I hope that everything works out well, peacefully and without scandal.

October 10.

* * *

Describe some subject in the foreword to a book, then say that the author has chosen a completely different subject for his book.

He looked to be about 36 years old, but in fact he was slightly less than 38.

* * *

On the radio:
Yenukidze, Molotov, a representative from the International, Chudov from the Leningrad NKVD, Kaganovich, Shaposhnikov, Petrovsky from Ukraine, Bagirov from Baku.
Carrying medals on a little red pillow.
Small procession.

* * *

[From notebook 31]

Mendelssohn's Trio
Bach's Chorale and Brandenburg Concerto No. 2.
The ending of Chaikovsky's Third Concerto, good.
Grieg, "The Hunter's Song," "The Storm" from *Peer Gynt*: in a single word, Chaikovskian.

* * *

December 9. Listening to *Scheherazade*, Albert Coates conducting. What an abominable thing!
The second movement is even more vile than the first. Difficult to listen to.
When he's calm, Coates can be very handsome.
The back and forth of the instruments is embarrassing.
Rimsky-Korsakov is an all time contemptible bugger.
The music of *Scheherazade* is fit for fiery pantomime in a circus, and even excerpts pulled out of various works would have been better than this.
The longer it goes, the worse it gets.
That Coates can conduct it without a score does not speak well of him.
Coates's left hand is puffy and at times disgusting.

The drum part is like rain tapping on a roof, while the tinkling of the triangle is simply indecent but perfectly worthy of the Philharmonic audience.

The violin solo is even worse than gypsies

Listening to *Scheherazade*, it's hard to think of a worse piece of music.

Movement III.

Ye gods, there's still a third movement! The violin solo is even worse than in the first two movements.

Aha! The bells have started ringing.

Scheherazade has exceeded all my expectations, it's simply a piece of trash without a break.

Again the bells!

The dance with the basses and the piccolo is slightly better.

Again the first theme (an important one, with questions and affirmations) is good. But then more trash.

Terrible depressing trash with harps and Oriental melodies.

* * *

Chaikovsky's Symphony No. 6
Coates.

1. Conductors put a handkerchief in their left pocket.
2. I don't like the gloomy beginning.
3. Coates has an unpleasant way of making slight movements with his left hand.
4. A shot.
5. Horns, good.
6. Percussion and trumpet effects, nice.
7. Again the cloying first theme.
8. I'm sitting in row 13, it's too far back for me.

   Second movement
1. The main theme, brilliant.
   The rest is worse.

   Third movement.
1. Much better than the first two. The March. The end is good.
2. Brilliant! That's the public.

448

Fourth movement.
1. Opening chords are very good.
2. Conductor is like a poodle who's managed to find the person to whom he's been sent.

* * *

For 5 months now I've been going to bed very late, between 3 and 6:30 in the morning.

Something's not right with Marina. It's already 2:15 in the morning and she's not home yet.
December 10, 1934.

* * *

Horosho pisatj latinskim shriftom.

Heinrich Karl Brugsh, *The History of the Pharaohs.*
James Henry Breasted, *A History of Egypt.*
The Ancient World in its Literary Monuments.
Charles Lenormant, *Egypt.*
Gaston Camille Maspero, *Egypt, Assyria.*

* * *

I couldn't write anything down about Oleinikov.

* * *

At the Hermitage Theater.
 Acis and Galatea. Handel ~~Brilliant~~ Didn't hear it.
 Comic opera by Adolphe Adam. December 24, 9 pm.

* * *

Homer, *The Iliad*
Georgy Vinogradov, *Russian Children's Folklore.*
Children's Satirical Lyrics, Irkutsk.
Viktor Zhirmunsky. *The Theory of Verse.*
Müller-Freienfels, *Poetics.* 1923.
Boris Tomashevsky, *Poetics.*

Science and Life, No. 1. Article on astronomy by Professor Polak
Jeans, *The Movement of the Planets*.
Polak, *Astronomy for Trade Schools*.
Suvorov, *Planets and Stars*.
Prianiashnikov, *Diverting Evenings of Planetary Observation*.

* * *

December 24. Marina is somewhere with Sergei Bezborodov.

Something's not right with Marina.

She comes to the Publishing house and just sits there.

If Marina leaves tomorrow morning without talking to me, that means's she's not worth much. December 25.

If Marina wants to leave me, that means she's not worth much. So it's better not to hold her back. December 25.

St. Nicholas the Wonderworker. The Great Martyr Tryphon. The Great Martyr John the Warrior.

December 26. Another round of quarrels with Marina.

Call Boba at noon.

[From notebook 31]

Saving money saving time
People running for the train
Lustily the last bell rings
Locomotive whistle sings
Semaphore picks up its face
Train starts talking picks up pace
You can hear the moan of steel
Banging clanging of the wheels
And the chatter of the ties
Means the train's begun to fly
Engine breathing quickly and
Lady drowses, nods her head
Lamps cast light upon the floor
Soldier's sleeping, no that's wrong
For at least the hundredth time
Scans the lady with bold eye
~~Fixed his eye upon her breast~~
~~Travels down to see the rest~~
~~Down his glance goes to her legs~~
~~And like knight who fears not death~~
~~Shouting, to the fray he flies~~
~~Slyly lowering his eyes~~.
Willing her to take a look
And the lady moves her foot.

January 1, 1935.

* * *

Louis-Ferdinand Céline. Translation by Elsa Triolet. *Journey to the End of the Night*. OGIZ 1934.

It's disgusting to have to depend on the mood of that conceited boor.
Oleinikov.
January 9, 1935.
That **shopkeeper** is still pretending not to notice.
The difference in income is growing.
My situation is miserable. What should I do?
I don't know how to make money. It's already hard to be with friends
because I'm so poor.

* * *

Beginning January 1, 1935, I have resolved on the following:
1. Write no fewer than 10 lines of poetry and one vaudeville per day.
2. On no account get up from bed later than noon. On no account go
   to bed later than 2 am (lights out).
3. Read the newspapers.
4. Keep a record every day of the number of hours spent doing nothing.

* * *

3	– ♃	Chaikovsky
4	– ♀	*Romeo and Juliet*
5	– ♄	
6	– ☉	Stravinsky
7	– ☽	*The Rite of Spring*
8	– ♂	
9	– ☿	
10	– ♃	
11	– ♀	
12	– ♄	

Lento – Medium

* * *

Aeschylus, *Prometheus Bound.*

Here I am gradually sinking into a cesspit.
Suspicion of me is growing.
There it is: disaster.
I can't see any way to climb out.

O God, how difficult to see indifference all around.

My poor, poor wife!

O God, what does the future have in store for me.

* * *

Merezhkovsky,
> 1. *The Death of the Gods*. Vols. 1-3.
> 2. *Michelangelo*.

* * *

Sitting with her back to me, but she can see me lighting matches.

* * *

[From notebook 38]

The Circus. Rehearsal. Freeze: everyone stays in their places. Parachute.
Flying of every sort.
The movement of objects.

May 8, 1935

If good weather		If bad weather	
9	get up.	10.30	get up.
10.30—5	beach.	11.30—1	read.
6—7	dinner.	1—3	write.
7—9	write.	3—4	read
		4—5	write.
		5—6	dinner.
		6—8	write.

Beach
10.30—12	read.
12—12.30	observe.
12.30—2	compose.
2—3	observe.
3—4	read.
4—5	compose.

* * *

In like fashion, set aside little lanes for solitary strolling, with seats for single people. Between the seats are shrubs. Children are forbidden, as are noise and loud conversation.

Good looking women don't take walks in public gardens.

O Lord, nourish me with Thy body,
So that thirst for the working of Thy spirit awakens in me.
O Lord, give me to drink of Thy blood,
So that the strength of My versification might be resurrected.

* * *

Malevich paintings:
    1. Bearded men.
    2. Eggs.
    3. Red house with stripes.
    4. Face with cross (pink background).
    5. Woman in green skirt.
    6. Egg-shaped man, in lemon-yellow shirt.
    7. Square. Black square.
    8. ~~Four~~ Five little houses. (silo)
    9. Black cross. Intersection of surfaces.
    10. Group of three men. Especially pure. 1914.
    11. Bearded men on blue background. 3 bearded men in white, green and white shirts.
    12. Self-portrait in multi-colored suit.

* * *

Union of Composers. End of May.
Secretary of the Union of Composers, Konstantin Arenkov.
The composer Zatoplitsky played 10 pieces.
Terrible impressionism. Most of all, I like the end of "Venetian Melody" and "Sleeping" without the march. But even that was weak.
The composer Morozov performed excerpts from two suites.
Boring.

May 6, 1935. Saw the picture *The Private Life of Peter Vinogradov*. At first I badmouthed it, saying it was *poshliatina*, but then I started to like it. I like the theme of a man who accomplishes great things as the result of intense labor.

Mendelssohn, "On wings of Song." Bad.
Brahms, "Double Concerto," third movement.

* * *

It's already been 2 days without a letter from Marina. I'm very worried.
May 25.

* * *

Robert Louis Stevenson, *Treasure Island*, May 13.
Stevenson and Osborn, *The Wrecker*, May 13.
Sigmund Freud, *The Psychopathology of Everyday Life*.
Yury Tynianov, *Young Vitushishnikov*.

* * *

I'm a tiny little bird who's flown into a cage with big angry birds. (At Popov's in Detskoe Selo, July 3, 1935).

Here's what's I don't like:
       Contemporary taste in culture.
       Tikhon Churilin.
       Pasternak.
       The artist Lebedev.
       The artist Akimov.
       Palekh craftsmen.
       "Academia" publishers.
       Slant-cut pockets.
       Broad lapels on men's jackets.
       The craze for skinny women.
       The tango.
       The cinema.
       The tone of spinsters: Back off!
       Ray Noble's orchestra.
       The gramophone, Jazz.
       Shortening "Metropolitan" to "Metro."

* * *

Owed to:

Marshak	- 150 r.	
Shvarts	- 100 r.	
Mutual Aid Bank	- 200 r.	
Illa	- 100 r.	900 r.
	- 8	
To Liza	- 30	
Moscow	- 300	
Gabbe	- 15	
Ebushints	- 3 r. 50 k.	
Elizaveta Alekseevna	- 1 r.	
Ester	- 11 r.	200
The tailor	- 20 r.	
Trepov	- 40 r.	
Nanny	- 15 r.	
Papa	- 10 r.	
	50	100 r.
Gernet	- 3 r.	
Lipavsky	- 2 r.	
Gomets	- 130 r.	
Nevsky Shvarts	- 30 r.	
Boba	- 50 r.	
Oleinikov	- 5 r.	

* * *

To buy	Expenses
Heater.	Book shelves.
Kerosene lamp.	Writing desk.
Repair spirit-lamp.	2 blankets.
Pot.	Shoes for Marina.
Frying pan.	Dress for Marina.
Move things.	

Georgian popular ditties. (good stuff).
The Azerbaijani dance is disgusting.

And that's what the Europeans imitate.
Ossetian *lezghinka*. Very good.
Commune Memorial Oriental Orchestra.
Chorus of Georgian Teamsters, directed by Shabulidze.

* * *

no respect.

Reading the French, I always experience a certain irritation and exasperation. A stupid race!

Right next to me, on the neighboring bench, a foolish woman in a covert coat is sitting and reading *A History of Literature* all the while ostentatiously underlining the text with a pencil. Stupid bitch!

* * *

Your doctor reminds me of one of those heads with eyeglasses you see on display in an optician's shop.

J. S. Bach, *The Passion of St. John*. I like *The Passion of St. Matthew* much better. The alternation of recitatives and chorals in *St. John* is monotonous.

Borrow *Don Quixote* from Druskin.
Victor Shklovsky, *Sentimental Journey*.
Ivan Zabelin, *The Everyday Life of the Russian People*. 2 vols. 1872.
Aleksei Ermolov, *The Agricultural Wisdom of the People as Expressed in Proverbs, Aphorisms, and Signs*. 1 vol.
The Calendar of Folk Beliefs. St. P., Suvorin. 1901. Vol. II, Signs.
Yury Tynianov, *Kiukhlia*.
Franz Werfel, *Verdi*.
Ivan Bunin, "Mitya's Love."

Aleksei Novikov-Priboi, *Tsushima*.   For Natasha.
Ilya Erenburg, *The Second Day*.

Edward Fuchs, *Erotic Art*.

* * *

[Scenes from the life of the poet]

"I Decided to Mess Up the Party…"

1

One day I arrived at State Publishing where I ran into Evgeny Lvovich Shvarts, who, as always, was badly dressed but with pretensions to something or other.

As soon as he saw me, Shvarts began cracking jokes but also, as always, without success.

I cracked some jokes with significantly greater success and soon, in an intellectual relation, I put Shvarts flat on his back.

Everyone around envied my wit, but undertook no measures whatsoever since they literally dropped dead from laughter. In particular, Nina Vladimirovna Gernet and David Efimovich Rakhmilovich, who for the sake of euphony calls himself *Eugene*, dropped dead from laughter.

Seeing that jokes don't work with me, Shvarts began to change his tune and finally, after swearing a blue streak at me, announced that in Tiflis everyone knows Zabolotsky, but almost no one knows me.

Here I got angry and said that I am more historical than Shvarts and Zabolotsky, that I will leave a bright spot upon history, while they will quickly be forgotten.

Having sensed my grandeur and major world significance, Shvarts gradually began to tremble and invited me over for dinner.

2

I decided to mess up the party, and that's exactly what I'm going to do.

I'll begin with Valentina Efimovna. This non-domestic personage invites us over to her place and instead of food puts some kind of sour stuff on the table. Now I love to have a bite and I know my way around food. You won't take me in with sour stuff! Now and again I'll even drop into a restaurant to see what kind of food they have there. And I can't abide it when this particularity of my character is not taken into account.

Now I turn to Leonid Savelievich Lipavsky. He wasn't ashamed to tell me to my face that every month he composes ten thoughts.

In the first place, he's lying. He composes not ten, but less.

And in the second place, I compose more. I haven't counted how many I compose in a month but it must be more than him. . . .

I, for example, don't rub it in everyone's nose that I possess, as they say, a colossal mind. I have all the grounds to consider myself a great man. And, by the way, I do consider myself to be such.

That's why it hurts and is painful for me to be among people placed lower than me in mind, and sagacity, and talent, and not to feel a completely deserved respect for myself.

Why, oh why, am I better than everyone?

3

Now I understand everything: Leonid Savelievich is a German. He even has German habits. Look at how he eats. A pure German, and there's nothing more to say! You can even tell by his legs he's a German.

Without bragging, I can say that I am extremely observant and witty.

Here, for example, if you take Leonid Savelievich, Yury Berzin and Wolf Erlich and line them up together on the sidewalk, then you can say, "small, smaller, smallest."

In my opinion, that's witty because it's fairly funny.

And still Leonid Savelievich is a German! I will certainly tell him that when I see him.

I don't consider myself an especially intelligent man, but all the same I have to say that I am smarter than everyone else. Perhaps there are more intelligent people on Mars, but on Earth, I don't know.

They say Oleinikov is very smart. But my opinion is that he's smart, but not very. He discovered, for example, that if you write 6 and turn it upside down, you get a 9. But, in my opinion, that's not smart.

Leonid Savelievich is absolutely correct when he says that a man's worth is his mind. But if there is no mind, there's no worth either.

Yakov Semyonovich objects to Leonid Savelievich and says that a man's mind is his weakness. But in my opinion, that's already a paradox. Why should mind be a weakness? Not at all! Rather a fortress. At least that's what I think.

We often get together at Leonid Savelievich's and talk about this. If an argument starts up, I always end up the winner of the argument. I don't know why myself.

For some reason, everyone looks at me with amazement. Whatever I do, everyone finds it amazing.

But I don't even try. Everything simply happens by itself.

Zabolotsky once said that it is inherent in me to govern the spheres. He was probably joking. Nothing of the like has ever occurred to me.

At the Writers' Union for some reason they consider me an angel.

Listen, friends! Really, there's no need to bow down before me like this. I'm just like the rest of you, only better.

4

I've heard the expression: "Seize the moment."

That's easy to say, but hard to do. In my opinion, the expression is meaningless. And really, it's wrong to call for the impossible.

I say this with confidence because I've tried it all on myself. I tried seizing the moment but couldn't catch it and ended up breaking my watch. Now I know that it's impossible.

To "seize the epoch" is just as impossible because it's the same as the moment, only bigger.

It's quite another thing to say: "Immortalize what happens in the moment." That's an entirely different thing.

Here's an example: one, two, three! Nothing happened. Here I've immortalized a moment in which nothing happened.

I told Zabolotsky about this. He really liked it, and all day long he sat counting: one, two, three! And noticing that nothing happened.

One day Shvarts came across Zabolotsky engaged in this activity. And Shvarts also became fascinated by this original way of immortalizing what is happening in our epoch, because, after all, an epoch is made up of moments.

But I ask you to note that the progenitor of this method is once again me. Once again me! Everywhere me! Simply amazing!

What comes to others with difficulty, comes to me with ease!

I even know how to fly. But I won't talk about that since, no matter what, no one will believe it.

5

When two men are playing chess, it always seems to me that one is making a fool of the other. Especially if they're playing for money.

In general, I find all games played for money disgusting. I forbid gambling in my presence.

And as for card players, I would put them to death. That's the most correct method of combating games of chance.

Instead of playing cards, it would be better to get together and read moralizing stories to each other.

But, on the other hand, morals are boring. It's more interesting to chase after women.

I've always been interested in women. Women's legs have always excited me, especially above the knee.

Many people consider women depraved creatures. But not me, not a bit! To the contrary, I even think they're in some ways quite nice.

A plumpish young woman! How is she depraved? Not at all depraved.

Now children are a different story. People say they're innocent. But I think, perhaps, they really are innocent, just terribly loathsome, especially when they dance. I always make myself scarce whenever children are around.

And Leonid Savelievich doesn't like children either. I was the one who instilled these thoughts in him.

In general, everything Leonid Savelievich says was already said by me some time before.

And it's not just Leonid Savelievich.

Everyone is happy to latch onto the merest scraps of my thoughts. Even I find it funny.

Yesterday, for example, Oleinikov came running to me saying that he has gotten completely tangled up in questions of existence. I gave him some advice and sent him on his way. He left, made happy by me, and in his best possible mood.

People look to me for support, repeat my words, are amazed at my actions, but they don't pay me any money.

Foolish people! Bring me some more money and you'll see how happy I'll be then.

6

Now I'll say a few words about Aleksandr Ivanovich.

A talker and a gambler. But what I value him for is that he's obedient to me.

Day and night he attends me, just waiting for the hint of an order on my part. I just have to give that hint and Aleksandr Ivanovich flies like the wind to do my will.

For doing this I bought him shoes and said: "Here, put them on!" And here he is wearing them.

When Aleksandr Ivanovich comes to State Publishing, they all laugh and say among themselves that Aleksandr Ivanovich has come for money.

Konstantin Ignatievich Drovatsky hides under the table. I say this in an allegorical sense.

Most of all Aleksandr Ivanovich loves macaroni. He always eats it with dry biscuits, he eats almost a full kilo, and perhaps even a great deal more.

Once he's finished eating his macaroni, Aleksandr Ivanovich says he feels nauseous and lies down on the couch. On occasion, the macaroni comes out the way it went in.

Aleksandr Ivanovich doesn't eat meat and doesn't like women. Although sometimes he does. Even, it seems, quite often.

But the women Aleksandr Ivanovich likes are, to my taste, all ugly and hence we will not even consider them women.

If I say something that means it's correct.

I defy anyone to argue with me: whatever happens, he'll come out looking like a fool because I will out-argue anyone.

And you're not the one to contend with me. Others, much better than you, have already tried. I laid them all low! It means nothing if it looks as if I can't really speak: once I get wound up, you won't stop me.

Once I got wound up at the Lipavskys' and just went on and on! I talked them all to death!

Then I went to the Zabolotskys' and talked their heads off too. Then I went to the Shvartses' and talked their heads off. Then I came home and at home I talked for half the night.

(1935-36)

[Scenes from the life of the poet]

"Once Marina Told Me . . ."

Once Marina told me that Sharik used to come visit her in bed. Who the hell, or what the hell this Sharik was, I wasn't able to figure out.

Several days later this Sharik came over again. Then he started coming fairly often, roughly every third day.

I wasn't home. When I got home, Marina told me that Sinderyushkin had telephoned and asked for me. Some Sinderyushkin, you see, needed me!

Marina bought some apples. We ate a few of them after dinner and, it seems, we left two apples for the evening. But when evening came and I wanted to get my apple, it turned out the apple was gone. Marina said that Misha the waiter had come by and taken the apples to put in the salad. He didn't need the apple cores, so he peeled them right in our room and threw the cores into the waste paper basket.

I figured out that Sharik, Sinderyushkin and Misha usually live in our stove. I don't quite understand how they settled in there.

I questioned Marina about Sharik, Sinderyushkin and Misha. Marina tried to wriggle out of answering directly. When I expressed my misgivings that this company was, perhaps, not completely respectable, Marina assured me that they were, in any case, "hearts of gold." I couldn't get anything else out of Marina.

In time, I learned that these "hearts of gold" did not all have the same education. More precisely, Sharik had a high school diploma, while Sinderyushkin and Misha had no education at all. Sharik even had some scholarly works to his credit. And for this reason he was somewhat condescending to the other "hearts of gold."

I was quite interested in what these scholarly works of Sharik's were. But that was to remain unknown. Marina says he was born with a pen in his hands, but she won't give me any more details about his scholarly activity. I started to get to the bottom of it and, finally, found out that he was more in the shoemaking line. But how this related to his scholarly activity, I never could find out.

Once I learned that these "hearts of gold" had a little party. They pooled their money and bought some marinated eel. And Misha even brought along a little jar of vodka. In general, Misha loves a drink.

Sharik's shoes are made of cork.

At some point in the evening, Marina told me that Sinderyushkin had cursed me out calling me a hooligan because I had stepped on his foot. I got angry too and asked Marina to tell Sinderyushkin not to hang around underfoot.

The Conversation of the "Hearts of Gold" Overheard by Me about Bechamel

The train was rushing from the hills,
Airs through the windows, noises swell.
That's when I hear their *tete-a-tete*,
a great debate on bechamel.

Night. And I can't see a face,
only by the sound I know:
all those little "golden hearts"!
Still I'm prepared to shake their hands.

I got up now I'm on my way,
rocking through the car's dark hall—
if I manage not to fall,
I'll find them, but won't touch them.

Suddenly there's no more dark,
a station flashes in the window,
a sudden tightness in my chest,
a shark jumped in my heart.

Then the brakes began to screech,
cutting short the wheels' revolving,
I look and see with all my eyes:
I'm all alone, the car is empty.

I no longer hear the words
About some sort of bechamel.
And suddenly, as in the woods,
winds through the windows, noises swell.

The train cars, having screeched,
move on. The light's gone out.
The train roars on, like a lion
running from the chase.

February 18, 1936

* * *

[Letter to Elizaveta Gritsyna]

February 28, 1936.

Dear Liza,

My best wishes to Kirill on his birthday, and also to his parents,
who are successfully fulfilling the plan prescribed by nature of
raising a human offshoot unable to walk up to the age of two
years, but then, with time, beginning to destroy everything in sight
and, finally, in the attainment of a young preschool age, using a
voltmeter stolen from his father's desk to smash the head of his
beloved mother who had failed to dodge an especially agile attack
conducted by her not as yet completely matured child, already
planning in his immature occiput that once having knocked off
his parents, he could turn all his most ingenious attention to his
grandfather, grizzled with silver hairs, thereby proving his mental
development, so abnormal for his age, in honor of which, on the
28th of February, some of the admirers of this truly extraordinary
phenomenon are gathering, among whom, to my great regret,

I will be unable to count myself, since I find myself at the given moment in a certain state of tension, going into raptures on the coast of the Gulf of Finland, with the ability characteristic of me since my childhood years, once I've grabbed a steel pen and dipped it into an inkwell, to express in short and distinct phrases my profound and, at times, even, to a certain extent, highly elevated thought.

Daniil Kharms

* * *

[Speech by Kharms on April 3, 1936]

I have difficulty in using the terms "formalism" and naturalism" in the range of meanings that they are now being used in literary discussion. The meaning of the term "formalism" is so varied and has been so idiosyncratically interpreted by each speaker that I cannot see any possibility of using it with any kind of definite meaning.

The term "naturalism" has become nearly synonymous with the concepts "cynicism" and "pornography."

The articles in *Pravda*, though most immediately concerned with music, possess an immense and principled significance for all the arts, and quite definitely and clearly point to a movement which, over the course of at least 50 years, has grown stronger and stronger and, finally, has come to dominate almost all contemporary art.

And now this movement, which until the present time seemed synonymous with high art, has, suddenly, lost all its strength. Before it seemed that this movement would lead culture out of the dead end in which, in my view, it found itself in the 19th century.

If in Pushkin's lines—

Through the wavy mists of night
The moon invades.
And doleful pours her wavering light
On doleful glades.

—you can feel a tension and a terrible energy in every line. (Everything here is calculated: the precision of description, the movement of meaning, the force of sound, and the tension in the voice, and much much else besides. Every word serves a specific purpose. Not a single line gets through on the back of the inspiration of the preceding line.)

Then Lermontov's—

> Wave rushed upon wave,
> Wave driving wave on. . .

Are lines that you want to read with your eyes closed, in an inspired voice. It's still beautiful but it's no accident that for many people at the end of the 19th century Lermontov seemed more trenchant, sharper and deeper than Pushkin. Frightful words: deeper, subtler, sharper, farther etc. etc. created remarkable writers like Dostoevsky and Tolstoy. They also created a remarkable writer like Chekhov.

And later on it turned out that a pencil sketch is sharper and subtler than a finished painting. There are people who know that, when visiting an artist, you can appear to be a subtle connoisseur of art by showing interest in unfinished pencil sketches rather than finished paintings.

I want to say that at the end of the 19th century the first clear signs of a decline in art appeared in the form of impressionism. I think that the academic art of the time was in a considerably more deplorable state than it seemed then.

For many, many reasons art had lost its way. And impressionism appeared to be the way of salvation.

It must have been that there was some insignificant bit of historical truth in impressionism, even in relation to such an immense writer as Tolstoy.

In any case, impressionism achieved magnitude and movement.

People at the end of the 19th century simply did not possess the immense creative energies of a Mozart or a Pushkin. And so, impressionism saved the day. Fragment, draft, sketch, all were much easier to fill with the creative energy they possessed.

An insufficiency of creative thought was replaced by aesthetic sensations. The sharpness, the piquancy of situation replaced strength of meaning. But that which yesterday appeared piquant today seems much less so.

Impressionism evolved and transformed with a frenzied rapidity. There were schools and counter-schools, aesthetics and counter-aesthetics.

The best people got caught up in this movement, really interesting things did in fact appear, which then at the time seemed great. Art had turned to the left.

Over the course of 20 years art covered so much ground that it seemed that in those 20 years more was accomplished than had been in many millennia. Devices were discovered that had been completely unknown up to that time. The questions of "sharpening," "de-familiarization," "distortion," "the creation of a complex image," etc. were brilliantly worked out.

Art galloped to the extremes. But something beyond that was demanded. But what could go further?

In 1927 Malevich said: the most important thing in art is to stop!

And really, stopping was the most left, the newest and the sharpest. Left art stopped.

A period began when it became clear that left art had come to a dead end. There are people who were never ever infected by this left art. I was in any case. And it wasn't so easy to recognize the insolvency of left art. I only realized it in 1929, or even 1930.

Even before that I had hated impressionism, decadence and symbolism. Left art seemed to me a force to counter impressionism And only in 1930 did I realize that it was all of the fruit of the same plant, that it was the last faded echo of the 19th century, the last bourgeois art, no less doomed to die, be it slowly or quickly, as is all bourgeois art.

And I began to hate every last drop of impressionism, even the most insignificant, every pointless ornament, every random leftist affectation.

Unfortunately, 50 years could not pass without leaving a trace in art. To this day works by Joyce, Schonberg, Braque, and so on are considered models of artistic technique.

It's a pointless, impotent artistry. And it's not even artistry. It's nothing but the clever trick of filling up an insignificant expanse with feeble strength. It's like the strength of a flea that can jump across a house.

If the decadents and the futurists have long ago exited the scene and no longer influence our art, then Joyce, Braque and Schonberg have remained completely legitimate models for imitation.

Art's dead end, which began in the 19th century, when impressionism seemed to be salvation, has come to an end. The time has come when art can again begin to evolve with the strength of classicism.

The articles in *Pravda* in an amazingly contemporary way have declared war on this incorrect movement in art.

I haven't published any new things in four years and have been working exclusively for children's journals, where I published short humorous captions, poems and stories.

I worked a fair amount during this time. And now, only towards the end of 1936, am I considering coming out with new things.

* * *

[Letter to Boris Zhitkov]

[End of September 1936?]

Dear Boris Stepanovich,

Every day as I sit down at the harmonium, I think about you. Especially when I play Handel's Second Fugue, which you used to like too. Remember how in places the bass harmonizes with the high voices by using a theme like this:

This fugue is the crown jewel of my repertoire. I've been playing it twice a day over the course of a month and now I can play it fluently. Marina is not especially well disposed to my practicing and since she almost never leaves the house, I practice for no more than one hour a day, which is exceedingly little. Other than the fugue, I play Palestrina's "Stabat mater" arranged for choir, a minuet by John Blow, "O field, field, who has sown you with dead bones" from *Ruslan and Liudmila*, the chorale in E major from the St. John Passion, and now I'm learning the C minor air from a Bach Partita. It's one of Bach's best pieces and is quite simple. I'm sending you the upper line for violin since, although I'm learning it with only one finger, it's been giving me great satisfaction. Druskin comes to see me often. But his remarkable technique on the piano keeps him from playing the harmonium well. On the other hand, a young conductor, a friend of Nikolai Timofeev, was visiting and he really showed what can be done on the harmonium. By changing registers or giving it more air, he attained such variety and conveyed an orchestral sound so precisely that I was simply amazed. In addition, he played from a score that included 22 parts as fluently as you can read a French book in Russian. What's more, he sings all the parts. He sang the sextet from *Don Giovanni* and moved so skillfully from voice to voice, emphasizing precisely the most important moments, that I was able to grasp the sextet in its entirety. What a pity that you've moved to Moscow. I am sure that this young conductor would have delighted you.

Write me, Boris Stepanovich, have you found an apartment and are you playing the violin?

About myself, I can only say that my material situation is worse than ever. I survived September exclusively by selling off my things, and even at that I could count on eating for two days and going hungry for one, but I do hope that someday things will be better. If you happen to be at Children's Publishing, and it's not too difficult for you, try to find out why I haven't received any money from Oleinikov's journal. Oleinikov says that he approved a payment of 500 rubles for me but I haven't gotten them. And also give me some advice here: I translated Wilhelm Busch for *Siskin*. The journal proposed publishing it as a separate book. But then Shvarts came back from Moscow and told me that Obolenskaya is proposing to publish the Busch in Moscow. Thinking that the honoraria and the print runs are bigger in Moscow, I turned down *Siskin*'s offer. I sent a letter to Obolenskaya with Oleinikov, where I write that I would like to publish the Busch in Moscow and ask to be informed about the terms. According to Oleinikov's story, it seems that Obolenskaya was insulted (that I asked about the terms?). Then she consulted with Vvedensky and seems to have refused to publish my Busch. And now I've received the following telegram from her: "Taking your translation of Busch. Terms 1000 rub. per 100 lines. Telegraph agreement. Send poems. Obolenskaya." If they had proposed these terms to me in Leningrad, I would have thought them acceptable, but for Moscow, I don't know. I really need money but don't want to sell my book too cheaply. The whole book is 200 lines. Perhaps it's better to demand payment for the whole thing from her? But how much? Perhaps what Obolenskaya proposes is quite good? Or perhaps quite bad? And how many copies? Boris Stepanovich, you know all this better than me. If you have an extra 5 rubles, send me a telegram. I've really lost touch with how things are done in publishing.

I remain yours,
Daniil Kharms
11 Mayakovsky Street, Apt. 8

* * *

[Letter to Boris Zhitkov]

Leningrad, October 3, 1936

Dear Boris Stepanovich,
          Thanks so much for your reply. I was beginning to feel that everyone who moves to Moscow changes and forgets their Leningrad acquaintances. It seemed to me that Muscovites consider Leningraders some sort of idealists with whom there's nothing to talk about. All that remained was my faith in your unchangeability. In the 10 years I've known you, everyone has changed. You, however, remained just exactly as you were, even though your external life changed more than any of my acquaintances. And then, suddenly, it seemed that you had become a Muscovite and wouldn't answer my letter. That would have been as improbable as if I had written a letter to Oleinikov and he had sent me a

reply. Therefore, when I got your letter today, I felt immense joy, something like "Hurray! Justice will triumph!"

When someone moves to Moscow, I, as a Leningrad patriot, take it as a personal affront. But your move to Moscow, my dear Boris Stepanovich, makes me infinitely sad. Among my acquaintances in Leningrad, not one real man or living human being remains. One will yawn if you start speaking about music, another doesn't even know how to unscrew an electric teapot, a third, upon awaking, won't even light up a cigarette until he's eaten something, while a fourth will deceive you and trip you up so that afterwards all you can do is marvel. The best of all of them is, perhaps, Nikolai Andreevich. I really really miss you, dear Boris Stepanovich.

I am amazed at your strength: to live for such a long time without your own room and yet to remain yourself. You're the one who used to say that the nicest gift is a dressing gown with 30 pockets! You remind me of an Englishman who's been drinking for 8 days and, as they say, can't see straight and still sits straight as a stick. It's even frightening. All this, of course, is because you have a million little habits and needs, but the most important are tea and tobacco.

In my next letter, I'll write you about my affairs. Just let me know to what address I should write.

Kharms

* * *

[Letter to Grigory Tsypin]

[Leningrad. September—October 1936]

Dear Comrade Tsypin,

I just received your letter. I agree with your proposal and will send you the text in the next few days.

But I have to say that your conditions aren't clear to me. Permit me to explain the lack of clarity. Obolenskaya has sent me the following telegram: "1000 rub. up to 100 lines." But what if, let's say, there are 175 lines?

You write: "1000 rub. for 100—120 lines." And as an exception you offer to pay me 1500 rub. For 120 lines or for the entire book?

I haven't yet finished chapter VII and do not know the exact number of lines. But I think there will be 250, and perhaps more. From Obolenskaya's telegram, I understood that one has to consider 10 rub. as the average payment per line.

In a word, to this point I still do not understand your conditions. But I agree, since it's nicer to receive a lot of money from Moscow than just a little. But it's nicer to receive a little money than nothing at all.

I remain yours,

Daniil Kharms

* * *

[Scenes from the life of the poet]

About Pushkin

It's hard to say anything about Pushkin to someone who knows nothing about him. Pushkin is a great poet. Napoleon is less great than Pushkin. And compared to Pushkin, Bismarck is nothing. And Alexanders I and II and III are simply squirts compared to Pushkin. And really everyone compared to Pushkin is a squirt. Only compared to Gogol, Pushkin himself is a squirt.

And so, instead of writing about Pushkin, I had better write about Gogol.

Even so, Gogol is so great that it's quite impossible to write anything about him, therefore I'll write about Pushkin anyway.

But after Gogol, it's somehow insulting to write about Pushkin. But it's impossible to write about Gogol. Therefore I had better write nothing about anyone.

December 15, 1936

* * *

Alaph! Today I didn't have time to tell you anything. All day long I felt like eating and sleeping. I walk around in a daze and nothing interests me.

When someone has grown accustomed to going to bed late, it's very difficult to break the habit. There's one correct way to get back on a normal schedule: skip a night. That is, go to bed later and later: first very late at night, then early in the morning, then in the daytime, and finally the next evening. That's the way to get back onto a normal schedule.

When falling into the muck, there's only one thing for a man to do: fall without looking back. It's important to do this with a certain interest and energy.

I once knew a watchman interested only in vice. Then his interest narrowed, and he began to take an interest in a single vice. And then when he discovered that this vice was his specialty and took an interest in this specialty alone, he began to feel himself a man again. He became self-confident, he required erudition, he had to look into adjoining disciplines, and the man began to grow. The watchman became a genius.

December 23, 1936.

* * *

Today I didn't finish my 3—4 pages. My handwriting looks this way because I'm writing lying in bed.
<u>Daniil Kharms</u>.

Yesterday Papa said to me that as long as I'm Kharms, I'll be hounded by harms.
<u>Daniil Kharms</u>.
December 23, 1936.

* * *

We propose dividing all works of art into two camps, Fire and Water.

Let us explain by way of examples:
1) If you walk through the Hermitage you get a Watery feeling from the galleries housing works by Cranach and Holbein and from

the galleries where gilt silver and wooden church sculptures are exhibited.

2) From the Spanish gallery you get a Fiery feeling, even though here too you will see examples of purely Watery phenomenon (monks with ribbons coming out of their mouths).

3) Pushkin is Watery.

4) The Gogol of *Evenings on a Farm near Dikanka* is Fiery, but later Gogol becomes more and more Watery.

5) Hamsun is Watery.

6) Mozart is Watery.

~~Bach has some fiery things, but overall Bach is more of a watery phenomenon.~~

7) Bach is both Fire and Water.

Table

Purely Watery	Combination Fire and Water	Purely Fiery
Pushkin	Gogol	Schiller
Mozart	Bach	Van Dyck
Hamsun	~~Leonardo da Vinci~~	Rembrandt
Holbein		Velasquez
Cranach		
Raphael		
Leonardo da Vinci		

* * *

Russian Literature	World Literature
1. Apocrypha.	1. Shakespeare.
2. John Damascene.	2. Ben Jonson (selections).
3. John Chrysostum.	3. Elizabethan dramatists.
4. Heroic Tales.	4. Blake.
5. The Lay of Igor's Campaign.	5. Dickens.
6. Feofan Prokopovich.	6. Mark Twain.
7. *Domostroi.*	7. E. A. Poe (selections).
8. Tretiakovsky.	8. ~~Browning~~.
9. Kantemir.	9. Longfellow (selections).
10. Lomonosov.	10. Edward Lear.

11. Derzhavin.

12. Karamzin.

13. Pushkin.

14. Baratynsky.

15. Gogol.

16. Dostoevsky.

17. Tolstoy (selections).

18. Leskov.

19. Nekrasov.

20. Tiutchev.

21. Sologub (selections)

22. Briusov (*The Fiery Angel*).

23. Bely (selections).

24. ~~Blok~~ Chekhov.

25. David Burliuk.

26. Khlebnikov.

27. Remizov.

28. Rozanov.

29. Prutkov.

30. Ershov.

31. Senkovsky.

32. Polezhaev.

11. Lewis Carroll.

12. A. A. Milne.

13. Kipling (selections).

14. Ballads.

15. Milton.

16. Sterne.

17. Richardson.

18. Conan Doyle (selections).

19.

20. Rabelais.

21. Scarron.

22. Corneille (selections).

23. Balzac (selections).

24. Maeterlinck (selections).

25. Marcel Proust.

26. Dante.

27. Swift (selections).

28. Cervantes (*Don Quixote*).

29. Leonardo da Vinci.

30. Calderon (selections).

31. Krasinski (selections).

32. Sholem Aleichem (selections).

33. Peretz (selections).

34. Mendel Mocher Sforim (selections).

35. Goethe.

36. Schiller.

37. Heine.

38. Novalis.

39. Hoffman.

40. Meyrink.

41. Hamsun.

42. Kalevala.

43. Munchausen.

44. Jerome.

"THE BLUE NOTEBOOK"

(August 23, 1936—October 26/27, 1937)

For the album.

Once I saw a fly fighting with a bedbug. It was so frightening that I ran out into the street and ran off devil knows where.

That's the way it is with the album: make a mess and it'll be too late.

Kharms
August 23 1936

1. My opinion about traveling in brief: when travelling, don't go too far, or you'll see something that later on will be impossible to forget. And if something gets stuck too stubbornly in memory, at first a man isn't quite himself, and then it's very difficult to remain in good spirits.

2. So, for example: one watchmaker, Comrade Badaev, couldn't forget a phrase he had heard once: "If the sky were askew, it wouldn't fall through." Comrade Badaev couldn't fully understand this phrase, it irritated him, he found it unreasonable, devoid of any meaning, even unhealthy, because it contained an obviously incorrect assertion (Comrade Badaev felt that a competent physicist could have said something about the sky "falling through" and would have found fault with the phrase "if the sky were askew." If Perlman got wind of the phrase, even comrade Badaev knew that Perlman would have torn it to shreds, as a puppy tears slippers to shreds) which was clearly hostile to normal European thought. And if the assertion in this phrase were true, it would be too unimportant and trivial to talk about. And in any case, once heard, the phrase should have been forgotten at once. But that's just what didn't happen: comrade Badaev constantly remembered the phrase and suffered terribly.

3. It's useful for a man to know only that which he ought to know. I can use the following episode as an example: one man knew slightly more, another slightly less, than they were supposed to know. So what of it? The one who knew slightly less got rich, while the one who knew slightly more lived his entire life no more than comfortably.

4. Since ancient times people have wondered what intelligence is and what stupidity is. In this regard I recall the following incident: when my aunt gave me a writing desk, I said to myself: "well now, I'll sit down at the desk and the first thought I compose at this desk will be especially intelligent." But I wasn't able to compose an especially intelligent thought. Then I said to myself: "OK. Since I haven't been able to compose an especially intelligent thought, I'll compose an especially stupid one." But I wasn't able to compose an especially stupid one either.

5. Everything extreme is very difficult to do. The middle parts come easier. The very center doesn't demand any exertion at all. The center is equilibrium. There's no struggle there at all.

6. Must one leave the state of equilibrium?

7. When traveling, don't give into daydreams, but fantasize and pay attention to everything, even the trivial things.

8. Sitting in place, don't swing your legs.

9. Every kind of wisdom is good, as long as someone has understood it. Wisdom not understood can get dusty.

10. There was once a redheaded man, who had no eyes or ears. He had no hair either, so people called him redheaded only in a manner of speaking. He couldn't speak, since he had no mouth. He also had no nose. He didn't even have arms or legs. And he didn't have a stomach, and he didn't have a back, and he didn't have a spine, and he didn't have any insides. He had nothing. So it's impossible to understand what we're talking about. Far better if we talk about him no longer. *Against Kant*

January 7, 1937

11. A certain grandmother had only four teeth in her mouth. Three teeth on the top, and one below. The grandmother couldn't chew with these teeth. Strictly speaking, they were of no use to her. So one day the grandmother decided to rid herself of all her teeth and to have a corkscrew inserted into

her lower gums and little tweezers into her uppers. The grandmother drank ink, ate beets, and cleaned her ears with matches. The grandmother had four rabbits. Three rabbits above, and one below. The grandmother caught the rabbits with her hands and put them in little cages. The rabbits cried and scratched their ears with their hind legs. The rabbits drank ink and ate beets. Shoo, shoo, shoo! The rabbits drank ink and ate beets!

12.   A certain Pantelei struck Ivan with his heel.
A certain Ivan struck Natalia with a wheel.
A certain Natalia struck Semyon with a muzzle.
A certain Semyon struck Selifan with a trough.
A certain Selifan struck Nikita with a coat.
A certain Nikita struck Roman with a plank.
A certain Roman struck Tatiana with a spade.
A certain Tatiana struck Elena with a jug.
And then the fight began.
Helena beat Tatiana with the fence.
Tatiana beat Roman with the mattress.
Roman beat Nikita with the suitcase.
Nikita beat Selifan with the tray.
Selifan beat Semyon with bare hands.
Semyon spit in Natalia's ears.
Natalia bit Ivan on the finger.
Ivan kicked Pantelei with his heel.
Ekh, we thought, what fine folk are fighting.

13.   One young girl said: "gva."
Another young girl said: "khfy."
A third young girl said: "mbru."
While Yermakov crunched and crunched cabbage from under the fence.

Clearly evening had already begun.
Motka finished playing with shit and went home.
It was drizzling.
Pigs were eating peas.
Ragozin took a look into the women's bathhouse.
Senka was riding Manka like a horse.

Manka had already begun to doze.
The sky darkened. Stars began to twinkle.
Rats gnawed at a mouse beneath the floors.
Sleep, my child, and fear not stupid dreams.
Stupid dreams are from the stomach.

14. Shave your beard and shave your whiskers!
You're not goats that you should wear those beards.
You're not cats that you should twitch your whiskers.
You're not mushrooms that you should have a cap.
Hey, young ladies!
Take your little caps off!
Hey, you beauties!
Take your little skirts off!
C'mon there Manka Marusina,
Sit right down on Petya Yelabonin.
Hey there little girls, cut your little braids off.
You're not zebras that you should run with tails.
Plump and pleasing little girls,
Invite us to your revelry.

15. Lead me on with eyes bound shut.
I won't go with eyes bound shut.
Unbind my eyes—I'll go myself
And don't you hold my hands,
I want to give my hands free play.
Step aside you stupid spectators,
I'm going to lash out with my feet.
I'll make my way along a floorboard and I won't wobble.
I'll run along the cornice and won't collapse.
Don't you cross me. You'll be sorry.
Your cowardly eyes are not pleasing to the gods.
Your mouths open wide just when they shouldn't.
Your noses do not know vibrating smells.
Eat your soup—for that's your occupation.
Sweep up your rooms—for that's your task from ages out of mind.

But take off all my bandages and bellybands,
I feed on salt and you on sugar.
I have my parks and have my gardens.
In my garden pasture goats
In my trunk there's a hat made of fur.
Don't you cross me. I am what I am, and you are nothing to me
but a quart of smoke.

January 8, 1937

16. Today I wrote nothing. That's not important.

January 9, 1937

17. Dmitry made querulous sounds. Anna sobbed, burying her head in the pillow. Mania cried.

18. −Fedya, hey Fedya!
   −What is it sir?
   −I'll show you "what is it sir"!
   (Silence)
   −Fedya, hey Fedya!
   −What's the matter?
   −Oh you son-of-a-bitch! You're asking me what the matter is.
   −But what do you want from me?
   −Did y'see? What do I want from him? Why I oughta give it to you, you bastard, for that kind of talk. . . . I'll smack you so hard you'll go flying you know where!
   −Where?
   −Into the shitpot!
   (Silence)

19. −Fedya, hey Fedya?
   −What's with you, auntie, have you lost your mind?
   −Ah! Ah! Say that again!
   −No, I won't repeat it.
   −That's more like it! You should know your place! I'll say! That's right!

February 23, 1937

20.   I was choking on a mutton bone.
      They took me by the elbows and led me out from behind the table.
      I fell to thinking.
      A mouse ran by.
      Ivan Ivanovich came running after the mouse with a long stick.
      A nosy old woman was watching from the window.
      As he ran past the old woman, Ivan hit her with the stick right in the snout.

21.   On my way home from a walk,
      Suddenly I said: Oh My God!
      I've been walking four full days
      Whatever will my kinfolk say?

22.   We're vanquished on the field of life.
      There's no more hope at all in sight.
      The dream of happiness is gone.
      But destitution lingers on.

      April 3, 1937

23. To possess only intelligence and talent is too little. You must also have energy, real interest, purity of thought, and a sense of duty.

24. Here I will write today's events, for they are astonishing. Or rather: one event is especially astonishing, I will underline it.

1) Yesterday, we had nothing to eat. 2) In the morning I withdrew 10 rubles from the bank, leaving 5 in the account, so as not to have to close it. 3) I stopped off at Zhitkov's and borrowed 60 rubles from him. 4) Went home, buying groceries on the way. 5) Beautiful, spring weather. 6) Went with Marina to the Buddhist temple, took a bag of sandwiches and a flask of watered-down red wine. 7) On the way home, we stopped at a second-hand shop and saw there a Schiedmayer harmonium, double manual, a copy of the one at the Philharmonic. The price was only 900 rubles! But half an hour ago someone had bought it! 7a) Saw an excellent pipe at Alexander's. 85 rub. 8) We went to Zhitkov's. 9) With Zhitkov, we found out who had

bought the harmonium and we drove to the address: 31 Pesochnaya Street, apartment no. 46, Levinsky. 10) Couldn't buy it off him. 11) We spent the evening at Zhitkov's.

April 4, 1937

25. Enough of laziness and idleness! Open this notebook every day and write down no less than half a page in it. If you have nothing to write, then at least take Gogol's advice and write that there's nothing to write today. Always write with interest and look on writing as a holiday.

April 11, 1937

26. ~~Fonarev suddenly got rich unexpectedly. He suddenly acquired the possibility of dressing well, fixing up his room, furnishing it with expensive things purchased in the commission store and, despite this, he had enough money remaining so that he could eat a meal every day at a good vegetarian cafeteria, then in the evening get into the "Caucasus" restaurant and stay there until closing. When Fonarev was poor still, he had a lot of friends. There would be days when Fonarev had nothing to eat. Then he would go to his friend Rubanov, and Rubanov would almost always feed Fonarev. But it also would happen that Rubanov would come to Fonarev hungry. And if Fonarev also had nothing, then they would go together to Weitel and Weitel would feed them. And if Weitel had nothing too, then all three of them would head out for Minaev's (relative of the well-known poet Minaev). But Minaev almost never had any money. However Minaev did have a library left to him by his famous relative.~~

27.   This is how hunger begins:
       In the morning you wake, feeling lively,
       Then begins the weakness,
       Then the boredom;
       Then comes the loss
       Of the power of quick reason—
       Then comes the calm—
       And then the horror.

October 4, 1937

28.   Dreaming will be your undoing.
Your interest in unyielding life
Like smoke will vanish. At that moment
Angelic envoys won't fly in.

And all your passions will have faded.
The ardent thoughts of youth will pass . . .
Leave off! Leave off, my friend, your dreaming
And liberate your mind from death.

October 4, 1937

29.   The Day
(Amphibrachs)

And little fish flash in the cool of the stream,
And a little house stands at the back of the scene,
And a dog barks and yaps at the herd of the cows,
And wheeling downhill in his cart comes Petrov,
And up on a rooftop a little flag waves,
And rip'ning in wheatfields the nourishing grain,
And flies with a whistle fly round without cease,
And pollen shines silver on every last leaf,
And girls warm themselves as they lie in the sun,
And bees in the garden contentedly buzz,
And geese dive and surface in shade-dappled ponds,
And the day rushes by in its usual works.

October 26/27 1937

To the remark: "You wrote that wrong," reply: "That's the way it always looks when I write it."

Since absolutely no thoughts have come into my head these last few days, I've written nothing down, neither here nor in the blue notebook. Reflections of sunbeams on the floors and walls torment me. I worked a bit on Radlov's album *Stories in Pictures*. J. Mornings I sit naked. Devoid of all pleasing force. Annoyed thanks to <u>A</u>.
April 1937.

O God! What's happening? I'm wallowing in poverty and dissipation. I've ruined Marina. O God, save her! God save my dear unhappy Marina.
May 12, 1937.

Marina's gone to Detskoe Selo to see Natasha. She's decided to divorce me. O God, help make it all painless and peaceful. If Marina leaves me, then may God send her a better life than the one she had with me.

An even more terrible time has begun for me. At Children's Publishing they've made an issue of some of my verses and have got their claws in me. They've stopped publishing me, and say they can't pay me because of some incidental glitches. I feel that some secret evil is taking place there. We have nothing to eat. We're starving.

I know the end has come for me. I'm going to Children's Publishing now so they can refuse to pay me. June 1, 1937. 2 hrs. 40 minutes.

Now they'll refuse to pay me at Children's Publishing.
June 1, 1937.

We're done for.

* * *

I've completely lost my edge. It's terrible. Complete impotence in all respects. You can see it even in my handwriting. But what insane stubbornness there is in my attraction to vice. I sit for hours, day after day, to get my own and I don't get it, but still I sit and sit. That's what you call genuine interest! Enough pretense: nothing interests me but this.

Inspiration and interest, they're one and the same thing.

To turn away from true inspiration is just as difficult as to turn from vice.

In the face of true inspiration everything else vanishes and it alone remains.

Therefore, vice is also its own kind of inspiration.

* * *

At the root of both vice and inspiration lies one and the same thing. At their root lies genuine interest.

Genuine interest is the most important thing in our lives.

A man with no interest in anything will quickly perish.

An overly one-sided and powerful interest increases the stress on life exponentially: just one more little push and a man goes out of his mind.

A man cannot fulfill his duty if he lacks true interest in it.

If a man's true interest coincides with his duty, he will become great.

June 18, 1937. In Illa's room.

* * *

July 5. A new disaster: Marina's found out that I've been cheating on her with Vvedensky's wife. That's not good.

July 5, 1937. You go to Marina with tenderness in your soul, and you come away annoyed. And the cause of it must be me.

I don't even know what to write, I'm so upset and confused. Terribly empty inside me. I have nothing to brag of. I'm inadequate in absolutely everything.

[From notebook 32]

You have to be cold-blooded, that is, know how to keep silent and not change the constant expression of your face.

When the person talking to you is being irrational, speak affectionately and agree with him.

Whenever someone says: "I'm bored," there's always a sexual question hidden there.

A woman who gives off no smell is revolting. A woman whose sexual organs give off a smell is attractive: she is arousing. A woman should not wash herself so often that the smell of her sexual organs is washed away: the stronger the smell of her sexual organs, the better. But a woman must take care that her sexual organs not smell of urine.

They say there's an incubus around here. He squashes bedbugs.
The incubus is Ator.

Create a pose for yourself and have the character to maintain it. There was a time when I'd pose as an Indian, then Sherlock Holmes, then a yogi, but now it's as an irritable neurasthenic. I'd rather not hold that last one. Have to think up a new one.

* * *

Compendium:

"Formerly when the desire to understand someone, or even myself, would come upon me, I would focus not on actions, in which everything is conventional, but on desires. Tell me what you desire, and I'll tell you who you are."

    Chekhov, "A Boring Story."

". . . in our age of aviation and wireless electricity. . ."

Reason would have me become a genius, while my feelings make me want to be naked among naked and ripe young women who smell strongly of sex organs and I want these women to get aroused looking at me.

Just try to remain calm and composed when the money runs out!
July 17.

Here's something interesting from the beach: there's an empty spot next to you. Who's going to lie down there? You wait. Usually your new neighbor turns out to be completely uninteresting.
July 21. The beach at the Peter-Paul Fortress.

* * *

From time to time I make notes here about my condition. Now I've fallen lower than ever. I can't think about anything. Utterly tormented by the reflections of sunbeams. A feeling of complete collapse. Body sluggish, stomach swollen. Digestion unsettled, voice hoarse. Terrible absent-mindedness and neurasthenia. Nothing interests me. No thoughts at all, or if a thought should flash through my mind, it's feeble, filthy or cowardly. I need to work but I do nothing, absolutely nothing. And there's nothing I can do. Sometimes, all I can do is a little light reading. I'm in debt up to my ears. I have around 10,000 rubles of inescapable debt. Not a single kopeck to my name, and in my fall I have no financial prospects whatsoever. I can see that I'm done for. And no energy left to fight. O God, I ask for Thy help. August 7, 1937.
Detskoe Selo

I can accurately predict that there will be no improvement at all for me and that in the near term I'm threatened by, and will suffer, a full-blown crash.

August 7.

* * *

For Nastya—nasty weather.

I have achieved a tremendous fall.
I've lost the ability to work.
Completely. I'm a living corpse.
Abba, Father, I have fallen. Help me. To Rise.
August 7, 1937.

Life is the sea, fate is the wind, while man is a ship. Just as an experienced helmsman can make use of a contrary wind and even sail against the wind without changing course, an intelligent man can make use of the blows of fate, and with each blow come nearer to his goal.
Example: A man wanted to become an orator ~~lawyer~~ but fate cut out his tongue and the man became mute. But he didn't give up and he learned to hold up boards with phrases written in large letters and also showing where

to snarl or howl along, and in this way he had a greater influence on his listeners than would have been possible with normal speech.

* * *

If the state can be likened to a human organism, then, in case of war, I would rather live in the heel.

* * *

Here it is already August 7. Up to now, I've done nothing. Now I'm in Detskoe Selo (since August 1). My condition is, if anything, worse. Neurasthenia, absent-mindedness, no joy in my soul, utterly unable to work, thoughts sluggish and scattered.

* * *

[Scenes from the life of the poet, and two letters to a philosopher friend]

About How I was Visited by Messengers

Something went bang in the clock and then the messengers came to me. I didn't realize right away that the messengers had come to me. At first I thought that the clock was broken. But then I saw the clock was still running and was, in all likelihood, showing the correct time. Then I decided that there was a draft in the room. And then I wondered: what kind of phenomenon is it that a clock running wrong and a draft in the room can equally serve as cause? As I thought this over, I was sitting on the chair near the couch and looking at the clock. The minute hand was on the nine and the hour hand near the four: consequently it was a quarter to four. Beneath the clock there was a tear-off calendar, and the pages of the calendar were rustling as if a strong wind were blowing in the room. My heart was pounding and I was afraid of losing consciousness.

–I have to drink some water,—I said. On the end table next to me there was a pitcher of water. I stretched out my arm and took the pitcher.

–Water may help,—I said and started looking at the water.

But here I realized that the messengers had come to me, but I could not distinguish them from the water. I was afraid to drink the water, because by mistake I might drink up the messengers. What does that mean? It means nothing. You can only drink a liquid. But really, are the messengers a liquid? That means I can drink the water and there's nothing here to fear. But I can't find the water. I went around the room looking for it. I tried shoving a belt into my mouth, but it was not water. I shoved the calendar into my mouth— it wasn't water either. I said the hell with the water and started looking for the messengers. But how could I find them? What do they look like? I remembered that I couldn't distinguish them from the water which means they look like water. But what does water look like? I stood there thinking. I don't know how long I stood there thinking, but suddenly I trembled.

Here's the water!—I said to myself.

But it wasn't the water, it was simply that my ear had begun to itch.

I started to root around under the dresser and under the bed, thinking at the very least to find there the water or a messenger. But all I found under the dresser in the dust was a ball that had been chewed through by a dog, and under the bed some shards of glass.

Under the chair I found a half-eaten cutlet. I ate it and I felt better. By now the wind had nearly stopped blowing, while the clock ticked calmly showing the correct time: a quarter to four.

−Well, that means the messengers have already left,—I said to myself and began changing my clothes to go and visit.

August 22, 1937

Five Unfinished Narratives

Dear Yakov Semenovich,

1. A certain man running full speed ahead smacked his head into a smithy with such force that the smith put aside the sledge hammer he was holding in his hands, took off his leather apron and, smoothing his hair down with his palm, went out onto the street to see what had happened. 2. Now the smith saw the man sitting on the ground. The man was sitting on the ground and holding onto this head. 3. "What happened?" asked the smith. "Ouch!" said the man. 4. The smith went up closer to the man. 5. We break off our narrative about the smith and the unknown man and begin a new narrative about the four friends of the harem. 6. Once upon a time there were four *amateurs* of the harem. They thought it pleasant to have

eight women each all at once. They would gather evenings and reason about harem life. They drank wine; they got as drunk as drunk could be; they collapsed under the table; they barfed. It was repulsive to look at them. They bit one another on the feet. They called one another bad words. They crawled upon their bellies. 7. We break off our story about them and take up a new story about beer. 8. There was once a keg of beer and next to it sat a *philosophe* and he reasoned: "This keg is filled with beer; Beer ferments and is fortified. And I by my reason wander the firmament above the stars and am fortified in spirit. Beer is a beverage flowing in space, while I am a beverage flowing in time. 9. When beer is enclosed in a keg, it has nowhere to flow. Time will stop and I will come to a stop. 10. But time will not stop, and my flowing is immutable. 11. No, far better that beer flow freely for it is contrary to the laws of nature for it to stop in one place. And with these words the *philosophe* opened the tap and the beer poured out onto the floor. 12. We've said enough about beer; now we'll say something about a drum. 13. A *philosophe* beat on a drum and shouted: "I am producing philosophic noise. This noise is not needed by anyone and it even disturbs everyone. But if it disturbs everyone, it means that it is not of this world. And if it is not of this world, then it is of that world. And if it is of that world, then I will keep producing it." 14. The *philosophe* made noise for a long time. But now we'll leave this noisy tale and go to the following quiet tale about trees. 15. A *philosophe* walked beneath the trees and was silent because inspiration had abandoned him.

(1937)

Connection

Philosopher!

1. I write you in reply to the letter you are planning to write me in reply to my letter which I wrote you. 2. A violinist bought himself a magnet and took it home. On the way hooligans fell upon the violinist and knocked off his cap. The wind picked up the cap and carried it down the street. 3. The violinist put the magnet on the ground and ran after the cap. The cap landed in a puddle of nitric acid and disintegrated completely. 4. But the hooligans meanwhile swiped the magnet and disappeared. 5. The violinist returned home without a coat and without a cap because the cap had disintegrated

completely in the nitric acid and the violinist, distressed by the loss of his cap, forgot his coat on a streetcar. 6. The conductor of that streetcar took the coat to the flea market and there he exchanged it for sour cream, groats, and tomatoes. 7. The conductor's wife's father gorged himself on the tomatoes and died. They put the conductor's wife's father's corpse in the mortuary, but then they mixed him up and in place of the conductor's wife's father they buried some old woman. 8. On the grave of the old woman they put up a white post with the inscription: "Anton Sergeevich Kondratiev." 9. Eleven years later worms gnawed this post through and it fell down. So the cemetery watchman sawed this post into four parts and burned it in his stove. And the wife of the cemetery watchman used the fire to cook up cauliflower soup. 10. But when the soup was ready the clock fell down off the wall right into the pot with this soup. They pulled the clock from the soup but there were bedbugs in the clock and they turned up in the soup. The soup they gave away to the beggar Timofei. 11. The beggar Timofei ate some soup with bedbugs and told the beggar Nikolai all about the goodness of the cemetery watchman. 12. The next day the beggar Nikolai came to the cemetery watchman and started asking for alms. But the cemetery watchman gave nothing to the beggar Nikolai and drove him off. 13. The beggar Nikolai got really furious and set fire to the house of the cemetery watchman. 14. Fire jumped across from the house to the church and the church burnt down. 15. An extensive investigation was undertaken but it was not possible to establish the cause of the blaze. 16. On the spot where there once was a church they built a club and, on the day the club opened, they arranged a concert in which was performing the violinist who lost his coat fourteen years ago. 17. And among the listeners sat the son of one of those hooligans who fourteen years ago had knocked the cap off this violinist. 18. After the concert they went home on the same streetcar. But in the streetcar coming behind them the driver was the very same conductor who had once sold the violinist's coat at the flea market. 19. And so here they are, riding around the city late at night: in front, the violinist and the hooligan's son; and behind them the driver, the former conductor; 20. They ride and don't know the connection between them and won't know it till the day they die.

September 14, 1937

Daniil Kharms

* * *

[From notebook 32]

Tibetan

    Kadakh: white silk shawl.

    Dalai Lama: ocean teacher.

    Taschi—Lama

    Taschi—Lunpo

    Lekso: thank you (Tibetan).

    Dymoena: hello.

    Za senu: hello (Mongolian).

    Mar: butter (Tibetan).

    Dzha: tea (Tibetan).

Mongolian

    Sai: Mongolian tea.

    Togo: butter.

    Makha: meat.

        Sugar.

        Bread.

        Butter.

    Ssu: Milk.

        Thank you.

    Ossa: Water.

    Ukho: drink.

    Itkha: eat.

    Khalun: hot.

    Bi: I.

    Shi: you.

    Abre: aunt.

    Sadda: son.

    Agvan Dorzhiev.

    Damáru boribanchin.

    Khambo Agvan—Lovsan Dorzhiev

    Potala Palace.

* * *

We've eaten well (hot dogs with macaroni) for the last time: because I don't expect any money tomorrow, and there won't be any ever again. And there's nothing left to sell. Three days ago I sold a score of *Ruslan and Ludmila* that wasn't mine for 50 rubles. I spent money that wasn't mine. In a word, the line has been crossed. And now we have no hope left. I tell Marina that I'm going to get 100 rubles tomorrow, but it's all lies. I won't get any money from anywhere. Thanks to Thee, O God, that till now Thou hast fed us. And after that, Thy will be done.
October 3, 1937.

* * *

I give thanks to Thee, O Christ our God, for Thou hast sated us with Thy earthly blessings. Neither deprive us of Thy Heavenly Kingdom.

October 4, 1937. We'll go hungry today.

October 4, 1937. Oh to sit in one's room, knowing that you're completely secure, making sketches of apartments.

October 9, Saturday 10 hrs. 40 m. morning. 1937.
Through Saturday, October 30, 1937, I pledge neither to dream of money, nor of an apartment, nor of glory.
Daniil Kharms

O God, now I have but a single request of Thee: destroy me, shatter me utterly, cast me into hell, do not stop me before my course is run, but deprive me of all hope and swiftly destroy me forever and ever.
Daniil
October 23, 1937. 6 hrs. 40 min evening.

* * *

October 31, 1937.
The only thing that interests me is "<u>nonsense</u>": only that which has no practical meaning. Life interests me only in its absurd manifestations. Heroism, pathos, daring, ethics, hygiene, morality, tenderness and fervor are odious to me as words and feelings.

However I fully understand and respect: ecstasy and exultation, inspiration and despair, passion and obsession, debauchery and chastity, sorrow and grief, joy and laughter.

* * *

November 13, 1937. I'm going to a meeting of the Children's Literature Section. I'm certain they'll refuse to help me and that they'll throw me out of the Union.

* * *

Here are my favorite writers:

		For Mankind:	For My Heart:
1.	Gogol	69	69
2.	Prutkov	42	69
3.	Meyrink	42	69
4.	Hamsun	55	62
5.	Edward Lear	42	59
6.	Louis Carroll	45	59

Just now Gustav Meyrink is especially dear to my heart.
November 14, 1937.

* * *

I don't want to live anymore. November 16, 1937.

I don't need anything anymore. I have no hope left. It's best not to ask anything of God: whatever He sends, let it be. If death, let it be death; if life, let it be life: all that God sends me. Into Thy hands, O Lord Jesus Christ, I commend my spirit. Preserve me, have mercy on me and grant me life eternal. Amen.

There's nothing I can do. I don't want to live.

Lipavsky asserts that we are made of matter destined for genius. November 22, 1937.

What am I grumbling about? I have been given everything I need to live life on a higher plane. But I am drowning in sloth, depravity and daydreams.

A person does not "believe" or "not believe," but rather "wants to believe" or "wants not to believe."

There are people who *do not believe* and do not *not believe* because they do not want to *believe* and do not want *not to believe*. So I *do not believe* in myself because I have neither the desire *to believe* nor *not to believe*.

I want to be in life what Lobachevsky was in geometry.

It's wrong to think that faith is something unmovable, and that it comes of its own volition. Faith demands intense effort and energy, perhaps greater than anything else.

Doubt is already a particle of faith.

Do miracles exist? There's a question to which I would like to hear an answer.

* * *

Marina naked, wearing nothing but a nightshirt, ran out onto the stairs and was talking to a woman. I think she caught a cold. I got terribly angry. November 23, 1937.

All night long I dreamt of A with whom—‖ November 22-23, 1937.

O God, what a horrible life, and what a horrible state I'm in. There's nothing I can do. I feel like sleeping all the time, like Oblomov. No hope left. We ate for the last time today. Marina is ill with a constant low-grade fever. I have no energy.
November 30, 1937.

I am astonished by man's powers. Here it is, already January 12, 1938. Our situation has become even worse and still we hang on. O God, send us death quickly.

      January 12, 1938.

Few fall as low as I have fallen. One thing is beyond doubt: I have fallen so low that now I can never rise again.

      January 12, 1938.

* * *

I really love my Marinochka.

It's now 9:30 in the morning. I just returned from the Petrograd side. First I was at Valentina Efimovna's. Mikhailov and Anna Semyonovna were there. A. S. went home at 1:30. I walked her home and then went to see the Lipavskys. Mikhailov and Valentina Efimovna showed up there too.
2 am. The Slonimskys were visiting the Lipavskys. Lots of vodka and beer. Around 4 o'clock everyone left. Marina Rzhevutskaya is spending the night at our apartment. I know that she's sleeping on my couch. I don't want to come home in the middle of the night and wake everyone up. That's why I stayed at the Lipavskys' for the night.
At 7:30 I woke up because the bedbugs were biting me. Couldn't sleep, couldn't turn on the light without waking my hosts, and had the urge to smoke. I sat there in the darkness till 9, smoked 2 pipes and then took off quietly for home. At home both Marinas were still sleeping. I sat down on the little sofa.
I really love my Marina.
Early morning, January 24, 1938.
Harmonius.

March 11, 1938. For 200r. I sold the Pavel Buré watch mama gave me.

* * *

March 20, 1938. I went up to the window naked. I could see that someone in the house across from us was outraged, the sailor's wife, I think. A policeman, the janitor and somebody else burst in on me. They stated that I have been upsetting the tenants in the house opposite for three years now. I put up curtains.

Things have gotten even worse for us. I don't know what we're going to eat today. And as for what we'll eat after that, I have no idea.
We're starving.
March 25, 1938.

My last days have arrived. I had a talk with Andreev yesterday. Very bad conversation. No hope. We're starving. Marina is getting weaker, and on top of that I have a vicious toothache.
We are perishing. God help us.
April 9, 1938.

May 25. Yesterday and today I went to the "Golden Birch" beach. Yesterday was for the first time this year. Olga arrived today. I went to the *banya*. Viktor Eduardovich left for Finland. I got into a fight with Marina because I felt that she really didn't want me to leave. Still, that evening, after a scene, I left.

May 26, 1938. Marina is in bed in a terrible mood. I love her so much, but how horrible to be married.

I am tormented by "sex." I go for weeks, sometimes months, without a woman.

* * *

What is more pleasing to the eye: an old woman in just her slip or a completely naked young man? And which is less likely to be allowed to appear in public that way?

1. Every human life has but one goal: immortality.
1-a. Every human life has but one goal: the attainment of immortality.
2. One person strives towards immortality by continuing his family, another undertakes great deeds on earth to immortalize his name, and only the third leads a righteous and holy life in order to attain immortality as life eternal.

3. Man has only 2 interests: the earthly—food, drink, warmth, women, rest; and the heavenly, that is, immortality.

4. Everything earthly bears witness to death.

5. There is a single line along which all that is earthly lies. And only that which does not lie along this line bears witness to immortality.

6. And therefore man looks for that which diverges from this earthly line and calls it "the beautiful" or a "thing of genius."

June 9, 1938. Marina has left me and is living for the time being at Varvara Sergeevna's.

[From notebook 38]

1939, Dec. 1 Evening edition late news:
11 hours 30 minutes from Moscow. Otto Kuusinen

* * *

Yura Firgang has been living with us since April 19, 1939.
Between April 8 and 19, I stayed at home with a cold, my tooth ached, and
had no shoes. Easter fell on the 9th, so Nikolai Vasilievich and I went to
Easter matins on the 8th.

* * *

[From notebook 22]

[In Oleinikov's handwriting]

Vvedensky's fate:
Vvedensky's fate is not enviable. Forgotten by everyone, he's dead
to the new life (there!).
When will this happen?
August 22, 1939
Certified true copy. Magus.
Nikolai Makarovich Oleinikov.

* * *

[From notebook 33]

Derzhavin. *Poems*. 1935. Poet's Library, ed. by M. Gorky. Leningrad.

* * *

"Do sit down and have some tea," said Shirin, extinguishing the
kerosene lamp and wiping his hands off on a long brown towel.

500

Manazov bowed and sat down at the table.

"Here's cheese," said Shirin, pointing at an empty plate, "and here's jam," and Shirin pointed at a small glass jar ~~in which~~ full of ~~clear~~ transparent water. Manazov ~~in amazement~~ looked at the empty plate and the water in the glass jar, then looked at Shirin but didn't say anything.

"Just a minute," said Shirin, and walked out of the room.

~~Manazov sat for a few minutes~~. Somewhere outside the window a rooster crowed.

"What are roosters doing here?" Manazov thought. But at that moment the door opened and Shirin crawled into the room on all fours.

Shirin's face was distorted and pale. Manazov looked at Shirin but lacked the strength to move. Shirin slowly crawled to the center of the room and stopped.

"What's the matter with you?" Manazov asked quietly.

Shirin opened his mouth.

Sheridan, *The School for Scandal*

* * *

[Note to Marina Malich]

Dear Marishenka,

I've gone to the station to meet you.

Kisses.

Danya
6 o'clock.
November 19, 1939

[Letter to Marina Malich]

Dear Fefulya,

I've gone out on various errands. As I was leaving, I dropped a brush and you suddenly stirred and began to smile in a very funny way, stretching your mouth open wide, and nodding to someone in your sleep.

I'll return home around 5 or 6.

Hugs and kisses,

Danya
January 19, 1940
2 hours 30 minutes

* * *

[From notebook 33]

On *poshliatina.*
Poshliatina can have its own theories and laws. We can even speak of it having its own gradations and levels. (In music an example of high grade *poshliatina* is Dunaevsky.)

Much consolation for various occasions can be found in the Psalms of King David. But a man who has discovered a complete lack of talent in himself will find no consolation, not even in the Psalms.
March 11, 1940.

* * *

Vsevolod Soloviev. *Works in 10 volumes*. St. Petersburg. Mertz Pub., 1903.
O. Bumke, *Common Misconceptions about the Mentally Ill*. Trans. from German, 1913.

Yu. Kannabikh. *What is Mental Illness*? Pg. 102. 1938.
Pavel Fedotov is the best Russian artist. *Niva*, 1897, pg. 32.
Niva, 1897, Konstantin Sluchevsky's "The Blue Kerchief" (about a madman).

* * *

Daniil Ivanovich
Kharms—Yuvachev
11 Mayakovsky Street, apt. 8.

My medical record card should be sent from the Clinic at 18 Pravda St.

* * *

11. man   111. white
12 woman   112. red
13.   113. yellow
                   114. black

1. Human.
2. Living but not human.
3. Vegetable.
4. Natural formation.
5. Created by man.

O God, I'm so sick of him already.

* * *

SONTES VURTO
COLLISTO VERTO
QUNAPTES

* * *

She's not looking at me.
Sitting between the windows.
Her back to me.
Clearly not looking this way.
Busy with her sewing.

Sitting behind the wall and
Not looking at me,
I haven't seen her
looking at me.

Sitting but not looking.
She finds me repulsive.
She's not looking at
Me. Clearly she finds me repulsive.

April 9, 1940 ♂
12:03 −
12:10 −
12:20 --   ♀
12:53   sitting but not looking.
1   gone.
1:04   she's there, but not looking at me.
1:10   gone.
Not sitting anymore at the window today.

April 10 ☿
12:12 −
12:20   not there.
12:30   glimpse of ♀.
12:33   ♀ sitting at window but not looking this way.
12:40-45   sitting, back turned.
12:50   sitting, back turned.
12:57   not looking.

April 11 ♃ 1940
12:08 −   ♃
12:17   empty.
12:20
12:28   not there.
12:37   glimpse of ♀
12:45   Die Zeit ist vergangen.

* * *

[From notebook 34]

April 12 ♀ 1940

For God's sake, don't pay attention to anyone and go quietly on your way.
No advice whatsoever: there's your motto for you.
You can't please everyone. Please yourself and you'll please everyone.

* * *

[From notebook 33]

13 April ♄ 1940.

1:00	Went for kerosene so she won't be sewing.
1:15	still not there.
1:16	glimpsed.
1:20	house glimpsed.
1:21	glimpses of something. Children.
1:23	not looking this way. Children there.
1:25	can see her hands, but can't see her face.
1:27	not her.
1:28	It is her, just got back with kerosene.
1:30	Children and a man there.
1:36	red and blue
1:37	can't see anyone.
1:50	glimpses of something, but not ladies.
1:56	The ladies aren't looking this way.

You'll never live long enough for the young ladies to look at you.
2 o'clock not there.
Now they'll look at you!!!

* * *

April 16, 1940 ♂

12:30	not there.
12:35	not there and probably won't be.
12:55	didn't come to the window once.

☿ April 17

10:06	I sat down and started to watch.
10:07	glimpse of her.

10:08	not there.
10:11	children.
10:20	went for a walk with children.

* * *

[From notebook 34]

Daniil Ivanovich Kharms

Whoever finds this note-pad, please return it to its RIGHTFULowner.

* * *

Diseases of the Brain. index 616.8

Emil Kraepelin

Kleines Schema

1. Mental disorder associated with traumatic brain injuries.

2. Mental disorder associated with other organic illnesses of the brain.

3. Mental disorder associated with toxemias:

A. Alcoholism.

B. Morphinism and narcomania.

C. Toxemia caused by poisons from impaired exchange of substances (uremia, eclampsia, diabetes, etc.).

D. Disordered functioning of endocrine glands (Graves disease, cretinism, myxedema, etc.).

4. Mental disorder associated with infectious diseases (typhus, etc.).

5. Syphilis of the brain, including diabetic psychosis. Progressive paralysis of the insane.

6. a). Arteriosclerosis. b). Pre-senile and senile mental disorders.

7. True epilepsy.

8. Schizophrenia (forms of early imbecility).

9. Manic-depressive psychosis.

10. Psychopathologies (obsessive conditions, psycho-neuroses, pathological characteristics, etc.).

11. Psycho-genetic conditions, including hysterical conditions (prison psychoses, traumatic neuroses and battle fatigue, neurotic fear, anxiety, etc.).

12. Paranoia.

13. Mental retardation (idiotism, imbecility, etc.).

14. Ambiguous instances.

15. Psychologically healthy.

The three circles of disease:

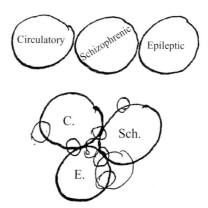

The smaller circles represent less serious forms of the disease, through which the fundamental circles not only adjoin but transition one into another.

* * *

Mustard Plaster, Medicine, Kerosene, bread, 1 kilo Pork, Potatoes, Onions. Nowadays in world events it's always the most boring and least interesting possibility that transpires. 1939.

Miracle alone is interesting in that it violates the physical structure of the world.

* * *

Charles Sorel, *L'histoire comique de Francion*. Trans. and commentary by G. I. Yarko.
Academia 1935.

* * *

~~Shashkin's wife ran way~~
~~Shashkin looked out the window and thought~~
Shashkin (standing in the middle of the stage): My wife ran away. Well, what can you do? Still, seeing she's run off, you won't get her back. You've got to be a philosopher and perceive every event wisely. Happy the man who possesses wisdom. That Kurov here doesn't possess any wisdom, but I do. ~~And then Kurov's not handsome, but I am. Kurov never goes to~~

~~the theater and doesn't read books while I, though I don't go to the theater, love to read books. And then I drink tea with milk and find use in it. While Kurov, that animal, he won't even take, heh-heh, kvass, much less tea, into his mouth. Complete lack of culture! Mediocrity! But me, I adore asparagus more than anything.~~ I even read a book twice at the Public Library. Everything was written about real cleverly there. ~~And why all this? Because my needs are broad. I have an intellectual cast of mind.~~ I'm interested in everything, even languages. I know counting in French and know what "belly" in German is. *Der Magen.* That's what! Even Kozlov, the artist, is friends with me. We drink beer together. And what about Kurov? He doesn't even know how to tell time. He blows his nose in his fingers, eats his fish with a fork ~~and spoon~~, sleeps in his boots, doesn't even brush his teeth . . . Phoo! That's what you call a peasant! Go ahead and show yourself in society with him: they'll toss you out and what's more cover you in filth: they'll say, don't you come around here with that peasant seeing you're an intellectual yourself. ~~I'm a self-forged man.~~ No way will you get to me. Bring on a count, I'll talk with a count. Bring on a baron, I'll talk with a baron too. ~~I'm even a count of sorts myself, only I don't parleyvous in French, although I know their numbers and then also I don't eat oysters.~~

~~Shashkin sat down on the sofa, and scratching his (butt) knees with his hand, he continued.~~ First off, you can't even understand who it is I am. ~~What, in fact, do I need?~~

Sure I don't know German so well, although I do know that belly is *der Magen*. But then they'll say to me "*der Magen findel mun,*" and I won't even know what the hell that is. ~~I'll just stand there flapping my ears.~~ But that Kurov doesn't even know *der Magen.*

And to run off with a clown like that! Bitch! Truly a bitch! That, you see, is what she needs! She doesn't even take me, you see, for a man. And how am I to blame if they gelded me as a child? It sure wasn't me who cut the things off! "You have," she says, "a woman's voice!" Not ever a woman's, but a child's! Thin and childlike, not like a woman at all. Stupid bitch! Why's she so stuck on Kurov? ~~He's what, got such a great voice? Ha-ha! Well the hell with her. She ran away, so the hell with her! I'll get myself another broad. The hell with her! Der Magen!~~

The artist Kozlov says I should sit for him so he can paint my picture: a genuine, says he, *castrato*. That's almost the same as a Pope! And she goes and leaves me for Kurov! What a joke!

~~Shashkin got undressed and walked up to the mirror. He studied~~ ~~himself for a long time and finally said:~~ Yes. ~~that's the sort of man I am!~~

* * *

Ich kam heraus mit 15r.
Den hab ich:
3.15   für Salat.
4   für Druck.
5.40   für Schnaps.
4   für Schnaps.
16.55

* * *

In der Bibliotek: Shklovsky, *Lieutenant Fedotov*.
Pierre Giffard. *The Infernal War*. Pub. Soikin. Illus. Albert Robida. World of Adventure, 1911 or 1912.

I have absolutely no need of family life. There's not a single aspect of family life that I need.

* * *

On *poshliatina.*
Poshliatina is not the result of an insufficiency of the exalted, or an insufficiency of taste, or in general, an insufficiency of anything.
Poshliatina is something independent, in and of itself, an entirely definite magnitude.

On collecting.
There are two principles of collecting:
1). Acquire objects in accord with your taste and desire, regardless of their objective value, rarity and quality.
This principle makes sense to me.
2). Acquire objects in accord with their objective value, rarity and quality, without regard to your own taste and desire.
This principle makes no sense to me.
Only the first principle, strictly speaking, is, in fact, collecting.

* * *

Introduction:

> "Schweigen lehre."
>
> Hypostasis

Concerning the goal.

"To him who has much, it shall be given."

"Seek and ye shall find."

Peccatum parvum.

Tractatus.

4 categories.

On the flow of will and happy stupidity.

On religion and humor as sources of art.

On norms.

On accumulation.

On the interlocutor.

On the ideal watchmaker.

On sacrifice.

On obstacles.

On Laocoön.

* * *

April 18 ♃ 1940.

There is always a certain unpleasantness hidden in a blunt formulation. Is it wise then, when making a blunt formulation, to allow the unpleasantness to function as a necessary consequence, without even trying to correct and suppress it?

* * *

[Letter to Marina Malich]

> Dear Fefulinka,
>
> I've gone off to do some errands with a heavy heart. I really hope to see you soon.
>
> Danya
> 10 o'clock ☿ June 26, 1940

* * *

On space.

1. Unified, uniform and continuous space does not exist.

2. Space begins to exist in our understanding subject to the law of tripartite-existence.

3. If it is not possible to say ~~here~~ there and there, then it is also impossible to speak about space.

4. If ~~here~~ there and there do exist, then there must be an "obstacle" between them: here. For if there were no "obstacle," then there and there would be one and the same and would not exist.

5. At its root, existence has 3 elements: there, the "obstacle" and there.

6. Thus, we see that for the formation of existence, the presence of three elements, which we call this, the obstacle and that, are necessary.

7. . . .

12. Or: a unified void encountering the obstacle splits into ~~two~~ parts, forming the trinity of existence.

13. The obstacle is like the creator who makes something out of nothing.

14. If this something amounts to nothing, then the "obstacle" also amounts to nothing.

15. But this can be something which does not exist in and of itself. Then, in that case the obstacle has to be something that does not exist in and of itself.

16. ~~The obstacle, something that does not exist in and of itself, as it becomes an obstacle in something that does not exist in and of itself, splits this non-existing something into 2 parts.~~

16. In this way there can be two non-existing somethings.

17. If there are two non-existing somethings, then one of them is the obstacle for the other, dividing it into parts.

18. In the same way, the other turns out to be the "obstacle" for the first thing, dividing it into two parts.

18. In this way, three parts are created which do not exist in and of themselves.

19. The three parts which do not exist in and of themselves constitute the three fundamental elements of existence.

20. The three fundamental elements of existence which do not exist in and of themselves, together form a certain existence.

21. If one of the three fundamental elements of existence were to disappear, then the whole would also disappear. For example, if the "obstacle" were

to disappear, then <u>this</u> and <u>that</u> would become one and the same and would cease to exist.

22. ~~Our world~~ The universe is made up of two somethings or of two somethings that do not exist in and of themselves: space and time.

24. Time, in its essence, is unified, uniform and continuous and therefore does not exist.

~~25.~~ 23. Space in its essence is unified, uniform and continuous and therefore does not exist.

~~24.~~ 25. But as soon as space and time begin to interact, they become an "obstacle" to each other and begin to exist.

~~25.~~ 26. As they begin to exist, space and time mutually become parts of one another.

~~26.~~ 27. When time encounters the "obstacle" of space, it divides into parts making up the trinity of existence.

~~27.~~ 28. Once divided, existing time comprises the three elements of existence: past, present and future.

~~28.~~ 29. As elements of existence, the past, present and future are always necessarily dependent on one other.

The past cannot exist without the present and the future, nor the present without the past and future, nor the future without the past and present.

* * *

[Letter to Aleksandr Vvedensky]

August 1940, Leningrad.

Dear Aleksandr Ivanovich,

I heard that you're saving money and have already saved five thousand rubles. For what? Why save money? Why not share what you have with those who don't have even a perfectly extra pair of trousers. For, after all, what is money? I've studied this question. I have photographs of the most common bank notes: one, three, four, and even five rubles in value. I've heard about bank notes that contain up to 30 rubles at once. But hoard them? What for? After all, I'm not a collector. I have always despised collectors of stamps, pens, buttons, little onions, and so on. They're stupid,

Дорогой Александр Иванович,

я слышал, что ты копишь деньги и скопил уже приличную пять тысяч. К чему? Зачем копить деньги? Почему не поделиться тем, что ты имеешь, с тем, у кого не имеют даже совершенно лишней пары брюк? Ведь, что такое деньги? Я изучал этот вопрос. У меня есть фотографии самых ходовых денежных знаков: в рубль, в три, в четыре и даже в пять рублей достоинством. Я слыхал о денежных знаках, которые содержат в себе разом до 30-ти рублей! Но копить их, зачем? Ведь я не коллекционер. Я всегда презирал коллекционеров, которые собирают марки, перышки, пуговки, луковки и т.д. Это глупые, тупые и суеверные люди. Я знаю, например, что так называемые «нумизматы», это те, которые копят деньги, имеют суеверный обычай класть их, как бы ты думал куда? Не в стол, но в шкатулку и... на книжки! Как тебе это нравится? А ведь можно взять деньги, пойти с ними в магазин и обменять на, ну скажем, не суп (это такая пища), или на соус кефаль (это тоже вроде хлеба)

Нет, Александр Иванович, ты такой же нетупой человек как и я, а копишь деньги и не меняешь их на разные другие вещи. Прости, дорогой Александр Иванович, но это не умно! Ты просто поглупел, живя в этой провинции. Ведь должно быть не с кем даже поговорить. Посылаю тебе свой портрет, чтобы ты мог хоть глядеть видеть перед собой умное, развитое, интеллигентное и прекрасное лицо. Твой друг Даниил Хармс

Letter to Vvedensky, 1940.

obtuse and superstitious people. I know, for example, that so-called "numismatists" are those who hoard money and have the superstitious habit of putting it, where might you think? Neither into the drawer, not into a little box, but . . . into little albums! How do you like that? After all, you can take money, go to the store with it and exchange it for, well, let's say for soup (that's a kind of food), or for grey mullet sauce (that's also something like bread).

No, Aleksandr Ivanovich, you are hardly any more obtuse than I, and yet you hoard money that you don't exchange for various other things. Forgive me, dear Aleksandr Ivanovich, but that's not smart! You have simply gotten stupid living in the provinces. For after all, there's probably no one even to talk to. I'm sending you my portrait so that you can, at least, see before you an intelligent, refined, intellectual and beautiful face. Your friend.

Daniil Kharms

* * *

[Letter to Nikolai Khardzhiev, September 9, 1940]

Dear Nikolai Ivanovich,

By this point I haven't seen you for longer than permissible. I have a request to make of you: please, write neither letters, nor articles on Khlebnikov, but concentrate on your own work. I fear that you are living among swine, before whom it's shameful even to write. For God's sake, take no account of them. If they praise your work, that would mean you've failed. I know that your constant concern for literature keeps you from writing. That's quite annoying. You're not at all a literary scholar, nor are you Khlebnikov's publisher. You are, for the most part, Khardzhiev. And I am convinced that your salvation lies in quantity. Please believe that, in this instance, I am a prophet: if, over the course of a year, you write 28 things (of any length), you will have fulfilled your mission. There are collectors of books, such are bibliophiles; there are collectors of money, such are rich men; and there are collectors of their own works, such are graphomaniacs and geniuses. Become a collector of your own works. Please remember that you are made of the dough of genius and that there are none such around you. If you do begin writing, read nothing to any one until you reach the eleventh piece.

To this I can also add that I would very much like to see you, my dear Nikolai Ivanovich.

Marina Vladimirovna says hello.

Yours, Khaarms
☽ ♏ 9 1940, SPB.

* * *

[Letter to Nikolai Khardzhiev, December 18, 1940]

♃ ♒ 18 1940

Dear Nikolai Ivanovich,

I presume that today is your nameday and, therefore, congratulations.

Daniil Kharms

[Letter to Marina Malich, August 9, 1941]

♄ 9 ♍ 1941, 11 h. 20 m.

Dear Marina,

I've gone to the Union. Perhaps, God willing, I'll get some money. Then by 3 o'clock I have to stop by The House of the Arts.

From 6 to 7, I've got the clinic. Before the clinic, I hope to drop by home.

Hugs and kisses,

God keep you.

Danya

[Letter from Marina Malich to Natalia Borisovna Shanko]

September 1

Dear Natalia Borisovna,

On the twenty-third of August, Daniil Ivanovich went to see Nikolai Makarovich, and I was left alone, with no work, no money, and a grandmother on my hands. I don't know what will become of me, all I know is that with his departure, life is over for me.

My dear, if only I had some hope left, but it vanishes with each passing day.

I can't even write you anything more, but if you get this postcard, answer it, it's still warmer somehow when you know you have friends. I never imagined that he could leave me right now.

All my love.

Yours, Marina.

Unknown years

[From notebook 38]

From May 20—23.

I feel like having a woman so I'm keeping my eyes open. May 23.

I'm very unlucky. May 25.

When in lines, always stand behind good-looking women.

Hot dogs	1r. 20k.
Grilled meat	1r. 85k. There's an interesting cashier at the restaurant of the Writers' Club. Not really interesting but interesting to flirt with.

It's horrible when a woman takes up so much room in your life.

July 1. J.

Ah, what a nice cashier at the restaurant of the Writers' Club. Her name is Shura. I would love to have her attention, her arousal and her lust. But she doesn't think I'm so nice. How nice she is.

* * *

Once I bought myself the score of Weber's opera *Oberon*. I didn't pay much, 18 rubles. On the other hand, the devil only knows what it's really worth. It's possible it's worth no more than 10 rubles.

Seek what is higher than you can find. Do not write words in vain.

You should do what you need to modestly and industriously. Don't be distracted, but focus on the task at hand and, keeping one eye always on your goal, go straight to it without a second thought and without getting sidetracked.

* * *

I hate people capable of speaking more than ~~to~~ 7 minutes on end.

There's nothing more boring on this earth than someone recounting his dreams, telling war stories or talking about his trips to the south.

Verbosity is the mother of mediocrity!

* * *

It is impossible to conceive of seven spheres, as in "one, two, three, four, five, six seven spheres." "Seven" designates only a certain quantitative quality.

* * *

There is no visionary without vice.

Spirits have no words.

Keys on a table mean a quarrel is on the way.

Sluts with big hips, a Jew, a wolf, a bear are good luck.

I'm observing the scary old hags at the hairdresser's. Grotesque faces, showing off, giggling. Horrible old bags!

Maria Konstantinovna is the proprietor, and Vera is the manicurist.

* * *

One of the fundamental principles that divide human beings is the passion either for thin or plump women.

It would be a good idea to set aside paths for quiet walks in public gardens, with little benches for two set at a distance of a couple of yards. Between the little benches you could plant bushes so that someone sitting at one would not be able to see what was going on at the next. The following rules would be established for these paths:

1. Children, either alone or accompanied by their parents, are not allowed on the paths.

2. All noise and loud conversations are forbidden.
3. Only a woman may sit down on a bench alongside a man, and only men may sit down next to women.
4. If the person sitting on the bench puts his or her hand or any other object on the seat, it is forbidden to sit down there.

Schedule:

Despite monetary failure or success, do the following every day:

1. Write no fewer than 10 lines of poetry.
2. Write no less than one page of prose in a notebook.
3. Read something about religion or God or the paths of achievement, no fewer than 3 pages. Meditate on what you've read.
4. Exercise in the evening as planned.
5. In the evening, write a leter to Iti.

* * *

[Note to my family members, Leningrad, no date]

Awaken me
At 11 am.

Danya.

I'll be very grateful, quite,
A Tartar with a knife of nights.

* * *

[Note to Boris Semyonov]

Boris Fedorovich, my dear, where have you been hiding? I looked for you under the sofa and in the closet, but couldn't find you anywhere. Very sad.
D. Kh.

* * *

[Note to Tamara Meier–Lipavskaya]

[no date, no place.]

Thank you, Tamara Alexandrovna, I just love *wa ter mel ons*. Better you should come see us.

* * *

[Letter to Natalia Koliubakina]

[Leningrad suburbs, no date]

Dear Natasha,
I won't be able to have coffee. Better I walk in the park for another hour to take advantage of what they call nature or, simply, "oneself."
D

Epilogue

On August 23, 1941, two months after the German invasion of the Soviet Union, Daniil Kharms was arrested by the NKVD for the third and final time. Based on the denunciation of an informer, the order for his arrest was drawn up and signed by representatives of the secret police and approved by the Office of the Leningrad Public Prosecutor:

Case No. *2196—1941*

On August 21-22, 1941, the deputy director of the NKVD for the Leningrad District, Major of State Security Makarov and Deputy Prosecutor L. Gribanov of the Office of the Leningrad Public Prosecutor affirmed the following document:

ARREST ORDER

Leningrad, August 20, 1941. I, the authorized representative of the I Division of the Counter-Revolutionary Department of the NKVD for the Leningrad district, Sergeant of State Security Burmistrov, having examined the available documents concerning criminal activity by:

Yuvachev-Kharms, Daniil Ivanovich, born 1905, native of Leningrad, Russian, no party affiliation, citizen of the USSR, children's writer in the City Committee of Writers, currently residing at 11/1 Mayakovsky Street, apt. 8.

HAVE FOUND THAT

Yuvachev-Kharms, D. I. has counter-revolutionary sympathies, and has disseminated within his circle slanderous and defeatist sentiments, in an attempt to cause panic and create dissatisfaction with the Soviet government among the populace.

Yuvachev-Kharms declares:

"The Soviet Union lost the war on the very first day. Leningrad will now either be besieged or will be starved to death,

or will be destroyed by bombing which will not leave one stone upon another. And then the Baltic fleet will surrender, after which Moscow will be handed over without a fight."

And further: "If I am given a draft notice, I will punch the commander in the face! Let them shoot me, but I will not put on the uniform and will not serve in the Soviet army, I don't want to be such a piece of crap. If they force me to shoot a machine gun from an attic during street fighting with the Germans, I will fire the gun at them, not the Germans!"

Yuvachev hates the Soviet government and is impatiently awaiting the replacement of the Soviet government, declaring:

"Better for me to be in a German concentration camp than to live under the Soviet regime."

On the basis of the above:

DO ORDER THAT

Yuvachev-Kharms be subject to search and arrest, and confined in the prison of the NKVD for the Leningrad district.

Representative of the I Division,
Sergeant of State Security,
Burmistrov.

Director of I Division of the Counter-Revolutionary
Department,
Lieutenant of State Security,
Kozhemiakin.

"Agreed." Director of the Counter-Revolutionary
Department of the NKVD for the Leningrad District,
Captain of State Security,
Zanin.

While witnesses differ on the exact details, it is known that Kharms was taken into custody on August 23, 1941. He was taken immediately to the "Big House" (NKVD headquarters on Liteiny Prospekt in Leningrad), where he was searched and the following protocol was drawn up:

PROTOCOL OF PERSONAL SEARCH

Leningrad, August 23, 1941.
NKVD, Leningrad District, Associate Tsyganov

On the basis of warrant No. 550 of *August 23, 1941*, in the presence of *Associate Korostelin*

In conformity with articles 175-185 of the Political Criminal Code, a search was carried out on the person of *Yuvachev-Kharms, Daniil Ivanovich in the building of the NKVD of the Leningrad District.*

In accordance with this order *Yuvachev-Kharms Daniil Ivanovich* was detained.

The following items were confiscated during the search:

1. *Passport Series XII No. 679339, issued by the Seventh Department of the Militia of the city of Leningrad in the name of Yuvachev-Kharms, Daniil Ivanovich on June 7, 1941.*
2. *Certificate of exemption from military service for medical reasons No. 49, issued December 3, 1939 by the Dzherzhinsky Region Commission for the city of Leningrad in the name of Yuvachev-Kharms, Daniil Ivanovich.*
3. *Copy of marriage certificate and various receipts in the name of Yuvachev-Kharms, D. I. 7 sheets.*
4. *Analysis No. 26248 from the Tuberculosis Dispensary No. 1. Excerpt from certification No. GN 396623 Labor-Medical Specialist Committee, and referral from Writers' Union.*
5. *Application from Daniil Kharms to the Leningrad Soviet, on one sheet.*
6. *A poem on two half sheets in manuscript entitled "Elegy" signed by Aleksandr Vvedensky.*
7. *Notebook with various jottings, one.*

8. *Member card No. 2330 of the Union of Soviet Writers issued December 1, 1934, in the name of Kharms, D. I.*
9. *Five sheets of paper with various colored drawings and with signatures.*
10. *6 photographic postcards, two of which were cancelled.*
11. *Book "New Testament," published in 1912 with markings and notations in the margins.*
12. *A wallet, old, calico, with a note on covering, inside divider, one.*
13. *Two railroad tickets numbers No. 0730 and 2350, used.*
14. *Magnifying glass with square brass mounting, one.*
15. *Pocket watch of white metal, no cover, No. 3232.*
16. *Ring, white metal with large yellow stone.*
17. *Ring, yellow metal.*
18. *Three tumblers and one shot glass, white metal.*
19. *Cigarette case made of white metal, one.*
20. *Amber cigarette holder, with yellow metal frame, one.*
21. *Two bronze, one wooden icon.*
22. *Brooch in shape of octagon with various colored stones and with inscription "Holy Jerusalem (Revelation, chapter XXI) April 22, 1907. St. Petersburg," yellow metal, one. Two matchboxes with initials D. Kh.*
23. *Icon (to be worn on neck, yellow material with inscription "May the Lord Bless You. To Daniil Yuvachev from Metropolitan Antony, August 22, 1906."*
24. *Small cross (to be worn on neck) homemade, white metal.*

The search was carried out between *13:20 hours and 14:00* hours. During the search the following complaints were made:

1. concerning irregularities allowed during the search including, in the opinion of the complainant, the following: *none made*
2. concerning the disappearance of objects not entered into the protocol, specifically: *none made.*

During the search the following were sealed: *nothing sealed.*

> Signature of the person searched:
>> *Dan. Kharms (Yuvachev-Kharms D. I.)*
>
> Witness   *N. Korostelin*
>
> Search conducted by Associate of the NKVD *Tsyganov*

All complaints and applications received have been entered into this protocol.

For all receipts showing the number of the order, the day of issuance, when the search was carried out, apply to the Office of the Commandant, NKVD for the Leningrad District, 6 Volodarsky Prospect, information office.

> *August 23, 1941 Associate Tsyganov*

A copy of this protocol was received by:

> *D. Kharms (Yuvachev-Kharms)*

Later on the same day, a search was carried out of his apartment in the presence of his wife, Marina Malich, and the building janitor, Ibrahim Kildeev, who had also been present when the police arrested Kharms in 1931. From surviving documents we know that the following items were confiscated:

1. Letters in opened envelopes, 22.
2. Notebooks with various jottings, 5.
3. Various religious books, 4.
4. One book written in a foreign language.
5. Various correspondence, 3 sheets.
6. One photo.

Late in the evening of August 25, Kharms was interrogated for the first time. The agent in charge of the interrogation confronted him with the charge of crimes against the state, which Kharms promptly denied. Although this interrogation lasted two hours—from 10 in the evening until midnight—only two questions and answers are listed in the protocol as we have it:

Testimony of the accused, *Yuvachev-Kharms, Daniil Ivanovich*

August 25, 1941

The interrogation began at 22:00 hours.

Question: *Tell me about your crimes against Soviet power.*

Answer: *In 1930 I was arrested by organs of the NKVD on a charge of counter-revolutionary activity, four months later I was freed and the case was closed. In 1935 I was arrested by organs of the NKVD on a charge of illegal commercial activity, a few days later I was freed and the case closed.*

I have never committed any crimes against Soviet power.

Question: *That's untrue. The investigation has at its disposal evidence that you conducted criminal anti-Soviet activity, and demands truthful testimony.*

Answer: *Once again I repeat that I never committed any crimes against Soviet power. The interrogation concluded at 24:00 hours. I have read the protocol, which was drawn up accurately from my words.*

Daniil Kharms

Interrogator: *Deputy Director of the Investigative Department Counter-Revolutionary Department, Leningrad NKVD Artemov*

There are several inaccuracies in Kharms testimony. He was arrested in 1931, not 1930, and rather than simply being released from prison when the case was closed, Kharms was duly convicted and sentenced to exile.

Beyond this, something must have happened during the two hours of the interrogation to raise serious doubts regarding Kharms's sanity in the mind of this interrogator. Two days later Artemov recommended that Kharms be transferred to a psychiatric hospital for testing:

DECREE

City of Leningrad, August 27, 1941. I, Deputy Director of the Investigative Division of the NKVD for the Leningrad District, Counter-Revolutionary Department, Artemov, having examined the investigation No. 2196-1941 concerning the accusation against:

Yuvachev-Kharms, Daniil Ivanovich,

HAVE FOUND THAT

Yuvachev-Kharms, D. I., was arrested for conducting counter-revolutionary and defeatist agitation within his circle.

Brought in for interrogation, Yuvachev-Kharms showed signs of psychological derangement and therefore, in conformity with articles 202 and 203 of the Political Criminal Code of the RSFSR,

DO ORDER THAT

Yuvachev-Kharms, Daniil Ivanovich be transferred to the Psychiatric Department of the Hospital for Prisoners under Investigation to determine his psychological condition.

The investigation into case 2196-1941 be suspended. A copy of this decree be forwarded to the office of the Leningrad City Public Prosecutor.

*Deputy Director of the Investigative Division of the NKVD,
Counter-Revolutionary Department
Artemov.*

*Agreed. Director of the Investigative Division,
Junior Lieutenant of State Security,
Baskakov.*

On September 2, Kharms was moved from the NKVD Detention Facility on Shpalernaya Street across the Neva to the psychiatric wing of the NKVD Prison Hospital on Arsenalnaya Street. Over the course of the next week, hospital psychiatrists examined him and, on September 10, drew up the following document describing the results of their examination:

Information based on the words of the subject: *father was an archeologist by profession, died at 83 years of age, was imprisioned for 12 years at Schlüsselburg Fortress, where he suffered a nervous breakdown. Mother died at 60 years of age. 4 children in the family, one died, of the remaining, the subject is the oldest. Childhood diseases, measles, scarlet fever, chicken-pox < . . . > Completed 9 years of schooling, then 3 years at the University in the Physics and Mathematics Department, but did not graduate. From the age of 20, he started earning a living as a writer for children, subsequently he also engaged in literary work, although for approximately the past 2 years as it became more difficult to write, he became obsessed with the idea of inventing (the elimination of the "peccatum parvum"). This year he was given a finding of second-class disability.*

In 1939 he was hospitalized in a psychiatric ward.

Exempted from military service in accordance with article no. 7.

Psychiatric condition and behavior: *thinks clearly, correctly oriented with respect to time, place and surroundings. Expresses floridly delusional notions concerning his inventions. Believes that he has invented a method of correcting "flaws," the so-called "peccatum parvum." Considers himself a special person with a delicate and highly developed nervous system, capable of eliminating "a disrupted equilibrium" by a creation of his own means. His delusions are characterized by absurdities, are devoid of consistency and logic, so, for example, he explains that the reason to wear headgear is the desire to hide thoughts, without which thoughts become "exposed" or "exteriorized." To keep his thoughts concealed, he wraps his head in a headband or a small rag. He gives a special name and terminology to each of his inventions. Diminished awareness of his own condition. Affect subdued, personal interactions with others selective or superficial. Passively submits to the regimen on the unit. Autonomic nervous processes exhibit no major deviations.*

Documentation: *case history for No. 410/11861 from Vasilievsky Island Psychiatric Dispensary indicates that Yuvachev-Kharms, Daniil Ivanovich was under treatment with a diagnosis of schizophrenia between September 29, 1939 and October 5, 1939. During the period of his hospitalization, the following was noted: delusional notions concerning his inventions and relations with others, paranoia; considers his "thoughts to be exposed and exteriorized" if he does not wear bands or rags around his head, displayed fear in the presence of others, made obsessive movements and would repeat what he heard. Discharged without improvement.*

Signature *Director Pakhomov.*

CONCLUSION

On the basis of the above, as well as the facts of the case and our observation of the subject, on September 10, 1941, the commission with the participation of Professor N. I. Ozeretsky, has concluded that Yuvachev-Kharms, Daniil Ivanovich, is suffering from psychological derangement in the form of schizophrenia.

The disease is of long standing, the prognosis is unfavorable.

As someone mentally ill, Yuvachev-Kharms cannot be held accountable for his incriminating act, that is, he is not culpable, and therefore requires treatment in a psychiatric hospital.

Director of Medicine	*Dr. Rodionova*
Professor of Psychiatry	*N. I. Ozeretsky*
Head of the Psychiatric Dept.	*Dr. Kelchevskaya*
Consulting Psychiatrists	*Dr. Volkova*
	Dr. Lastovetsky

September 10, 1941

There are several inaccuracies recorded in this document: Kharms's father had worked most of his adult life as a bank examiner, not an archeologist; he had spent four years in Schlüsselburg, not twelve; he was 80 at the time of his death, not 83; Kharms himself had never attended the University of Petersburg. Rather than lapses in memory, they may well have been part what can be interpreted as a ploy by Kharms to evade judicial punishment for his "anti-Soviet" behavior. By convincing the doctors that he was suffering from mental illness, he could avoid a sentence of death and summary execution. He had employed this strategy successfully in 1939 to gain exemption from military service. Whether this is sufficient to account for the strange statements recorded by the hospital staff is a matter of conjecture.

Although the psychological testing was completed by September 10, Kharms remained in the prison psychiatric wing for more than a month. Perhaps the NKVD was unsure what to do with his case. The fall of 1941 was an extremely difficult period for blockaded Leningrad with its constant bombing, unusually cold weather, declining daily bread rations, and increasing mortality among the population. While Kharms was incarcerated in an NKVD psychiatric ward, his wife and friends had no idea where he was. In late November, Kharms's wife was apparently told that he had been evacuated to Novosibirsk. On November 30, she wrote to the Schvartses who had been evacuated to Perm, asking their help in locating Kharms.

Shortly before that, the NKVD had reopened Kharms's case, and more incriminating evidence came to light through the interrogation of Antonina Oranzhireeva. She had met Kharms at the apartment of a common friend in 1940 and had been serving as an informant for several years. Interrogated on November 26, Oranzhireeva, who may have been the source for the anonymous denunciation leading to his arrest in August, stated that Kharms was "*a person hostile to the Bolshevik Party and Soviet power, someone engaged in anti-Soviet activity.*" She went on to detail Kharms's alleged anti-Soviet activity:

> *I know that Yuvachev-Kharms had anti-Soviet sympathies and that, after the invasion of the Soviet Union by Fascist Germany, he systematically engaged in counter-revolutionary defeatist agitation and disseminated provocative anti-Soviet fabrications among his friends. Among his acquaintances, Yuvachev-Kharms asserted that the defeat of the USSR in the war with Germany was supposedly*

inevitable and unavoidable. Yuvachev-Kharms said that without private capital there could be no order in the country. Describing the situation at the front, Yuvachev-Kharms stated that the entire city of Leningrad was mined and that unarmed fighters were being sent to defend the city. Soon nothing will remain of Leningrad but its stones, and if there is street fighting, Kharms will go over to the German side and fight the Bolsheviks. Yuvachev-Kharms said that to improve living conditions in the country, it was necessary to eradicate the entire proletariat or to make them slaves. Yuvachev-Kharms expressed his sympathy for the enemies of the people Tukhachevsky, Yegorov and others, saying that, were they alive, they would have saved Russia from the Bolsheviks. At this time I cannot recall other specific statements by Kharms in an anti-Soviet vein.

Immediately after this, Kharms's NKVD investigators recommended that his case be sent to the Leningrad NKVD Military Tribunal:

DECREE

City of Leningrad, November 28, 1941, I, Deputy Director of the 9 Division of the Counter-Revolutionary Department, NKVD, Leningrad District, Junior Lieutenant of State Security Artemov, having examined investigation no. 2196-41 in the matter of the accusations against—

Yuvachev-Kharms, Daniil Ivanovich, born 1905, native of Leningrad, Russian, citizen of the Soviet Union, no party affiliation, writer, currently residing at 11 Mayakovsky Street, apt. 8.

HAVE FOUND THAT

The Leningrad Division of the NKVD has received information that Yuvachev-Kharms, resident of Leningrad, has been conducting counter-revolutionary activities.

On this basis Yuvachev-Kharms, D. I. was arrested on August 23, 1941.

Subsequent investigation determined that Yuvachev-Kharms, Daniil Ivanovich, since the beginning of the war between the USSR and Fascist Germany, did in fact conduct counter-revolutionary defeatist agitation among his acquaintances with the purpose of undermining the military might of the Soviet Union and disrupting and demoralizing the rear of the Red Army.

Summoned to an interrogation as the accused, Yuvachev-Kharms, D. I. manifested clear signs of psychological disorder, in connection with which he was transferred to the Psychiatric Department of the Hospital for Prisoners under Investigation in order to determine his psychological state.

In accordance with the conclusions of the Forensic-Psychiatric Commission, Yuvachev-Kharms, Daniil Ivanovich has for some time been suffering from mental disorder in the form of schizophrenia and as "non compos mentis" was and remains legally not culpable, neither at the time of the commission of his crimes nor at present, and is remanded to the Psychiatric Hospital for treatment.

On the basis of the above, in accordance with article 11 of the Criminal Code of the RSFSR,

DO ORDER THAT

Investigation file No. 2196-41, in the matter of the accusation against Yuvachev-Kharms, Daniil Ivanovich, under article 58, paragraph 10, part II of the Criminal Code of the Russian Federation, with the agreement of the office of the Leningrad Public Prosecutor, be sent for consideration to the NKVD Military Tribunal, Leningrad District, to undertake any and all measures necessary in regard to the mandatory treatment of Yuvachev-Kharms, D. I.

> *Deputy Director, 9 Division, Counter-Revolutionary Department, NKVD, Leningrad District*
> *Junior Lieutenant of State Security*
> > *Artemov*

> *Director of 9 Division, Counter-Revolutionary Department, NKVD, Leningrad District*
> *Senior Lieutenant of State Security*
> > *Podchasov*

On December 5, 1941, this recommendation was approved by Procurator Gribanov, who ordered that it be forwarded to the Military Tribunal of the Leningrad NKVD, where two days later, in closed session, the Tribunal concluded that Kharms was a danger to society and recommended that he be kept in the prison hospital for mandatory psychiatric treatment:

> *In view of the fact that, in accordance with the judicial-psychiatric expert opinion of September 10, 1941, although the accused Yuvachev-Kharms is acknowledged to be mentally ill and not responsible for the charge for which he has been incriminated, nonetheless, due to the character of the crime which he has committed, he remains a danger to society. According to article II of the Criminal Code of the Russian Federation, Yuvachev-Kharms should be remanded to a psychiatric hospital for mandatory treatment until such time as he is cured and the case returned to the I Special Division of the Leningrad NKVD.*

The final official document concerning Kharms's fate that we know of is dated December 8, 1941:

> *To the commander of the NKVD Internal Prison,*
>
> *You are being sent a copy of the protocol of the preliminary meeting of the Military Tribunal of the Leningrad NKVD from December 7, 1941 concerning case No. 989, ordering that prisoner D. I. Yuvachev-Kharms be remanded to a psychiatric hospital for compulsory treatment.*
>
> *Senior secretary of the Military Tribunal*
> *Military jurist 3rd class Bochkov*

In mid-December, as the first reports of cannibalism were spreading among Leningrad's starving population, Kharms was transferred to the psychiatric wing of Leningrad's Prison No. 1, known as the "The Crosses." By that time Marina Malich had learned that her husband had remained in prison in Leningrad. She was able to drop off small packages of food for him twice, but when she returned to the prison on February 9, she was informed that her husband had died a week earlier.

FINALE

"I was born among the rushes . . ."

I was born among the rushes. Like a mouse. My mother bore me and put me into the water. And off I swam. Some kind of fish with four whiskers circled round me. I started to cry. And the fish started to cry. And suddenly we saw kasha swimming through the water. We ate the kasha and began to laugh. We were very happy and off we swam with the current and came upon a crab. It was an ancient, great crab; in his claws he held an axe. A naked frog came swimming after the crab. "Why are you always naked," the crab asked her, "aren't you ashamed?" "There is nothing shameful here," answered the frog, "Why should we be ashamed of the good body nature has given us when we are not ashamed of the loathsome deeds we ourselves have done?" "You speak rightly," said the crab. "And I don't know how to answer you. I suggest we ask man about it, because man is cleverer than we are. We are clever only in the fables man writes about us, and so again it turns out that man is clever, and we are not. But just then the crab saw me and said: "And we don't even have to swim anywhere, because here he is—man." The crab swam up to me and asked: "Need we be ashamed of our naked body? You are a man so answer us." "I am a man and and I will answer you: we need not be ashamed of our naked body."

(1934)

Chronology

1903

March: Nadezhda Ivanovna Koliubakina marries Ivan Pavlovich Yuvachev.

1905

Revolution of 1905: Uprisings in cities and countryside lead to the October Mani-festo, granting limited freedoms and creating of Russia's first Parliament (Duma).

December 17 (new style December 30): Daniil Ivanovich Yuvachev is born in Saint Petersburg.

1909

Sister Elizaveta is born.

1912

Sister Nadezhda is born.

1914

August: Russia enters World War I against Germany and the Austro-Hungarian Empire – Saint Petersburg is renamed Petrograd.

1916

March 3: According to family tradition, young Daniil writes his first story.

1917

February Revolution: Abdication of Emperor Nicholas II and the end of autocracy in Russia.

Daniil enrolls in Peterschule, one of the oldest and most prestigious schools in Petrograd, where German is the language of instruction. After the Revolution, the school is renamed "Unified Labor School No. 4."

October Revolution: Bolshevik government led by Lenin and Trotsky takes power.

1918

Civil War begins in Russia.

To escape famine in Petrograd, Daniil and Elizaveta are sent to Saratov Province in the Volga region, where maternal relatives live.

1919

Spring—Summer: As Civil War and famine spread to the Volga region, Daniil and Elizaveta return to Saint Peterburg and spend summer in Tsarskoe Selo with aunt Natalia Koliubakina.

Daniil creates his earliest surviving drawings.

1920

January: Yuvachev family moves into former laundry of the Botkin Hospital.

Daniil resumes studies at Peterschule.

Civil war intensifies.

Sister Natasha dies.

1921

Kharms is forced to leave Peterschule because of poor academic performance.

1922

Civil War disrupts food supply: famine in Petrograd, winter 1921-22.

September: Kharms moves to Tsarskoe Selo, lives in his aunt Natalia's house, and attends "Children's Village [Detskosel'skaya] Unified Labor School," where she is director and teacher.

1924

January 21: Death of Lenin – Petrograd is renamed Leningrad.

July 14: Kharms graduates from secondary school in Tsarskoe Selo and moves back in with his parents in Leningrad.

September: Kharms enrolls in First Leningrad Electro-Technical College.

Kharms meets Ester Rusakova.

Autumn: Kharms appears in public regularly reading his own and others' poems. After reading a poem by Nikolai Gumilev (executed in 1921 on charges of counterrevolutionary activity), Kharms is detained and interrogated by the state security service (OGPU), but later released.

Kharms participates in avant-garde "actions," e.g., walking down Nevsky Prospect with painted face, etc.

1925

March: Kharms is invited to join Aleksandr Tufanov's "Order of *Zaumniki* DSO."

March—April: Kharms meets Aleksandr Vvedensky, Yakov Druskin, Leonid Lipavsky, who will remain close friends and literary collaborators his entire life.

Summer: Kharms joins Vvedensky, Lipavsky, Oleinikov, Druskin in *Chinari*.

December: With Vvedensky, Kharms founds short-lived group "Left Flank," later renamed "Flank of Leftists" and "Academy of Left Classics," in hope of uniting all "Left" artists of Leningrad.

1926

February 13: Kharms is expelled from the Electro-Technical College.

March 26: Kharms is accepted into the Leningrad division of the All-Russian Union of Poets.

September 17: Kharms enrolls in cinema division of the Institute for the History of the Arts although he never graduates.

September—November: Kharms begins collaboration with theater collective "Radiks," which rehearses play by Kharms and Vvedensky, *My Mama's all in Watches*, at Malevich's Institute of Artistic Culture, but the group collapses before the play is performed.

Second half of the year: Kharms's poetic debut, "An Incident on the Railroad," is published in a collection of the Leningrad Union of Poets.

1927

March 28: Public reading by the *Chinari* at the Institute for the History of the Arts. A review attacking the performance provokes Kharms and Vvedensky to write to the Leningrad Union of Poets to defend their conduct.

December: Kharms, Vvedensky and Zabolotsky are invited to join newly formed Association of Children's Writers.

Kharms's "The Poem of Peter Yashkin" is published. This is the second and last time any of his works written for adults will be published during his lifetime.

1928

January: The OBERIU Declaration is published.

January 24: The celebrated OBERIU public performance, "Three Left Hours," staged at the Leningrad Press House.

January 25: A negative review of "Three Left Hours" is published.

February: First issue of *Hedgehog* is published, including several poems by Kharms.

March 5: Kharms marries Ester Rusakova.

March 7: Kharms is called up for temporary military service, although he continues to live at home.

December 5: Ester threatens to divorce Kharms.

1929

February 18: Kharms's mother dies of tuberculosis.

March 10: Kharms is expelled from Leningrad Union of Poets for failure to pay his membership dues.

1930

January: First issue of *Siskin* is published.

April 1: OBERIU (Kharms, Levin, Vladimirov) performs in Leningrad University student dormitory.

April 9: A negative review of what turns out to be the final public performance by OBERIU is published in student newspaper.

1931

October 4: Yury Vladimirov dies.

December 10: Kharms, along with Vvedensky and Tufanov, is arrested by the OGPU as part of an anti-Soviet group of children's writers.

1932

March 21: Kharms is sentenced to 3 years imprisonment in labor camp.

April 23: The Central Committee of the CPSU orders the establishment of a single Union of Soviet Writers.

June 18: Thanks to intervention by his father, Kharms is released from preliminary detention and the camp sentence is replaced by exile.

July—October: Kharms is in exile in Kursk and shares rooms with Vvedensky.

October 12: Kharms returns to Leningrad.

November: Kharms is involved in an affair with Frau René.

End of November: Kharms begins an affair with Alisa Poret.

1933

February: Kharms's romance with Alisa Poret ends.

March: Victor Serge (Kibalchich) is arrested as Trotstkyite sympathizer.

Summer: The *Chinari* (Kharms, Vvedensky, Druskin, Zabolotsky, and Oleinikov) begin to meet regularly at apartment of Leonid and Tamara Lipavsky.

Autumn: Kharms engages in a "romance in letters" with actress Klavdia Pugacheva.

1934

April 26: Konstantin Vaginov dies of tuberculosis.

August 8-24: First All-Union Congress of Soviet Writers.

July: Kharms marries Marina Malich

December 1: Sergei Kirov, Leningrad Party boss, is assassinated.

1935

May: Malevich dies. Kharms participates in funeral service at the artist's apartment and reads the poem "On the Death of Kazimir Malevich" at the official memorial service at the Artists' House, where he also helps carry the coffin.

1936

April 3: Kharms gives speech at Second Conference of Union of Writers criticizing Formalism.

April: Victor Serge (Kibalchich) allowed to leave the USSR due to pressure from international communists.

End of summer: Vvedensky leaves Leningrad for Kharkov.

September 7: Rusakov and Kibalchich family members are arrested and sentenced to the Gulag for connections with Trotskyite Victor Serge. Ester is sentenced to five years in the Gulag, where she dies in 1943. Ester's sister and brother will survive and live to see rehabilitation.

1937

The "Great Terror" in Leningrad reaches a peak.

Second half of the year: Kharms's translation of *Max und Moritz* is criticized for "wrecking activity" in the journal *Children's Literature.*

July 3: Oleinikov is arrested.

November 24: Oleinikov is executed.

1938

March 19: Zabolotsky is arrested, and sentenced to 5 years in the camps.

1939

September 1: Germany invades Poland.

Autumn: Kharms checks into psychiatric clinic on Vasilievsky Island on September 29. He is released from the hospital a week later with a diagnosis of schizophrenia.

December 3: Kharms is exempted from military service based on mental illness.

1940

May 1: Kharms's father Ivan Yuvachev dies.

1941

June 22: Germany invades USSR

Late summer—late fall: Kharms is arrested by the NKVD and accused of spreading panic and dissatisfaction with Soviet Government. After psychiatric examination, he is found to be suffering from schizophrenia, hence not responsible for his "criminal" behavior. The military tribunal concludes that, because of his mental illness, Kharms is dangerous to society and should be transferred to the psychiatric division of Prison no. 1 ("The Crosses").

1942

February 2: Kharms dies in Leningrad NKVD prison hospital.

1956

Kharms is rehabilitated posthumously.

Selected Bibliography

WORKS OF DANIIL KHARMS IN RUSSIAN

Izbrannoe. Edited and introduced by George Gibian. Würzburg: Jal-Verlag, 1974.

Sobranie proizvedenii, 4 volumes. Edited by Mikhail Meilakh and Vladimir Erl'. Bremen: K-Presse, 1978-1988.

Polet v nebesa. Edited by Aleksandr Aleksandrov. Leningrad: Sovetskii pisatel', 1988.

"Dnevnikovye zapisi Daniila Kharmsa," edited by A. Ustinov and A. Kobrinskii, *Minuvshee: Istoricheskii almanakh,* 11 (1992): 417-583.

Polnoe sobranie sochinenii, 6 volumes. Edited by Valerii Sazhin. Saint Petersburg: Akademicheskii proekt, 1997-2002.

"...Sborishche druzei ostavlennykh sud'boiu" A. Vvedenskii, L. Lipavskii, Ia. Druskin, D. Kharms, N. Oleinikov: "Chinari" v tekstakh, dokumentakh i issledovaniiakh, 2 volumes. Edited by Valerii Sazhin, Moscow: Ladomir, 1998.

Dnei katybr: Izbrannye stikhotvoreniia, poemy, dramaticheskie proizvedeniia. Edited by Mikhail Meilakh. Moscow-Cayenne: Hylea, 1999.

Sluchai i veshchi. Saint Petersburg: Vita Nova, 2004.

Risunki Kharmsa. Edited by Iu. S. Aleksandrov. Saint Petersburg: Izd. Ivana Limbakha, 2006.

Sobranie sochinenii, 3 volumes. Edited by Valerii Sazhin. St. Petersburg: Azbuka, 2011.

BIOGRAPHIES

Kobrinskii, Alekdsandr. *Daniil Kharms.* Moscow: Molodaia gvardiia, 2008.

Shubinskii, Valerii. *Daniil Kharms: Zhizn' cheloveka na vetru.* Saint Petersburg: Vita Nova, 2008.

KHARMS IN ENGLISH

Russia's Lost Literature of the Absurd: Selected Works of Daniil Kharms and Alexander Vvedensky. Edited and translated by George Gibian. Ithaca, NY: Cornell University Press, 1971.

The Man with the Black Coat: Russia's Literature of the Absurd. Translated by George Gibian. Evanston, IL: Northwestern University Press, 1987.

The Plummeting Old Woman. Translated by Neil Cornwell. Dublin: Lilliput Press, 1989.

Incidents. Translated by Neil Cornwell. New York: Serpent's Tail, 1993.

"Lapa." Translated by Matvei Yankelevich. *PAJ: A Journal of Performance and Art* 23, no. 2 (May 2001): 89-101.

The Blue Notebook. Translated by Matvei Yankelevich. Brooklyn, NY: Ugly Duckling Press, 2005.

OBERIU: An Anthology of Russian Absurdism. Edited by Eugene Ostashevsky. Evanston, IL: Northwestern University Press, 2006.

Today I Wrote Nothing: The Selected Writings of Daniil Kharms. Edited and translated by Matvei Yankelevich, et. al. New York: Ardis and Overlook Duckworth, 2009.

CRITICISM

Carrick, Neil. "Daniil Kharms and the Art of Negation." *The Slavonic and East European Review* 72 (1994): 622-43.

Cornwell, Neil, ed. *Daniil Kharms and the Poetics of the Absurd: Essays and Materials*. London: MacMillan, 1991.

Jaccard, Jean-Philippe. *Daniil Harms et la fin de l'avant-garde russe*. Bern: Peter Lang, 1991.

Jakovljevic, Branislav. *Daniil Kharms: Writing and the Event*. Evanston, IL: Northwestern University Press, 2009.

Levin, Ilya. "The Fifth Meaning of the Motor-Car: Malevich and the Oberiuty." *Soviet Union/Union Sovietique* vol. 5 part 2 (1978): 287-300.

Millner-Gulland, R. R. "'Left Art' in Leningrad: The OBERIU Declaration." In *Oxford Slavonic Papers: New Series 3* (1970): 65-75.

Nakhimovsky, Alice Stone. *Laughter in the Void: An Introduction to the Writings of Daniil Kharms and Alexander Vvedensky. Wiener Slawistischer Almanach*. Special volume 5. Vienna: Institute fur Slawistik der Universitat Wien, 1982.

Roberts, Graham. *The Last Soviet Avant-Garde: OBERIU—Fact, Fiction, Metafiction*. Cambridge: Cambridge University Press, 1997.

Scotto, Susan. "Xarms and Hamsun: *Staruxa* Solves a Mystery?" *Comparative Literature Studies* 23 (1986): 282-96.

Sokol, Elena. *Russian Poetry for Children*. Knoxville: The University of Tennessee Press, 1984.

Vishevsky, Anatoly. "Tradition in the Topsy-Turvy World of Parody: Analysis of Two OBERIU Plays." *Slavic and East European Journal* 30, no. 3 (1986): 355-66.

Commentary

Although it is not without lacunae and errors, the Collected Works (*PSS*) in 6 volumes edited by Valery Sazhin and published between 1997 and 2002 by the Petersburg publishing house *Akademicheskii proekt* remains the standard edition of Kharms's writings. Although excerpts from Kharms's notebooks had appeared in print and on-line for a number of years, in these volumes all of the surviving notebooks and most of Kharms's letters were published with scholarly rigor for the first time. Although we have not hesitated to use other editions, or to amend Sazhin's readings when it seemed warranted, the bulk of our translation derives from this edition. Without this work, our task would have been impossible. In addition, we have supplemented our translation with Kharms's "quasi-autobiographical" writings, contemporary reviews and documents, and the records of Kharms's two arrests and interrogations by the Soviet state security services.

Preliminaries

Both "And so they put me into the incubator" (page 51) and "Incubation period" (52) are typical of Kharms's "quasi-autobiographical" mode, in which he freely combines the autobiographical with the fantastic to create a uniquely Kharmsian self-mythology. Kharms uses the same technique in some of his letters (see, for example, the letter to Lipavskaya of June 28, 1932, page 305).

1924–1925 (pages 55–82)

Notebook 1. Autumn 1924—April 1925. The earliest surviving notebook, consisting largely of lecture notes from his physics and mathematics classes (not translated), was written while Kharms was a student at the Electro-Technical College. We have included a selection of Kharms's jottings on various subjects, plus his quixotic attempt to apply the laws of mathematics to the problem of human individuality.

Page 57. "Phrenology." While studying to become an electrician, Kharms was already interested in the arts of divination.

Page 58. "Sacher Mädchen." Perhaps a note to Ester Rusakova, whom Kharms had recently met. In moments of stress and crisis, Kharms would sometimes resort to German in the notebooks. Ester would remain at the center of Kharms's life for the next seven years. In our edition, an English translation follows the original German in italics.

Page 59. "3rd of July Street." In 1923, Sadovaya Street was renamed 3rd of July Street to commemorate a bloody battle fought at its intersection with Nevsky Prospect during the so-called "July Days" of 1917.

Page 59. "25 October Prospect": Nevsky Prospect, Leningrad's main avenue, was renamed 25 October Prospect in October 1918, on the first anniversary of the Bolshevik revolution.

Page 60. ". . . at Marcel's." Paul Marcel, see Glossary.

Page 60. "Today is March 18, 1925." The centerpiece of notebook 2 is this brilliant fragmentary letter, probably addressed to Ester Rusakova, in which confessional prose turns into a Joycean tour-de-force in which, despite the violations of Russian grammar, semantics, word-formation, and syntax, Kharms's intentions are quite apparent.

Page 62. "H. Bergson. *Introduction to Metaphysics.*" No philosopher was closer to the young Kharms than Henri Bergson, whose ideas on free will, causality, intuition, laughter, and creativity were all central to Kharms's life and his writings. In a 1925 autobiographical note written for the Institute for the History of the Arts, Tufanov, Kharms's poetic mentor at the time, wrote that "closest of all to me now is Bergson" [Aleksandr Tufanov, *Ushkuiniki*, ed. Jean-Philippe Jaccard and Tatiana Nikol'skaia (Oakland: Berkeley Slavic Specialists, 1991), 173].

Page 63. "Bernstein, A. *Clinical Methods for the Psychological Study of the Mentally Ill.*" Kharms's reading of books like these will come into play at several crucial moments in his life when, threatened by military conscription or arrest and imprisonment, he will feel forced to simulate mental illness.

Page 63. "The sexual question." While Kharms's interest in sex is hardly unusual for someone his age and reflects the rejection of traditional mores characteristic of the Soviet Union in the 1920s, in later years this interest will become an obsession with non-normative sexuality.

Page 64. "Resembling pinion wheels and cogs." An early attempt to include contemporary Soviet thematic material in his experimental poetry: here Kharms incorporates several lines from a well-known military march of the 1920s (Budyonny's March).

Page 65. "Holy Cross and Mary." Kharms will repeat this prayer as a mantra in moments of crisis throughout his life.

Page 65. "Ich fuhlte mich . . ." Although at this point Kharms's problems at the Technical College are purely academic in nature, later entries in this same notebook suggest broader problems.

Page 66. "Shakyamuni, Dhanwantari and Maitreya." This list of Hindu-Buddhist deities suggests both Kharms's interest in Eastern religions and the poet's interest in words and, especially, their sounds.

Page 67. *"Ushkuiniki. River Pirates."* While Aleksandr Tufanov published a collection of poems with this title in 1927, this entry suggests that the author may have shared something of this work with Kharms prior to its publication. In *Ushkuiniki*,

Tufanov experiments with a form of *zaum* that uses Old Russian and Protoslavic etymologies to overcome time and space.

Page 67. "Dear friend." Kharms's interest in graphology was typical of his period: in 1933, Walter Benjamin wrote that "Graphology has taught us to recognize in hand-writing images that the unconscious of the writer conceals in it."

Page 69. "Several accusations . . ." Kharms is apparently preparing for an interview with College authorities concerning his possible expulsion. Although after this interview he was allowed to continue at the College, he was officially expelled on February 13, 1926. In the original, this passage is crossed out.

Page 70. "With her eyes she raised an arrow up." These four lines are taken from Vladimir Mayakovsky's narrative poem *Man* (*Chelovek*, 1917-18).

Page 70. "Volkov-Davydov. A Brief Guide to Melodeclamation." In preparation for becoming a professional reader of poetry, Kharms not only memorized poems, but also studied the theory and practice of public speech. The poems he has memorized are mostly by the central figures of Russian Modernism, including Symbolists (Blok, Bely, Sologub), Acmeists (Mandelstam, Gumilev, Akhmatova), Futurists (Kruchenikh, Severianin, Mayakovsky, Khlebnikov, Aseev, Tufanov), plus a few of his friends (Vigiliansky, Mart, Martynov).

Page 72. "Pushkin *500 New Jokes and Puns*." In this classic of Futurist "literary criticism," published in 1924, Kruchenykh subverted Pushkin's poetry by shifting word boundaries in well-known lines, thereby creating unexpected and often humorous readings.

Page 72. "A nasal ananas. . ." The first of several "monoverses" or one-line poems that Kharms recorded in this notebook. Playful, highly alliterative, often close to palindromes, they are reminiscent of Kruchenykh's futurist wordplay in his *500 New Jokes*. We offer two versions.

Page 73. "ESTHER." When Kharms writes Ester Rusakova's name in Latin letters, we transcribe it as "Esther"; when in Cyrillic letters, we transliterate her name as "Ester." The distinction was clearly meaningful to Kharms; see his letter of November 2, 1931 to Poliakovskaya (page 285).

Page 74. "The fourth Michael." Sketches for a 1925 poem (*poema*) entitled "The Mikhails" (*Mikhaily*) names three Michaels without giving last names. The fourth Michael registered here possibly refers to Mikhail Chernov, Ester Rusakova's first husband and Kharms's rival for her affection.

Page 76. *Zangezi* is a major 1922 work by Velimir Khlebnikov, "a poetic union of the linguistic, mythological, historical, and mathematical quests of his life" (Kasack, *Dictionary of Russian Literature since 1917*, 171).

Page 77. "Now the factory wakes up." Another attempt by Kharms to use Soviet material in his early poetry. Some readers have noticed similarities between this poem and Kharms's later poems for children.

Page 79. "Lord, I made so bold." This is the first use in the notebooks of the hieroglyph ⊟ to stand for Ester Rusakova. For Kharms's explanation of the symbol, which he calls a "window," see his letter of November 2, 1931 to Poliakovskaya (page 285-286).

Page 81. "Verbal art is temporal." The important notion of "fluidity" presumably derives from Tufanov, who himself was influenced by Bergson. In her *Bergson and Russian Modernism, 1900-1930,* Hilary Fink writes that "Tufanov's emphasis on the "fluidity" (*tekuchest'*) of time and poetry (which he seems to have appropriated from the Bergsonian notion of consciousness/duration/life) may have been one of the concepts that Kharms "adopted" from his elder teacher." Writing in 1930, Kharms states: "One person thinks logically; many people think *fluidly*. Even though I am only one person, I think *fluidly*" ("Odinnadtsat' utverzhdenii Daniila Ivanovicha Kharmsa," *PSS*, vol. 2, 205).

This entry has been one of the most challenging to translate. We think it likely that these are notes that Kharms jotted down quickly during the "Evening of *Zaumniki*" (described in the passage that follows it), perhaps for a statement he intended to make before reading his poems. As presented in the *Complete Works*, this passage is more erratically punctuated than is usual even for Kharms, and several words are only half written out. To make sense of this passage, we have made an emendation: where the *Complete Works* reads "и понимает" ("even understands") we read "н понимает" ("doesn't understand"), taking the "н" as an abbreviated version of the negation "не."

Page 81. "An evening of *Zaumniki.*" The original is a handwritten unsigned manuscript and was published in Vvedenskii, *PSS*, vol. 2, 1984, 238-239. Despite the protestation in the 1928 OBERIU declaration ("There exists no school more hostile to us than trans-sense poetry"), the influence of his first literary mentor, Aleksandr Tufanov, one of the founders and theorists of trans-sense "sound" poetry in Leningrad, was a constant in Kharms's poetry.

1926 (Pages 83–114)

Page 83. "Letter to Pasternak." As a well-known and established "left-wing" poet, Boris *Leonidovich* Pasternak was a potentially valuable ally to the young Kharms and Vvedensky as they tried to establish themselves in the Russian literary world. Pasternak, however, never replied to the letter, perhaps upset that the young poets got his patronymic wrong.

Page 84. "Chinar 1926." This is the first usage in Kharms's notebooks of the word *chinar*. For more information on the term, see footnote 31 to the introduction.

Page 84. "In all likelihood . . ." Kharms died at the age of 36.

Page 84. "Tamara Aleksandrovna Meier' s. . ." After Ester Rusakova, Tamara Meier was the most important woman in Kharms's life, as well as the addressee of several of his poems and letters. See Glossary for more information.

Page 85. "9 Vorovsky Square." Between 1923 and 1944, St. Isaac's Square in Leningrad was called Vorovsky Square in honor of Marxist revolutionary Vaclav Vorovsky (1873-1923).

Page 87. *"Chastushki."* Popular four-line rhyming verses, often humorous, pornographic or satirical in intent. Though their origins go back to the late-nineteenth-century peasant village, in the early twentieth century *chastushki* move to the city, where they are appropriated by poets such as Blok and Mayakovsky. In 1923, Tufanov published a piece on the rhythmical and metrical structure of *chastushki.*

Page 89. "11 Nadezhdinskaya Street, apt. 9." On December 24, 1925, Kharms's entire family moved to a large apartment on Nadezhdinskaya Street (since January 16, 1936 Mayakovsky Street), where they continued to live together until the apartment was bombed in the first months of World War II. When first Kharms and then his sister Elizaveta ("Liza") married, their spouses moved here as well.

Page 90. "Monday." Schedule of lectures in Cinema Studies that Kharms was attending at the Institute for the History of the Arts ("IHA"), one of the premier academic institutions in Leningrad in the 1920s and a stronghold of Russian formalism.

Page 90. "Foxtrot at Igor's." The foxtrot craze of the 1920s did not pass by Soviet Russia. Kharms was not only intensely interested in popular European and American music of the time, he was also unusually knowledgeable about musical trends of the 1920s.

Page 93. "To call up a thunderstorm." Kharms combined serious study of the history and bibliography of occultism, mysticism, and magic with a naïve belief in magic spells.

Page 93. "Chess bibliography." Like many Russian men, then and now, Kharms was devoted to chess.

Page 94. "Radiks." From the Latin word for "root" and associated with the idea "radical." Short-lived avant-garde theater group founded in 1926 by Georgy Katsman, Boris Levin, Sergei Tsimbal, and Igor Bakhterev, several of whom were later to become members of OBERIU. Looking for a suitable text to perform on the stage, they commisioned a play from Kharms and Vvedensky, who jointly wrote "My Mama's All in Watches." Although he was not one of the founders of the group, Kharms instantly took on himself the main organizational responsibilities: he convinced Kazimir Malevich, the director of Leningrad's Institute of Artistic Culture ("INAC"), to provide rehearsal space for the group, dealt with the censor, scheduled rehearsals, secured the necessary props, etc. Although the play was never produced, the text subsequently lost, and the group disbanded, Kharms's experience with "Radiks" proved valuable when it came time to organize the OBERIU. After the collapse of "Radiks," its members renamed themselves, first as the "Flank of the Left" (*Flang levykh*) and then the "Academy of Left Classics" (*Akademiia levykh klassikov*). In 1927, the group was invited to perform at Leningrad's Press House by its director Nikolai Baskakov on the condition that they come up with a new name: since Stalin was then engaged in the struggle against Leon Trotsky and the so-called "Left Oppositionists," the word "left" or "leftist" had become politically suspect. The group finally settled on the name OBERIU.

Page 94. "Les Six." In 1920, a French music critic coined the name for six French composers, Honegger, Milhaud, Poulenc, Auric, Durey and Tailleferre to contrast with the group of five late 19th-century Russian composers known as "Les Cinq" or "The Mighty Handful" (*Moguchaia kuchka*) that included Balakirev, Borodin, Cui, Rimsky-Korsakov and Mussorgsky.

Page 95. "Using ether." Kharms was introduced to ether by Vvedensky, who, like many other writers of the nineteenth and twentieth centuries, was convinced that ether could help one attain those "mysteries of a higher order" that were inaccessible to the rational mind.

Page 96. "Began reading Ramacharaka's *Paths* . . ." Ramacharaka was one of the many pseudonyms of William Walker Atkinson (1862-1932), American lawyer, merchant, and author who, writing as "Yogi Ramacharaka," published a number of influential books on Yoga and Hindu belief and occult practice. His *Advanced Course in Yogi Philosophy and Oriental Occultism* (1904) remains in print to this day.

Page 97. "On Friday, November 12 . . ." Only part 2 of Kharms's play *The Comedy of the City of Petersburg* has survived.

Page 97. "Speransky. *The Gates of Aristotle, or the Secret of Secrets.*" This is a translation of a mid-twelfth century Latin treatise, the *Secretum Secretorum*, itself a translation of the Arabic *Kitab sirr al-asrar*. An encyclopedic work, it covers a wide range of topics including statecraft, ethics, and medicine, as well as physiognomy, astrology, alchemy, and magic (the latter grouping being of great interest to Kharms.) It also contains charts for divination based on assigning a numerical value to the letters of a person's name, a divinatory method practiced both by Pierre Bezukhov in *War and Peace* and Kharms in his notebooks.

Page 97. "What should I do!" Beginning with poems whose central emphasis was on pure sound, Kharms gradually moved towards a greater appreciation and understanding of the role (and value) of semantics in poetry. Kharms clearly felt himself caught between the "pure" poetry of his mentors and friends Tufanov and Vvedensky and the more traditional semantic experimentation of Zabolotsky. On Zabolotsky's opposition to "trans-sense" or "*zaum*" verse, see N. Zabolotskii, "Moi vozrazheniia A. I. Vvedenskomu, Avto-Ritetu bessmyslitsy. Otkrytoe pis'mo," in Vvedensky, *PSS*, vol. 2, 252-53.

Page 98. "For this Friday." Every public reading in which Kharms participated was planned in detail in advance. The elements of nonsense, parodies of critical analysis, and play were constant in the public performances of the *Chinari*, the "Left Flank," the "Academy of Leftist Classics," and, most notably, the OBERIU.

Page 100. "That's all." In order to mark a completed poem or story, Kharms would write "That's all" (*vse*) or sign his name at the end, allowing us to know with reasonable certainty which works in his notebooks he considered fragmentary or incomplete.

Page 100. "I.D." Kharms may have been collecting documents to prepare for an official check on Soviet citizens.

Page 101. "Reply of Nikolai Zabolotsky and Evgeny Vigiliansky." Both Kharms's friends and literary collaborators were then serving in the Red Army.

Page 102. "Gustav Meyrink (Austrian) . . ." Meyrink (1868-1932) was the author of *The Golem* (1913-1915), one of Kharms's favorite novels: based on Jewish legends about a living being created from inanimate matter, the story was so popular that it was adapted for the silent cinema 3 times between 1914 and 1920. *The Golem* stimulated Kharms's interest in Jewish mysticism and the occult generally. See Anna Gerasimova and A. T. Nikitaev, "Kharms i "Golem." Quasi una fantasia," *Teatr*, no. 11 (1991): 60-72.

Page 102. "I am Athanasius Pernath." Athanasius Pernath was the protagonist of Meyrink's *The Golem*.

Page 103. "Can visit the short-termers . . ." Zabolotsky and Vigiliansky were on short-term duty in the Red Army.

Page 103. "Fred Niblo . . ." Notes taken in connection with Kharms's study of cinema at the Institute for the History of the Arts.

Page 105. "Make up a little anthology . . ." Denied the possibility of publishing his poems, Kharms resorted to preparing manuscript copies of his works, which he shared with friends and family members.

Page 106. "Sokolsky's Daughter." This entry allows us to follow closely Kharms's process of revising the poem.

Page 113. "Eliphas Levi" was the "magical name" of French occultist Alphonse Louis Constant (1810-1875). A major figure in the occult movement of the nineteenth century, he published his *Dogme de la Haute Magie* in 1855, and followed it a year later with a companion volume, *Ritual de la Haute Magie*. The two were later combined into a single book titled *Dogme et Rituel de la Haute Magie*, published in Russian as *Uchenie i ritual vyshei magii* in 1910.

Page 113. "Conversation with K.S. Malevich." Malevich presented Kharms with a copy of his 1922 book *God Is Not Cast Down: Art, Church, Factory*, which he inscribed: "Go and stop progress." In the late 1920s, Kharms looked to Malevich not only as a mentor but as the key to uniting the left artists of Leningrad into one organization, in which Kharms would, of course, play a central role. Kharms's most ambitious attempt to unite the left-wing artists and writers in Leningrad around Malevich failed with the closure of the Institute of Artistic Culture in 1926.

Page 116. "A collection of poems. . . " The collection of Kharms's poems for which these materials were prepared was never published. Until he started publishing for children, Kharms saw no more than two of his poems appear in print.

Page 118. "Material for publication." One of Kharms's many ideas for publications that never appeared in print.

Page 121. "Ether's the chicken in reverse." Perhaps a reference to a method of Yuletide divination practiced by Russian peasant girls (a version of which is recorded in Zhukovsky's ballad "Svetlana.") Unmarried girls would sprinkle grain on the floor and set a chicken loose: the girl whose grain was the first to be pecked would be the first to marry. Kharms may be suggesting that sniffing ether, after reducing human intelligence to that of a fowl ("the chicken in reverse"), may produce insights that are as random as the choices made by the chicken.

Page 125. "Some part of the Celts. . ." While there exist legends that the Celts may be descended from one of the lost tribes of Israel, we can find nothing similar to Kharms's fantastic account of the Jews descending from the Celts. In his review of the *Complete Works*, Mikhail Meilakh mentions that Kharms's *druidessy (*read in the *Complete Works* as *brundessy)* is a neologism deriving from the Russian word for druids. We can find no record of a Celtic tribe called the *bodonoi*.

Page 127. "The Numeration of Jerome Cardan." This quote is taken from one of the numerous occult works by Eliphas Levi.

Page 129. "Material for the first Radiks collection." Another ambitious but failed attempt to unite the left artists of Leningrad: this miscellany would have included poetry, prose and drama of the *Chinari*, the "Left Flank," and "Radiks," critical articles by the Formalist critics, and graphic work by Pavel Filonov.

Page 132. "The Literary Scene." The first article in the Soviet press reviewing a public performance by Kharms and his colleagues.

Page 133. "A statement to the Leningrad . . ." Although this "statement" apparently achieved its purpose and nothing came of the complaint, a few years later such articles in the press would normally be followed by, at the very least, expulsion from the Writers' Union and often arrest.

Page 136. "Jearning just for you." Entered by Kharms in English. A popular 1924 song by Joseph Burke and Benny Davis, "Yearning just for you" has been recorded by the likes of Tommy Dorsey and Bob Wills, Vince Gill, and the Quebe Sisters band, among many others.

Page 139. "Conjoining literary phases." The influence of the formalist critics, with whom Kharms was in close contact in these years, first as a student at the State Institute for the History of the Arts and later as a colleague, can be felt here. The problem of causality will become a major focus of Kharms's later prose.

Page 142. "Feast of the Annunciation." The feast of the Annunciation is celebrated on March 25.

Page 143. "Be a tsar." A reference to Pushkin's sonnet of 1830 "To the Poet." As translated by James E. Falen in Alexander Pushkin, *Selected Lyric Poetry* (Evanston, IL: Northwestern University Press, 2009):

"O poet! Scorn the people's quick acclaim:
The moment of impassioned praise will cease,
The frigid crowd will laugh and fools defame
But keep your firm resolve and be at peace.

Be czarlike – live alone and feel no shame.
Allow your inner freedom to increase:
Refine the fruits your cherished thoughts release,
Asserting for your noble deeds no claim.

For you alone must judge the work you do:
The strictest court of all resides in you.
And if you find it worthy, and your own?

Then let the motley crowd in fury curse
And spit upon the vessel of your verse
And try in puerile sport to shake your throne."

Page 154. "Meeting of the Oberiuts." The first mention of the OBERIUTS in Kharms's notebooks. As usual, Kharms takes the main role in planning and preparing meetings of this group.

Page 154. "Oleinikov and Zhitkov have been organizing. . ." This is the beginning of Kharms's career as a writer for children, which will be his only source of income for the rest of his life.

1928 (Pages 158–219)

Page 158. "Declaration of the OBERIU." The group OBERIU represented the culmination of the experimental literary path that Kharms had been following since his association with Tufanov in the "Order of *Zaumniki* DSO." Consistent with his earlier attempts to unite the experimental writers and artists of Leningrad, the OBERIU combined literary, theatrical, artistic, and cinematic sections, and their public performances, often noted in Kharms's notebooks, were a major factor in the artistic life of Leningrad between 1928 and 1930. Largely written by Nikolai Zabolotsky, this defense of experimental and revolutionary art represents the last public statement of the avant-garde in Leningrad before independent literary organizations were dissolved by order of the Central Committee in 1932. The notebooks represent a major source for the history and activities of the OBERIU.

Page 164. "Tuesday, at 6:00 at my place, meeting about play." Kharms's play *Elizaveta Bam* was being rehearsed and prepared for the notorious OBERIU performance, "Three Left Hours," that took place on January 24, 1928. Kharms's notebook entries for January represent the most detailed account we have of the preparations for this evening, including rehearsal schedules, props, cast list, invitations, advertising, finances, etc.

Page 165. "Poster." This entry records several elements that went into the design of the printed poster for "Three Left Hours." According to Bakhterev, the production of the poster was overseen by a "quartet" made up of Zabolotsky, Kharms, Razumovsky, and himself. As he recalls it: "Working together with the compositors, we chose, much to their amazement, type fonts that had already gone out of use but were, nonetheless, quite pretty: together we laid out the text, we even involved ourselves in the business of the poster hangers: Following Zabolotsky's suggestion they put up two posters side by side, one the right way, the other upside down" [I. Bakhterev, "Kogda my byli molodymi. Nevydummanyi rasskaz," *Vospominaniia o Zabolotskom* (M.: Sovetskii pisatel', 1984), 93]. A copy of the printed poster is reproduced in this edition on page 23.

Page 177. "Natalia Tarpova." A play directed by Igor Terentiev at the Press House Theater that premiered on February 4, 1928.

Page 178. "Speak to Kashnitsky about makeup." Preparations for another public performance of the OBERIU.

Page 179. "By March 1." In November, 1927, Kharms was invited to collaborate in the recently established Children's Section of the State Publishing House in Leningrad, which would go on to publish these and other books of Kharms's poetry for children.

Page 179. "For Daniil." Entered around the time of Kharms's wedding to Ester Rusakova, this note may list clothing that the newlyweds intended to purchase. Although the contents of this list are completely plausible, later in the notebooks Kharms will construct purely fantastic lists of clothing.

Page 180. "The torments of Tantalus." Presumably, Kharms is explaining this to Ester because, born and raised in France until the age of 10, her knowledge of Russian was never perfect.

Page 182. "On March 7 . . ." These entries provide the most detailed information we have concerning Kharms's short stint in the Red Army. Although the service requirement was quite limited, and Kharms was able to return home after several hours of daily military drill and instruction, the notebook entries show he was both constitutionally unsuited for military life and alienated from the new order.

Page 183. "Comrades, no spidding . . ." In this entry, Kharms is apparently reproducing spelling errors in a sign posted at his place of military service.

Page 186. "Stupid empty words." A fragment from Kharms's play *Elizaveta Bam*.

Page 188. "Tuesday, March 13, 1928." "Mishenka" is Misha Chernov, Ester's first husband.

Page 194. *Republic of Shkid* (1927), a semi-autobiographical account of life in a special school for "unsupervised children" (*bezprizorniki*) written by Grigory Belykh and L. Panteleev.

Page 196. "With God's Help, Deliver "The Old Woman" to State Publishing." Kharms's poem for children entitled "A Story about how an Old Woman Bought some Ink," not the better known story "The Old Woman," which was written in 1939.

Page 197. "For August 15, 1928." Kharms never completed his intended translations of the fairy tales of the Grimm brothers.

Page 198. "Sent with Mansurov." Frustrated by their inability to see their works published in the Soviet Union, Kharms and the other members of the OBERIU decided to send manuscript copies of some of their works abroad with the artist Pavel Mansurov, who was travelling to Italy for an exhibition of his works. Unfortunately, this plan to publish their works in the Russian émigré press came to nothing. Mansurov never returned to the USSR, and the manuscripts by Kharms, Vvedensky, Vaginov, Zabolotsky, Bakhterev, and Levin subsequently disappeared.

Page 200. "At restaurants." The restaurant and café were traditional venues where the Russian avant-garde would undermine "normal" bourgeois ways of thinking, behaving and eating. One critic has written that such examples of absurd behavior were intended "not so much to shock as to perplex the public by the alogicality of what was happening, to give a twist in the public's consciousness to normal causal-investigatory notions, having exposed reality in all its illogicality." See Tatiana Nikolskaia, "The Oberiuty and the Theatricalisation of Life," in *Daniil Kharms and the Poetics of the Absurd*, ed. Neil Cornwell (New York: Macmillan, 1991), 195-99.

Page 203. "Marshak's brother . . ." See glossary: *Marshak, Ilya Yakovlevich*.

Page 203. "I'm observing October 10, 1928 . . ." The increasingly dire economic circumstances of a marginal Soviet writer will be a central theme of the notebooks from the late 1920s and 1930s.

Page 205. "1. Number of performers . . ." Concerning an upcoming public performance by the OBERIU.

Page 207. "The clever boy . . ." Advertising copy for a new literary journal for children, *Hedgehog* (*Ezh*), whose first edition appeared in print in February, 1928. Kharms was one of its main contributors and sometimes its editor. Increasingly, Kharms will use his notebooks to record drafts, ideas, projects for children's poems.

Page 211. "Take *The Castle*. . ." Franz Kafka's novel *Das Schloss* was published in 1926.

Page 211. "Go to . . . Smolny and the GPU." These visits to the headquarters of the Leningrad Party at the former Smolny Institute and to the GPU were possibly connected to the arrest and expulsion from the Party of Kharms's brother-in-law, Victor Serge.

Page 212. "Marshak is angry with me . . ." That is, because Kharms did not complete the translation.

Page 217. "Daniel, I've gone to the wedding registry. . ." Apparently, Ester did not go through with this threat to divorce Kharms less than a year after they were married.

According to Kharms biographer, Valery Shubinsky, Ester divorced Kharms sometime in the middle of 1932, while he was still in exile in Kursk.

1929 (PAGES 220–241)

Page 221. "With a name like Bukharin . . ." Nikolai Bukharin (1888-1938) was a leading Bolshevik intellectual, the editor of *Pravda*, and one of the most popular Party leaders in the 1920's. Arrested in 1937, he was convicted of espionage and counter-revolutionary activity in one of the great Moscow show trials. He was executed on March 15, 1938.

At the time he receives mention in Kharms's notebooks, Bukharin was locked in a power struggle with Stalin over the direction of the Soviet economy, placing his career in considerable jeopardy: having publicly criticized plans for forced collectivization in an article appearing in September 1928, in January 1929 he submitted a declaration to the Politburo protesting plans to squeeze the peasantry and the absence of real Party democracy. His views were denounced as a "direct slander of the Party" and a "direct slander of Comrade Stalin," and in April of 1929 he was removed from all Party posts, including the editorship of *Pravda*.

The precise force of Kharms's remark is not clear to us.

Page 223. "Poetry." *Archimedes' Bath*, an ambitious collection of poetry, prose, and criticism by the leading representatives of the avant-garde of the literary world, was never published. It should not be confused with a similarly-titled anthology of OBERIU writings published in 1991.

Page 225. "I know of a no more disgraceful bunch than the Writers Union." Formerly the center of a relatively free literary life in Leningrad, the local division of the Union of Writers was increasingly coming under the sway of the Stalinist Leningrad Association of Proletarian Writers (LAPP), whose first order of business was to curtail publishing and performance opportunities for experimental writers like Kharms and the OBERIU.

Page 226. "I was sitting on the roof of the State Publishing House." State Publishing was located in the former Singer building on Nevsky Prospect, the so-called "*Dom knigi*" (House of the Book).

Page 229. "Magic tricks." Kharms's skill at magic tricks was well known not only to his friends but apparently to the local NKVD as well. According to Marina Malich, Kharms was once summoned to the local NKVD office: instead of arresting him, the NKVD agents wanted to know how he did a certain magic trick! Unfortunately, Kharms was so terrified, and his hands shook so much, that he was unable to demonstrate the trick.

Page 232. "Bukhshtab. 'On the Social Command.'" Well-known essay by the young formalist critic on a Marxist theory, popular in the late 1920s and 1930s, that literature fulfills the "command" of society or particular social groups. During the first Five-Year Plan, for example, writers obeyed the social command by travelling to collective farms and factories, where they were to report on the "construction of socialism" in the country.

Page 236. "I think that . . ." For writing a poem that satirized the aristocracy in the aftermath of the Decembrist revolt, Aleksandr Polezhaev (1804-38) was arrested and drafted into the army, where he spent the rest of his short life.

Page 238. "Twist together . . ." Spells like this one, intended to bring Ester back to him, suggest how Kharms's life intertwines with his philosophical and literary interests. A search on the internet reveals, surprisingly, that the spell remains extremely popular today.

1930 (pages 242–259)

Page 244. "Zvenigorodsky." Pseudonym of Evgeny Shvarts.

Page 244. "T. A. R. A." While T. A. refers to Tamara Aleksandrovna Meier-Lipavskaya, the identity of R. A. is a mystery.

Page 245. "O why do you twinkle." This is our English rendition of Kharms's Russian translation of Lewis Carroll's "Twinkle, twinkle little bat" from *Alice's Adventures in Wonderland*. Kharms turns Carroll's trochees into amphibrachs, and it should also be noted that the Russian word for bat, *letuchaya mysh'*, like the German *Fledermaus*, literally means "flying mouse."

Page 248. "An evening of natural thinkers." For much of his adult life, Kharms "collected" interesting and extravagant people he met in pubs and on the street whom he called "natural wisemen" (*estestvennye mudretsy*) or "natural thinkers" (*estestvennye mysliteli*). Among them were barroom philosophers and primitive artists, some of who suffered from mental illness, whom Kharms planned to include in public performances of the OBERIU.

Page 249. "A Reactionary Circus." This article spelled the end of the public performances by the OBERIU. Concerning the author of this review, see Introduction, note 37.

Page 251. "The Master of Ceremonies with a dog." Notes for a meeting with children to promote an animated film based on Samuel Marshak's poem "The Mail."

1931 (pages 260–290)

Page 262. "They *chibu chibu* in us." In a notebook entry for the previous year (page 248), in a list of animal sounds, Kharms identified "*chibu chibu*" as a way of speaking to colts. Later in the same poem, Kharms uses a *zaum* word (*chiberias*), which Meilakh suggests is derived from this phrase. If this is correct, *chiberias* may refer to the colts themselves.

Page 276. "Tycho Brahe had an artificial nose." The famous Danish astronomer (1546-1601) did, in fact, wear an artificial nose. He lost the bridge of his nose in a sword duel with his third cousin, fought over the legitimacy of a mathematical formula.

Page 276. "May 6, 1931." In some numerological belief systems, the number 11 is considered a "master number" associated with insight, intuition, and poetry, and is known as The Illuminator, The Messenger, or The Teacher. Kharms could have derived 11 as a personal talisman by combining the dates of his birth Old Style (17 December) and New Style (30 December): $1+7 = 8$, $3+0 = 3$; $8+3 = 11$. Although he never wrote the work outlined here, in 1930 he did write "Eleven Assertions of Daniil Ivanovich Kharms."

Page 279. "Scenes from the life of the poet." Under this heading we include texts that, although not recorded in the notebooks themselves, straddle the boundary between fiction and autobiography.

Page 282. "A 27-year-old physicist from Leningrad G. A. Gamov." Georgy Antonovich Gamov (1904-1968) was a brilliant theoretical physicist and cosmologist, responsible for numerous discoveries concerning the Big Bang, star formation, and radioactivity. At an international physics conference in Brussels in 1933, he and his wife defected from the USSR. As George Gamow, he spent the rest of his life in the United States, where in addition to teaching at George Washington University, the University of California, Berkeley, and the University of Colorado, Boulder, he wrote the popular *Mr. Tomkins* series of science books for children.

Page 283. "The adventures of a lazy boy." More ideas for poems for children.

Page 285. "Dear Raisa Ilinishna." Were it not for these letters, we would know absolutely nothing about Raisa Poliakovskaya. Clearly, Kharms was infatuated with her in the autumn of 1931, although apparently the relationship was never consummated. The letters turn on the coincidence of "*Raia*" (a diminutive form of the name "*Raisa*") with "*rai*", the Russian word for "paradise." The second letter explains Kharms's use of the window symbol (⊟) to represent Ester.

Arrest by OGPU. December 1931 (pages 291–300)

Beginning on December 10, the members of a literary circle that met at the apartment of biologist and writer, Peter Kalashnikov, were arrested by agents of the OGPU. Although members of the circle, which included Kharms, Vvedensky and Marshak, were critical of the present state of politics, especially in regard to literary policy, they were arrested in connection with an orchestrated campaign directed against children's writers in Leningrad. The first note of this campaign was sounded at a meeting of the All-Russian Union of Writers in late October, where Leningrad's most successful writers for children, including Kharms, Vvedensky, and Marshak, were criticized for rejecting the Soviet need to educate children in the spirit of class-consciousness and collectivism. As is clear from the interrogation protocols, the OGPU transferred the alleged anti-Soviet beliefs of the Kalashnikov circle to the children's writers, and fabricated a group of writers working to infect the younger generation with counter-revolutionary thoughts and beliefs.

Following the preliminary questions at the arrest, Kharms was interrogated four times between December 18, 1931, and January 18, 1932, by two OGPU agents,

Lazar Kogan and Aleksei Buznikov. The texts that we have translated were written out in Kharms's own hand. The Soviet procedure was that, at the end of each interrogation, the accused would draw up a summary of the evidence against him, which he would then sign. Although this was intended to "prove" that the evidence had not been coerced, such summaries were often written at the dictation of the interrogator. In the protocols of Kharms's interrogations, for example, one senses the style of an experienced OGPU interrogator, obsessed with interpreting playful poetry as part of an entirely fantastical conspiracy to undermine the education of Soviet young people. Clearly, Kharms decided that his best chances lay in agreeing with the picture painted by his interrogator, no matter how absurd.

In the end, Kharms was proven right. The arrested were found guilty of introducing politically harmful ideas into children's literature, of composing "trans-sense" poetry as a way of agitating against Soviet power, and of disseminating anti-Soviet literature, that is, their own works. By the end of March, the verdict was confirmed by the Leningrad Procurator and they were sentenced to various terms of imprisonment and exile: while Vvedensky was exiled to Kursk, Kharms was sentenced to 3 years in a prison camp. Thanks to the efforts of his father, himself a political prisoner during the Tsarist regime, Kharms's sentence was eventually reduced to exile. After six months in prison, Kharms was released on June 18, 1932, and he joined Vvedensky in exile in Kursk a month later. All in all, he spent slightly less than 3 months in Kursk and returned to Leningrad on October 12.

1932 (pages 301–325)

Page 301. "June 18, 1932." Kharms was freed from the Leningrad Preliminary Detention Prison. He was given a month to prepare for exile.

Page 302. "Discuss with Kogan." That is, Lazar Kogan, the "intellectual" OGPU interrogator in charge of his case, with whom Kharms developed a surprisingly close relationship.

Page 303. "AGLA." A kabbalistic acronym for "You, O Lord, are mighty forever."

Page 311. "Black suit (3)." The first of several fantasy lists of clothing.

Page 313. "Saturday, August 13." Kharms's health, exacerbated by poverty, poor food, loneliness, inactivity, obsessive masturbation and, perhaps, a degree of hypochondria, will be the major concern of his writings in exile.

Page 320. "I'm reading the Negro novel *Home to Harlem*." Published in 1928, this is an influential novel by Jamaican-American writer Claude McKay (1889-1949), one of the seminal figures of the Harlem Renaissance and the author of novels, stories, poems and memoirs. In 1922-23, McKay spent 8 months in the Soviet Union, where several of his books were translated into Russian.

Page 326. "Reading Hamsun." Norwegian writer Knut Hamsun (1859-1952) was one of Kharms's favorite writers and an important influence in his work.

Page 334. "From Kursk, late 1932, early 1933." This description of his exile was found in Kharms's archives written on a separate sheet of paper, strictly speaking not part of the diary entries. It is possibly the draft of a lost letter.

Diary 1932 - 1933 (pages 336–351)

This diary, the only example of a true diary in Kharms's surviving papers, describes his first year back in Leningrad after his return from exile. Due to the exertions of his father, Daniil was released after serving 6 months of a 3-year sentence. He returned to Leningrad on October 12, 1932, and picked up his life precisely where he had been forced to abandon it in the summer of 1932: back to scraping a living out of his work in children's literature.

Page 337. "Exhibition of All the Artists." Kharms's name for the exhibition "Artists of the RFSFR for the Last Fifteen Years" then on display at the Russian Museum.

Page 340. "I was sitting next to Frau René. . ." The situation, described here and elsewhere in the diary, of a poverty-stricken lover, hyper-conscious next to his beloved, is eerily familiar to readers of Gogol and Dostoevsky.

Page 349. "At the end of January. . ." Beginning in January 1932, every Soviet citizen over the age of 16 was required to carry a so-called "internal passport," which included the *propiska*, or official registration, granting the bearer the right to live in cities like Moscow and Leningrad. This presented a problem for Kharms, since the official prohibition against residing in Leningrad that went along with his exile sentence had never been officially removed. Although his return to Leningrad had taken place with the knowledge and approval of the Leningrad OGPU, he had no official documents permitting his residence in Leningrad.

1933 (pages 352–427)

Page 353. "Chapters." Apparently the first sketch of a novel that remained unwritten.

Page 353. "Public performances." While Kharms was unable to perform or publish his works for adults, he remained quite popular as a reader of his works for young audiences.

Page 357. "What I've written about *Professor Trubochkin*. . ." In fact, this story about the eccentric professor was the only work by Kharms that appeared in *Siskin* in 1933. As becomes clear from the notebooks, Kharms survived this period thanks to loans from his friends and family.

Page 367. "KOU." Linguistic tomfoolery by Kharms: the "pronoun" КЫ in the original is an invented word that violates the phonetic norms of Russian.

Page 378. "What interests me." A version of Kharms' response to the question posed to the members of the "Club of Poorly Educated Scholars," which included Kharms's closest friends and literary colleagues (i.e., Vvedensky, Zabolotsky, Oleinikov, Lipavsky, Druskin, and Dmitry Dmitrievich Mikhailov) and which met at the apartment of Leonid Lipavsky to discuss literature, life and philosophy. See Leonid Lipavskii, *Issledovanie uzhasa* (Moscow: Ad Marginem, 2005), 307-423.

Page 380. "My wife and I." Unlike the other fantasy lists in Kharms's notebooks (e.g., clothing, pipes, etc.), this fantasy of pre-revolutionary living conditions for the Yuvachev family includes an obvious political dimension.

Page 391. "As they decrease, numbers do not end . . ." Over the years, Kharms's childhood love of mathematics and technology turned into a lifelong fascination with various mystical and occult numerological systems. Here we see one of numerous short quasi-mathematical tracts that Kharms wrote in the early 1930s, in which he tries to move beyond the ordinary ways of thinking about numbers. The concept of the Cisfinitum is treated at length by Jean-Philippe Jaccard in his *Daniil Harms et la fin de l'avant-garde russe*.

Page 397. "Thanks for Zhemchuzhnikov's poems . . ." Aleksandr Zhemchuzhnikov (1821-1908) was, along with his brothers Aleksei and Vladimir, his cousin Aleksei Tolstoi, and their friend Petr Ershov, one of the co-creators of the fictional poet Kozma Prutkov. First published in the 1850s and 1860s, Prutkov's hilarious and often absurd poems were a major inspiration to Kharms and the other members of the OBERIU.

Page 407. "Dear Nikandr Andreevich." While at least one of Kharms's Russian editors considers this text an "imitation of the epistolary genre," we have decided to include it, whether or not it was ever sent to its addressee. Nikandr Tiuvelev (1905?-1938?) was a poet and friend of Kharms, who at one point was considered for membership in the Left Flank.

Page 408. "Messengers and their Conversations." A reference to Druskin's essay entitled "The Conversations of Messengers," which had just been read and discussed by the *chinari*. The notions of "neighboring worlds," and "visitors" or "messengers" from these worlds, derive from the *chinar* philosophy of Lipavsky and Druskin, where they were useful as thought experiments for imagining the world from an entirely external (i.e., non-human) point of view. By the 1930s, this notion came to play an increasingly important role in Kharms's thought in relation to his notion of "miracle." For Kharms, miracle was primarily neither a religious nor a supernatural event, but the real intrusion of another world into our earthly existence, and the messenger was the vehicle through whom the miracle was accomplished. The notions of miracle and miracle-worker play a central role in Kharms's most famous story, "The Old Woman" (1939).

Page 411. "October 5, 1933." Combined with a renewed interest in Bach, Mozart, and Goethe, this letter, in which Kharms distances himself from contemporary "left" art for the first time, shows signs of his evolution towards an aesthetic of "classicism." Valery Shubinsky uses this letter to argue that, rather than seeing himself and his fellows as the last stage of the Russian avant-garde, Kharms thought that he was standing at the beginning of a great new period in Russian art.

Page 414. "Monday, October 16, 1933." In one of his most important letters, Kharms describes his ideas about art more directly and openly than anywhere else in his writings.

Page 418. "E. Sno . . ." Evgeny Eduardovich Sno, not his son Evgeny Evgenievich Sno, who may have been the author of "A Reactionary Circus."

1934 (pages 428–450)

Page 431. "Pugachev visitation." In the original, Kharms writes *pugachevshchina,* a punning reference to the eighteenth-century Cossack revolt against Catherine the Great, headed by Yemelyan Pugachev (1742-1775).

Page 431. "*Pouliages.*" While the word Kharms uses here, *pul'iazhi,* is recorded in all editions of this letter, after diligent search and inquiry we have been unable to locate it in any language with which we are familiar.

Page 432. "Daniil Sharon." Kharms never tired of testing alternate pseudonyms.

Page 435. "It's absolutely unbearable . . ." It is unclear whether this comment should be understood in a political or psychological sense.

Page 436. "Olga Forsh . . ." Kharms uses the real names of famous contemporary Soviet writers in this grotesque story, one of his most famous.

Page 436. "As everyone knows . . ." Aleksandr Ilich Bezimensky (1898-1973) was another famous contemporary Soviet writer.

Page 438. "Have to learn Russian grammar." While this statement need not be understood literally, it is true that Kharms never mastered the rules of Russian orthography, and his notebooks contain numerous spelling errors (usually phonetic spellings) on many pages. We have chosen not to reproduce them.

Page 440. "Not alive." Here and below, Kharms is playing a version of the game "20 Questions."

Page 443. "Haygang." Kharms is playing with more pseudonyms apparently based on Daniil Wolfgang (see above).

Page 446. "Constitution." Although Kharms wrote this list with his tongue firmly in his cheek, his views on women were, like those of most of his literary friends and colleagues, definitely patriarchal.

Page 446. "You who would censure the poet but vainly." Although crossed out in the original, this poem anticipates, in both its diction and its perfectly regular dactyls, the new poetic style that Kharms would call "Exercises in Classical Meters" (*UKR, Uprazhneniia v klassicheskikh razmerakh*). The several poems that Kharms wrote in this style in January 1935 mark an important stage in his turn from avant-garde poetics. Not only had the verbal and semantic experiments in the young Kharms's poetry all but disappeared in such poems as "To Oleinikov" ("*Konduktor chisel, druzhby zloi nasmeshnik*"), but, as Pushkin did almost exactly 100 years previously, Kharms was simultaneously turning his pen to "stern prose."

Page 447. "On the radio." This reference to the funeral of Sergei Kirov (real name: Sergei Mironovich Kostrikov, 1886-1934), the popular Party boss in Leningrad, assassinated by Leonid Nikolaev in his offices at the Smolny Institute on December 1, is one of the very few overt references to the political life of the Soviet Union contained in the surviving notebooks. The mysterious circumstances of the assassination have led many to conclude that Stalin, jealous of Kirov's popularity, had a hand in the assassination. Under the pretext of eliminating those implicated in Kirov's assassination, Stalin initiated a massive purge of dissident Bolsheviks in Leningrad while laying the foundation for the Great Terror of 1937. Among the many victims of this campaign was the Rusakov family which, together with Ester, was swept away into the Gulag.

Page 449. "Something's not right with Marina." In her memoirs, Marina Malich complains of Kharms's serial affairs with other women, which brought her to contemplate divorce and even suicide.

1935 (PAGES 451–462)

Page 453. "The circus." Kharms's scenario for the puppet theater in Leningrad called "Circus Shardam," first presented in the autumn of 1935, continues to be performed in puppet theaters in Russia today.

Page 454. "At first I swore it was *poshliatina. . .* " The quality *poshlost'*, the occurrence of which would be called *poshliatina*, was revealed to the English-speaking world by Vladimir Nabokov in his brilliant *Nikolai Gogol*, where he famously defines *poshlost'* as "not only the obviously trashy but also the falsely important, the falsely beautiful, the falsely clever, the falsely attractive."

Page 455. "Here's what's I don't like." Tikhon Vasilievich *Churilin* (1885-1946) was an avant-garde poet and actor. Vladimir Vasilievich *Lebedev* (1891-1967) was an artist and is considered the founder of the Leningrad school of book illustration. Between 1924 and 1933, he directed the art division of Children's Section of State Publishing. Nikolai Pavlovich *Akimov* (1901-1968) was an important avant-garde theater director and artist, book illustrator and, later in life, pedagogue. He directed the premieres of numerous plays by Evgeny Shvarts. *Palekh* is a village located approximately 350 kilometers to the North East of Moscow. A center of icon painting in the nineteenth century, after 1917 its painters turned to illustrating miniature *paper-mâché* boxes with scenes predominantly from folk tales. Founded in 1922, *"Academia"* was a major publisher of classics of World literature; in 1938, it was merged with State Publishing.

1936 (PAGES 463–484)

Page 466. "Speech by Kharms." With the publication in *Pravda* on January 28, 1936, of a harshly critical review of Dmitry Shostakovich's opera "Lady Macbeth of the Mtsensk District," an official campaign against "formalism and naturalism" in the arts was begun. Although the article, "A Muddle instead of Music," was unsigned, it was widely believed that the attack on Shostakovich for rejecting "simplicity, realism, comprehensible images, [and] the natural sound of the word" belonged to Stalin himself. This was followed by a 3-month-long campaign against "formalism and naturalism" orchestrated by the Union of Writers, in which many writers were coerced to participate. Kharms gave this speech at a session devoted to formalism and children's literature. The campaign's major accomplishment was to drive the young Leonid Dobychin, one of the most interesting and talented prose writers living in Leningrad in the 1930s and a target of much fanatical criticism for his novel *The Town of N*, to suicide. Carol Any discusses this episode at greater length in her admirable *Boris Eikhenbaum: Voices of a Russian Formalist*.

Page 468. "In 1927 Malevich said . . ." In February 1928, Malevich presented Kharms with a copy of his book *God Is Not Cast Down: Art, Church, Factory*, in which he had written: "Go ahead and stop progress." At the artist's funeral in 1935, Kharms read one of his most famous poems, "On the Death of Kazimir Malevich."

Page 470. "John Blow." English Baroque composer and organist (1649-1708).

Page 472. "Dear Comrade Tsypin." Samuil Evgenievich Tsypin was a Moscow official responsible for the publication of children's literature. The discussion concerns the terms for Kharms's translation of *Plisch und Plum,* an illustrated book for children by the prolific Wilhelm Busch (1832-1908), whose 1865 *Max und Moritz,* served as the inspiration for the Katzenjammer Kids.

Page 477. "The Blue Notebook." This title translates *"Golubaia tetrad',"* a title conventionally assigned to a cycle of works contained in a hardbound blank book covered in light-blue watered silk [Kharms, *Sobranie sochinenii* (2011), 2:428]. A mixture of aphorisms, diary entries, reflections, miniature stories, poetry, and advice, it so closely mirrors the structure and content of the notebooks (*zapisnye knizhki*) that we have chosen to include it here as a way of calling into question the boundaries between the notebooks and his other works. It is one of Kharms's most famous, and most often translated, texts.

Page 483. "This is how hunger begins." One of Kharms's favorite books was *Hunger,* the 1890 novel by the great Norwegian writer Knut Hamsun (pseudonym of Knud Pedersen, 1859-1952) that made his reputation. The novel tells the story of a young writer's struggle with poverty, hunger, and madness, and is remarkable for its absolute focus on the psychology of the young man and its avoidance of any hint of social criticism: in striving to remain true to his ideals and his calling as a writer, the young man comes close to madness at several points, but by novel's end enlists on a ship leaving the city. There is no question that Kharms identified himself with Hamsun's self-destructive yet proud writer, caught between the conflicting needs of his art and his body.

1937 (pages 485–496)

Page 485. "To the remark . . ." Kharms was obviously aware of his inability to spell correctly, either in Russian or German.

Page 485. "Annoyed thanks to A." Valery Sazhin, the editor of the *Collected Works*, suggests that this is a reference to Anna Semyonovna Ivanter, Vvedensky's wife, with whom Kharms had an affair. See entry for July 5, 1937, below.

Page 485. "An even more terrible time . . ." Kharms is referring to the scandal provoked by his poem "A Man Once Walked Out of His House" (*Iz doma vyshel chelovek*), published in *Siskin*, 1937, no. 3. Following the publication of this poem, which describes the unexplained disappearance of a man and was taken as a reference to the arrests of Leningrad citizens during the purges, *Siskin* refused to publish any of Kharms's poems until 1938. The poem has been well translated by Matvei Yankelevich and Eugene Ostashevsky in *OBERIU: An Anthology of Russian Absurdism*.

Page 486. "I've completely lost my edge." Nevertheless, Kharms managed to compose many of his best stories in these years of acute hunger.

Page 489. "If the state can be likened . . ." The first hint in Kharms's notebooks of the coming war with Germany.

Page 489. "About How I was Visited . . ." See note above on "Messengers."

Page 494. "October 31, 1937." This often quoted passage conveys some of Kharms's essential ideas.

1938 (pages 497–499)

Page 498. "March 20, 1938." One of the elements of Kharms's sexuality was a definite predilection to exhibitionism.

1939 (pages 500–501)

Page 500. "1939, Dec. 1." This cryptic note refers to the announcement that, slightly more than 2 months after the outbreak of World War II and the Soviet invasion of Poland, Soviet forces had just invaded Finland. The so-called Winter War proved a debacle for the Soviets who, despite overwhelming military superiority, were unable to overcome stiff Finnish resistance. When the Moscow Peace treaty was signed on March 13, 1940, the Finns were forced to make territorial concessions, but retained their sovereignty. Otto Kuusinen (1881-1964) was one of the leaders of the Finnish socialists who, after the victory of the Whites during the Finnish Civil War of 1918, had fled to Russia, where he lived and worked for the rest of his life. As the Red Army invaded Finland, he was handpicked by Stalin to be the president of the planned Finnish Democratic Republic to be set up after the victory. Instead, he returned to the Soviet Union and served as chairman of the newly formed Karelo-Finnish SSR for 15 years.

Page 500. "Vvedensky's fate." In 1937, Vvedensky left Leningrad and moved with his wife Galina Borisovna Viktorova (1913-1985) to Kharkov, where he lived apart from the Leningrad literary world until his arrest and death in the first months of the Second World War. For a recent collection of Vvedensky's works and biographical documents, see Aleksandr Vvedensky, *Vse*, ed. Anna Gerasimova (Moscow, 2011).

1940 (pages 502–515)

Page 503. "She's not looking at me." In addition to his exhibitionism, Kharms was also an obsessive voyeur. Over the course of several days, he watches a woman in a neighboring apartment, recording what she is doing.

Page 506. "Diseases of the brain." Kharms was once again studying books on mental illness apparently to avoid conscription into the Red Army.

Page 510. "Introduction." This plan for a collection of various "theoretical" writings, obviously, never amounted to anything.

Page 510. *"Peccatum parvum."* According to Druskin, the universe (existence, time, and space) was composed of two main principles existing in a state of equilibrium except for a certain flaw, defect, or obstacle. He expressed the whole as *quaedam equilibritas cum peccato parvo*. By dividing an undifferentiated whole into parts, the "obstacle" (*peccatum parvum*) allowed the whole to be perceived: neither time, nor space, nor existence could be perceived by man without the distinctions introduced by demonstratives like "this and that," "here and there," and "now and then." Kharms returned to these ideas in numerous works in prose and poetry [see, for example, "Notnow" (*"Neteper'*," 1930), "About equilibrium" (*"O ravnovesii*," 1934), and "About existence, time, space" (*"O sushchestvovanii, o vremeni, o prostranstve*," 1940)]. That Kharms's attitude towards Druskin's "philosophy" was not without an element of irony is suggested by Kharms's founding of "The Order of Equilibrium with a Slight Flaw" in 1938: according to Aleksandr Kobrinsky, Kharms and Vvedensky would sing the Latin to the tune of a polka.

Page 512. "Dear Aleksandr Ivanovich." Kharms's last surviving letter to Vvedensky, written shortly before the outbreak of the Second World War. While Kharms was remarkably passive in the face of hunger and the increasing difficulty of publishing his poems and stories, Vvedensky, driven by the need to provide for his wife and young son, was resilient and tireless in seeking out publishing possibilities.

1941 (page 516)

Page 516. "Dear Natalia Borisovna." Written a week after Kharms was arrested, this letter is one of several Marina Malich wrote describing her increasingly desperate situation in besieged Leningrad to her friend Natalia Shanko, who had earlier been evacuated to Perm with Anton Shvarts (of the "Nevsky Shvartses"). In this context, going "to see Nikolai Makarovich" was code for "getting arrested by the secret police." Oleinikov had been arrested in 1937 and executed in 1938.

Glossary of Names, Places, Institutions and Concepts

A

A.I.   See: ***Vvedensky, Aleksandr Ivanovich***

"Academy of Left Classics"
    See: ***"Flank of the Left"***

Aleksandr Ivanovich
    See: ***Vvedensky, Aleksandr Ivanovich***

Alice   See: ***Poret, Alisa Ivanovna***

Alisa, Alisa Ivanovna
    See: ***Poret, Alisa Ivanovna***

Andronikov, Irakly Luarsabovich (1908-1990)
    Writer, editor, memoirist; contributor to ***Hedgehog*** and ***Siskin***; 1931 arrested along with Kharms, **Vvedensky**, and **Tufanov**, although after preliminary interrogation, he was freed for lack of evidence.   342, 367

Anna Semyonovna
    See: ***Ivanter, Anna Semyonovna***

B

Badmaev, Nikolai Nikolaevich (1879-1939)
    Specialist in Tibetan medicine; arrested 1938; convicted of anti-Soviet and terrorist activity; shot 1939.

Bakhta, Iraida Genrikhovna (?-1963)
    Ballet instructor; student of Isadora Duncan; in memoirs, Anatoly Krasnov-Levitin remembers her as the daughter of a distinguished aristocratic family whose home was host to "Silver Age" luminaries and futurist avant-garde; Levitin describes her as a "mystic" with a strong interest in spiritualism and Eastern religion, esp. Buddhism.   223, 232

Bakhterev, Igor Vladimirovich (1908-1996)
    Poet, playwright, artist; meets Kharms in the 1920s; with **G. Katzman** and **S. Tsimbal** organizer of **"Radiks"**; member of **"Left Flank"** and **OBERIU**; 1930 begins work in children's literature; arrested 1931; freed 1932 and exiled 3 years; later publishes reminiscences of Kharms and other acquaintances from 1920s-30s.   22, 41n33, 88, 90, 98, 111-113, 117, 118, 121, 124, 125, 129-131, 136, 138, 140, 160, 164, 165, 167, 168, 172-174, 180, 199, 206, 208, 210, 219, 234, 254, 293, 342, 367, 376, 547, 552, 553, 556

Balnis, Vladimir

Identified by Sazhin as a staff member of the agricultural institute in *Children's Village* and a close acquaintance of Kharms.

Barmin, Aleksandr Gavrilovich (1900-1952)

Author of numerous books for children on science and history. 350

Baskakov, Nikolai Pavlovich (1896-1937)

Journalist, also active in publishing; member, Communist Party, 1917-28; 1920s, director of Leningrad **Press House**; at the end of April 1928 sentenced to three years in the camps for his alleged involvement in a "Leningrad underground center"; sentenced to death and executed in 1937 for "counter-revolutionary Trotskyite activity." 164-167, 171, 178, 220, 527, 547

Bashilov, Aleksandr Alekseevich

Tailor, artist, "**natural thinker**"; According to accounts by contemporaries, a "small, slightly hunchbacked man" of "indeterminate age." His "artfully painted wooden blocks" decorated with "abstract colorforms" were reportedly much appreciated by **Malevich**. 248, 308, 329, 348, 438

Belykh, Grigory Grigorievich (1906-1938)

Writer, best known as co-author of *The Republic of SHKID* (1927), a semi-autobiographical account of life in a special school for "unsupervised children" (*bezprizorniki*) written with **L. Panteleev**; sentenced to three years imprisonment for anti-Soviet agitation, 1936; 1938 died in a Leningrad prison hospital. 338

Bezborodov, Sergei Konstantinovich (1903-1937)

Journalist and popular children's writer; arrested and executed for espionage, 1937. 450

Bianki, Lev Valentinovich (1884-1938)

Zoologist and entomologist; older brother of **Vitaly Bianki**. 348, 350

Bianki, Vitaly Valentinovich (1894-1959)

Author of over 300 stories, tales, and articles for children compiled in 121 books, which sold some 40 million copies; son of naturalist Valentin Lvovich Bianki (1857-1920); focused his work on the life of plants, animals, and people in nature; arrested 6 times.

Boba   See: **Levin, Boris Mikhailovich**

Bogaevsky, Georgy Leonidovich

Engineer, poet-dilettante. 83, 219

Bogdanovich, Sofia Aniolovna (1900-1987)

Children's writer; her mother Tatiana Aleksandrovna Bogdanovich (1872-1942) was head of the children's section of the Writers Union 1920s-30s. 153

Bondi, Aleksei Mikhailovich (1892-1952)

Actor and dramatist; began career on stage, later moving to film; during 1920s appeared at Leningrad cabaret "The Crooked Mirror."   128

Braudo, Isaiah Aleksandrovich (1896-1970)

Organist, pianist, music historian and pedagogue; from 1923 taught at Petrograd (later Leningrad) conservatory. Joseph Brodsky dedicated a poem to him, entitled "To the Memory of Professor Braudo," 1970.   343, 348, 420

Braun, Nikolai Leopoldovich (1902-1975)

Poet; attended **Institute for the History of the Arts**; first collection of poetry published 1926; active in Leningrad branch of Writers Union.   90, 131

Briantsev, Aleksandr Aleksandrovich (1883-1961)

Founder and chief director of the Leningrad **Children's Theater** 1921-26.   431

Brodsky, Isaak Izrailevich (1884-1939)

"Kremlin court painter" whose iconic portrayals of Lenin and Stalin and heroic canvases depicting the Revolution and Civil War provided a blueprint for Socialist Realism in art.   337

Buddhist Temple

Tibetan-style Buddhist temple in the northern reaches of Saint Petersburg planned and constructed 1909-15 at the initiative of *Agvan-Lovsan Dorzhiev*. A favorite spot for Kharms's walks.

Budogoskaya, Lydia Anatolievna (1898-1984)

Popular children's writer; among her best-known works is "The Tale of a Red-Haired Girl" (1929).   212

Bukhshtab, Boris Yakovlevich (1904-1985)

Literary scholar and critic; student of prominent formalist critic **Boris Eikhenbaum**; scholar of nineteenth-century Russian poetry; during the second half of the 1920s produced work on **Khlebnikov**, Mandelstam, **Pasternak,** and **Konstantin Vaginov.**   129, 223, 232

C

Champions of the New Art

See: *UNOVIS.*

Chernov, Mikhail (Misha, Mishenka)

First husband of Ester Rusakova, and a lightning rod for Kharms's obsessive jealousy.   146, 188, 191, 220, 463, 464, 552, 545, 552

Cherny, Boris Konstantinovich (1904-?)

Writer, critic; member of Moscow "Guild of Poets"; attended meetings of the **"Order of *Zaumniki* DSO"** as well as the **"Left Flank."**   80, 82, 83, 86

Children's Publishing (*Detgiz* or *Detskoe gosudarstvennoe izdatel'stvo*)
From 1933, state-run publishing house responsible for all children's publishing activities in the Soviet Union. See also: **State Publishing House**. 20, 485

Children's Theater (*Teatr iunykh zritelei*, "Theater for Young Viewers")
Established in Petersburg in 1922, one of the first professional theaters for presenting plays to children.

Children's Village
See: ***Detskoe selo***

Chinar, pl. ***Chinari*** ("*Spiritual authorities*")
Founded in 1922 by **Aleksandr Vvedensky, Leonid Lipavsky, Yakov Druskin** and **Nikolai Oleinikov** as a venue for these writers and friends to discuss radical literature, art and philosophy, the group assumed final form when Kharms joined in 1925. Both Kharms and Vvedensky used the term to differentiate their own version of avant-garde poetics from that of their nearest rivals, the ***zaumniki***. Kharms's association with the group, the longest and most influential of his life, lasted into the 1930s. Transcripts of some of their meetings, as recorded by Lipavsky, have been published as *Razgovory* (see bibliography).

Chukovskaya, Lydia Korneevna (1907-1996)
Author, editor, memoirist; close friend and confidante of Anna Akhmatova; daughter of **Kornei Chukovsky**; attended lectures in the literature division of the **Institute for the History of the Arts** 1924-25; from 1928 editor in children's section of **State Publishing House**; compiled first posthumous collection of Kharms' poetry for children, 1962. 41n40

Chukovsky, Kornei Ivanovich (1882-1969)
Prominent poet, writer, children's author, translator (esp. from English), critic, and literary scholar. 336

D

Detskoe selo ("*Children's Village*")
Name used for the town previously known as *Tsarskoe selo,* one-time royal residence south of Saint Petersburg, 1918-37; renamed *Pushkin,* 1937; home to Kharms's aunt, **Natalia Koliubakina**.

Dobychin, Leonid Ivanovich (1894-1936)
Promising young writer, author of three books of prose published between 1927 and 1935; driven to suicide by criticism leveled against him as part of the campaign against Formalism at the 1936 conference of the Union of Soviet Writers. 223, 561

Dorzhiev, Agvan-Lovsan (1854-1938)
Buddhist teacher and scholar; spiritual adviser to the Dalai Lama; from 1901 Tibetan representative to Russia and later to the Soviet Union; initiated and oversaw construction of Saint Petersburg **Buddhist Temple**; active in Saint Petersburg-Leningrad 1920s-30s; arrested and imprisoned, 1937; died in prison hospital, 1938. 493

Druskin, Yakov Semyonovich ("Yashka") (1902-1980)

Philosopher, musician and writer; founding member of *Chinari*; author of important diaries and memoirs; responsible for saving Kharms's archives during World War II and preserving them for 30 years, thereby making the rediscovery of Kharms possible.   10, 17, 20, 30, 32, 36, 37n4n5, 38n5n6, 40n32, 41n32, 86, 256, 350, 367, 384, 399, 408, 430, 457, 470, 536-538, 558, 559, 563, 564

DSO   See: *Order of Zaumniki DSO*

Dunaevsky, Isaak Osipovich (1900-1955)

Popular composer of operettas, ballets, songs, films; considered the Russian Irving Berlin; wrote the music for Grigory Aleksandrov's musical comedies *The Happy-Go-Lucky Fellows*, *Circus*, *Volga-Volga*, and *The Radiant Path*; 1937-1941 director of the Leningrad Union of Composers.   502

Dzhemla

See: *Vigiliansky, Evgeny Ivanovich*

E

Eikhenbaum, Boris Mikhailovich (1886-1959)

Leading Formalist literary scholar, critic and known proponent of "Left" art; Kharms attended his lectures at the **Institute for the History of the Arts** and repeatedly tried to gain his cooperation for joint publishing ventures.   72, 90, 169, 219, 221, 223, 561

Erbshtein, Boris Mikhailovich (1901-1963)

Theatrical designer, painter, eccentric; student of Petrov-Vodkin and Meyerhold; acquainted with Kharms from 1920s; arrested with **Elena Safonova** and **Solomon Gershov**, 1932; sent to exile in Kursk, later Borisoglebsk, Petrozavodsk, Saratov; returned to Leningrad, 1936; re-arrested, sentenced to five years in camps for espionage, 1941; freed without right of residence in major cities, 1947; rehabilitated 1958; committed suicide in Kuibyshev, 1963. Throughout a long and difficult career Erbstein continued to produce notable work for the theater, ballet and opera in both Leningrad and regional theaters.   167, 316, 318, 324, 326, 333

Ermolaeva, Vera Mikhailovna (1893-1937)

Artist, illustrator, teacher; one of the organizers of **"The Champions of New Art" (UNOVIS)**; director of color laboratory at **Institute of Artistic Culture**; helped design the banner for "Three Left Hours"; illustrator for *Hedgehog* and *Siskin*; illustrator of several of Kharms's books for children; organized exhibits of fellow artists' work at her apartment, 1929; arrested for "anti-Soviet activity," December 24, 1934; sentenced to 3 years in labor camp in Kazakhstan; executed 1937.   101, 134, 157, 164, 207, 209, 341

Ester, Esther

See: *Rusakova, Ester Aleksandrovna*

F

FEKS *(Fabrika èktsentricheskogo aktera:* Factory of the Eccentric Actor*)*
> Founded in 1921 by fledgling directors **Grigory Kozintsev** and **Leonid Trauberg** to provide training and experience for aspiring theatrical and film actors, FEKS became a center of the Saint Petersburg avant-garde and was responsible for notable Russian theatrical and cinematic productions in the 1920s.

Filonov, Pavel Nikolaevich (1883-1941)
> Leading Russian avant-garde painter, theorist, pedagogue, poet; one of the organizers of the **Institute of Artistic Culture**; founder of "Analytical Art"; supervised a painting studio where **Alisa Poret** and **Tatiana Glebova** studied. After his death, his works were not exhibited in Saint Petersburg until 1988.   130, 159, 167, 170, 550

"Flank of the Left"
> Short-lived grouping of avant-garde writers, artists, musicians, and dancers organized in mid-1920s by Kharms as a way of establishing his independence from his first poetic master, **Aleksandr Tufanov**. For reasons that remain obscure, the group was renamed several times, first as the **"Left Flank"**, then as the **"Academy of Left Classics"**.

Formalism
> 1) A school of literary criticism and theory that emphasized the formal properties of a work of art as inseparable from its content. 2) In Soviet literary politics, a term of abuse for any approach to literature or art that was not deemed to emphasize its social-political content.   130, 159, 167, 170, 466, 539, 547, 550, 561

Frau René
> See: ***O'Connell-Mikhailovskaya, René Rudolfovna***

Froman, Mikhail Aleksandrovich (real name Frakman) (1891-1940)
> Writer, poet, translator; secretary of the Leningrad Union of Poets in the 1920s.   19, 117, 125, 128, 131

G

Gaga   See: ***Katsman, Georgy Nikolaevich***

Gershov, Solomon Moiseevich (1906-1989)
> Artist, student of Chagal and Malevich; arrested with **Elena Safonova** and **Boris Erbshtein**, 1932; exiled to Kursk, then Borisoglebsk; re-arrested, 1948; rehabilitated, 1956.   316, 324, 337, 341

GINKHUK
> See: ***Institute of Artistic Culture***

Ginzburg, Lydia Yakovlevna (1902-1990)
> Prominent literary scholar and critic; when enrolled in the ***Institute for the History of the Arts***, she was invited to participate in several never-published collections planned by Kharms.   129, 223, 231

Glebova, Tatiana Nikolaevna (1900-1985)

Painter and graphic artist; friend and roommate of **Alisa Poret**; friend of musicians **Isaiah Braudo** and **Maria Yudina**; from 1926 in the studio of painter **Pavel Filonov;** contributor to *Hedgehog* and *Siskin*; illustrated several of Kharms's works; 1932-33 exhibits at "Artists of the RFSFR for the Last 15 Years" (Kharms: "Exhibition of All the Arists").   336, 339, 343, 348, 349

Goldina, Valentina Efimovna (married name Kamenskaya) (1902-1968)

Artist, close friend of **Tamara Lipavskaya**; mentioned in numerous letters by Kharms.   255, 257, 277, 278, 307, 309, 310, 319, 331, 391, 420, 441, 458, 497

Gorodetsky, Sergey Mitrofanovich (1884-1967)

Symbolist poet, translator, critic, journalist.   85

GPU (*Gosudarstvennoe politicheskoe upravlenie*: State Political Directorate)

Soviet state security apparatus responsible for rooting out counter-revolution and espionage, 1922-23. See also: **OGPU, NKVD.**   211, 307, 332, 553

Grits, Teodor Solomonovich (1905-1959)

Writer, literary scholar with a strong interest in **Khlebnikov.**   355

Gritsyn, Kirill Vladimirovich ("Kirill") (b. 1933)

Son of Vladimir Gritsyn and step-son of Kharms's sister, **Elizaveta Yuvacheva**; provided information about Kharms to biographers and scholars.   350, 465

Gritsyn, Vladimir Iosifovich (1900-1976)

Electrical engineer; first husband of Kharms' sister, **Elizaveta Yuvacheva**; father of **Kirill Gritsyn.**   347, 348

Gritsyna, Elizaveta

See: *Yuvacheva, Elizaveta Ivanovna*

H

Hedgehog and *Siskin* (*Ezh* and *Chiz*)

Leading Soviet children's magazines, in which Kharms's work for children was published from 1928 to 1941. *Hedgehog* (1928-33) was conceived by **Samuel Marshak** and intended for school-age children. First edited by **Nikolai Oleinikov** and **Evgeny Shvarts**, it included among its contributors **OBERIU** members **Nikolai Zabolotsky** and **Aleksandr Vvedensky,** in addition to Kharms. *Siskin* (1930-41) was intended for preschool children and appeared originally as a supplement to *Hedgehog.*   25, 27, 155, 208, 222, 295, 357, 366, 438, 470, 537, 538, 553, 558, 562

I

Igor   See: *Bakhterev, Igor Vladimirovich*

IHA   See: *Institute for the History of the Arts*

Illa   See: *Smirinskaya, Lydia Alekseevna*

Ilyin   See: *Marshak, Ilya Yakovlevich*

INAC   See: *Institute of Artistic Culture*

Ink, Emilia Vladimirovna (real name, Vanshtein) (1899-1994)
>Ballerina, actress, director; in the 1920s, performed as a dancer in Leningrad restaurants; actor in **Terentiev's** theater in Press House.   167

Institute for the History of the Arts, IHA (*Institut Istorii Iskusstv*)
>The site of the first **"Left Flank"** performance in December 1925. Kharms enrolled here in the fall of 1926 after his expulsion from the Electro-Technical College in February. Founded by Count Platon Zubov in 1912 and located in his family mansion at 5 St. Isaac's Square in Saint Petersburg, the Institute was one of the most important institutions for cultural study in Russia, occupying a central place in the literary life of Leningrad in the 1920s. Re-organized in 1921 as a research institute, it conducted research and offered free instruction in art, theater, music, and verbal art, adding a film division in 1925. It numbered among its instructors the formalist critics **Boris Eikhenbuam** and Yury Tynianov, and film directors **Grigory Kozintsev** and **Leonid Trauberg**. Friends and associates of Kharms who studied at the Institute include **Igor Bakhterev, Sergei Tsimbal, Boris Levin, Klimenty Mints, Aleksandr Razumovsky**, and **Lydia Chukovskaya**. As part of an ongoing campaign against "formalism," a government commission concluded toward the end of 1929 that the Institute was a "nest of ideology hostile to the proletariat," and its ranks were subsequently purged. In 1931 the Institute was restructured, merged with other institutions, and given a different name. In 1992 the Institute regained its independence and was reconstituted as the Russian Institute for the History of the Arts.   19, 100, 130, 132, 179, 206, 218, 537, 547, 549

Institute of Artistic Culture, INAC
(*Gosudarstvennyi institut khudozhestvennoi kultury, GINKHUK*)
>A research institute devoted to the theory and methodology of art conceived in universal terms. Founded in 1923 by **Kazimir Malevich** and his followers and located on 9 St. Isaac's Square in Saint Petersburg, it was merged with the **Institute for the History of the Arts** in 1926 after being attacked in the press for using state funds to support projects of no discernable utility. In addition to Malevich, important figures associated with INAC include poet **Igor Terentiev** (head of the phonology division), painter **Pavel Filonov** (head of the division of general ideology), and architect **Vladimir Tatlin** (head of the division of material culture). Among Kharms's friends and acquaintances associated with INAC are **Vera Ermolaeva** (director of the color laboratory) and **Aleksandr Vvedensky** and **Yakov Druskin** (both of whom worked in the division of phonology).   82, 85, 94, 113, 115, 121, 130, 537, 547, 549

Ivan Ivanovich
>See: *Sollertinsky, Ivan Ivanovich*

Ivanter, Anna Semenovna ("Niurochka")

Second wife of **Aleksandr Vvedensky** from 1930-34; published reminiscences of Vvedensky and Kharms, 1991. According to her own account she became acquainted with Vvedensky at an **OBERIU** evening at the **Institute for the History of the Arts** in 1928, and was romantically involved with Kharms in the late 1930s at the time of his marriage to his second wife, **Maria Malich**. 210, 308, 343, 344, 562

K

Kalashnikov, Petr Petrovich (1893-?)

Biologist and writer at whose apartment Kharms and a number of his friends met to discuss literature in the late 1920s; December 1931 arrested along with Kharms, Vvedensky, Tufanov and others, implicated in anti-Soviet activities; convicted and condemned to 3 years in a labor camp. 257, 293, 299, 556

Katsman, Georgy Nikolaevich ("Gaga"; pseud. Georgy Kokh-Boot) (1908-1985)

Writer, theater director; member of **"Left Flank"** and **"Academy of Left Classics"**; co-founder and director of experimental theater group **"Radiks"**; director of failed production of *My Mama's all in Watches (Moia mama vsia v chasakh),* jointly written by Kharms and Vvedensky; arrested 1927, sentenced to labor camp in Arctic Russia, where he remained after release and continued working in theater. 94, 98, 104, 116, 117, 124, 125, 131, 135, 138, 143, 355

Kaverin, Veniamin Aleksandrovich (real name: Zilber) (1902-1989)

Writer, novelist, author of important memoirs of literary Leningrad in the 1920s; member of the Serapion Brotherhood; taught at the **Institute for the History of the Arts**. 223, 224, 230

Khardzhiev, Nikolai Ivanovich (1903-1996)

Distinguished literary scholar, art historian, writer, and collector; authority on history of Russian avant-garde, esp. **Khlebnikov**. 412, 514, 515

Khlebnikov, Velimir (real name: Viktor Vladimirovich) (1885-1922)

Russia's greatest Futurist poet; one of the creators of *zaum*; poetic idol of Kharms. 68, 71, 109, 129, 130, 223, 231-233, 356, 411, 476, 514, 545

Kibalchich, Viktor Lvovich (pseud. Victor Serge) (1890-1947)

Russian revolutionary and writer; married to Ester Rusakova's sister Liubov; opponent of repression of Stalin's Soviet Union; expelled from Communist Party for support of Left Opposition, 1928. He was arrested twice, briefly in 1928 and again in March 1933, when he was sentenced to 3 years in a camp near Orenburg. Thanks to pressure from international communists and writers sympathetic to the Soviet Union, including Maxim Gorky, Andre Gide, and Romain Rolland, he was released and allowed to leave the Soviet Union in 1936. He settled in Belgium, which he abandoned for Mexico City at the beginning of World War II. 344, 539

Koliubakina, Nadezhda Ivanovna ("Mama") (1869-1929)

Kharms's mother; born in Saratov district into a noble family that included military and government figures, writers, and poets in its lineage; graduate of Smolny Institute for Noble Girls; worked as head laundress at H. I. H. Princess of Oldenburg Asylum for Woman Released from Petersburg Prisons, later becoming its director; married **Ivan Yuvachev**, 1903; relocated with her husband and children to the family estate in Saratov, 1917; returned to Petrograd, 1919, and worked as head of housekeeping at the Botkin Hospital.   10, 12, 51, 54, 105, 123, 128, 129, 144, 145, 146, 177, 247, 497, 535

Koliubakina, Natalia Ivanovna ("Natasha") (1868-1945)

Kharms's godmother and aunt; elder sister of his mother, **Nadezhda Koliubakina**; a philologist who knew many languages and taught Russian at the Mariinsky Girls' Grammar School, then served as principal when it became the 2nd Children's Village (*Detskoselsky*) Unified Labor School, from which Kharms graduated; frequently hosted literary evenings; an influential figure in both Kharms's early education and his creative life; was often consulted on creative questions; is mentioned in his poetry.   13, 15, 39n19, 75, 105, 155, 179, 231, 256, 301, 308, 320, 322, 323, 325, 340, 346-348, 350, 381, 397, 400, 457, 485, 520

Kozintsev, Grigory Aleksandrovich (1905-1973)

Eminent film director, pedagogue, writer; with **Leonid Trauberg**, founded and directed the "Factory of the Eccentric Actor" (**FEKS**) and directed numerous classics of early Soviet film; Kharms attended his lectures at the **Institute for the History of the Arts** in the 1920s.   90

Kruchenykh, Aleksei Eliseevich (1886-1968)

Major first-generation Futurist poet; along with **Velemir Khlebnikov**, one of the originators of the theory and practice of *zaum*.   68, 72, 545

Kruchinin, Valentin Yakovlevich (1892-1970)

Soviet-era composer; prolific author of popular songs, dance music, films scores, marches.   60

Krug (Krugovtsy) (The Circle of Artists)

Group of young painters and sculptors, active in Leningrad between 1926 and 1930, whose self-proclaimed program was to "create the style of the era." Rejecting the individualism of "left art," they emphasized a collective approach to art. **Alisa Poret** was one of the founding members of the group.   337

Kuzmin, Mikhail Alekseevich (1872-1936)

Leading modernist poet of Silver Age Petersburg and Leningrad in the 1920s; known for his support of talented young poets; Kharms and his literary colleagues sought his approval of their poetry.   19, 41n39, 48, 83, 85, 101

L

"Left Flank"

See: *"Flank of the Left"*

Leonid Savelievich
> See: *Lipavsky, Leonid Savelievich*

Levin, Boris Mikhailovich ("Boba," pseud. of Ber Mioshelevich Doivber) (1899-1941)
> Writer, member of the **OBERIU**; theatrical director of *Three Left Hours*; performed in numerous **OBERIU** evenings.   22, 154, 161, 164, 168, 172, 174, 180, 199, 200, 205, 206, 208, 219, 228, 235, 249, 250, 278, 287, 301, 308, 337-339, 341, 342, 345, 347, 355, 367, 450, 456, 538, 542, 547, 553

Library of New Books (Biblioteka novykh knig)
> Located at 40/42 25 October Prospect (Nevsky Prospect), a lending library opened in 1925 by Antonina Yakovlevna Golovina.   62, 73, 74, 84, 89, 93, 117, 170

Lipavskaya, Tamara Aleksandrovna
> See: *Meier-Lipavskaya, Tamara Aleksandrovna*

Lipavsky, Leonid Savelievich (pseud. Leonid Saveliev) (1904-1941)
> Philosopher and children's writer; with Druskin and Vvedensky one of the original *Chinari*, whose conversations he preserved; married Tamara Meier, Vvedensky's former wife, 1932; killed in the first months of the war with Nazi Germany. His philosophical works have recently been published for the first time.   20, 35, 40n32, 41n32, 123, 129, 136, 168, 172, 176, 177, 194, 256, 257, 301, 305, 343, 344, 346, 347, 355, 384, 399, 409, 445, 456, 458, 495, 536-538, 558, 559

Livshits, Benedikt Konstantinovich (1887-1938)
> Futurist poet, translator; author of one of the best memoirs of the Futurist movement, *The One-and-a-half Eyed Archer*; arrested 1937; shot as "enemy of the people."   86, 169

Liza   See: *Yuvacheva, Elizaveta Ivanovna*

M

Malevich, Kazimir Severinovich (1879-1935)
> Major Russian artist and theoretician; founder of Suprematism; a leading figure in "left" art organizations in the post-1917 period in Vitebsky and Leningrad; one of Kharms's heroes; leader of **UNOVIS**, the **Champions of the New Art**, 1919-22; director of GINKHUK, the **Institute of Artistic Culture**, 1923-26, from which position he authorized the members of **"Radiks"** to rehearse the play *My Mama's all in Watches* in the organization's building.   94, 110, 112, 113, 118, 140, 156, 159, 167, 170, 337, 454, 468, 537, 539, 542, 547, 549, 561

Malich, Marina Vladimirovna (1909 or 1912-2002)
> Kharms's second wife, 1934-41. She left an account of her extraordinary life as told to Vladimir Glotser, which was published in 2002 as *Marina Durnovo: My Husband Daniil Kharms*.   10, 29, 31, 37n5, 437, 449, 450, 455, 456, 463, 464, 469, 482, 485, 486, 494, 496-499, 501, 502, 510, 516, 525, 533, 539, 554, 560, 564

Mama   See: ***Koliubakina, Nadezhda Ivanovna***

Mansurov, Pavel Andreevich (1896-1983)

Artist, director of the experimental division of Malevich's **Institute of Artistic Culture**; emigrated to Western Europe, 1928; his efforts to publish poems by Kharms and other members of **OBERIU** in émigré press failed.   76, 156, 167, 196, 198, 199, 553

Marcel, Paul (real name: Paul Aleksandrovich Rusakov) (1908-1973)

Brother of **Ester Rusakova**; musician, pianist, composer of popular songs and ballads with texts by Russian poets in 1920s; arrested 1936, sentenced to 10 years in labor camp in the Far North, where he worked in the camp musical theater. In 1947, his sentence was reduced for "evidence of highly productive labor." He was released from the camp and, thanks to a petition by **Dmitry Shostakovich**, was allowed to return to Leningrad, where he worked as the musical director and conductor of the Leningrad circus. He was rehabilitated in 1956.   34, 60, 80, 91, 344, 345

Margulis (Margolis) Aleksandr Osipovich (1898-1938)

Translator from French, German; poet; close friend of Osip and Nadezhda Mandelstam and mentioned in latter's memoirs; active in Leningrad Writers' Union; arrested and imprisoned.   427, 430

Marina   See: ***Malich, Marina Vladimirovna***

Maro   See: ***Rappoport, Tamara Romanovna***

Marshak, Ilya Yakovlevich (pseud. Ilyin) (1896 -1955)

Brother of **Samuil Marshak**; children's writer, who wrote a regular column for *Siskin*; suffered from tuberculosis in the late 1920s.   203

Marshak, Samuil Yakovlevich (1887-1964)

Eminent poet, dramatist, translator, literary critic, children's writer; founded studio for children's writers in Petrograd and began work as first literary director of Leningrad **Children's Theatre** 1922; from 1924-25 worked as editor of children's magazine *The New Robinson Crusoe (Novyi Robinzon)*, in which work by writers **Boris Zhitkov**, **Vitaly Bianki**, and **Evgeny Shvarts** appeared among others; de-facto head of children's literature section of **State Publishing House,** into whose orbit he drew Kharms in 1928; in 1933 became first editor-in-chief of newly-formed **Children's Publishing,** which published work by Kharms, **Aleksandr Vvedensky, L. Panteleev, Viktor Shklovsky** and **Aleksei Tolstoy,** in addition to work of the earlier mentioned authors.   25, 41n39, 154, 155-157, 164, 167, 172, 177, 203, 212, 218, 222, 231, 251, 309, 313, 329, 333, 338, 339, 341, 355, 400, 401, 424-426, 456, 553, 555, 556

Matiushin, Mikhail Vasilievich (1861-1934)

Leading Futurist painter and musician; 1918-1934 director of the division of organic culture at the **Institute of Artistic Culture.**   165, 167

Meier-Lipavskaya, Tamara Aleksandrovna ("TAM," "T.A.M.") (1903-1982)
Schoolmate (1919-21) of **Yakov Druskin** and **Aleksandr Vvedensky**; married to Vvedensky (1921-30) and a major influence in his life; marries **Leonid Lipavsky**, 1932, and their apartment becomes an important gathering place for Kharms and friends in the 1930s; the recipient of several of Kharms's most-important surviving letters. 35, 84-86, 125, 138, 177, 196, 211, 214, 244, 254, 257, 258, 277, 278, 305, 308, 309, 318, 322, 323, 331, 332, 344, 346, 520, 538, 543, 546, 555

Mints, Klimenty Borisovich (1908-1995)
Director; member of **OBERIU**; co-director with **Aleksandr Razumovsky** of first (and only) OBERIU film, *The Meatgrinder*, screened at "Three Left Hours." 22, 162, 168, 180

N

Nadezhina, (Nadezhdina) Lydia Aleksandrovna
Emigrated from Russia before 1917; in America, worked as editor of various Russian newspapers; visited Leningrad, 1929, where she met Kharms and took an interest in the **OBERIU**. Following her return to America, she corresponded with Kharms and other young Russian writers. 223, 291, 412

Nadejina, Lydia
See: *Nadezhina, Lydia Aleksandrovna*

Natasha
See: *Koliubakina, Natalia Ivanovna*

"natural thinker"
See: note to page 248 (Commentary, 555).

Nikolai Makarovich
See: *Oleinikov, Nikolai Makarovich*

Niurochka
See: *Ivanter, Anna Semenovna*

NKVD (*Narodnyi kommisariat vnutrennykh del:* People's Commissariat for Internal Affairs)
Soviet state security apparatus responsible for rooting out counter-revolution and espionage, 1934-46. See also: **GPU**, **OGPU**. 9, 10, 26, 29, 35, 447, 521-523, 525-528, 530-533, 536, 538, 540, 554

Nosovich, Sofia Dmitrievna (1896?-after 1988)
Vocalist; graduate of Smolny Institute; among the first women to attend Saint Petersburg Capella conservatory after it began admitting women in 1920; in exile with Kharms in Kursk. 330, 332, 333

O

OBERIU (*Ob"edinenie real'nogo iskusstva*: Association of Real Art)
Active between 1927 and 1930, OBERIU, whose main members included Kharms, **Aleksandr Vvedensky**, **Nikolai Zabolotsky** and **Konstantin Vaginov**, rejected all traditional notions of art in favor of a new poetics of

the absurd. The publication of their manifesto in January 1928 was followed by numerous public performances like "Three Left Hours," at which they provoked generally uncomprehending audiences with poetry, prose and drama devoid of ordinary logic and all social concerns. The carnivalesque spirit of their public performances, heavily indebted to the circus, was an affront to the Stalinist vision of the role of art in a socialist culture. Their works branded in several newspaper reviews as "counter-revolutionary" and themselves as "class enemies," the group broke up in 1930. Ignored by Soviet literature and forgotten by the public, OBERIU was gradually rediscovered in the late 1960s and is today considered one of the most significant episodes in the Russian avant-garde of the early 20th century.

Oleinikov, Nikolai Makarovich (1898-1937)

Poet, writer, editor; "unofficial" member of **OBERIU** and *Chinari*; organizer and editor of *Hedgehog* **and** *Siskin*; arrested as Trotskyite oppositionist and executed, 1937; posthumously rehabilitated, 1957. His poems for adults were published for the first time in Russia in the late 1980s. By turns ironical and philosophical, they are now considered a major contribution to twentieth-century Russian poetry.   20, 38n6, 41n32, 48, 154, 177, 217, 243, 278, 301, 337, 343, 347, 348, 354, 362, 377, 409, 438, 449, 452, 456, 459, 461, 470, 471, 500, 537, 538, 539, 541, 551, 558, 560, 564

O'Connell-Mikhailovskaya, René Rudolfovna ("Frau René") (1891-1981)

Painter, ceramicist, graphic artist, theatrical designer; student, later instructor at the Society for the Encouragement of the Arts; married to artist Ivan Bilibin, 1912-17; later married to Sergei Nikolaevich Mikhailovsky with whom she had two children; friend of **Alisa Poret** and **Tatiana Glebova**; "repressed" mid-1930s.   336-338, 340, 341, 343, 348, 538, 558

Olimpov, Konstantin (pseud. of Konstantin Konstantinovich Fofanov) (1889-1940)

One of the founders of Ego-Futurism; delusions of grandeur in his poetry have been variously interpreted as stylistic technique or as signs of mental derangement; arrested in a round-up of an "anti-Soviet group of bohemian writers," 1930; sentenced to 3 years in prison camp; sentence increased to 10 years, 1931; released 1938. His last years were spent in obscurity and poverty.   86, 113, 248

OGPU (Ob"edinennoe gosudarstvennoe politicheskoe upravlenie: Unified State Political Directorate)

Soviet state security apparatus responsible for rooting out counter-revolution and espionage, 1923-34. See also: **GPU**, **NKVD**.   41n37, 291, 291, 556-558

"Order of Zaumniki DSO"

Short-lived group of experimental poets, founded in 1925 by **Aleksandr Tufanov**; members included Kharms, **Vvedensky**, and **Vigiliansky**. "DSO," written in Latin letters, has been variously understood: Tufanov himself interpreted it as an equation expressing an expanded perception of time and space; others, including the **OGPU** agents who interrogated him in 1931, saw the Order as an anti-Soviet conspiracy, possibly thinking of the Distinguished Service Order of the British military. See also: *zaum*. 81, 536

Oranzhireeva, Antonina Mikhailovna (1897-1960)
Great-granddaughter of the Decembrist Baron Andrei Rosen; educated at the Saint Petersburg Archeological Institute; her first husband, engineer and poet Nikolai Oranzhireev, executed 1925; her second husband, archeologist Aleksandr Aleksandrovich Miller was arrested in 1933 and died in 1935. Having been diagnosed with epilepsy and mental illness and unable to hold a job, in November 1941 she provided evidence against Kharms to **NKVD** interrogators. Following the war, as a member of Akhmatova's inner circle, she is known to have informed on Akhmatova who, never suspecting this, wrote a touching poem in honor of her death (*"Pamiati Anti"*). 530

P

Papa See: *Yuvachev, Ivan Pavlovich*

Panteleev, L. (pseud. of Aleksei Ivanovich Yeremeev) (1908-1987)
Writer, co-author with **Grigory Belykh** of *The Republic of SHKID*, a semi-autobiographical account of life in a special reform school for "unsupervised children" (*bezprizorniki*); regular contributor to *Hedgehog*. 224, 308, 312, 329, 338, 345, 425, 552

Pasternak, Boris Leonidovich (1890-1960)
Poet, novelist, winner of the 1958 Nobel Prize in Literature; with Mandelstam, Akhmatova, and Tsvetaeva, considered one of Russia's greatest modernist poets; associated with Moscow Futurism in the 1920s. 21, 48, 83, 455, 546

Peter Pavlovich
See: *Snopkov, Peter Pavlovich*

Polotsky, Semyon Anatolievich (1905-1952)
Poet, playwright, children's writer. 67, 68, 73, 86

Poret, Alisa Ivanovna ("Alisa," "Alice") (1902-1984)
Painter and graphic artist; studied drawing at the Society for the Encouragement of the Arts and the Academy of Arts with K.S. Petrov-Vodkin; from 1926 in the studio of painter **Pavel Filonov**; worked in children's literature section of **State Publishing House**, contributor to *Hedgehog* and *Siskin*, illustrates works by Kharms, **Vvedensky**; married (?-1927) to art historian Arkady Matveevich Pappe, later to artist **Peter Snopkov** (1933-35); shared an apartment with **Tatiana Glebova** up to the time of her second marriage. 24, 274, 336, 338-343, 345-353, 428, 538

Press House (*Dom Pechati*)
Umbrella organization for the arts, emphasizing literature, poetry, and theater; from 1920 to November 1928 located at 21 Fontanka River Embankment, Saint Petersburg; site of first **OBERIU** performance, January 24,

1928, and subsequent performances. 22, 87, 89, 127, 130, 134, 154, 155, 156, 157, 158, 164, 169, 172, 177, 180, 206, 218, 220, 246, 257, 279, 283, 293, 358, 537, 547, 552

Pugacheva, Klavdia Vasilievna (1906-1996)
Actress; graduated from Leningrad Children's Theater Studio, 1924; at Leningrad **Children's Theater**, 1924-33; from 1933-73 in Moscow theaters. 355, 394, 411-414, 421, 422, 424, 427, 430, 538

Pushkin, Aleksandr Sergeevich (1799-1837)
Russia's greatest poet; irritatingly unavoidable during the centennial year of 1937 and for months leading up to it; adopted at that time by the literary establishment as a proto-Soviet mascot. 9, 15, 17, 37n1, 43n1, 70, 72, 122, 344, 345, 416, 466, 467, 473, 475, 545, 551, 560

R

"Radiks"
Short-lived avant-garde theatrical collective founded by **Igor Bakhterev**, **Georgy Katsman** and **Sergei Tsimbal**, which commissioned a play based on excerpts from the poetry of Kharms and **Aleksandr Vvedensky** called *My Mama's All in Watches*. As entries in the notebooks record, during rehearsals for the play, the group fell apart and the play's manuscript was lost. The membership of "Radiks" formed the basis for the **OBERIU**.

Rappoport, Tamara Romanovna ("Maro")
Friend of Kharms; sister of theater director and playwright V. A. Rappoport. 69, 80, 86

Razumovsky, Aleksandr Vladimirovich ("Sasha") (1907-1980)
Director, screenwriter, playwright, children's writer, journalist; member of **OBERIU**; co-director with Klimenty Mints of first (and only) OBERIU film, *The Meatgrinder*, screened at "Three Left Hours"; author of cinema section of OBERIU declaration. 22, 162, 168, 172, 174, 180, 293, 355, 367, 431

Rozhdestvensky, Vsevolod Aleksandrovich (1895-1977)
Poet; leading member of the Leningrad Union of Poets in the 1920s; studied at the **Institute for the History of the Arts**. 128, 131, 168

Rusakov, Aleksandr Ivanovich (real name: Sender Ioselevich) (1872-1934)
Father of **Ester Rusakova**, father-in-law of Kharms and **Victor Serge**; revolutionary activist; emigrated 1905, settled in France; in 1919 deported from France for pro-Soviet activity, returned to Petrograd; briefly arrested for assault on party member in 1928. 59, 539

Rusakova, Ester Aleksandrovna ("Esther") (1909-1943)
Kharms's first wife (1928-32) and object of his obsessive romantic and erotic fantasies for 7 years; born to Russian revolutionary parents living in France; returns to Russia, 1919; meets Kharms in 1924; sister of composer **Paul**

Marcel and sister-in-law of novelist and regime critic **Victor Serge**; arrested 1936, allegedly for collaborating with her brother-in-law, and sentenced to five years, transported to Kolyma in the Far East; died in Magadan. 26, 34, 35, 47, 49, 79, 90, 119, 134, 135, 141-151, 176, 177, 179, 181, 182, 186-188, 190-193, 195, 196, 204, 209, 211, 212, 217, 219-222, 230-239, 243, 245-247, 259, 285, 286, 308, 337-339, 341, 342, 344, 345, 347, 348, 350, 351, 367, 376, 412, 456, 536, 537, 539, 543-546, 552-554, 556, 560

S

Safonova, Elena Vasilievna (1902-1980)
Artist, illustrator; daughter of musician V. I. Safonov; worked as illustrator for *Hedgehog* **and** *Sisken*, 1928-35, later collaborated with Kornei Chukovsky; illustrated children's books by Kharms, **Vvedensky**, and **Oleinikov**; arrested and exiled to Kursk with **Solomon Gershov** and **Boris Erbshtein**; afterward continued work in illustration and as stage designer; rehabilitated 1958. 315-318, 322, 323, 327, 329, 332, 333, 378

Selvinsky, Ilya Lvovich (1899-1968)
Poet, leader of the Constructivist movement in poetry; active in literary polemics in the late 1920s. 156, 221

Semyonov, Boris Fyodorovich (1910-?)
Artist, memoirist; illustrator for children's magazines. 519

Serge, Victor
See: *Kibalchich, Viktor Lvovich* 34, 538, 539, 553

Shapo Poet, eccentric doctor who treated Kharms and **Poret**; Kharms considered him a **"natural thinker."** 354, 355, 397

Shostakovich, Dmitry Dmitrievich (1906-1975)
One of the greatest composers of the twentieth century. "A Muddle instead of Music," a critical review of his opera *Lady Macbeth of Mtsensk District*, was published in *Pravda* on January 28, 1936, signaling the beginning of a campaign against **Formalism** in the arts. Although the article was unsigned, it was widely believed to have been written by Stalin. 418, 421, 561

Shura, Shurka
See: *Vvedensky, Aleksandr Ivanovich*

Shvarts, Anton Isaakovich (1896-1954)
Actor, professor, reader of poems; called "Nevsky Shvarts" in Kharms's notebooks to distinguish him from his cousin **Evgeny Shvarts**; in later years, famous for his dramatic readings of Gogol on the radio. 64, 456, 564

Shvarts, Evgeny Lvovich (pseud. Zvenigorodsky) (1896-1958)
Writer, playwright, worked in **Children's Publishing**; close friend and associate of members of **OBERIU**. 25, 177, 301, 308, 346, 350, 353, 354, 356, 367, 399, 413, 456, 458, 460, 470, 555, 561

Siskin   See: *Hedgehog* **and** *Siskin*

Smirinskaya, Lydia Alekseevna ("Illa") (1868?-1942)
Governess to Yuvachev children before 1917; after the Revolution, worked as the family servant, living with the family from 1925 until her death during the Leningrad blockade.   176, 177, 231, 243, 346, 347, 369, 425, 437, 456, 486

Sno, Evgeny Eduardovich (Snow) (1880-1941?)
Writer, poet, journalist; zither-playing Englishman who moved to Russia at the turn of the century; according to memoirs, one of Kharms's **"natural thinkers."**   418, 559

Sno, Evgeny Evgenievich (Snow) (1901-1938)
Sociologist; son of Evgeny Eduardovich Sno; identified by Bakhterev as an *agent-provocateur* working for the **OGPU** responsible for the arrest of the **OBERIU** writers in late 1931 (Kobrinskii, *Daniil Kharms*, 411-412.).   41n37, 559

Snopkov, Peter Pavlovich (1900-1942)
Painter, graphic artist, theatrical designer; married (1933-35) to **Alisa Poret**; arrested and later died in camp.   350, 351

Sofia Aniolovna
See: *Bogdanovich, Sofia Aniolovna*

Sollertinsky, Ivan Ivanovich (1902-1944)
Leading musicologist in Leningrad of the 1920s and 1930s; artistic director of the Leningrad Philharmonic.   167, 367, 377

State Publishing, State Publishing House
(*Gosizdat* or *Gosudarstvennoe izdatel'stvo*)
First large-scale Soviet state publishing house, founded in 1919 with the goal of bringing all publishing activity in Soviet Russia under unified control. Publishing for children was the responsibility of the Children's Division (*Detskoe otdelenie* or *Detskii sektor*), which from 1924 was headed by **Samuel Marshak**, and which provided employment for Kharms and other young writers. After the purge of the children's literature section in 1931-32, publishing activities for children in the Soviet Union were reorganized in 1933 into a separate entity, **Children's Publishing** (*Detgiz* or *Detskoe gosudarstvennoe izdatel'stovo*). In Leningrad, the offices of State Publishing were located at 28 Nevsky Prospect, famously known as *Dom Knigi* ("Book House" or "House of the Book").   138, 157, 164, 170, 173, 177, 178, 196, 197, 204, 208, 210, 211, 213, 217, 222, 226, 232, 234, 237, 257, 283, 329, 391, 398, 458, 462, 552-554, 561

Stenich, Valentin Osipovich (real name: Smetanich) (1897/98-1938)
Poet, literary critic, translator of Joyce's *Ulysses*; arrested and charged with conspiracy to commit terrorist act, 1937, executed shortly afterwards; posthumously rehabilitated, 1957.   228, 436

Storitsyn, Petr Ilyich (real name: Kogan) (1894-1941)
    Poet, theater critic, journalist, memoirist.   247

T

T.A.M.   See: *Meier-Lipavskaya, Tamara Aleksandrovna*

Tatlin, Vladimir Evgrafovich (1885-1953)
    Artist and architect, central figure in Russian avant-garde art; illustrated Kharms's book for children *In the First Place and the Second* (1929).   157

Terentiev, Igor Gerasimovich (1892-1937)
    Influential Futurist poet, playwright, leading avant-garde theater director; leading theorist of *zaum*; director of phonetic laboratory in **Institute of Artistic Culture**; in 1926 organized experimental theater at the Leningrad **Press House**; arrested 1931, found guilty of being a spy for England, served 3 years of 5-year sentence working on construction of White Sea Canal; after release, invited to organize an "agitation brigade" to highlight the remaking of criminals laboring at the construction of the Moscow-Volga canal; arrested again 1937, and executed.   135, 136, 159, 165, 167, 169, 180, 197, 552

Tikhonov, Nikolai Semyonovich (1896-1979)
    Poet, translator, editor; one of the most popular and influential Soviet poets of the 1920s; instrumental in getting Kharms accepted into the Leningrad Union of Poets.   131, 223

trans-sense (language, poetry)
    See: *zaum*

Trauberg, Leonid Zakharovich (1902-1990)
    Eminent film director, scenarist, pedagogue; with **Grigory Kozintsev** founded and directed the **FEKS** (*Factory of the Eccentric Actor*) and directed numerous classics of early Soviet film. Kharms attended his lectures at the **IHA** in the 1920s.   90

Tsarskoe selo
    See: *Children's Village*

Tsimbal, Sergei Lvovich (1907-1978)
    Writer, theater director; one of the organizers of **"Radiks,"** co-director of *My Mama's All in Watches*; participant in performances by Kharms and members of the **OBERIU**.   91, 98, 112, 129, 130, 164, 166, 168, 180, 547

Tufanov, Aleksandr Vasilievich (1877/1878-1941)
    Futurist poet, theorist of *zaum*; mentor and major influence on the poetic styles of **Vvedensky** and Kharms; founder of the **"Order of *Zaumniki* DSO"**; in 1931 arrested with Kharms and Vvedensky for supposed anti-Soviet activity, sentenced to 3 years in a prison camp in Mordova; never returned to Leningrad.   19, 46, 60, 71-73, 76, 82, 83, 85, 112, 131, 167, 216, 234, 248, 536, 538, 544-548, 551, 556

U

UNOVIS (Utverditeli novogo iskusstva: Champions of the New Art*)*
Influential group of avant-garde artists established by **Kazimir Malevich** in Vitebsk in 1919. One of the first government-sponsored groups of artists after the Revolution, they facilitated exhibitions, organized philosophical debates, participated in revolutionary holidays, etc. By the early 1920s, UNOVIS had spread to Moscow and a number of other cities, and in 1922 the group relocated from Vitebsk to Petrograd, where they were incorporated into the State **Institute of Artistic Culture** (GINKHUK), also directed by Malevich. As the political climate in the 1920s quickly turned against the radical experiments of the avant-garde, their freedom of activity was drastically curtailed.   110, 113

V

Vaginov, Konstantin Konstantinovich (real name: Vagengeim) (1899-1934)
Poet and novelist; member of **OBERIU** in 1927-1928; participant in OBERIU performances, including "Three Left Hours;" left OBERIU when he moved from poetry to prose at the end of the 1920s. His novels *The Satyr's Song* and *The Works and Days of Svistonov* contain satirical descriptions of the carnivalesque atmosphere and personalities of OBERIU. His untimely death from tuberculosis fueled Kharms's obsessive fear of the disease in the 1930s.   22, 88, 112, 118, 129, 130, 136, 140, 160, 164, 165, 172, 173, 197, 199, 205, 206, 208, 283, 293, 538, 553

Valentina Efimovna
See: **Goldina, Valentina Efimovna**

Vigiliansky, Evgeny Ivanovich ("Zhenka"; pseud. Dzemla) (1903-1942?)
Poet, member of the **"Order of Zaumniki DSO"** and the **"Left Flank"**; played the role of Papa in *Elizaveta Bam* at "Three Left Hours."   71, 75, 76, 79, 83, 85, 94, 101, 112, 168, 174, 180, 200, 205-208, 210, 219, 367, 545, 549

Vladimir Iosifovich
See: **Gritsyn, Vladimir Iosifovich**

Vladimirov, Yury Dmitrievich (1909-1931)
Writer, joined **OBERIU** in 1929; participant at final OBERIU performance on April 1, 1930. In addition to his works for children, only one story for adults, "The Gymnast," has survived.   22, 228, 132, 250, 293, 308, 323, 538

Vulfius, Pavel Aleksandrovich (1908-1977)
Composer, musician; studied at **Institute for the History of the Arts**; author of music for *Elizaveta Bam.*   165, 166, 168, 171, 174, 205

Vvedensky, Aleksandr Ivanovich ("Shura," "Shurka") (1904-1941)
Poet and writer; Kharms' closest friend and collaborator; meets Kharms summer 1925; member of **"Radiks,"** *Chinari,* **"Left Flank," "Academy**

of Left Classics"; founding member of **OBERIU**; contributor to *Hedgehog and Siskin*; 1931 arrested; in exile in Kursk with Kharms in 1932, where they share a house for several months while their relationship begins to fray; later to Vologda, then Borisoglebsk; from 1936 in Kharkov; arrested in September 1941 on charges of counter-revolutionary agitation; dies December 1941 on railway prison transport from Kharkov to Kazan. Vvedensky's wife destroyed his archive after his arrest in 1941.   20-22, 25, 27, 35, 38, 40n32, 41n32, 43n1, 48,73-76, 80-83, 88, 89, 95, 97, 100, 101, 104, 112, 113, 118, 120, 121, 125, 126, 128-131, 133, 134, 136, 138, 140-142, 144, 154, 157, 160, 167, 168, 173, 175, 177, 178, 199, 206, 208, 210, 217, 219, 220, 223, 224, 228, 231, 234, 244, 254, 256-258, 278, 293, 294, 296, 298, 299, 309, 310, 314, 315, 317, 318, 320, 422, 325, 337, 339, 342-344, 349, 350, 356, 367, 370, 411, 430, 431, 445, 461, 462, 471, 486, 500, 512-514, 517, 523, 536-539, 541, 542, 546-548, 553, 556-558, 562-564

Y

Yakov Semyonovich
> See: *Druskin, Yakov Semyonovich*

Yudina, Maria Veniaminovna (1899-1970)
> Distinguished pianist, cultural figure, and critic of the Soviet regime; maintained a broad range of contacts in the literary, musical, and artistic world; for many years, her "evenings" were fixtures of Leningrad cultural life.   274, 342

Yurkun, Yury Ivanovich (pseud. of Juozapas Jurkūnas) (1895-1938)
> Writer, artist, collector, dandy, and eccentric; close friend of **Mikhail Kuzmin**; literary debut in 1914; his writing did not appear in print after 1923; arrested 1938, sentenced to death, shot. His artwork was the subject of a 2010 exhibition at the Akhmatova Museum in Saint Petersburg.   88

Yuvachev, Ivan Pavlovich ("Papa") (1860-1940)
> Kharms's father; son of floor polisher at the Anichkov Palace in Saint Petersburg; naval officer, arrested in connection with plot to assassinate Alexander III August 1883; convicted and sentenced to death September 1884, although sentence commuted to 15 years hard labor. At Peter- Paul and Schlüsselburg Fortresses, he became a devout Christian, studied Hebrew, and began to write poetry; transferred to Sakhalin Island penal colony in the Russian Far East 1887, where after a brief stint as a laborer he conducted scientific research. Released in 1895 and returned to European Russia in 1897; elected Corresponding Member of the Academy of Sciences for his scientific work in 1899; published accounts of imprisonment and exile as well as devotional works, often under the pseudonym Miroliubov ("Peace and Love"). Married **Nadezhda Koliubakina** in 1903; served as a financial examiner in the Directorate of Savings Banks; after October 1917 worked as a senior inspector in the budgetary and accounting division of

the People's Commissariat of Finance; head of the accounting department at the Volkhov River Hydroelectric Power Station construction project 1923-24. Corresponded with Chekhov, Tolstoy, and Voloshin. 10, 12, 38n7n8, 39n16, 51-55, 74, 75, 99, 107, 115, 120, 141, 187, 224, 231, 235, 240, 256-258, 308, 320, 381, 429, 437, 456, 474, 535, 639

Yuvacheva (married name Gritsyna), Elizaveta Ivanovna ("Liza") (1914-1994)
Younger sister of Kharms; married electrical engineer **Vladimir Gritsyn** and adopted his son **Kirill Gritsyn**; left reminiscences about Kharms, family, and friends. 37n5, 38n5, 39n18, 39n19, 54, 180, 209, 233-235, 239, 240, 243, 245, 256, 291, 350, 355, 381, 394, 418, 456, 465, 547

Z

Zabolotsky, Nikolai Alekseevich (1903-1958)
Poet; member of **OBERIU** and main author of OBERIU Declaration; participant in "Three Left Hours;" worked in children's publishing in the early 1930s; arrested 1938, sentenced to 5 years in labor camp; released 1945; returned to Moscow 1946, where he became a successful Soviet poet and translator. 22, 25, 85, 97, 101, 112, 115, 118, 123, 124, 130, 131, 136, 141, 154, 161, 167, 170, 173, 175, 177, 180, 185, 205, 206, 210, 218, 219, 223, 243, 259, 293, 296, 301, 308, 326, 337, 345, 347, 354, 367, 384, 399, 409, 416-418, 458, 460, 537, 538, 539, 548, 549, 551-553, 558

zaum (zaum')
Variously translated as "trans-sense" or "trans-rational" language or poetry, *zaum* can be broadly understood as an attempt to detach language from conventionally assigned meaning. Originally a project of Russian Futurism, *zaum* was interpreted in a variety of ways by a variety of practitioners employing a variety of means. Whatever the differences, all sought to revitalize language by liberating it from established phonetic, phonemic, grammatical, syntactical, or semantic structures and strictures, and in doing so gain for it a renovated relationship to reality. Among the founders of *zaum* are **Aleksandr Kruchenych** and **Velimir Khlebnikov**. 24, 30, 41n32, 46, 48, 76, 81, 82, 132, 159, 160, 175, 293, 294, 299, 300, 545, 546, 555, 557

zaumnik, pl. *zaumniki*
A practitioner of trans-sense or *zaum* poetry. 41n32

Zhenka See: *Vigiliansky, Evgeny Ivanovich*

Zhitkov, Boris Stepanovich (1882-1938)
Prominent children's author; spent early career in scientific research, maritime pursuits; 1922 began literary career in Petrograd with encouragement of **Samuil Marshak** and **Kornei Chukovsky**; contributor to *Siskin and Hedgehog*; in 1927 organized the Association of Children's Writers (*Assotsiatsiia detskikh pistatelei pri Dome pechati*) with Kharms; died of pulmonary cancer, 1938. 154, 177, 194, 301, 308, 321, 336, 337, 339, 340, 341, 343, 348, 350, 372, 469, 471, 482, 483, 551

Printed by BoD™in Norderstedt, Germany